DIVERSE APPROA
TEACHING, LEA
AND WRITING ACROSS THE
CURRICULUM: IWAC AT 25

PERSPECTIVES ON WRITING

Series Editors, Rich Rice, Heather MacNeill Falconer, and J. Michael Rifenburg

The Perspectives on Writing series addresses writing studies in a broad sense. Consistent with the wide ranging approaches characteristic of teaching and scholarship in writing across the curriculum, the series presents works that take divergent perspectives on working as a writer, teaching writing, administering writing programs, and studying writing in its various forms.

The WAC Clearinghouse, Colorado State University Open Press, and University Press of Colorado are collaborating so that these books will be widely available through free digital distribution and low-cost print editions. The publishers and the Series editors are committed to the principle that knowledge should freely circulate. We see the opportunities that new technologies have for further democratizing knowledge. And we see that to share the power of writing is to share the means for all to articulate their needs, interest, and learning into the great experiment of literacy.

Recent Books in the Series

Hannah J. Rule, *Situating Writing Processes* (2019)

Asao B. Inoue, *Labor-Based Grading Contracts: Building Equity and Inclusion in the Compassionate Writing Classroom* (2019)

Mark Sutton and Sally Chandler (Eds.), *The Writing Studio Sampler: Stories About Change* (2018)

Kristine L. Blair and Lee Nickoson (Eds.), *Composing Feminist Interventions: Activism, Engagement, Praxis* (2018)

Mya Poe, Asao B. Inoue, and Norbert Elliot (Eds.), *Writing Assessment, Social Justice, and the Advancement of Opportunity* (2018)

Patricia Portanova, J. Michael Rifenburg, and Duane Roen (Eds.), *Contemporary Perspectives on Cognition and Writing* (2017)

Douglas M. Walls and Stephanie Vie (Eds.), *Social Writing/Social Media: Publics, Presentations, and Pedagogies* (2017)

Laura R. Micciche, *Acknowledging Writing Partners* (2017)

Susan H. McLeod, Dave Stock, and Bradley T. Hughes (Eds.), *Two WPA Pioneers: Ednah Shepherd Thomas and Joyce Steward* (2017)

Seth Kahn, William B. Lalicker, and Amy Lynch-Biniek (Eds.), *Contingency, Exploitation, and Solidarity: Labor and Action in English Composition* (2017)

Barbara J. D'Angelo, Sandra Jamieson, Barry Maid, and Janice R. Walker (Eds.), *Information Literacy: Research and Collaboration across Disciplines* (2017)

DIVERSE APPROACHES TO TEACHING, LEARNING, AND WRITING ACROSS THE CURRICULUM: IWAC AT 25

Edited by Lesley Erin Bartlett, Sandra L. Tarabochia,
Andrea R. Olinger, and Margaret J. Marshall

The WAC Clearinghouse
wac.colostate.edu
Fort Collins, Colorado

University Press of Colorado
upcolorado.com
Louisville, Colorado

The WAC Clearinghouse, Fort Collins, Colorado 80523

University Press of Colorado, Louisville, Colorado 80027

ISBN 978-1-64215-036-0 (PDF) | 978-1-64215-037-7 (ePub) | 978-1-64642-023-0 (pbk.)

DOI: 10.37514/PER-B.2020.0360

Printed in the United States of America

Library of Congress Cataloging-in-Publication Data

Names: International Writing Across the Curriculum Conference (2018 : Auburn, Alabama) author. | Bartlett, Lesley, editor. | Tarabochia, Sandra, editor. | Olinger, Andrea R., 1983– editor. | Marshall, Margaret J., editor.
Title: Diverse approaches to teaching, learning, and writing across the curriculum : IWAC at 25 / edited by Lesley Erin Bartlett, Sandra L. Tarabochia, Andrea R. Olinger, Margaret J. Marshall.
Description: Fort Collins : The WAC Clearinghouse, 2020. | Includes bibliographical references. Identifiers: LCCN 2020014423 (print) | LCCN 2020014424 (ebook) | ISBN 9781646420230 (paperback) | ISBN 9781642150360 (pdf) | ISBN 9781642150377 (epub)
Subjects: LCSH: English language—Rhetoric—Study and teaching (Higher)—Congresses. | Interdisciplinary approach in education—Congresses.
Classification: LCC PE1404 .I5285 2018 (print) | LCC PE1404 (ebook) | DDC 808/.0420711—dc23
LC record available at https://lccn.loc.gov/2020014423
LC ebook record available at https://lccn.loc.gov/2020014424

Copyeditor: Don Donahue
Designer: Mike Palmquist
Series Editors: Rich Rice, Heather MacNeill Falconer, and J. Michael Rifenburg
Consulting Editor: Susan H. McLeod
Associate Editor: Jonathan P. Hunt
Cover Photo: "Huángshān Vista" by Mike Palmquist

The WAC Clearinghouse supports teachers of writing across the disciplines. Hosted by Colorado State University, and supported by the Colorado State University Open Press, it brings together scholarly journals and book series as well as resources for teachers who use writing in their courses. This book is available in digital formats for free download at wac.colostate.edu.

Founded in 1965, the University Press of Colorado is a nonprofit cooperative publishing enterprise supported, in part, by Adams State University, Colorado State University, Fort Lewis College, Metropolitan State University of Denver, Regis University, University of Colorado, University of Northern Colorado, Utah State University, and Western Colorado University. For more information, visit upcolorado.com. The Press partners with the Clearinghouse to make its books available in print.

CONTENTS

ACKNOWLEDGMENTS

This book celebrates the twenty-fifth anniversary of the International Writing Across the Curriculum (IWAC) conference, held in June 2018, and marks that significant moment in time. It would not have been possible without the efforts of many different people and organizations. We are grateful to the IWAC 2018 conference organizers at Auburn University for hosting a conference that brought together such a diverse group of researchers and practitioners from across disciplines to share scholarship and move ideas forward.

We cannot thank the contributors enough for their energy and enthusiasm throughout the publication process. Every chapter went through extensive reviews and revisions to go from conference presentation to book chapter, and our contributors approached this process with brilliance, persistence, and commitment to a collaborative effort that enacts the spirit of connection and diversity at the heart of WAC.

We are grateful to Mike Palmquist, Sue McLeod, and Rich Rice at the WAC Clearinghouse for their support and guidance throughout this process. We also appreciate Abby Dubisar for her thoughtful feedback and Lori Peterson and Don Donahue for their indispensable editorial work. Michele Eodice and Mya Poe offered sage advice at key points throughout the process, and the book is undoubtedly better for it.

Finally, 40 reviewers graciously provided detailed, supportive feedback for contributors. The collective years of experience and expertise our reviewers possess have enriched each chapter and the book as a whole. They include Natasha Artemeva, Laura Aull, Jacob Babb, Kristin Marie Bivens, Glenn Blalock, Marilee Brooks-Gillies, Barbara D'Angelo, Rob Detmering, Norbert Elliot, Dan Emery, Chris Gallagher, Marilyn Gray, Michelle Hall Kells, Brian Hendrickson, Bruce Horner, Sandra Jamieson, Zak Lancaster, Suzanne Lane, Danielle Lillge, Thomas McNamara, Barry Maid, Dan Melzer, Michael Michaud, Rebecca Moore Howard, Terry Myers Zawacki, Trenia Napier, Stephanie Norander, Talinn Phillips, Jessica Rivera-Mueller, Alisa Russell, Lisa Russell-Pinson, Carol Rutz, Ghanashyam Sharma, Allie Sockwell Johnston, Stacey Sheriff, Raymond Smith, Jerry Stinnett, Chris Thaiss, and Janice Walker.

Working together on this project has been a joyful experience. Since our first official coeditors' meeting in May 2017, we have grown as scholars, teachers, editors, mentors, and friends. Over this time, we have celebrated two weddings, the birth of a child and grandchild, publication of a monograph, promotion to tenure, and countless other life-work experiences that we've shared amid reading and responding to chapters, corresponding with reviewers and contributors, and shaping the book you now hold in your hands. We are so grateful for the opportunity to have worked on this project, with this team, at this moment in time.

FOREWORD.
WAC TODAY: DIVERSITY AND RESILIENCE

Mya Poe
Northeastern University

In their 1992 collection, *Writing, Teaching, and Learning in the Disciplines*, Anne Herrington and Charles Moran began their introduction by noting that "movements such as writing in the disciplines have histories: at some point they were not; at another point they were; and somehow there was a progress from not-being to being" (p. 3). In framing WAC as a historical development, Herrington and Moran suggest multiple possible histories of WAC's origins; they asked Nancy Martin and David R. Russell to compare different histories of WAC—Martin's British history of WAC (1992) and Russell's U.S. history of WAC (1992). For Russell, the difference in history was in the "social and institutional forces that shaped" the WAC movements in the UK and U.S. (p. 4). Martin located those forces as the mid-twentieth century U.S. desire for "adequate standards of written language" and the British conversation about educational content necessary for the new clientele of school students (p. 4).

Russell's and Martin's comments 27 years ago are instructive in the context of this collection. *Diverse Approaches to Teaching, Learning, and Writing Across the Curriculum: IWAC at 25* suggests that the U.S. debate about "adequate standards of written language" has come full circle. Rather than working toward "adequate standards of written language" or even the idea that WAC helps students become compliant community members, WAC researchers today are resisting the notion that there is a single standard by which all students should write or that community membership is a one-way venture into an academic community or the workplace. Instead, WAC researchers today are thinking about expanded trajectories for literate action—trajectories that invite diverse identities and languaging practices.

In short, while WAC has been incredibly resilient over the last two decades, it is now that diversity is really beginning to shape the field.

It's been a long time coming. When I was a graduate student in the late 1990s and reading the Herrington and Moran collection, I thought of it as a window into the world of WAC. I was enamored by their inclusion of Bonnie Spanier's chapter "Encountering the Biological Sciences: Ideology, Language, and Learning." Spanier, who held a Ph.D. in microbiology and molecular genetics

DOI: https://doi.org/10.37514/PER-B.2020.0360.1.2

from Harvard and was a professor of women's studies at SUNY Albany, was committed to making "feminism and science work together for social change and evidence-based medicine" (Spanier, n.d.). Her chapter in the Herrington and Moran collection put forth a bold vision for WAC:

> writing-across-the-curriculum projects that address ideology in the discourse and practice of science are potentially transformative and may help to alleviate the exclusion of women and people of color from the scientific professions, the crisis in scientific literacy in the United States, and the vast gulf between scientific experts and the public in issues of science and society. (p. 193)

Spanier's feminist vision of science, one that acknowledged its Western, racialized history, was exciting. I scrawled notes over every inch of Spanier's chapter. This is what I wanted WAC to do!

But little would come of Spanier's vision, despite the occasional critique such as those by LeCourt (1996), Villanueva (2001), or Hall Kells (2007). WAC remained seemingly unchangeable when it came to critical theory, second-language research, and approaches to culturally sustaining pedagogy (Paris & Alim, 2014). But things have begun to change with offerings like Michelle Cox's (2010) WPA-CompPile research bibliographies on WAC-WID and second language writers, Michelle Cox and Terry Myer Zawacki's (2011) special issue in *Across the Disciplines* on second language writing and their subsequent collection, *WAC and Second-Language Writers: Research Towards Linguistically and Culturally Inclusive Programs and Practices* (Zawacki & Cox, 2013), which brought internationalization and second-language writing research to the field. Chris Anson's "Black Holes: Writing Across the Curriculum, Assessment, and the Gravitational Invisibility of Race" in Race and Writing Assessment, and Frankie Condon and Vershawn Ashanti Young's (2016) *Performing Antiracist Pedagogy in Rhetoric, Writing, and Communication*, which was an expansion of their 2013 Across the Disciplines special issue on Anti-Racist Activism: Teaching Rhetoric and Writing, brought attention to race and racism.

And here we are today. *Diverse Approaches to Teaching, Learning, and Writing Across the Curriculum: IWAC at 25* is a peer-reviewed collection edited by women—women who not just bring expertise in linguistics, student writing development, and feminist rhetoric to WAC work but who also bring a commitment to making higher education more inclusive. Spanier would be pleased.

From early chapters in Diverse Approaches to Teaching, Learning, and Writing Across the Curriculum: IWAC at 25 that narrate the formation of the field and the professional organizations that serve faculty and graduate students to later chapters that take up anti-racism and culturally sustaining approaches, the contributors in this collection foreground inclusivity. For example, the three-part goals of energizing, demystifying, and connecting for WAC-GO place access at the center of the organization that serves new members of the community.

WAC is about people making texts together, not studying texts in isolation, and forming meaningful collaborations has long been central to successful WAC programs. Today, in the diverse, global world of higher education, WAC collaborations can be even more expansive as they respond to language policy changes in locations such as Hong Kong. In expanding these horizons, the potential is enormous. For example, as Marcela Hebbard and Yanina Hernández write, becoming *transfronterizo* collaborators "demands learning to traverse across disciplinary and linguistic borders in order to develop . . . *transborder thinking,* the intellectual openness that considers that perspectives and methods in one's discipline have come from and/or been influenced by perspectives and methods outside one's discipline." In doing so, discussions about adequate standards for writing that fueled WAC long ago now become discussions about negotiation, perspective, and change.

The final chapters of *Diverse Approaches to Teaching, Learning, and Writing Across the Curriculum: IWAC at 25* in Attending to the Human Element: Antiracism, Emotional Labor, and Personal Connection in the Teaching of Writing leave a large footprint for the future of the field. Here, we do not see a focus solely on the changing demographics of U.S. higher education. Instead, we see authors wrestling with changing the deep structures of inequality that have long fueled U.S. higher education (and higher education globally). From Neisha-Anne Green and Frankie Condon's powerful epistolary on the effects of racism to Shannon Madden and Sandra L. Tarabochia's research on the emotional labor involved in mentoring, contributors document the many ways that cultural and social forces shape disciplinary knowledge-making practices. When we ignore racism, emotion, and culture, WAC remains complicit in a cycle of disempowerment. The contributors offer us hope. They explain how to make assignments culturally sustainable and meaningful to students. Such approaches ask us not to simply teach students disciplinary genres or discourses but to ask broader questions such as: What would it mean to teach students how to use grant writing skills for preservation of their own communities? How might students tap into knowledge about their communities to bring people together to talk about topics such as water quality? Such "expansive framing" puts students' interests and passions for the subject matter at the center of disciplinary language learning (Kareem, this volume).

Diverse Approaches to Teaching, Learning, and Writing Across the Curriculum: IWAC at 25 is proof that WAC has remained resilient over the last 25 years, but it also profoundly changing. With those changes, new histories—with new perspectives—remain yet to be written.

REFERENCES

Condon, F. & Young, V. A. (Eds.). (2016). *Performing antiracist pedagogy in rhetoric, writing, and communication.* The WAC Clearinghouse; University Press of Colorado. https://wac.colostate.edu/books/atd/antiracist/.

Cox, M. (2010). WAC-WID and second language writers, WPA-CompPile research bibliographies, No. 8. *WPA-CompPile Research Bibliographies.* https://wac.colostate.edu/docs/comppile/wpa/Cox.pdf .

Cox, M. & Zawacki, T. M. (Eds.). (2011). WAC and second language writing: Cross-field research, theory, and program development [Special Issue.] *Across the Disciplines, 8*(4). https://wac.colostate.edu/atd/special/ell/.

Herrington, A. & Moran. C. (Eds.). (1992). *Writing, teaching, and learning in the disciplines.* Modern Language Association.

Kells, M. H. (2007). Writing across communities: Deliberation and the discursive possibilities of WAC. *Reflections: A Journal of Writing, Service-Learning, and Community Literacy, (6)*1, 87–109.

Kells, M. H. (2012). Welcome to Babylon: Junior writing program administrators and writing across communities at the University of New Mexico. *Composition Forum, 25.*

LeCourt, D. (1996). WAC as critical pedagogy: The third stage? *JAC, 16*(3), 389–405.

Martin, N. (1992). Language across the curriculum: Where it began and what it promises. In A. Herrington and C. Moran (Eds.), *Writing, teaching, and learning in the disciplines* (pp. 6–21). Modern Language Association.

Paris, D. & Alim, H. S. (2014). What are we seeking to sustain through culturally sustaining pedagogy? A loving critique forward. *Harvard Educational Review,* 84(1), 85–100.

Russell. D. (1992). American origins of the writing-across-the-curriculum movement. In A. Herrington and C. Moran (Eds.), *Writing, teaching, and learning in the disciplines* (pp. 22–44). Modern Language Association.

Spanier, B. (n.d.) *Bonnie Spanier.* Retrieved 22 February 2020 from http://bonniespanier.blogspot.com/p/about.html

Spanier, B. (1992). Encountering the biological sciences: Ideology, language, and learning. In A. Herrington and C. Moran (Eds.), *Writing, teaching, and learning in the disciplines* (pp. 193–212). Modern Language Association.

Villanueva, V. (2001). The politics of literacy across the curriculum. In S. McLeod, E. Miraglia, M. Soven & C. Thaiss (Eds.), *WAC for the new millennium* (pp. 165–178). National Council of Teachers of English.

Zawacki, T. M. & Cox, M. (Eds.). (2013). *WAC and second-language writers: Research towards linguistically and culturally inclusive programs and practices.* The WAC Clearinghouse; University Press of Colorado. https://wac.colostate.edu/books/perspectives/l2/ .

DIVERSE APPROACHES TO TEACHING, LEARNING, AND WRITING ACROSS THE CURRICULUM: IWAC AT 25

INTRODUCTION.

ON CONNECTION, DIVERSITY, AND RESILIENCE IN WRITING ACROSS THE CURRICULUM

Lesley Erin Bartlett
Iowa State University

Sandra L. Tarabochia
University of Oklahoma

Andrea R. Olinger
University of Louisville

Margaret J. Marshall
Auburn University

This volume emerged out of a desire to celebrate the twenty-fifth anniversary of the International Writing Across the Curriculum (IWAC) conference and mark this significant moment in time. When the call for proposals to host the 2018 conference came out, Margaret and Lesley were working together in the Office of University Writing (OUW) at Auburn University. IWAC had played a significant role in launching and sustaining the still-young WAC program at Auburn, and both OUW staff and other campus stakeholders agreed that it was time to give back to the community that had been so helpful to Auburn's writing initiative.

The OUW staff appreciated the wide range of work represented at IWAC that happens at all levels and in all disciplines, work that supports a broad understanding of literate practices, so they proposed the theme of "Making Connections" and sought to continue the tradition of bringing many people with different types of expertise out of their institutional silos to learn together. When Margaret realized that the 2018 conference would mark its twenty-fifth anniversary, she suggested that Lesley invite other early-career colleagues whose work focused on WAC to co-edit a volume to commemorate this important milestone. Sandra and Andrea accepted Lesley's invitation, and the results of their collaboration are in the pages that follow. Like the IWAC 2018 conference

DOI: https://doi.org/10.37514/PER-B.2020.0360.1.3

at Auburn University, this volume seeks to connect the diverse ideas, practices, teachers, students, and other stakeholders that make up the rich WAC community. The conference call for papers captured this spirit:

> Our theme, "Making Connections," emphasizes how WAC fosters connections within and across institutions and programs, between people and positions, and among ideas and practices. In a historical moment when divisiveness, rancor, and disconnection are so pervasive on the national and international stage, our theme aims to underscore the power of collaboration, integration, inclusion, and the search for common ground. We invite participants to remember together why we chose—and continue choosing—our work, and then to envision more connected futures.

> To say that work in education too often happens in silos is to state the obvious. Recognizing that teaching and research are often isolated (and isolating), we aim to continue IWAC's long tradition of bringing many different kinds of people together and valuing the wide range of important work that happens at all levels, in all disciplines, and both inside and outside traditional classroom settings. Perhaps especially we want to foster curiosity about how the values of disciplinary faculty connect to the values of writing specialists and vice versa. For our students' sake as well as for our own, we aim to create a conference experience where people with differing expertise can connect, learn from each other, and carry that learning back to their classrooms, labs, faculty meetings, offices, and learning centers.

The diverse chapters collected here represent the spirit of connectedness that the IWAC 2018 conference emphasized. With the exception of Martha Townsend's invited essay, each chapter in this volume started as a session or keynote at IWAC 2018. While we invited submissions from all session types, the majority of submissions originated as panel presentations. We asked that each conference presentation be revised into a chapter submission. The co-editors reviewed all submissions and selected which ones to send to external reviewers. Because of the wide range of theoretical and methodological traditions our contributors explored under the umbrella of WAC—from translingualism to emotional labor to learning analytics—each selected submission was reviewed by no fewer than two external reviewers in addition to the co-editors (see acknowledgments page for a complete list of reviewers).

The emphasis on connection and common ground that felt so important to highlight when the OUW staff wrote the IWAC 2018 call for papers in early 2017 begs for complication and nuance now in response to escalating divisiveness, rancor, and disconnection—and in response to the diverse chorus of our contributors' work. The chapters collected here remind us that there is strength in difference. And while connection and common ground are sometimes worthy goals, they are not inherently virtuous. Thus, the collection highlights *both* connection *and* diversity—of ideas, strategies, approaches, and values. We hope the chapters collected here illustrate that connection and diversity are mutually enriching, not mutually exclusive. In fact, we argue that connection and diversity are keys to sustainability in WAC at this moment in time.

Sustainability has long been a concern for WAC. In their opening chapter to *WAC for the New Millennium*, Susan H. McLeod and Eric Miraglia (2001) wrote, "As an educational reform movement, [WAC] has had remarkable staying power, outlasting other institutional initiatives in higher education and enduring beyond the life expectancy that might have been predicted given the fate of similar movements in the past" (p. 1), and they noted reasons that WAC would likely endure, including "its institutionalization in many universities, its capacity to link up with and inform other initiatives in higher education, and the positive effect teachers say it has on their pedagogy" (p. 1). Of course, McLeod and Miraglia were right: WAC certainly had a future. At the same time, challenges continue to abound, making the search for sustainable practices a perennial pursuit for WAC. Recently, in *Sustainable WAC: A Whole Systems Approach to Launching and Developing Writing Across the Curriculum Programs*, Michelle Cox, Jeffrey R. Galin, and Dan Melzer (2018) provided a framework for addressing WAC program sustainability. The work in this volume complements their approach by demonstrating WAC's sustainability at various other levels, from explorations of individual teachers' classroom practices—what Cox et al. identified as the traditional focus of WAC scholarship (pp. 8–9)—to discussions about the preparation of future WAC scholars, to descriptions of how WAC is implemented throughout a university. This volume, indeed, is a testament to the durability and persistence of WAC.

In the chapters collected here, we see another useful lens for understanding and pursuing sustainability in response to this moment in time: resilience. Resilience has become a buzzword in fields as diverse as environmental studies, computer science, and economics. In a basic sense, resilience refers to the ability of a system (a person, an economy, a habitat) to weather adversity or disturbance and maintain its fundamental function or structure (Walker & Salt, 2006, p. xiii). Although resilience might seem inherently positive, as Chris W. Gallagher, Deborah Minter, and Shari J. Stenberg (2019) pointed out in the introduction to their recent special issue of *Pedagogy*, in our neoliberal age, it is important to remain "sharply critical of notions of resilience as a personal attribute or panacea" (p. 190). Nevertheless, they argue, and we agree, that a nuanced view of resilience can be valuable, even necessary, in this moment in time when higher education is faced with increasing austerity measures. In that vein, we suggest bringing the notion of resilience to complement a focus on sustainability in WAC.

In particular, we sense a deep resonance in the interplay of connection and diversity in WAC and in some definitions of resilience. From an environmental perspective, diversity is a necessary component of resilience because it determines "a system's capacity to respond to change and disturbance in different ways" (Walker & Salt, 2006, p. 145). A system with too much homogeneity may not respond well to disturbance; every component either responds well or succumbs to adversity. Diversity, however, increases the chances that some aspects of a system will respond or adapt to disturbance, sustaining the system in the long term. We invite readers of this volume to consider how diversity in approaches to WAC make it a resilient system, one able to weather the (in many ways) unprecedented adversity characterizing the climate of higher education at this moment in time. How might that resilience allow the connections, the foundational common ground that defines the WAC movement (values and commitments such as collaboration, for example) to sustain? At the same time, we might ask how diversity in WAC enacts critical definitions of resilience "that hold out promise not just for survival or riding out the status quo but for resistance, critique, and transformation" (Gallagher et al., 2019, p. 190). We invite readers to observe ways that WAC efforts captured in this volume not only adapt, bend, and compromise but also dig in, push back, and doggedly pursue systemic change.

The chapters that follow exemplify the keen capacity of WAC scholars and practitioners to embrace both connection and diversity as we work within the constraints of austerity and neoliberalism and simultaneously push on those constraints in pursuit of meaningful transformation. These contributions show WAC has met and continues meet that challenge by inspiring diverse agents and stakeholders to establish common ground on which to build momentum and resilience in response to an ever-changing educational landscape.

SUSTAINING MOMENTUM: HISTORIES AND FUTURES OF WAC

Chapters in the opening section describe and examine important developments in WAC, such as the evolution of the IWAC conference, the formation of professional organizations, and the exploration of learning analytics. In "A Personal History of WAC and IWAC Conferences, 1993–2020," Martha A. Townsend highlights a major feature of the grassroots WAC movement that has contributed to its staying power—the biennial conference, held for the first time in 1993. In the beginning, the conference was a way for a budding field to bring together early practitioners, build camaraderie, and share pedagogical and eventually programmatic practices. Today the conference represents "the key to WAC's overall ethos," what she calls a "capacious spirit for collaboration" as participants share "methods, data, teaching practices, and administrative acumen." Collaborative ethos and the drive to integrate diverse approaches, perspectives, and expertise remain the backbone of the WAC movement, our enduring point of connection.

Despite a foundational common ground, the evolution of WAC has, of course, historically been diffuse. As Christopher Basgier, Michelle Cox, Heather M. Falconer, Jeffrey Galin, Al Harahap, Brian Hendrickson, Dan Melzer, Mike Palmquist, and Stacey Sheriff explain in their chapter, "The Formation of a Professional Organization for Writing Across the Curriculum," the lack of a central organization constrained what WAC was able to accomplish in terms of membership, leadership, social agenda, and funding. In response, the Association for Writing Across the Curriculum (AWAC) was founded in 2018 to provide the WAC community with more of a voice, with procedures and support for developing new leaders, and with mechanisms for increasing the diversity of WAC scholars and practitioners. Basgier et al. recount the emergence of AWAC and highlight its historical significance to the movement.

In a similar vein, Alisa Russell, Jake Chase, Justin Nicholes, and Allie Sockwell Johnston, in "The Writing Across the Curriculum Graduate Organization: Where We've Been, Where We Are, and Where We're Going," explain how graduate students are "turning these conversations about the sustainability of WAC as a movement toward WAC as a field" by asking who will carry forward the vision of WAC as our founding leaders move toward retirement. They describe the establishment of WAC-GO, a formal organization developed to ensure the sustainability and diversification of the movement and field by pursuing a three-part mission to *energize*, *demystify*, and *connect*. Together, the establishment of the first graduate student organization and professional association for WAC constitutes new ways to sustain momentum by building on common ground. These organizations mark a turning point in the history of the field and attest to the ability of WAC to address the myriad challenges characterizing this moment in time—some unique and others sadly familiar—and to endure.

Mike Palmquist's chapter, "Learning Analytics in Writing Instruction: Implications for Writing Across the Curriculum," also illustrates a key resilience strategy for WAC: the ability to critically assess emerging trends in higher education and creatively adapt them to align with our values and commitments. Palmquist outlines and reflects on the slow but growing adoption of learning analytics tools in the field of writing studies. He examines the potential of writing analytics tools to process instructional data in order to predict, inform, and ideally enhance student learning. In addition to lauding the potential of these increasingly popular tools, Palmquist raises concerns about their use, opening the door for WAC scholars and practitioners to critically consider if, when, and how learning analytics might meaningfully support our work.

TEACHING AND LEARNING IN THE DISCIPLINES: DIVERSITY AND PARTICULARITY OF DISCIPLINARY PRACTICES AND GENRES

The chapters in this section model the key role of diversity in the context of WAC pedagogy. The contributors address one of WAC's primary concerns, the situated nature of writing practices in particular disciplinary cultures, and center on WAC's historical focus, how these practices are taught and learned in classrooms. In addition to simply being exemplars of pedagogical innovation, these chapters illustrate the epistemic, rhetorical nature of specific genres; the relationship between writing and the construction of one's scholarly or professional identity (what Kamler & Thomson, 2014, called "textwork/identitywork"); and the creative ways in which students come to learn about, adapt, and transform particular genres, not merely reproduce them.

Christy Goldsmith's teacher-research study, "Making Connections Between Theory and Practice: Pre-Service Educator Disciplinary Literacy Courses as Secondary WAC Initiation," examines a commonly ignored site of WAC teacher training: disciplinary literacy courses for secondary education majors that prepare them to teach writing-infused subjects, such as math and social studies, to high school students. The unique challenge of teaching disciplinary literacy pedagogy to preservice teachers, Goldsmith recounts, is that the preservice teachers themselves are not yet, and do not feel like, disciplinary experts. She quickly learned, through an introductory assignment called the "Reading and Writing in My Discipline Essay," that her students viewed reading and writing as generic academic practices. Yet because of Goldsmith's revisions to the curriculum, students eventually reconsidered what counted as knowing in their disciplines and began to see themselves as teachers of their disciplines. Goldsmith argues that "a campus culture which cultivates college students' disciplinary literacy identities from the moment they step into their math, science, literature, and history (and more) classrooms . . . produces stronger teachers which, in turn, produces stronger university students in the years to come." In this way, Goldsmith demonstrates, teacher education courses are important allies with the campus WAC community.

The rest of the chapters in this section respond to Goldsmith's call and illustrate—for the undergraduate mathematics proof, the engineering résumé, the social science literature review, and a graduate-level genre called the publication-based thesis—how and why these genres are patterned the way they are, ways to teach them, and/or students' processes of learning to produce them. In "What If It's *All* Common Knowledge? Teaching Attribution Practices in an Undergraduate Mathematics Classroom," Malcah Effron explores the role of attribution in mathematics courses where undergraduates write proofs. As Effron describes it, students' proofs usually re-prove established facts in the field—i.e., common knowledge, which typically wouldn't be cited—and paraphrasing may distort the accuracy of the proof. Effron asks, in what ways, then, can professional attribution be taught? She describes a series of pedagogical interventions she and colleagues have made to model professional practice. Her chapter illustrates how the seemingly generic concept of attribution is enacted in mathematics scholarship and how these practices can be applied to what is arguably a "mutt genre" (Wardle, 2009) that does not resemble authentic scholarly or professional communication.

In "Quantification of Disciplinary Discourse: An Approach to Teaching Engineering Résumé Writing," Mary McCall, Gracemarie Mike Fillenwarth, and Catherine G. P. Berdanier offer a pedagogy for résumés that is counter to the typically adisciplinary advice that emphasizes form (e.g., parallel structure) over content. Based on their research into the discourse of engineering résumés (e.g., Fillenwarth et al., 2018), this chapter describes the classroom activities they have designed that emerged from this research. They ask undergraduate engineering students to code their résumés for "disciplinary discourse" using the American Association of Engineering Societies Engineering Competency Model, calculate a "density" score, revise their résumés accordingly, and reflect on their professional identity development. In addition to demonstrating how Technical and Professional Communication (TPC) courses are a valuable site of WID research (Russell, 2007), the authors share how these exercises can be adapted for students in other majors.

Also exploring the discourse-level choices that help professionals recognize a particular genre as valid in the field, Misty Anne Winzenried focuses on students in a junior-level geography course learning to produce a literature review. In "Learning to Argue about the Literature: Discourse Choices and Students' Iterative Learning of Literature Reviews in Geography," Winzenried observed classes, collected artifacts, and conducted multiple semi-structured interviews with focal students. These interviews, done at multiple points in the semester as students were preparing a mini-literature review and then a more extensive literature review on a topic of their choosing, uncovered students' learning processes over time, revealing when and how they discovered the discursive signposts their instructors expected to see in the genre of the social science literature review, which the instructor described as "an argument" that is "about the literature." Winzenried's microanalysis of students' texts and talk—about their interactions with TA feedback, the assignment rubric, and genre models—gives WAC/WID instructors and scholars a window into student learning and ways of valuing students' still-developing genre knowledge.

Whereas Effron, McCall et al., and Winzenried discuss long-standing genres common to academic and workplace writing, Rachael Cayley's chapter, "Using Genre to Teach the Publication-Based Thesis," describes a genre that has long been used in European and Scandinavian universities (Guerin, 2016) but is increasingly common in North America: the publication-based thesis or dissertation (PBT). The PBT, which, according to Cayley, is composed of a number of publishable articles along with linking texts that "articulate how the whole project coheres," responds to the fact that many fields publish articles, not books, and privilege speed in communicating results. It also responds to an increasingly competitive job market in which publications strengthen one's marketability and to audit culture, which encourages the production of "'countable' research" (Guerin, 2016, p. 32). As Cayley points out, the purpose of the PBT purpose is pedagogical, not solely professional, in asking writers to demonstrate "the ability to articulate a sustained research agenda and the formation of an identity as an academic writer to communicate that research." Cayley argues that since most North American writing specialists have been trained in the humanities, which does not require the PBT, specialists and their students need a deeper understanding of PBT as a genre. She fills this gap by providing a discussion of the challenges and patterns of the PBT genre.

APPROACHING DIFFERENCE TOGETHER: CREATIVE COLLABORATIONS ACROSS UNITS, DISCIPLINES, LANGUAGES, AND EXPERTISE

From the beginning, WAC has been a movement rooted in collaboration across disciplines and institutional units. Barbara Walvoord's (1996) prognostication, cited in the introduction to *WAC for the New Millennium*, remains true today: "in an atmosphere of changing institutional priorities and funding opportunities, those of us involved in WAC must learn to collaborate with those involved in new initiatives, to 'dive in or die'" (p. 70, as quoted in McLeod & Miraglia, 2001, p. 3). As the call for papers for IWAC 2018 makes clear, our historical moment resonates in many ways with the "general atmosphere of gloom" (McLeod & Miraglia, 2001, p. 2) WAC faced almost two decades ago. The chapters in this section attest that WAC continues to meet the challenge of sustainability and resilience in part through creative approaches to collaboration.

In "'Something Invisible . . . Has Been Made Visible for Me': An Expertise-Based WAC Seminar Model Grounded in Theory and (Cross) Disciplinary Dialogue," Angela Glotfelter, Ann Updike, and Elizabeth Wardle describe ways in which the Howe Writing Fellows program at Miami University of Ohio fosters collaborations both within and across departments. Departmental teams work on projects together, including identifying threshold concepts for their fields and developing writing resources for their students, but the seminars foster collaborations between individuals from different departments in a number of innovative ways. From their ongoing program evaluation, the authors found that these cross-disciplinary collaborations, along with exposure to theories about writing and learning, have expanded faculty's conceptions of writing, helped them see that disciplinary writing is inseparable from disciplinary threshold concepts, and shifted teaching practices.

Similarly, in "Attempting to Connect Disciplinary Principles of 'Effective Writing' with Students' Prior Writing Experiences in Four Disciplines," James Croft, Phyllis Conn, Joseph Serafin, and Rebecca Wiseheart illustrate the value of cross-disciplinary collaboration for revealing, problematizing, and changing students' and instructors' assumptions about good writing. The four authors, all faculty at St. John's University, share insights from their years-long collaboration which began in local WAC workshops and programs and expanded to joint presentations at IWAC conferences. Juxtaposing their separate efforts to teach disciplinary writing in a legal writing course, history seminar, chemistry lab and clinical research writing course, the authors reflect on similarities and differences in disciplinary conventions. Cross-disciplinary collaboration, they show, usefully troubles assumptions about universally "effective writing" for students and faculty alike.

In a related vein, "Embrace the Messiness: Libraries, Writing Centers, and Encouraging Research as Inquiry Across the Curriculum" demonstrates how a collaboration among writing center staff and librarians helped students learn to embrace the necessarily messy entanglement of research and writing in and across disciplines and course levels. Jaena Alabi, James C. W. Truman, Bridget Farrell, and Jennifer Price Mahoney argue that "proximity does not necessarily result in productive collaborations; simply having similar practices and goals does not guarantee that separate units coordinate their activities. Rather, an increased intentionality is necessary to connect and integrate the practices of writing center consultants and librarians." As these two chapters show, collaborations across disciplines and institutional units can meaningfully integrate various types of expertise in service of empowering students to navigate disciplinary and academic discourses in more sophisticated and agential ways.

Two additional chapters in this section, "English Across the Curriculum Collaborative Projects: A Flexible Community of Practice Model at The Chinese

University of Hong Kong" and "Becoming *Transfronterizo* Collaborators: A Transdisciplinary Framework for Developing Translingual Pedagogies in WAC/WID," argue for the role of collaboration in sustaining WAC trends that have intensified in the new millennium. The first, by Jose Lai, Elaine Ng, Laura Man, and Chris Rozendaal, speaks to the internationalization of WAC by describing collaborative efforts at The Chinese University of Hong Kong. The authors explain a campus-wide English Across the Curriculum initiative that employs a Community of Practice approach to build teams of applied linguists, ESL specialists and disciplinary content experts to discover and address the unique needs of students in statistics, information engineering, music, and psychology, needs shaped in part by the diversity of students and a flexible university language policy. Their model offers a collaborative framework for U.S. WAC initiatives that don't always consciously include linguists and language specialists.

"Becoming *Transfronterizo* Collaborators: A Transdisciplinary Framework for Developing Translingual Pedagogies in WAC/WID" also emphasizes the role of language in WAC by modeling and advocating for a transdisciplinary framework for developing translingual pedagogies based on the notion of *transfronterizo* collaboration. Building on the growing demand for pedagogical approaches to WAC that challenge dominant language ideologies, Marcela Hebbard and Yanina Hernández argue that faculty must first come to terms with assumptions, experiences, and identities rooted in their linguistic and disciplinary histories. Drawing on their own experience, they elaborate a process of collaboration rooted in "border thinking" that has the potential to transform how faculty collaborators perceive their linguistic histories and abilities, challenge/enrich their instructional practices, and expand/complicate their scholarly knowledge. Along with Lai et al., Hebbard and Hernández show how issues introduced in *WAC for the New Millennium*, including Ann M. Johns' (2001) description of the "diverse needs" of "varied populations" of ESL learners and Victor Villanueva's (2001) discussion of the politics of literacy across the curriculum, have continued to evolve over time and how WAC faculty have responded by theorizing new means of collaboration.

ATTENDING TO THE HUMAN ELEMENT: ANTI-RACISM, EMOTIONAL LABOR, AND PERSONAL CONNECTION IN THE TEACHING OF WRITING

While all of the collected chapters attend to students in various ways, the chapters in our final section prioritize the human element of WAC work and the potential of an activist stance. These chapters call attention to and question the status quo in curriculum, programmatic outcomes, mentoring practices, and writing assignments and instruction.

In their epistolary chapter based on their IWAC 2018 keynote address, "Letters on Moving from Ally to Accomplice: Anti-Racism and the Teaching of Writing," Neisha-Anne S. Green and Frankie Condon name and challenge racism in academic spaces and curricula across disciplines. In naming linguistic supremacy's relationship to racism and white supremacy, they invite readers to move from the role of ally to the role of accomplice. Such a move entails learning about and teaching code-meshing, "the practice of braiding or blending languages, discourses, and rhetorical traditions within a single text—particularly those historically marginalized or excluded languages, discourses, and rhetorical traditions such as African American and Chicanx Englishes." Ultimately, Green and Condon argue that anti-racist work is WAC/WID work.

Like Green and Condon, Jamila M. Kareem's chapter, "Sustained Communities for Sustained Learning: Connecting Culturally Sustaining Pedagogy to WAC Learning Outcomes" invites readers to join the work of anti-racist writing pedagogies. In particular, Kareem argues for culturally sustaining pedagogies in the teaching of writing in the disciplines. Building on existing WAC scholarship, such as Writing Across Communities (Kells, 2018), Kareem argues that writing teachers across disciplines can go further in our work for students from raciolinguistically marginalized communities. Kareem offers concrete suggestions for revision of WAC outcomes to incorporate culturally sustaining pedagogies.

In "Emotional Labor, Mentoring, and Equity for Doctoral Student and Faculty Writers," Shannon Madden and Sandra L. Tarabochia focus on a population understudied by WAC scholars: emerging scholars, or writers who are late-stage doctoral students and early-career faculty. Their analysis of survey and interview data details how high-stakes mentoring situations can cause unwanted emotional labor that interferes with writers' development and productivity. The cause of this labor, they argue, is not solely poor individual mentors but also "structural issues that limit access to mentoring and that compel particular emotional performances as the cost of participation in institutional discourses." Their recommendations can help WAC leaders at colleges and universities improve the culture of writing for all writers on campus, not just undergraduates.

In their chapter based on their IWAC 2018 keynote address, "Meaningful Writing and Personal Connection: Exploring Student and Faculty Perspectives," Michelle Eodice, Anne Ellen Geller, and Neal Lerner returned to the data from their work on *The Meaningful Writing Project* (2017) to focus on the role of personal connection in writing. They invite readers to consider "pedagogies [that are] inclusive of students' identities and experiences—recognizing what students bring with them and where they are in their own development of academic literacies." Like the other chapters in this section, Eodice et al.'s work challenges conventional notions about what it means to teach writing well and makes visible the crucial role that identity plays in learning to write.

CONCLUSION AND ALTERNATIVE MAPS

This collection emphasizes making connections across diverse ideas, approaches, and people to build resilience in writers, teachers, and WAC programs and initiatives. We believe the lens of resilience complements and extends WAC's long-standing commitment to sustainability by highlighting the reciprocal relationship between connection and diversity, and we invite readers to view the chapters collected here with the following questions in mind: How does each chapter illustrate the importance of both connection and diversity as crucial elements of resilience? In what ways does each chapter work within and against conventional notions of resilience? How does a critical resilience lens open up possibilities for WAC scholars and practitioners and our students?

The chapters collected here offer an exciting picture of some of the important WAC work that is happening as the IWAC conference celebrates its twenty-fifth anniversary. Though we aim to mark this important moment in time, a collection like this cannot possibly offer a comprehensive picture. One important limit is that only presentations originally delivered at IWAC 2018 were considered for inclusion, and conference attendance requires resources that not everyone committed to WAC work has access to. Additionally, despite efforts to recruit diverse conference participants—from K–12, community colleges, museum studies, outreach and extension, international institutions, etc.—attendance still skewed toward writing specialists from four-year institutions in the United States. With these limitations notwithstanding, this collection offers a rich variety of ideas, approaches, methodologies, and programs for readers who are invested in the work of teaching writing across the curriculum in a wide range of institutional and disciplinary contexts. Indeed, there are many other points of connection between the essays that exceed our four sections: particular pedagogical, disciplinary, and geographical locations; specific empirical methodologies and methods or conceptual essays; chapters that focus on graduate or faculty writers, and teacher/mentor preparation. Readers who are interested in any of those areas can thus consult these alternative maps.

PEDAGOGICAL LOCATIONS

A number of chapters describe particular pedagogical practices that happen in common locations, from courses to WAC seminars to libraries.

- WID courses (Croft et al., Effron, Winzenried)
- Spanish as a Heritage Language courses (Hebbard and Hernández)

- English across the Curriculum courses (Lai et al.)
- First-year writing courses (Alabi et al., Hebbard and Hernández)
- Technical/professional communication courses (McCall et al.)
- Literacy methods courses for education majors (Goldsmith)
- Libraries (Alabi et al.)
- Writing centers (Alabi et al., Cayley)
- Partnerships between language/writing specialists and disciplinary faculty to teach and/or revise particular courses (Effron, Glotfelter et al., Lai et al.)
- WAC seminars (Glotfelter et al.)

Disciplinary Locations

The following is a list of writing-intensive courses that are explored in various chapters. As it happens, all of these courses are at the undergraduate level. Note that the courses are listed as they are described, and the authors provide more or less detail about the courses depending on their focus.

- Applied Nonparametric Statistics (Lai et al.)
- Communication Sciences and Disorders (Croft et al.)
- Disciplinary Literacies (Goldsmith)
- Engineering Clinic (McCall et al.)
- Experimental Physical Chemistry (Croft et al.)
- First-Year Writing (Hebbard and Hernández)
- Geography (Winzenried)
- Gerontology (Glotfelter et al.)
- History (Croft et al.)
- History of Western Music (Lai et al.)
- Information Engineering (Lai et al.)
- Legal Research and Writing (Croft et al.)
- Philosophy (Glotfelter et al.)
- Psychology of Consciousness (Lai et al.)
- Real Analysis (Effron)
- Spanish as a Heritage Language (Hebbard and Hernández)
- Writing in the Technical Professions (McCall et al.)

Geographical and Institutional Locations

Although the majority of authors do not focus on institutional and geographical location and are based in four-year colleges and universities in North America, the work of the authors of two chapters are intricately tied to their geographical and institutional locations.

- The Chinese University of Hong Kong (Lai et al.)
- The University of Texas Rio Grande Valley (Hebbard and Hernández)

EMPIRICAL RESEARCH CHAPTERS

Seven chapters report on empirical studies of teaching and learning.

- Classroom-based ethnography (Winzenried)
- Qualitative and quantitative analysis of interviews and surveys (Eodice et al., Madden and Tarabochia)
- Teacher research (Croft et al., Goldsmith)
- Program evaluation (Glotfelter et al., Lai et al.)

CONCEPTUAL CHAPTERS

Eleven chapters focus on what Liggett, Jordan, and Price (2011) called "conceptual inquiry," which encompasses historical, critical, and theoretical inquiry.

- Histories (Basgier et al., Russell et al., Townsend)
- Pedagogical narrative and analysis (Alabi et al., Cayley, Effron, McCall et al.)
- Critical/theoretical discussions (Green and Condon, Hebbard and Hernández, Kareem, Palmquist)

FOCAL PARTICIPANTS

The majority of the chapters focus on teaching and learning with undergraduates. A few chapters, however, center on the learning and development of graduate students and faculty, whether as writers, teachers, or WAC scholars.

- Graduate students (Cayley, Russell et al., Madden and Tarabochia)
- Faculty (Eodice et al., Glotfelter et al., Hebbard and Hernández, Madden and Tarabochia)

PREPARING FACULTY AS TEACHERS AND MENTORS

A few chapters focus on, or discuss implications for, the preparation of faculty and faculty mentors.

- Glotfelter et al.
- Goldsmith
- Madden and Tarabochia

REFERENCES

Cox, M., Galin, J. R. & Melzer, D. (2018). *Sustainable WAC: A whole systems approach to launching and developing Writing Across the Curriculum programs*. National Council of Teachers of English.

Eodice, M., Geller, A. E. & Lerner, N. (2017). *The meaningful writing project*. Utah State University Press. https://doi.org/10.7330/9781607325802.c001.

Fillenwarth, G. M., McCall, M. & Berdanier, C. G. P. (2018). Quantification of engineering disciplinary discourse in résumés: A novel genre analysis with teaching implications. *IEEE Transactions on Professional Communication, 61*(1), 48–64. https://doi.org/10.1109/TPC.2017.2747338.

Gallagher, C. W., Minter, D. & Stenberg, S. J. (2019). Introduction. *Pedagogy: Critical Approaches to Teaching Language, Literature, Composition, and Culture*, 19, 189–193. https://doi.org/10.1215/15314200–7295849

Guerin, C. (2016). Connecting the dots: Writing a doctoral thesis by publication. In C. Badenhorst & C. Guerin (Eds.), *Research literacies and writing pedagogies for masters and doctoral writers* (pp. 31–50). Brill. https://doi.org/10.1163/9789004304338_003.

Johns, A. M. (2001). ESL students and WAC programs: Varied populations and diverse needs. In S. H. McLeod, E. Miraglia, M. Soven & C. Thaiss (Eds.), *WAC for the new millennium: Strategies for continuing Writing Across the Curriculum programs* (pp. 141–164). National Council of Teachers of English. https://wac.colostate.edu/docs/books/millennium/chapter6.pdf.

Kamler, B. & Thomson, P. (2014). *Helping doctoral students write: Pedagogies for supervision* (2nd ed). Routledge. https://doi.org/10.4324/9781315813639

Kells, M. H. (2018). Writing across communities. In J. Liontas (Ed.), *The TESOL encyclopedia of English language teaching* (pp. 1–7). Wiley & Sons. https://doi.org/10.1002/9781118784235.eelt0152.

Liggett, S., Jordan, K. & Price, S. (2011). Mapping knowledge-making in writing center research: A taxonomy of methodologies. *The Writing Center Journal, 31*(2), 50–88.

McLeod, S. H. & Miraglia, E. (2001). Writing Across the Curriculum in a time of change. In S. H. McLeod, E. Miraglia, M. Soven & C. Thaiss (Eds.), *WAC for the new millennium: Strategies for continuing Writing Across the Curriculum programs* (pp. 1–27). National Council of Teachers of English. https://wac.colostate.edu/docs/books/millennium/chapter1.pdf.

Russell, D. R. (2007). Rethinking the articulation between business and technical communication and writing in the disciplines. *Journal of Business and Technical Communication, 21*, 248–277. https://doi.org/10.1177/1050651907300452.

Villanueva, V. (2001). The politics of literacy across the curriculum. In S. H. McLeod, E. Miraglia, M. Soven & C. Thaiss (Eds.), *WAC for the new millennium: Strategies for continuing Writing Across the Curriculum programs* (pp. 165–178). National Council of Teachers of English. https://wac.colostate.edu/docs/books/millennium/chapter7.pdf.

Walker, B. & Salt, D. (2006*). Resilience thinking: Sustaining ecosystems and people in a changing world*. Island Press.

Walvoord, B. E. (1996). The future of WAC. *College English, 58*(1), 58–74. https://doi.org/10.2307/378534.

Wardle, E. (2009). "Mutt genres" and the goal of FYC: Can we help students write the genres of the university? *College Composition and Communication, 60,* 765–789.

PART 1. SUSTAINING MOMENTUM: HISTORIES AND FUTURES OF WAC

CHAPTER 1.

A PERSONAL HISTORY OF WAC AND IWAC CONFERENCES, 1993–2020

Martha A. Townsend

University of Missouri

The biennial WAC and IWAC Conferences have become WAC's foremost conference for scholarly exchange. Yet no history of them exists for newer scholars to consult for help in understanding their role in WAC's becoming a subfield within Writing Studies. This article compiles a complete history to date, including how they began; what prompted the hosts to volunteer to take them on; how the conferences operated and were financed; the potentially confusing name change from WAC to IWAC; the value of the conference to the field as seen through a sampling of keynote addresses; and a look ahead. Beginning in 2020, the conference will for the first time come under the aegis of the newly formed Association for Writing Across the Curriculum (AWAC), making this an appropriate time to record conference history from 1993 to now.

My history of WAC and IWAC Conferences began as one third of a keynote address for the 2016 IWAC Conference hosted by the University of Michigan. I call this a personal history because, as I announced in the keynote, my goal was modest. I wasn't looking to make any grand claims. I simply wanted to document this one particular aspect of WAC culture so that it could be better known. Not long before the Michigan conference, I had taught a WAC graduate seminar for which students researched the conferences so as to better understand WAC as a subfield within Writing Studies. Although the students easily found information online, numerous gaps made forming a coherent picture problematic. The students and I realized that newer, younger scholars were likely not to ferret out the history either.

I say "one third" of a keynote address because the hosts of Michigan's conference, Anne Gere and her colleagues at the Gayle Morris Sweetland Center for Writing, were intent on "mak[ing] sure that the newest members of our profession feel that they have a place in IWAC" (A. Gere, personal communication, May 9, 2015). Gere's team assembled three keynote addresses, featuring multiple co-presenters ranging from doctoral students, postdoctoral fellows, and assistant professors to research and emerita professors. Gere invited me to "share the podium [and] engage the newcomers in a discussion . . . about where they see IWAC going." Andrea Olinger, one of the co-editors of this volume, was a co-presenter with me. As my review of WAC and IWAC Conferences shows, earlier conferences also featured multiple keynote addresses, often with two or more presenters (more on this later).

Table 1.1 summarizes the history of all WAC and IWAC Conferences, showing years held; locations held (which are sometimes different from the hosting institution); themes, if one was designated (the 1st, 2nd, 8th, 9th, and 10th conferences did not); attendance, if known; and conference hosts. Some of the information presented here is available at The WAC Clearinghouse (https://wac.colostate.edu), which hosts IWAC Conference archives from 2006 through 2018, and the Rice University website (https://nationalwac.rice.edu), which hosts WAC Conference archives from 1993 through 2004. The archives contain limited material, but offer reasonable places to begin exploring.

Table 1.1 A history of WAC and IWAC conferences

Year	Location	Theme	Attendance	Institution(s)	Conference Host(s)
2020	Fort Collins, CO	Celebrating Successes, Recognizing Challenges, Inviting Critique and Innovation	TBD	Colorado State University	Mike Palmquist, Caleb Gonzalez, and Matthew Klingstedt
2018	Auburn, AL	Making Connections	339	Auburn University	Margaret Marshall
2016	Ann Arbor, MI	Writing Across Difference	402	University of Michigan	Anne Gere
2014	Minneapolis, MN	Shifting Currents/ Making Waves	401	University of Minnesota	Pamela Flash
2012	Savannah, GA	The Future is WAC	453	Georgia Southern University	Michael Pemberton, Randall McClure, and Janice Walker
2010	Bloomington, IN	10th International WAC Conference	319	Indiana University	Laura Plummer and Jo Ann Vogt

Year	Location	Theme	Atten-dance	Institution(s)	Conference Host(s)
2008	Austin, TX	9th International WAC Conference	470	University of Texas Austin	Joan Mullin and Susan "George" Schorn
2006	Clemson, SC	8th International WAC Conference	420	Clemson University	Art Young and Kathleen Blake Yancey
2004	St. Louis, MO	WAC From an International Perspective	360	University of Missouri	Martha Townsend, Martha Davis Patton, and Jo Ann Vogt
2002	Houston, TX	Writing the Future: Leadership, Policies & Classroom Practice	un-known	Rice University	Linda Driskill
2001	Blooming-ton, IN	Writing, Teaching & Learning in New Contexts	418	Indiana University, Purdue University, and University of Notre Dame	Raymond Smith
1999	Ithaca, NY	Multiple Intelligences	400+	Cornell University	Jonathan Monroe
1997	Charleston, SC	Celebrating 27 Years of WAC	750	The Citadel, Clemson University, and College of Charleston	Carl Lovitt, Sylvia Gamboa, Angela Williams, and Art Young (advisor)
1995	Charleston, SC	2nd National WAC Conference	500	The Citadel, Clemson University, and College of Charleston	Carl Lovitt, Sylvia Gamboa, Angela Williams, and Art Young (advisor)
1993	Charleston, SC	1st National WAC Conference	150	The Citadel, Clemson University, and College of Charleston	Carl Lovitt, Sylvia Gamboa, Angela Williams, and Art Young (advisor)

For information not available through these archives, I turned to conference hosts themselves, most of whom I've come to know over the years and several of whom are treasured colleagues and friends. I also talked with one nonhost, Roy Andrews, editor of *The WAC Journal*, due to his longtime involvement with the field. All but one of the conference hosts provided personal recollections in semi-structured phone or in-person interviews in May 2016 and January to March 2019.

I was seeking basic background material, not in-depth information that would lead to a scholarly analysis. I spurred hosts' memories by asking such questions as: What was the impetus for your hosting the conference? What were your goals and did you achieve them? Did you "pay forward" any of the proceeds from your conference to help the next host mount her or his event? And—often their favorite—do you have any special memories from hosting? All interviewees seemed pleased to be discussing "their" conference and chatted freely about their experiences. One host declined to be interviewed due to that grant-funded program having ended and the host's retirement.

Taking a "personal" approach allows me to recognize and honor my own good fortune in having found an over 30-year academic home in WAC. As I think back on the WAC and IWAC Conferences I have attended (all except 1993), I am grateful for the intellectual and professional acculturation they have offered. A personal approach also allows me to integrate some of the hosts' reactions that would not necessarily appear in a more formal history but which illustrate the WAC and IWAC Conference ethos: friendly, open, congenial, good-natured—qualities that characterize the field of WAC itself.

The Association for Writing Across the Curriculum (AWAC), newly formed in 2019, will surely alter some of the conference's traditions, making this a propitious time to record the history. Basgier et al., in "The Formation of a Professional Organization for Writing Across the Curriculum" (this volume), describe how and why AWAC has taken shape. At the same time, some of AWAC's new leaders will come from WAC-GO, the relatively new graduate-student-led organization, which is concerned, as they say, not simply with the sustainability of WAC as a movement but also WAC as a field (see Russell et al., "The Writing Across the Curriculum Graduate Organization: Where We've Been, Where We Are, and Where We're Going," this volume).

Knowledge of one's professional history provides newcomers a way to build stronger relationships, construct disciplinary identity, nurture a sense of pride in one's work, and educate those who follow. Even though WAC-focused sessions have proliferated at the Conference on College Composition and Communication (4C's) over the years, the biennial WAC and IWAC meetings have become WAC's foremost conference for scholarly exchange. To invoke the old adage, and as the WAC-GO co-authors' title suggests, if we don't know where we've come from, how do we know where we're going?

CONFERENCE ORIGINS

WAC conferences began in 1993 in Charleston with the support of Art Young, one of WAC's foremost founders, scholars, and practitioners. Young, then a professor of both English and Engineering at Clemson University, was in Charleston to consult for Angela Williams at The Citadel and Sylvia Gamboa at College of Charleston, both of whom "were making a major commitment to WAC." (All quotations, unless otherwise indicated, are personal communications, taken directly from phone or in-person interviews.) Gamboa had been asked to "start a WAC program . . . to help evaluate writing across the disciplines." Having neither a WAC background nor a budget to travel to other programs, she "pushed for a conference in Charleston to bring WAC information there." Young took the idea back to Clemson, where Carl Lovitt was directing the Pearce Center for Professional Communication, with the suggestion that Lovitt help them organize it. "Gamboa ran it and Williams supported her," Lovitt recalls, while he "assembled the program all three years from Clemson," some 240 miles away. Lovitt fondly remembers that this assembly was accomplished by his "moving piles of paper around on the living room floor. *There was no technology.*" When the Charleston-based conference manager wanted Lovitt to send a program draft by email attachment, Carl had no idea how to do it.

Lovitt, Gamboa, and Williams' goals were straightforward: "to bring together practitioners in WAC and CXC (Communication across the Curriculum) and offer a forum for exchange of best practices." The first two conferences saw no emphasis on research or assessment, but participant feedback in 1995 indicated strong interest, and by the 1997 conference, research on WAC programs, especially in assessment, was added. By the time of the third in 1997, the attendance had grown so large—some 750—the three-way consortium had begun looking for a new host to take over.

Jonathan Monroe at Cornell eagerly assumed the role of next in line. Then in his second year of directing the Knight Writing Program (later the John S. Knight Institute for Writing in the Disciplines), Monroe "wanted to start realizing a fuller potential" for Cornell's writing program. Akin to Gamboa, Monroe, a comparative literature scholar, reasoned that, "hosting a conference would bring scholarship to campus from non-lit disciplines." The Cornell conference's 1999 theme "Multiple Intelligences" could be seen as solidifying the turn from "best practices" to a more scholarly oriented academic conference. One of Cornell's plenary addresses was delivered by a Nobel Prize winning chemist on their faculty. Monroe subsequently edited two volumes featuring his colleagues' work: *Writing and Revising the Disciplines* (2002) and *Local Knowledges, Local Practices: Writing in the Disciplines at Cornell* (2006).

From Cornell onward, the conferences have seen a continually increased focus on research, assessment, transfer of student knowledge from first-year composition to writing-intensive courses, interdisciplinarity, translingualism, and more—while also maintaining WAC's initial, primary focus on classroom pedagogy and student learning.

The sole exception to the WAC conference's biennial timing occurred in 2002, when Rice University hosted just one year after Indiana University's 2001 conference. Rice organizers hoped that henceforward conferences would be held annually, as they had done. However, the University of Missouri which was selected as the next host, recognized that one year's lead time was insufficient to identify a conference venue and lodging; issue a Call for Proposals; plan a program; and attend to the myriad other details required in mounting the conference. With Missouri's 2004 event, the conference returned to a biennial calendar.

IMPETUS AND ETHOS

As expected, all hosts demonstrated a scholarly commitment to the field of WAC, albeit from differing perspectives. All had been working in WAC for some time, and their ability to mount a large professional conference likely derived from having steered into being the complex, campus-wide curricular programs under their direction.

Hosts had strategic reasons for hosting that were not necessarily foregrounded in their Calls for Proposals (CFP). Of course, all aimed to create and disseminate scholarly knowledge about WAC. But they also used the conference to showcase their institutions, programs, faculty accomplishments, and ongoing research. Some capitalized on hosting to garner the attention of their local administrators, while others, like Gamboa and Monroe, used the conference as an occasion to educate themselves or influence their own faculty's thinking.

All hosts exhibited a capacious spirit for collaboration. Key to WAC's overall ethos is sharing methods, data, teaching practices, and administrative acumen. This collaborative spirit of WAC in general is clearly evident in hosts' comments about mounting their conferences. Hosts paying forward a portion of their proceeds to assist subsequent hosts in mounting their conferences is a good example, as are the freely offered suggestions of how to run them efficiently and offers to help vet the hundreds of participant proposals submitted.

Not surprisingly, all 15 WAC and IWAC Conferences have been (or will be) hosted by institutions with a strong WAC presence. All but three—Cornell, Notre Dame, and Rice, private institutions with endowed programs—are large public, research-based universities. Michigan is the single public exception in holding endowed status. Most are situated in the South and Midwest. No two-year institutions have hosted, presumably because WAC's presence and resources have traditionally been concentrated at four-year institutions.

OPERATIONS AND FINANCING

Until 2020, WAC conferences have been undertaken without an official organizational imprimatur. Each conference was organized and funded independently by a volunteer host and institution or group of institutions. The gatherings followed the general pattern of academic conferences (keynote addresses, plenary and concurrent sessions, workshops, publishers' exhibits, a reception, a proceedings document), with local hosts determining their own theme. Hosts usually engaged their institution's central conference office to manage enrollment, publicity, hotel contracts, meal arrangements, program printing, etc. But each local host remained responsible for establishing a budget; soliciting external funding; issuing a CFP; and inviting plenary speakers to address each conference's unique theme.

Each year, a committee of former hosts convened to review proposals for hosting the subsequent conference and select the next location. Each prospective host submitted a proposal demonstrating that institution's ability to mount a successful conference—dates, venue, lodging, institutional and financial backing, travel options, theme, perhaps tentative plenary speakers, and the like. As a participant in those deliberations every year from 2006 onward, I was always reassured by the proposals' quality and the commitment represented in them. Selections were made unanimously and with confidence. As with the fiscal philosophy of "paying forward," former hosts have generously advised new hosts on myriad logistics.

Because each host institution operated without a backing organization, each conference needed to break even to avoid sustaining a loss. So, in WAC's spirit of sharing *pedagogical* resources, a tradition took hold early on that each conference "paid forward" a portion of its proceeds to help the new host mount the succeeding conference—a tradition that continued through 2018. A portion of the monies remaining at the end of Auburn's 2018 conference was transferred into AWAC's new budget. Effective with the 2020 conference at Colorado State University, hosting institutions will be supported by the new professional organization.

WAC VERSUS IWAC NAMING: A CONFERENCE CONUNDRUM

Building on its work at multiple sites abroad, Missouri designated "WAC From an International Perspective" for the 2004 conference in St. Louis. Rather than re-naming the conference outright by declaring it an "international" conference, the previous-WAC-host committee waited to see how the international community responded. When 10% of the 2004 participants—36 of 360 registrations—came from institutions beyond U.S. borders, with panels featuring WAC work abroad, the committee added "International" to the title. Thus, the 2006 event hosted by Clemson, and all that follow, are referred to as International WAC Conferences or IWAC.

WAC advocates in the US have long noted substantial interest in WAC theory and pedagogy from non-U.S. locales. Mike Palmquist, WAC Clearinghouse founder (and host for the upcoming 2020 IWAC Conference), reports: "Of 2.7 million visits to the website, nearly 54 percent come from outside the US." (email to Townsend, April 10, 2019). The visits track closely to downloads, he adds, although he does not have data matching downloads to countries. In another sign of international interest, robust exchanges have been taking place between WAC scholars in the US and their international colleagues for more than two decades.

WAC Clearinghouse statistics and scholarly exchanges across borders, however, do not ensure IWAC conference participation. To my knowledge, no consistent records of international participation have been kept. Gamboa reports that two foreign countries were represented at the 1995 conference. Seventeen years later, Michael Pemberton's international response for 2012 in Savannah was "relatively small," with most of the non-U.S. participants coming from Canada. Pamela Flash reports that, despite significant recruiting, her 2014 efforts for the Minnesota conference were "not successful." In a significant uptick, Michigan host Anne Gere's staff reports that 22 countries were represented in 2016. Auburn host Margaret Marshall, reports that the 2018 international response was "thin." She notes that the English Across the Curriculum conferences sponsored by Hong Kong Polytechnic University (2016, 2018) and the Writing Research Across Borders conferences, sponsored by the International Society for the Advancement of Writing Research, held or forthcoming in Paris, France (2014), Bogota, Colombia (2017) and Xi'an, China (2020) offer opportunities that may be more cost effective for international travelers.[1]

Others, however, cite productive international collaborations that have developed in conjunction with IWAC events, such as Clemson's former project with Chalmers University of Technology in Sweden. Flash reports that her

---

1 Regrettably, the 2020 China event was cancelled due to the COVID-19 pandemic.

Writing-enriched Curriculum (WEC) Program at Minnesota has had collaborations with universities in Germany and Norway. From as far back as 1996, we at Missouri have hosted over a dozen international scholars for several weeks to as long as a full year.

Consideration was given some years ago to selecting a conference site in Canada, but concern for travel cost for the predominantly U.S. audience led to a U.S. site being chosen. As the conference continues to mature, organizers may wish to track international participation. Eventually, organizers and hosts may need to grapple with the conundrum of an "international" conference that is held only in the US.

To close this section on an upbeat note, a favorite memory from Art Young of hosting the first-designated International WAC Conference, at Clemson, involves inviting more than a dozen international participants to an impromptu dinner at his home after the conference ended. These conference goers couldn't leave town until the following day and he was eager to ensure they enjoyed a hospitable closure to their travels. The South Carolina skies poured forth with heavy rain that day, but the camaraderie wasn't dampened. Wine and beer and barbecue are just as easily served on the carport as in the dining room.

CONFERENCE VALUE AND NOTABLE KEYNOTES

Conference hosts believe that the WAC conferences have contributed to the field of WAC practice and theory. As Mullin succinctly puts it, "The conferences situate us as valid researchers and teachers." Pemberton says the conferences "have demonstrated sustained, ongoing interest in WAC; [helped to grow] the international connections; offer format and opportunity to share research, experiences, innovations; they inspire, respect, and value what *all* disciplines can bring."

Roy Andrews who, as editor of *The WAC Journal*, has observed the field closely since 1995 and attended most of the biennial meetings, reeled off a list of the conferences' contributions to WAC: "It's a good place to recruit 'frontier' articles for the journal, like Carol Rutz's interview series with prominent WAC figures; to meet people from disciplines like ESL and STEM (as opposed to writing center conferences, where participants are more homogeneous); and to foster research in addition to pragmatics."

A complete history of keynote addresses from 1993 through 2018, and the scholars who delivered them, would say much about the 14 WAC and IWAC Conferences so far. But inasmuch as most conferences featured multiple keynotes—and many of those talks featured two or more speakers delivering co-authored remarks—such an accounting isn't possible here. Still, the following

29

selection of keynote addresses illustrates the range and depth of issues that conference goers have been asked to ponder.

In 1995, Jacqueline Jones Royster, then at The Ohio State University, posed a provocative question about the emerging field in her talk "Writing Across the Curriculum: Whose Story Is This?" Whose experience, exactly, is being enacted, she wanted participants to consider. As a listener in that Charleston audience, I felt undeniably challenged. Even before the advent of today's diversity-driven agendas and institutionally appointed diversity officers, I was personally called to examine more closely who my students were and whether I was teaching them ethically.

Four years later, Charles Bazerman, University of California, Santa Barbara, took up Cornell's theme of Multiple Intelligences to pose "An Unfinished History of Intelligences, or Just Where Is This Curriculum We're Supposed to Cross?" He brought to Cornell the external scholarship that Monroe had sought in order to empower that institution to think more deeply about using writing to teach discipline-based modes of thinking. The two books Monroe subsequently edited featured a cross-section of Cornell faculty from neurobiology, psychology, philosophy, law, physics, history, chemistry, classics, government, and more.

Befitting its 2004 theme of "WAC from an International Perspective," Missouri featured the WAC Conference's first international keynoter, Professor and Dean of Education Richard Bates from Deakin University in Australia. In "Can We Live Together? Towards a Global Curriculum," Bates took up French sociologist Alain Touraine's assertion that the major global problem is not economic, but social, to argue that a global curriculum conceived in social terms would be possible if certain criteria were met. Bates' keynote was published in 2005 in Arts and Humanities in Higher Education, (4)1, 95–109.

Bazerman, founder of the Writing Research Across Borders (WRAB) initiative, was back as a WAC Conference keynoter again in 2008, this time at University of Texas at Austin. Bazerman's plenary panel, "Writing Across International and Curricular Borders," featured colleagues from Université Stendahl, Grenoble, France; Central European University, Budapest, Hungary; Loyola College, Baltimore, Maryland, US; and Institute of Education, University of London, England, who offered WAC Conference goers a cross-section of research that had been represented at WRAB conferences. WRAB's work has been subsumed by the new International Society for the Advancement of Writing Research (ISAWR).

In Michigan in 2016, conference participants considered the impact of WAC on non-native students through that year's focus on difference. A three-speaker keynote panel comprised of Jonathan Alexander, University of California-Irvine; Paula Carlino, University of Buenos Aires; and Jonathan Hall, York College, CUNY, presented "World-Wide WAC?: Encountering Difference Across Places,

Languages, and Technologies." Among other topics, they examined the transnational and translingual identities students bring to our classrooms.

In numerous ways, many of these keynotes seem as current today as when they were originally presented. An analysis of as many of the addresses as could be found would make for a worthwhile master's thesis.

LOOKING AHEAD

Both the field of WAC and its academic conference have come a long way since their respective origins in the 1970s and 1993. To put WAC conference history into context with the field as a whole, see "Fifty Years of WAC: Where Have We Been? Where Are We Going?" presented by the new WAC Standing Group at the 2019 4C's, available at https://wac.colostate.edu/standing-group/. As the 4C's presentation and other recent developments make clear, the study of writing in and across the disciplines, both in the United States and abroad, is proliferating via AWAC, WAC-GO, ISAWR, WEC, and the WAC Standing Group.

These, combined with already familiar locations where writing teachers converge—K–12, NWP, CAC, ECAC, writing centers, regional WAC associations, Consortium on Graduate Communication, and others—indicate a continued need to come together to discuss and share what we know and do. As scholars in the US and abroad continue to pursue an understanding of how writing, and language use writ large, affects student learning—particularly of the burgeoning number of second-language users—IWAC is well positioned to continue as a site for scholarly exchange. With the infusion of new leadership through AWAC and new leaders rapidly coming up through WAC-GO, new young scholars will surely find the conference as affirming and intellectually stimulating as I have. They will also find a welcome environment for making their own contributions to the field. Personally, I'm excited to observe and take part.

ACKNOWLEDGMENTS

Thanks to Pamela Flash, Anne Gere, Carl Lovitt, Jonathan Monroe, Joan Mullin, Martha Davis Patton, Michael Pemberton, Raymond Smith, Art Young (whom I interviewed in 2016), and Sylvia Gamboa, Margaret Marshall, Mike Palmquist, Naomi Silver, and Jo Ann Vogt (whom I interviewed in 2019) for providing personal recollections and historical data.

REFERENCES

Monroe, Jonathan. (2002). *Writing and revising the disciplines.* Cornell University Press.

Monroe, Jonathan. (2002). *Local knowledges, local practices: Writing in the disciplines at Cornell.* University of Pittsburgh Press.

Palmquist, Mike, Childers, Pamela, Galin, Jeffrey R., Maimon, Elaine, Mullin, Joan, Rice, Rich, Russell, Alisa & Russell, David R. (2019). Fifty years of WAC: Where have we been? Where are we going?" Presented at the Conference on College Composition and Communication, Pittsburgh, PA, March 13–16, 2019. https://wac .colostate.edu/standing-group/.

CHAPTER 2.

THE FORMATION OF A PROFESSIONAL ORGANIZATION FOR WRITING ACROSS THE CURRICULUM

Christopher Basgier[1]
Auburn University

Michelle Cox
Cornell University

Heather M. Falconer
Curry College

Jeffrey Galin
Florida Atlantic University

Al Harahap
University of Oklahoma

Brian Hendrickson
Roger Williams University

Dan Melzer
University of California, Davis

Mike Palmquist
Colorado State University

Stacey Sheriff
Colby College

---

1   Authorship is alphabetical

DOI: https://doi.org/10.37514/PER-B.2020.0360.2.02

In this chapter, we describe the rationale for and development of the Association for Writing Across the Curriculum (AWAC), which held its first meeting for members at the 2018 International Writing Across the Curriculum Conference. We first provide a historiography of previous WAC/WID-related efforts, including the specific contributions of each one, leading up to the more formalized process of establishing this new organization. Finally, we explain our aspirations of AWAC's role in supporting a sustainable and inclusive scholarly WAC/WID community.

Writing across the curriculum (WAC) has been recognized as the longest-standing curricular reform movement in U.S. higher education (Russell, 2002). It is widely adopted across the United States and, to a lesser but growing extent, in other countries. It is also recognized as one of the original high-impact practices (Kuh, 2008). A 2009 survey of WAC programs found that 64% of responding U.S. institutions either had or were planning to start a WAC or WID program (Thaiss & Porter, 2010). WAC enjoys substantial international strength as well, as indicated by reports in *Writing Programs Worldwide* (Thaiss et al., 2012) and presentations at conferences sponsored by organizations such as the European Association of Teaching Academic Writing and Writing Research Across Borders.

Despite its widespread adoption, WAC had not given rise to a formal professional association until 2018. Certainly, informal efforts such as the International Network of Writing Across the Curriculum Programs (INWAC), which began holding its annual meetings in 1981 at the Conference on College Composition and Communication (CCCC), played a central role in bringing WAC scholars together. And a wide range of WAC initiatives have served as a focus for this important educational movement. Until late 2018, however, members of the WAC community lacked a formal membership-based organization with bylaws that provided clear procedures for joining, entering into leadership roles, and funding initiatives.

This observation is not intended to diminish the success of WAC or the support it has enjoyed in higher education in the US and elsewhere. Indeed, one challenge we have faced, both as members of the working group that established the organization we discuss in this chapter and as the authors of the chapter, is how to accurately and appropriately recognize efforts that came before—and in some ways led to—the formation of the Association for Writing Across the Curriculum (AWAC). These include several important initiatives and groups:

- Since its founding in 1981, the INWAC Board of Consultants led an annual INWAC Special Interest Group (SIG) meeting at CCCC.

During this meeting, consultants met with small groups to discuss WAC program design, assessment, and administration, thus facilitating numerous mentoring relationships between experienced WAC scholars and those new to WAC. INWAC also facilitated the creation of a directory of WAC programs, managed and published annually by Chris Thaiss and later moved to the WAC Clearinghouse.

- In 2017, this INWAC SIG became the CCCC WAC Standing Group (https://wac.colostate.edu/standing-group), which meets annually at CCCC. It supports relationships between WAC and the broader writing studies community and provides resources to CCCC members interested in WAC.
- In addition to the attention it receives in national, regional, and international writing and education conferences, two biennial conferences bring together WAC scholars: the International Writing Across the Curriculum Conference (IWAC) and the Critical Thinking and Writing Conference held at Quinnipiac University.[2] More recently, the English Across the Curriculum conference, hosted by Hong Kong Polytechnic University, has also brought together international WAC scholars.
- Since 1997, the WAC Clearinghouse publishing collaborative (https://wac.colostate.edu) has offered access to a large number of open-access publications and resources, including monographs, edited collections, scholarly journals, and textbooks.[3] In addition to several book series, the Clearinghouse publishes *Across the Disciplines*, *The WAC Journal* (with Clemson University and Parlor Press), and *The Journal of Writing Analytics* and makes available several other open-access journals in current or archival forms, including *Double Helix*, *Language and Learning Across the Curriculum*, and the *Journal of Basic Writing*.
- The WAC-L email discussion list supports communication among WAC scholars (https://lists.illinois.edu/lists/info/wac-l).
- The Writing Across the Curriculum Graduate Organization (WAC-GO) provides a professional organization for graduate students focusing on WAC (https://wac.colostate.edu/go).

Regional organizations such as the Northeast Writing Across the Curriculum Consortium (https://newacc.colostate.edu) have been or are being formed.

Certainly, these WAC-related initiatives and groups do much of the work

---

2   For a thorough history of IWAC with reflections on the influence that the formation of AWAC will have on the conference and WAC more generally, see Townsend (this volume).

3   For an analysis of the publishing collaborative model, see Palmquist et al. (2012).

Joshua Kim (2018) identified in an *Inside Higher Education* blog as the province of professional associations. However, for much of its existence, WAC has resembled writing program administration before the formation of the Council of Writing Program Administrators (CWPA) and writing center studies before the formation of the International Writing Centers Association (IWCA). The lack of a formal professional organization—a hub, such as those provided by the CWPA and the IWCA—has arguably limited what this collection of WAC groups has been able to accomplish.[4] Barbara Walvoord (1996), for example, observed that a central organization would better position WAC to take part in national movements that impact writing and to support new and existing WAC programs (p. 74). Similarly, Thaiss (2006) noted that without a formal organization, WAC had been unable to "create an agenda to focus efforts, issue position statements, establish and publish standards, conduct statistical surveys of members, and, maybe most basic, ensure continuity through an orderly process of succeeding leadership" (p. 139).

Moreover, the informality of the structures that have emerged has had unintended consequences, including a lack of clearly defined pathways for getting involved and perceptions, particularly among those new to the WAC community (including graduate students, junior scholars, and seasoned scholars who unexpectedly find themselves in the position of leading institutional WAC efforts), that the existing constellation of WAC organizations has not met their needs. In "The Writing Across the Curriculum Graduate Organization: Where We've Been, Where We Are, and Where We're Going" (this volume), Alisa Russell, Jake Chase, Justin Nicholes, and Allie Sockwell Johnston attribute the motivations for forming WAC-GO to a desire to contribute to the sustainability of WAC and the need to develop clearer pathways for involvement:

> WAC-GO is the result of turning these conversations about the sustainability of WAC as a *movement* toward WAC as a *field*. Many of the founders and key figures of the WAC movement who have ensured its sustainability so far are moving (or have moved) into retirement. As a new organization in the field, then, WAC-GO contends that the question of who will replace these founders and key figures should be one of central focus. WAC-GO also contends that replacing and diversifying key figures in WAC will take more than informal measures. . . . We believe that a formal organization

---

4   For an analysis of WAC organizations and the impact of the lack of a hub on the sustainability of a field, see Cox et al., 2018, pp. 218–233.

like WAC-GO can provide the structures graduate students need for successful socialization, which we further believe is necessary to both sustain and diversify the field.

The establishment of a formal organization makes it easier for those new to the field to obtain mentoring, engage in professional development, collaborate on scholarly work, and participate in leadership efforts. It also allows WAC as a field to increase the diversity of scholars who participate in WAC initiatives. Making a commitment to diversifying WAC not only promises to strengthen the field but also aligns with broader calls to address the disparity between the lack of diversity in faculty and leadership positions in higher education and an increasingly diverse student demographic nationwide (Taylor et al., 2010).

A formal organization can (1) provide codified structures for active membership in the WAC community, (2) ensure equitable pathways for scholarly and professional development in WAC, (3) establish procedures for cultivating new leadership, (4) envision and build new resources for the WAC community, and (5) include faculty from WAC programs who would not likely have become involved without institutional membership opportunities. Thus, a formal organization increases the likelihood that the diverse perspectives associated with a wide range of member experiences, backgrounds, institutional affiliations, and instructional goals can enhance the vitality of the WAC movement, its constituent organizations, and its scholarship. The inclusion of these diverse perspectives also makes it likely that the WAC movement itself will remain responsive to shifting student demographics and associated changes in the landscape of higher education. A formal organization can also seek status as a government-sanctioned 501(c)(3) entity, allowing it to address pragmatic concerns such as the establishment of bank accounts for constituent organizations. Finally, and perhaps most importantly, a formal organization can ensure that emerging scholars see WAC as a welcoming, intentionally inclusive community that is committed to the growth of WAC scholars, WAC scholarship, and WAC programs.

ESTABLISHING AWAC

AWAC emerged from conversations at and following CCCC 2015, CCCC 2016, IWAC 2016, CCCC 2017, and CCCC 2018, as well as Skype discussions involving a fairly large group of interested participants who volunteered to help draft the organization's mission, goals, bylaws, and descriptions of committees.

These conversations were prompted by a change in leadership of the INWAC Board of Consultants, combined with the impending retirements of many of the leaders of the WAC movement. At the CCCC 2016 INWAC SIG meeting, participants agreed (1) to move forward with a CCCC Standing Group application, which would give the SIG more stability, and (2) to host a broad discussion about a larger WAC organization at the upcoming IWAC conference in Ann Arbor.

At the IWAC 2016 meeting—which included stakeholders representing INWAC, the WAC Clearinghouse, WAC-GO, various WAC journals, and directors of the IWAC and Critical Thinking/Writing conferences—participants expressed a great deal of respect for those who had created the foundations for WAC. However, they also identified limitations, such as perceived barriers to participation and the need to engage critically with the diversity and future of WAC. Attendees discussed how WAC might benefit from the coordination and collaboration a formal organization could foster.

INWAC Co-Chairs Michelle Cox, Jeff Galin, Anne Ellen Geller, and Dan Melzer subsequently created a survey to solicit feedback from the wider WAC community about the structure and goals for a new national organization. The survey results were presented at an open meeting at the CCCC 2017. Most survey respondents supported the idea of creating a new professional organization, noting that this organization could create pathways into leadership positions, promote research, and provide more visibility for the field and those who identify with it professionally. During the meeting, some participants expressed concern about the potential loss of the informal spirit that has characterized WAC culture, others expressed concern that an organization emerging from the field of Writing Studies might discourage membership from scholars in other fields, and still others argued that formal structures would allow the field to be more inclusive and diverse.

The CCCC 2017 meeting concluded with a proposal to form a working group to draft the prospective WAC organization's mission, goals, and bylaws. Invitations were sent to a number of email discussion lists. The resulting group, composed of more than 20 new and seasoned stakeholders, worked for 18 months to develop AWAC's foundational documents. Subsequently, feedback was solicited on AWAC's mission statement, bylaws, and associated documents on the web, via email discussion lists, and at an open meeting at CCCC 2018. In the AWAC working group's subsequent Skype discussions, initial dates were set for a membership call, approval of the bylaws, election of officers, and incorporation of AWAC both as a state nonprofit and as a 501(c)(3) organization.

In the spring of 2018, more than 250 members joined the organization and plans were made to host a fourth face-to-face open meeting at IWAC 2018. This timing was opportune: IWAC 2018 was the conference's twenty-fifth anniversary, so it was fitting that the inaugural meeting of the growing organization coincided with this milestone for the larger WAC community. AWAC also embodies the conference theme, "Making Connections." We saw such connections at work in the organization's IWAC 2018 session, during which available AWAC working group members offered a brief overview of the organization and then invited members to meet in committee working groups, to discuss committee descriptions, goals, and objectives, and to share ideas and insights. Each committee group reported back to the larger group, suggesting ways that AWAC could help support and grow existing WAC initiatives as well as strategies for the committees to work with each other. This participatory process mirrored the WAC community's long-standing commitment to grassroots action and the inclusion of diverse perspectives, including those of the many scholars, administrators, disciplinary faculty, librarians, high school teachers, and community members who attended IWAC 2018.

One important conversation that took place during and following the IWAC 2018 meeting addressed the nature of affiliations with other organizations. The key concern was how, if AWAC were to act as a hub, affiliations with other organizations would function. Four groups were interested in formal affiliations: IWAC (see Townsend, this volume), the recently organized WAC-Graduate Organization (see Russell et al., this volume), the WAC Clearinghouse, and the newly launched WAC Summer Institute. These groups sought formal affiliation not only for the organizational support but also to manage funds more effectively than they had been able to do as less formal (i.e., non–501(c)(3)) organizations. At first, the intention was to create Memoranda of Understanding to define the relationships between these organizations and AWAC. However, in working through the process of filing for 501(c)(3) status, it became clear that this option wasn't tenable. In the end, three of the organizations decided to become part of AWAC by forming committees within it, giving each organization representation on the AWAC Executive Board and full access to AWAC's infrastructure. The WAC Clearinghouse, which had been involved in the discussions, was unable to affiliate using the committee model because of the nature of its funding structure.

In November 2018, the state non-profit organization was created, the first slate of officers was elected, and the AWAC website (https://www.wacassociation.org) went live. Dues-paying membership was opened in January 2019, committees held their first official meetings that February. In March, the 501(c)(3) application was filed, committees drafted proposals for their first year of work, and the organization held its first business meeting, which took place at the CCCC.

ORGANIZATIONAL STRUCTURE AND NEXT STEPS

The Executive Board of AWAC is comprised of Past-, Current-, and Incoming-Chairs; a Secretary and Treasurer; three Members-at-large; and Committee

Chairs. The inaugural Executive Board (elected in November 2018) is charged with developing the foundation on which the organization will build over time.

Central to the organizational structure of AWAC are the committees, through which much of the work of the organization moves forward (see Table 2.1).

Table 2.1. AWAC's standing committees

Committee	Primary Purpose
Advocacy	To advocate for WAC organizations, programs, and practices
Communications	To communicate and disseminate the work of AWAC
Diversity and Inclusion	To promote diversity and inclusion within AWAC and the field of WAC
International Collaborations	To foster collaborations between AWAC and WAC organizations, conferences, and scholars outside of the US
International Writing Across the Curriculum (IWAC) Conference	To host a biennial conference focused on WAC
Mentoring	To facilitate mentorship opportunities for a range of WAC stakeholders
Partnerships	To develop and sustain formal and informal partnerships with higher education and K–12 organizations whose purposes align with the goals of AWAC (i.e., CCCC, CWPA, NCTE, NWP)
Research and Publications	To support, disseminate, and develop research related to WAC
Writing Across the Curriculum Graduate Organization (WAC-GO)	To provide networking and mentorship opportunities for graduate students interested in WAC
Writing Across the Curriculum Summer Institute (WACSI)	To host an annual summer institute for novice WAC program directors

Two of the AWAC committees, IWAC and WACSI, are comprised of those who organize the events associated with these committees. The remaining eight committees are open to all AWAC members, who may select the committees they wish to join when registering with the organization. It is important to note that while the WAC-GO committee is focused on creating opportunities for graduate students, membership on this committee is not limited to graduate students. In fact, the committee chairs hope that experienced WAC scholars join this committee. Furthermore, graduate students are encouraged to join other committees, so that they may have a voice in the important conversations that have implications for the future of the field. AWAC also encourages cross-fertilization among committees by allowing members to join two committees. The inclusive nature of these committees creates opportunities for all members to have a hand in shaping and contributing to the organization.

Immediately following its launch, AWAC charged each committee to begin its work. On an ongoing basis, the chairs of each committee will collaborate with committee members to identify specific, measurable, and achievable goals, and the committee members will then work to achieve these goals. Initially, these efforts have been built on the ideas gathered during the AWAC meeting at IWAC 2018. For example, the members of the Research and Publications Committee began exploring initiatives for supporting WAC scholarship, such as mentoring, mini-grants, and cross-institutional research collaborations. The Diversity and Inclusion (D&I) Committee explored ways to hold AWAC accountable to issues of demographic, disciplinary, and institutional diversity and inclusion, such as having D&I committee members sit on other committees and inviting members of other committees to do D&I work. The Partnerships Committee brainstormed potential partnerships between AWAC and other WAC and writing-related organizations as well as among WAC programs. The Mentorship Committee brainstormed the idea of establishing mentoring "pods" of colleagues from similar institutions who seek support for their ongoing programs with seasoned WAC program directors. This committee also began exploring how to formalize a WAC consulting board to take on one of the roles that the INWAC board of consultants used to serve, providing consultations for universities building WAC programs. The Advocacy Committee began thinking about how AWAC might advocate for WAC programs and practices, as well as what AWAC's role should be in advocating for more equitable working conditions for the graduate students and adjunct faculty who often teach WAC courses. In conjunction with the aforementioned efforts, WAC-GO considered ways to inform and integrate graduate students and junior scholars into the field, with the goal of establishing a pipeline of mentoring and professional development that might lead to a more dynamic, accessible, supportive, sustainable, and robust WAC community.

Through these collaborative and strategic efforts, AWAC aims to provide a structure through which WAC scholars, educators in diverse contexts, and other interested stakeholders can access research and practices related to the field, as well as build networks of like-minded individuals. Even if it means forgoing some of its informal, grassroots ethos, the larger WAC community stands to gain much from this new professional organization. AWAC can ensure that the field continues its broad mission of curricular and pedagogical reform, even in the face of generational changes in leadership and fluctuations in funding and institutional support. What's more, it can provide an accessible network of seasoned WAC professionals and newly interested graduate students, teachers, administrators, and researchers who can promote the work of writing across disciplinary, curricular, professional, institutional, and international contexts.

NOTE

The authors of this chapter were part of the 23-member working group that led the formation of AWAC until the Executive Board was elected. All members of the group were invited to co-author this chapter. In addition to the chapter authors, the other members of the working group are Chris Anson, Melissa Bender, Ann Blakesley, Laurie Britt-Smith, Pamela Childers, Jonathan Hall, Margaret Marshall, Maureen Ann Mathison, Siskanna Naynaha, Federico Daniel Navarro, Joseph Pizzo, Justin Rademaekers, Nicole Severino, and Terry Myers Zawacki. We express our gratitude to our colleagues in the working group as well as to the many individuals and groups who have helped shape this moment along the way, some of whom are mentioned by name in this chapter.

REFERENCES

Cox, M., Galin, J. & Melzer, D. (2018). *Sustainable WAC: A whole systems approach to launching and developing Writing Across the Curriculum Programs.* National Council of Teachers of English.

Kim, J. (2018, June 18). What do higher ed professional organizations do? And who is studying them? [Blog post]. *Inside Higher Education.* https://www.insidehighered .com/blogs/technology-and-learning/what-do-higher-ed-professional-associations -do?utm_content=bufferf176d&utm_medium=social&utm_source=facebook& utm_campaign=IHEbuffer.

Kuh, G. D. (2008). *High-impact educational practices: What they are, who has access to them, and why they matter.* Association of American Colleges and Universities.

Palmquist, M., Mullin, J. & Blalock, G. (2012). The Role of activity analysis in writing research: Case studies of emerging scholarly communities. In L. Nicholson & M. P. Sheridan (Eds.), *Writing studies research in practice: Methods and methodologies* (pp. 231–244). Southern Illinois University Press.

Russell, D. R. (2002). *Writing in the academic disciplines: A curricular history.* Southern Illinois University Press.

Taylor, O., Apprey, C. B., Hill, G., McGrann, L. & Wang, J. (2010). Diversifying the faculty. *Peer Review, 12*(3). https://www.aacu.org/publications-research/periodicals /diversifying-faculty.

Thaiss, C. (2006). Still a good place to be: More than 20 years of the National Network of WAC Programs. In S. H. McLeod & M. I. Soven (Eds.), *Composing a community: A history of writing across the curriculum* (pp. 126–141). Parlor Press.

Thaiss, C., Bräuer, G., Carlino, P., Ganobcsik-Williams, L. & Sinha, A. (Eds.). (2012). *Writing programs worldwide: Profiles of academic writing in many places.* The WAC Clearinghouse; Parlor Press. https://wac.colostate.edu/books/perspectives/wpww/.

Thaiss, C. & Porter, T.. (2010). The state of WAC/WID in 2010: Methods and results of the U.S. survey of the international WAC/WID mapping project. *College Composition and Communication, 61*, 534–570.

Walvoord, Barbara E. (1996). The future of WAC. *College English, 58*(1), 58–74. https://doi.org/10.2307/378534.

CHAPTER 3.

THE WRITING ACROSS THE CURRICULUM GRADUATE ORGANIZATION: WHERE WE'VE BEEN, WHERE WE ARE, AND WHERE WE'RE GOING

Alisa Russell

University of Kansas

Jake Chase

AIM Academy

Justin Nicholes

University of Wisconsin-Stout

Allie Sockwell Johnston

University of Tennessee, Knoxville

This chapter provides a brief overview of the Writing Across the Curriculum Graduate Organization (WAC-GO)'s history, from an initial listening tour of graduate student needs to a recent roundtable discussion at IWAC 2018. The chapter focuses on three verbs that illustrate WAC-GO's mission: energize, demystify, and connect. The authors explore how these verbs have activated WAC-GO projects across the past and present, and they conclude by imagining the organization's future. Ultimately, this chapter recognizes these three verbs (energizing, demystifying, and connecting) as goals of not only WAC-GO, but WAC as a field.

A graduate student organization in Writing Across the Curriculum (WAC) follows from a long line of conversations about the sustainability of our work and of our field. WAC scholar-practitioners have been urged to make purposeful choices toward sustainability ever since McLeod (1989) recognized that WAC had progressed from a primarily grassroots movement to a "second stage" of increasing institutionalization. Since then, most conversations about the sustainability of WAC have revolved around the dynamic landscape of higher education and institutionalization (Condon & Rutz, 2012; Malenczyk, 2012; Townsend, 2008; Walvoord, 1996). However, the Writing Across the Curriculum Graduate Organization (WAC-GO) is the result of turning these conversations about the sustainability of WAC as a movement toward WAC as a field. Many of the founders and key figures of the WAC movement who have ensured its sustainability so far are moving (or have moved) into retirement. As a new organization in the field, WAC-GO makes a statement that the question of who will replace these founders and key figures should be one of central focus.

WAC-GO also makes a statement that replacing and expanding key figures in WAC will take more than informal measures. Within writing studies, WAC is unique in its strong interdisciplinarity, its locally shaped administrative components, and its range of methodological approaches. It is also unique since not every university or even writing studies program has faculty who specialize or offer coursework in WAC. This means that, in most cases, a graduate student's development as a WAC scholar-practitioner must be sought out. Further complicating graduate-student entrance into WAC, WAC researchers historically have too often ignored graduate students' and new faculty members' efforts to write their ways into disciplines and academic careers (Madden & Tarabochia, this volume). In their discussion of graduate student socialization, John Weidman, Darla Twale, and Elizabeth Stein (2001) described a field of study as a "guarded enclave," but they also noted that entrance into this enclave "comes more easily" through formal structures like assistantships, fellowships, etc. (p. 77). Moreover, the intentionality of these formal structures becomes a significant factor in recruiting and increasing retention of diverse and/or underrepresented student populations (Mullen, 2008). We believe that a formal organization like WAC-GO can provide the structures graduate students need for successful socialization, which we believe is further necessary to sustain and diversify the field.

To accomplish this sustainability and diversification, three verbs activate WAC-GO's mission: *energize, demystify,* and *connect.* How do we energize the momentum of the field by encouraging fresh and diverse graduate student perspectives? How do we demystify entry points into WAC work and spaces for graduate students? And how do we connect graduate students to peer and faculty mentors and collaborators? Where we've been, where we are, and where we're going is driven by how we can best put these verbs into action, and, as our readers will see in this brief history, the International Writing Across the Curriculum (IWAC) Conference is often poised at their intersection. Of course, constructing a narrative of WAC-GO's inception, development, and possible future in this short piece is one we approach enthusiastically, but cautiously. While we turned to the organization's meeting records, documented files, and collective memory to build this narrative, we cannot fully capture the myriad emails, informal conversations, moments of inspiration, and encouraging words that stitch these discrete pieces together. Thus, we offer what we hope you'll consider three snapshots—where we've been, where we are, and where we're going—that capture but moments of WAC-GO's history and possible future.

WHERE WE'VE BEEN

Our story begins at the 2014 Conference of Writing Program Administrators where Michelle LaFrance couldn't help but notice the strong and integrated graduate student presence. She traced this presence back to the Writing Program Administrator Graduate Organization (WPA-GO), a graduate student-led organization that linked graduate students with mentors, helped them find financial support, and encouraged them to actively participate at the conference. She wondered if the field of WAC Studies would benefit from a similar graduate student organization. After an enthusiastic response from several established scholar-practitioners in WAC, Michelle brought the idea to then-graduate students and WPA-GO officers, Brian Hendrickson and Al Harahap (and later Alisa Russell). Before these founders could launch a full-scale WAC graduate organization, though, they simply needed to listen. Over the next several semesters, the founders created space to listen to established scholar-practitioners in WAC, leaders of other WAC entities, and, most important, graduate students interested in WAC.

The first stop on this listening tour occurred a year before IWAC 2016. Michelle, Brian, Al, and Alisa met with upcoming conference host, Anne Gere, to collaboratively consider what it would mean to highlight graduate student voices at the conference (in other words, *energize*). However, the founders' conversation with Anne stumbled upon a more pressing issue. For the closing plenary talk, Anne wanted a long-time scholar-practitioner paired with a graduate student. A long-time scholar-practitioner was easy to locate, but Anne hit a roadblock in locating this mythical graduate student. Neither she, nor the members of her conference planning team, knew where to look for a graduate student doing WAC work. The founders recognized this dilemma as an intriguing tipping point in the field: WAC had become an epistemic category and a professional identity in its own right, but graduate education and mentorship in writing studies (and related disciplines) had not developed commensurately to foster emerging WAC identities. They immediately recognized the need for something more formal, more concrete, and more visible to demystify entry points and connect graduate students to those already established in the field.

For the next stop on the founders' listening tour, they met with a newly assembled advisory board of WAC scholars and administrators from across institutions that was working to guide the founders toward a mission statement and organizational details. The conversation quickly unearthed a complicated facet of WAC: As the founders and the advisory board tried to decide where a WAC graduate organization could fit among the already-existing WAC entities, they realized there was no overarching umbrella for WAC organizations. For example, most of the major WAC entities—the WAC Clearinghouse, the WAC Special Interest Group (now the WAC Standing Group), the International Writing Across the Curriculum (INWAC) Board, the IWAC conference, etc.—had developed in response to specific needs, and thus played important but different roles in the field. And while they often collaborated, these entities tended to operate independently of one another. The advisory board considered how these varying structures could lead to confusion about entry points and involvement, especially for graduate students, which folded into initial conversations that ultimately resulted in the Association for Writing Across the Curriculum (Basgier et al., this volume). The need for a formalized graduate organization that could energize graduate student involvement, demystify entry points, and connect graduate students to these organizations seemed evident.

After these conversations with trusted advisors in the field, the founders were ready to hear from graduate students themselves. On September 25, 2015, the founders hosted an introductory video meeting to share their vision for WAC-GO and learn more about graduate student needs. Many graduate students shared their experience of "stumbling" into WAC work; for example, one graduate student who had developed a ten-week workshop for graduate teachers in the disciplines realized that this was a major WAC project only after the fact. Graduate students also noted that they wanted to "see" more of what WAC work looks like across institutions, both because many did not have formal WAC programs at their institutions or because they had only experienced their own institution's model. Encouragingly, one graduate student asked how much WAC scholarship addresses language issues, and the other attendees jumped in enthusiastically with references and summaries. The founders noted that this was exactly the kind of connecting that WAC-GO could facilitate.

With the listening tour coming to a close, the founders' first steps in launching a sustainable organization focused on building visible structures. They built this visibility through hosting a social at IWAC 2016 in Ann Arbor; assembling an Executive Committee with clearly demarcated roles and responsibilities; creating an organizational logo; drafting and voting on official bylaws; building a central web presence on a WAC Clearinghouse page; launching social media profiles on Facebook and Twitter; and growing a member list. As WAC-GO's visibility and member list grew, the Executive Committee still wanted to ensure that our fledgling initiatives were meeting the needs of our members. We thus distributed a Resource Survey in February 2017 to our member list and to various organizational writing listservs, receiving 20 responses. Some findings were expected—for example, graduate students found WAC-related conferences cost prohibitive, and they thus highly valued travel grants. However, some findings took us by surprise: Of the 11 respondents whose programs did not offer coursework in WAC, 10 of them were already involved in WAC research or administration. Likewise, only three respondents indicated they do not have access to mentors in WAC/WID, but 11 indicated that they do not know how to find or cultivate mentoring relationships in WAC/WID. These findings became fundamental in developing the founders' original short- and long-term goals as an organization.

WHERE WE ARE

As the current Executive Committee, we've found translating the founders' goals of energizing, demystifying, and connecting into concrete initiatives both challenging and invigorating. One major revelation of the listening tour was that most graduate students are not able to take coursework in WAC, or they find themselves doing WAC-focused theses and dissertations without realizing there's a whole field with an exciting body of literature and developed methodologies waiting for them. Thus, we have collected resources for graduate students interested in WAC work on our Clearinghouse page (https://wac.colostate .edu/go/) to connect them to the resources they need for success. For example, our Research Support section offers resources such as "Research Questions and Methods in WAC Scholarship," as well as a Post-C's webinar recording, "Quantitative Design in WAC Studies." In these resources, we draw from landmark WAC studies to suggest what WAC/WID-related research questions and methodological approaches might look like. Relatedly, we know from experience that graduate students are not always explicitly introduced to occluded genres or processes of the academy. Therefore, our Professionalization Corner offers resources such as a "New to WAC Studies" info-doc; "Advice on Writing Your IWAC Proposal," contributed by our advisory board; annotated conference proposals that point out salient rhetorical moves; and a Post-C's webinar recording, "Publishing as a Graduate Student."

Another major initiative to energize and connect graduate students interested in WAC is our bimonthly newsletter. The WAC-GO Newsletter is foremost a point of shared experience: We want to provide our members (and the larger writing studies community) with a recurring touchstone of common readings and key announcements. The newsletter is a way for graduate students to see what others are up to, stay briefed on recent WAC initiatives, and maybe even feel less alone. Second, the newsletter provides a low-stakes forum for graduate students to test out their ideas. We encourage graduate students (and junior faculty) to submit ideas for two of the newsletter standing sections: "Engagement with WAC," in which the author engages with or reflects on a recent issue, trend, or idea in WAC/WID studies, and "What I'm Working On," in which the author can provide an overview of their current WAC projects, including the purpose and methods, and can also ask a question or two to the community to help move the project forward. The third standing section, "From the Desk Of," serves as word from a more experienced scholar-practitioner in WAC/WID to grad students interested in WAC/WID. Our hope is that graduate students realize other graduate students are interested in similar work, sparking collaborative enterprises and institutional crosstalk (you can find our newsletter archives at wac.colostate.edu/go/wac-go-newsletter-archives/).

One of our most recent initiatives, The Cross-Institutional Mentoring Program, connects a graduate student interested in WAC work with an established scholar-practitioner at a different institution. This program is especially meant to provide one-on-one mentorship to graduate students who do not have access to WAC mentors, WAC coursework, or WAC opportunities in their graduate programs to further demystify WAC work. Participants in this program define and develop their mentoring relationships by setting their own goals, expectations, and activities over two semesters (Fall and Spring). Some of these activities might include video chatting regularly, sharing drafts of recent work, emailing regularly, collaborating on projects, or socializing at conferences. Some of our initial findings from the program's pilot year show that both mentors and mentees greatly value close mentoring relationships, but both parties don't always know what they can get out of these relationships. Our findings also show that WAC work is very much fueled by these mentoring relationships, both for graduate students wading through the complex world of writing studies and for junior faculty navigating new institutional contexts, and that these mentoring relationships are especially key for cultivating diversity and supporting underrepresented students. Encouragingly, both mentors and mentees in our pilot program were deeply committed to structures and initiatives that increase the diversity of our field. (You can find a white paper on the pilot program at https://drive.google.com/file/d/1THwS3lQJ3oVaYt8w5BBMmvg8Bodhhyry/view.)

Finally, we seek to energize the presence of graduate students at writing studies conferences, but especially at IWAC. Thanks to the generous support from the Auburn University hosts and our donors (Macmillan, the WAC Clearinghouse, and Fountainhead Press), WAC-GO was able to host a conference-wide cocktail hour at IWAC 2018 that explicitly encouraged cross-generational networking. We were also able to connect with many graduate students throughout the conference at our hospitality table. These are exciting starts that we plan to continue at future conferences.

WHERE WE'RE GOING

WAC-GO's nearest future (the 2018–2019 academic year, at the time of writing) is at least in focus. We already have a number of initiatives lined up, some of which include compiling job-market resources, designing a budget and application process for travel and research grants, and launching a social media campaign to feature graduate student scholarship. However, our vision gets fuzzier the further into the future we look. What will it mean to energize, demystify, and connect in 5, 15, even 30 years? To consider this question, we hosted a roundtable discussion at IWAC 2018 about these future possibilities for WAC-GO as an organization.

Roundtable attendees first brainstormed ways that WAC-GO could not only provide support for graduate students, but also harness (or energize) the passion of these graduate students to significantly contribute to the field in lasting ways. For example, one roundtable attendee suggested the newsletter could take on some of our field's bigger questions and explore generational changes: What does WAC mean in the world right now? What's missing from our conversations about WAC? Additionally, we discussed recruiting graduate students to compile an oral-history-of-WAC project or a web series in which established scholar-practitioners share their experiences and advice. Graduate students would benefit from the experience of conducting these projects, but then the whole field would also benefit by archiving these narratives.

Our roundtable discussion soon turned toward issues of sustaining the organization itself. As one roundtable attendee noted, by the time a problem becomes clearly defined, the Executive Committee members may no longer be graduate students. We emphasized, then, the need for clearly defined structures (like the bi-monthly newsletter and the Post-C's webinar) and roles (like the rotating Executive Committee positions) that can be handed off from generation to generation. Additionally, after enough time, we expect our resource development and project initiatives could either reach a critical mass or no longer answer the changing needs of graduate students. Future Executive Committee members will need to remain self-reflexive to strike a balance between maintenance and creation, as well as flexibility and structure.

Through our roundtable discussion, we also realized that, for sustainability as an organization, it is just as important to recognize what we *cannot* do as it is to recognize what we *can* do. It seems obvious, but it's worth saying: We cannot provide graduate students with everything they will need to know before they go into a WAC position. We can't know the institutional context graduate students will move into or what kind of research projects will ultimately result from their questions. What we *can* do, though, is provide introductions—to the field, to the range of methods available to WAC scholars, to some stories of what it can be like to run a WAC program. What we can also do is *demystify* the paths for mentorship and networking: Hopefully a new faculty member can call up their old cross-institutional mentor when they run into an issue, or collaborate with that other WAC-GO member on a new research project.

CONCLUDING THOUGHTS

Energize. Demystify. Connect. When working through an earlier version of this draft, we as co-authors realized in a moment of clarity that these three WAC-GO goals echo the very mission of WAC as a movement. From the beginning, Writing Across the Curriculum has been about energizing faculty and students to engage with writing as a mode of learning; demystifying genres and writing processes across rhetorical spaces; and connecting individuals to their various communities through writing. Is it any wonder that we, the Executive Committee of WAC-GO, realized the significance of applying these values to the field's own graduate students?

Being a graduate student is overwhelming, daunting, and sometimes isolating. But as Executive Committee members for WAC-GO, we have a home base to share advice, triumphs, failures, and laughter. Yes, we have had the chance to form relationships with some of the "big-wigs" in WAC: Regularly emailing those whose scholarship we know by heart is an opportunity we are sure few graduate students receive! Even more importantly, though, are the relationships we've formed with each other and with other peers who will eventually become our colleagues. In short, we have experienced a process of socialization into a WAC community that would not have been easy to achieve otherwise. For the future, we hope that WAC-GO continues to provide this important space for newcomers to construct themselves as WAC folk, but we also hope the relationships built in WAC-GO contribute to a more inclusive and connected field as a whole.

ACKNOWLEDGMENTS

We would like to thank Terry Myers Zawacki, Michelle LaFrance, Dan Melzer, and our anonymous reviewer for their excellent and generous feedback on previous drafts. We would also like to thank the WAC-GO Advisory Board, the WAC Clearinghouse, and AWAC for the incredible support and guidance they have offered WAC-GO.

REFERENCES

Condon, W. & Rutz, C. (2012). A taxonomy of writing across the curriculum programs: Evolving to serve broader agendas. *College Composition and Communication, 64*, 357–382.

Malenczyk, R. (2012). WAC's disappearing act. In K. Ritter & P. K. Matsuda (Eds.), *Exploring composition studies: Sites, issues, and perspectives* (pp. 89–104). Utah State University Press. https://doi.org/10.2307/j.ctt4cgjsj.9.

McLeod, S. (1989). Writing across the curriculum: The second stage, and beyond. *College Composition and Communication, 40*, 337–343. https://doi.org/10.2307 /357778.

Mullen, C. A. (2008). Conclusion: Mentoring, change, and diversity: Findings and lessons. In C. A. Mullen (Ed.), *The handbook of formal mentoring in higher education* (pp. 297–319). Christopher-Gordon.

Townsend, M. (2008). WAC program vulnerability and what to do about it: An update and brief bibliographic essay. *The WAC Journal, 19*, 45–62. https://wac.colo state.edu/docs/journal/vol19/townsend.pdf.

Walvoord, B. E. (1996). The future of WAC. *College English, 58*(1), 58–79. https:// doi.org/10.2307/378534.

Weidman, J., Twale, D. & Stein, E. (2001). Socialization of graduate and professional students in higher education: A perilous passage? *ASHE-ERIC Higher Education Report, 28*, 2–135.

CHAPTER 4.

LEARNING ANALYTICS IN WRITING INSTRUCTION: IMPLICATIONS FOR WRITING ACROSS THE CURRICULUM

Mike Palmquist

Colorado State University

*Learning analytics tools process data collected from instructional appli-
cations and learning systems to estimate the likelihood of student success
in a given course or program of study and to identify points at which
interventions might increase the likelihood of student success. They can
also be used to carry out retrospective analysis of student success for
course redesign. While these tools are widely used in many disciplines
in higher education, their adoption in writing and writing-intensive
courses has been slow. Nonetheless, a subset of learning analytics tools,
characterized as writing analytics tools, have seen growing use in the
field of writing studies. This chapter explores the uses of learning analytics tools and writing analytics tools within composition and writing
across the curriculum, considers concerns about their use in instructional
contexts, and discusses factors likely to shape their adoption and use.*

Learning analytics—the analysis of data drawn from a wide range of sources
including learning management systems, adaptive quiz tools, student information systems, and communication tools, among others—has been a growing area
of discussion and concern among faculty across the curriculum (Daniel, 2015;
Fournier et al., 2011; Siemens & Long, 2011; Viberg et al., 2018). While the use
of data to gain insights into student learning performance has long been a common practice in educational research, improvements in our ability to assemble
and analyze large sets of data from learning tools and communication tools promise to enhance our ability to understand how various learning behaviors, instructional practices, and instructional material shape student success in our courses.

The primary purposes for which learning analytics data and tools are used
include

DOI: https://doi.org/10.37514/PER-B.2020.0360.2.04

- identifying students who may be in danger of failing or performing poorly in a course while the course is being offered
- predicting the likelihood of success of students prior to the start of a course
- identifying learning behaviors that are correlated with student success (or the lack thereof) in a course (typically after the course has been completed)
- identifying course materials and assignments that are correlated with student success (or, again, the lack thereof)

The findings from these kinds of analyses can be used to understand patterns of student performance in a course after it has been offered, typically with the goal of modifying or substantially redesigning a course. They can also be used to understand the differential impact of new assignments, learning materials, and assessments on students during and after the academic term in which a course is offered. Learners can benefit from the reports generated by learning analytics tools, both by gaining a sense of their progress in a course and by obtaining information about activities they might engage in to advance their progress. For example, a student who is struggling in a writing or writing-intensive course might be given advice regarding resources, such as writing centers or relevant digital learning materials, that they could make use of while the course is in progress.

In writing-across-the-curriculum (WAC) courses, the data made available through learning analytics tools have the potential to help program leaders and instructors understand the differential impact of particular instructional methods and materials in a course. For example, data about student behaviors as they worked on a staged writing assignment—one, for instance, that involved a topic proposal, a review of literature, contributions to web discussion forums, a research plan, and multiple drafts—would support analysis of the relative success of students who engaged at higher or lower levels (or did not engage at all) during various stages of the assignment. Those data might also allow comparison of behaviors across writing assignments and, in turn, those behaviors might be considered in light of particular instructional practices employed before or during work on assignments. In addition, the data might allow comparison of both the behaviors and success across groups of students, such as majors and non-majors, upper-division and lower-division students, and students from various demographic groups. In turn, this data could be used to assess the overall impact of the WAC program on student learning and success at the institution.

Learning analytics tools are increasingly included in digital learning applications and platforms. Learning management systems such as Canvas and Blackboard, for example, allow instructors to view a basic but nonetheless informative set of learning analytics reports, some of which allow customization. Among other information, instructors can view completion of assignments, logins, scores on quizzes and exams, and activity on discussion forums. Similarly, the learning analytics tools built into learning systems offered by textbook publishers, such as McGraw-Hill's Connect and Macmillan's Achieve platforms, support the analysis of student learning behaviors, typically with the goal of identifying students who might benefit from intervention by the instructor. More powerful learning analytics systems, such as Barnes and Noble Education's LoudSight, provide predictive analyses based on course performance data, student demographic information, and student performance in past courses. These systems offer customizable reports, support one-to-one and one-to-many messaging between instructors and students, and can send automatic "nudges" (brief messages delivered through email or text messaging) to students whose behavior (or lack of behavior, such as failing to complete assignments or neglecting to log in regularly to a learning management system) suggests that they are in danger of performing poorly in the course.

In addition to these types of learning analytics tools, a related set of tools—such as EAB's Navigate—are being used to help institutions identify courses in which students struggle and, perhaps more importantly, to reveal course combinations within an academic term or course sequences across academic terms that appear to be correlated with lack of success.

The growing sophistication and predictive accuracy of these analytics tools have allowed instructors to become aware of and intervene to address student behaviors that undermine learning and success. In some cases, institutions have used this information during course redesign to inform efforts to improve teaching effectiveness, student learning, and student success. For WAC leaders, it is difficult to overstate the importance of learning analytics data and the uses to which such data can be put in pursuing the goals of a WAC program. On a purely instructional basis, these data can be used to identify courses that might benefit from the use of writing-to-learn, writing-to-engage, and writing-to-communicate assignments; to assess the effectiveness of those assignments; and to determine whether to continue to use them and, if so, how they might be enhanced. On a more pragmatic programmatic level, these data can also play an important role in determining institutional funding priorities and, consequently, can shape decisions about continuing and enhancing institutional support for WAC initiatives.

SOURCES OF LEARNING ANALYTICS DATA

Learning analytics data are related primarily to the behavior, products, and performance of students within a course. This can include data drawn from

- learning management systems, such as logins, access to files, and quiz tools and discussion forums, among other tools (Daniel, 2015; Zhang et al., 2018)
- eReaders, video players, and other tools for accessing and interacting with course content (Junco & Clem, 2015; Shoufan, 2018)
- learning tools provided by vendors and publishers, such as adaptive quiz tools and interactive exercises (Lewkow et al., 2015)
- "multimodal" data sources, which can reveal student location and other activities in real time, such as posting to social media and accessing wireless networks, by drawing on data from the Internet of Things, cloud data storage, and wearable technologies (Di Mitri et al., 2018)
- writing carried out in formal and informal assignments, including journaling and posts on discussion forums (McNely et al., 2012; Shum et al., 2016; Wise et al., 2013; Yu et al., 2018)

These data are often analyzed in combination with academic information, such as scores on college entrance examinations and performance in high schools, as well as demographic information drawn from a student information system, such as race, ethnicity, gender, and family income. In some cases, learning analytics data from a specific course will be analyzed in combination with data about student participation in institutionally supported activities, such as attending tutoring and study group sessions and meeting with faculty and academic advisors. In rare cases, these data might also be considered in light of activity on social networks and location data that might be derived from connections to a campus network or access to mobile phone data.

LEARNING ANALYTICS DATA AND TOOLS: PRACTICAL AND ETHICAL CONCERNS

While recognizing the insights afforded by the use of learning analytics tools, a number of scholars have called attention to the potential misuse of information they produce. Slade and Paul Prinsloo (2013), for example, observed that predictions about the likelihood of successful course completion could lead instructors and advisors to discourage students from taking courses or pursuing programs of study in which they are likely (but by no means guaranteed) to fail. Their caution is particularly important given the difficulty faced by students—often first-generation college students and/or members of historically underrepresented groups—who might enter higher education courses with comparatively lower levels of academic preparation than students who are members of majority group, whose families enjoy higher socio-economic status, or whose families include members with college degrees. Slade and Prinsloo also expressed concern that inappropriate conclusions might be drawn about the teaching effectiveness of faculty members, a concern that echoes arguments made by a number of scholars about the reductive nature of student evaluations of teaching (see, for example, the 2017 meta-analysis by Uttl et al., 2017). Other scholars have argued that learning analytics tools are too immature to be used without a great deal of caution, citing privacy concerns (Jones & Salo, 2018; Pardo & Siemens, 2014), reservations about issues related to privacy and the potential commercialization of student data (Flavin, 2016; Rubel & Jones, 2016), and concerns about the reductivism inherent in any analysis of "big data" (Stephens, 2017).

The importance of these concerns for scholars involved with learning analytics are addressed in the editor's introduction to a recent issue of *The Journal of Learning Analytics*:

> Questions related to privacy and ethics in connection to learning analytics have been an ongoing concern since the early days of learning analytics. Examples of some of the major questions are related to the ownership and protection of personal data, data sharing and access, ethical use of data, and ethical implications of the use of learning analytics in education. It is well recognized that these issues lie at the very heart of the field and that great care must be taken in order to assure trust building with stakeholders that are involved in and affected by the use of learning analytics. (Gašević et al., 2016, p. 2)

With these concerns in mind, numerous proposals have been made regarding ethical principles and practices related to both the analyses that learning analytics tools produce and access to the data on which they are based. In 2013, George Siemens suggested that we look not only at data ownership and retention but also at the issue of learner control over the uses to which that data should be put. One year later, Abelardo Pardo and Siemens (2014) proposed an ethical framework for learning analytics that focused on four aspects of privacy that had emerged in response to the growing collection of digital user data over the past two decades: "transparency, student control over the data, security, and accountability and assessment" (p. 448). More recently, Andrew Cormack (2016) has argued that we should draw on ethical frameworks used in medical research to separate "the processes of analysis (pattern-finding) and intervention (pattern-matching)" so that we can protect learners and teachers from "inadvertent harm during data analysis" (p. 91). Hendrik Drachsler and Wolfgang Greller (2016) proposed DELICATE, an eight-point checklist based on recent legal principles and the growing literature on ethical use of learning analytics data that supports a "trusted implementation of learning analytics" (p. 89). And in a promising approach to preserving privacy while ensuring benefits to learners and teachers, Mehmet Emre Gursoy, Ali Inan, Mehmet Ercan Nergiz, and Yucel Saygin (2017) have developed and tested a framework that for the development and enforcement of "privacy-preserving learning analytics (PPLA)" (p. 69).

Building on these efforts, a small but growing number of higher education institutions (e.g., Charles Sturt University, 2015; Colorado State University, 2018; University of Michigan, 2018), professional organizations such as the Society for Learning Analytics Research (Gašević, 2018, personal communication) and the Reinvention Collaborative (Jensen & Roof, 2016), and nongovernmental organizations such as Jisc (Sclater, 2014; Sclater & Bailey, 2015) have developed frameworks to inform the ethical use of learning analytics data and tools. Other institutions and organizations are currently adapting existing or developing new frameworks. While no large breaches of learning analytics data had yet been reported at the time this chapter was completed, it seems almost inevitable that breaches will occur. Similarly, while no reports of harm to students or faculty as a result of using learning analytics tools and data had been made by the time this chapter was completed, sufficient expressions of concern have been made to suggest that some institutions might find evidence of unethical behaviors.

Even as these ethical frameworks have been developed, however, many of the scholars who point to the potential benefits of collecting and analyzing student learning data—including some who have participated in the development of the ethical frameworks—have argued that it is both far too early to draw strong conclusions about the effectiveness of learning analytics tools and data and that we should continue to explore how they might be used effectively and appropriately. These scholars have observed, for example, that the quantitative data provided through learning analytics are used most effectively in combination with qualitative data (Pardo et al., 2015), suggested that students can benefit from "nudges" and other automated communications that might promote self-regulated learning (Howell et al., 2018; Pilgrim et al., 2017), and pointed to promising approaches that can help students use learning analytics to succeed in courses in which they might otherwise struggle (Drachsler & Greller, 2016; Macfadyen et al., 2014).

LEARNING ANALYTICS IN WRITING INSTRUCTION: WRITING ANALYTICS

Within writing studies, the use of learning analytics tools in writing courses and writing-intensive courses has only recently received consistent scholarly attention. As Joe Moxley and Katie Walkup noted in 2016, "Despite a growing interest in the applications of WA [Writing Analytics], and several conferences on these applications, including LAK (Learning Analytics and Knowledge) and EDM (Educational Data Mining), there remain surprisingly few foundational pieces on WA" (p. 1). Indeed, while Moxley (2013) and others had long addressed questions about the role of "big data" in writing research, the term "writing analytics" did not come into use until 2015, when Simon Buckingham Shum (2015), a cognitive psychologist with a strong interest in learning analytics, coined the term. By 2016, Shum et al. had defined writing analytics as "the measurement and analysis of written texts for the purpose of understanding writing processes and products, in their educational contexts, and improving the teaching and learning of writing" (p. 481).

Since 2016, Shum has conducted a series of workshops on writing analytics at the annual Learning Analytics and Knowledge conference, which is sponsored by the Society for Learning Analytics Research (SoLAR). Shum, who has focused largely on reflective writing, has shown a strong interest in the use of automated scoring of texts within specific pedagogical contexts. His work is informed largely by work in latent semantic analysis, corpus linguistics, and cognitive psychology. It does not appear to be informed in any meaningful way by work in the field of writing studies.

The limited attention paid by writing and WAC scholars to learning analytics (and, more recently, writing analytics) does not reflect a reluctance to use data to inform decisions. For decades, these scholars have drawn on the kind of data now being used in learning analytics both to carry out WAC program evaluations and as sources of information in scholarly work. In the 1980s, for example, Art Young and Toby Fulwiler (1986) and their colleagues at Michigan Tech University drew heavily on institutional and student data, such as course completion data, grades, and graduation rates, as well as analysis of student writing, to inform their comprehensive evaluation of the first five years of Michigan Tech's WAC program. Similarly, in an effort that significantly predates the development of predictive analytics tools, many first-year-writing programs have relied on student performance data—such as high school GPA and class rank as well as scores on the verbal portions of the SAT and ACT examinations—to place students into or exempt them from introductory composition courses. More recently, Eodice, Geller, and Lerner (this volume) have employed a range of data collection and analysis methods to explore and attempt to understand what students and faculty members bring to their work as writers. And importantly, corpus linguistics and content analysis, which can be used to search for patterns in large collections of texts, have long played important roles in the study of student writing (see, for example, Carley & Palmquist, 1992; Palmquist, 1990, 1993).

The reluctance of writing and WAC scholars to embrace the tools offered through more mainstream learning analytics tools and systems, such as those included in learning management systems, may have its roots in both the metaphors on which these tools are based (the standard lecture classroom with its heavy reliance on quizzing and testing) and a long-standing awareness that the assessment of student writing performance is not well served by reductive analysis of written text. That said, the growing capabilities, speed, and accuracy of computer-based text analysis have significantly reduced the time and labor required to carry out analyses of collections of student writing—such as those produced by students in one or more classes. And writing and WAC scholars have taken notice of these tools. Examples of scholar work that employs these tools can be found in *The Journal of Writing Analytics*, established in 2016 by the editorial team of Joe Moxley, Norbert Elliot, Dave Eubanks, and Meg Vezzu and published through the Colorado State University Open Press and the WAC Clearinghouse (https://wac.colostate.edu/jwa/). The journal publishes articles that typically work with data drawn from one or more of five areas:

- corpus linguistics
- automated text analysis (often based on latent semantic analysis and natural language processing)
- content analysis
- student course behaviors
- student demographic and academic background

To date, the data analyzed in most articles published in the journal have been drawn from the first three areas. Eventually, the editors of the journal expect the data to be drawn from the other areas as well.

Several articles in the 2018 volume of *The Journal of Writing Analytics* used automated text analysis tools to explore issues of concern to writing scholars. Susan Lang (2018) studied more than 140,000 instructor comments on writing assignments completed by more than 12,000 students over a five-year period. Her findings, while restricted to a single institution, suggest the formation of a local lexicon or "canon" that shaped instructor feedback. Focusing on student writing, Thomas Peele (2018) used corpus analysis tools to explore students' use of objection, concession, and counterargument in argumentative essays. His analysis of roughly 550 source-based argumentative essays suggests that while "students introduce objections to their arguments at about the same rates as in other corpora, they are significantly less likely to concede to those objections." Moreover, he noted, "when students made counterarguments they used only a limited range of the linguistic resources available to them" (2018, p. 79).

Genie Giaimo, Joseph Cheatle, Candace Hastings, and Christine Modey (2018) explored the work of tutors in writing centers, a key partner in many WAC programs, by analyzing more than 44,000 sessions notes written by writing center tutors at four institutions over a multi-year period. While their study serves primarily as a proof of concept that demonstrated the viability of a particular corpus analysis tool, it offers a promising path for subsequent analysis of tutor feedback to student writers. Similarly, Noah Arthurs' (2018) study of more than 15,000 texts created by student writers for courses across the disciplines used text analysis tools—in this case, a topic modeling algorithm—to explore how undergraduate student develop as writers over time.

The similarity of the terms *learning analytics* and *writing analytics* is intentional, according to the founders of *The Journal of Writing Analytics* (N. Elliot, personal communication, November 9, 2018). Both focus on automated analysis, both can employ statistical and text analysis methods that can be applied at scale, and both have strong application to student learning.

While many learning analytics tools focus primarily on relatively easily observed student behaviors, such as logins to a learning management system, time-stamp data for completion of assignments, and scores on quizzes and exams, researchers who employ a writing analytics approach focus on the structure and/or content of student writing to explore student engagement and attitude. Liang-Chih Yu and his colleagues (2018), for example, explored the use of sentiment analysis of student writing early in the academic term to improve predictions of student success in courses. Vasileios Kagklis, Anthi Karatrantou, Maria Tantoula, Chris Panagiotakopoulos, and Vassilios Verykios (2016) studied the content of and sentiment expressed in posts to a class discussion forum to determine whether strongly negative or positive sentiments were related to success in the course. While they saw only a modest correlation between sentiment and success, their results offer a promising means of tracking student engagement and attitude as a course unfolds. Working with the much larger group of students made available through a MOOC (massive open online course), a team of Carnegie Mellon researchers (Wen et al., 2014) analyzed the sentiment expressed in discussion forum posts from more than 5,000 students who participated in three MOOCs. They found that higher sentiment rates were correlated with lower dropout rates in the course.

These studies underscore the importance of written work as an indicator of student attitudes toward the learning situation in which they find themselves. While they focus primarily on the emotional content of words and phrases, they suggest that more complex analyses might one day be used to help instructors identify students who are struggling with a course. If so, it will provide an additional rationale for using writing in courses. Work in this area has already begun, particularly in the areas of natural language processing and latent semantic analysis (Ericsson & Haswell, 2006; Perelman, 2014; Shum et al., 2016). For example, in their study of students who had completed at least one course assignment and written posts totaling at least 50 words, Scott Crossley, Luc Paquette, Mihai Dascalu, Danielle McNamara, and Ryan Baker (2016) found that combining click-stream data with natural language tools to assess student sentiment led to predictions of student course completion with 78 percent accuracy. They argue that continued work in this area is likely to lead to tools that can provide automated notifications regarding student performance in courses.

Within writing studies, the use of computer-based analytical tools is increasingly combined with more traditional learning analytics approaches, such as Moxley's (2013) analysis of correlations between course outcomes (as revealed through grades), instructor ratings of student texts, and student's rubric-based evaluations of more than 100,000 student essays. While scholars within the field of writing studies have not to date published work that has drawn on data from student information systems, click streams, and other sources of student behavioral information, we can expect that future studies will likely combine automated text analysis tools with these other sources of data. It seems likely that we will see a significant emphasis on the development of analytics tools that draw on data from student writing, their other behaviors in their courses, and their academic and demographic backgrounds.

We can also expect to see a number of tools used to support peer review, such as Eli Review, contributing data that could be used in a learning analytics dashboard. If these tools are compliant with the Learning Tools Interoperability standard (https://www.imsglobal.org/activity/learning-tools-interoperability), as Eli Review is, they could be configured to provide data to emerging data platforms, such as the Unizin Consortium's data platform (http://unizin.org). Dashboards and other analytics tools built to draw data from such platforms could then combine data from student peer review sessions with other data collected from students in a course.

For writing and WAC scholars, writing analytics in particular and learning analytics more generally have the potential to enhance our use of writing in courses across the discipline. It can help us identify students who are struggling in a writing or writing-intensive course. It can contribute to our assessments of the effectiveness of writing and writing-intensive courses. It can help us identify courses in which writing might be used to enhance student learning and success. And it can help us understand the contributions made by efforts associated with writing across the curriculum, including writing centers and writing fellows programs.

ETHICAL USES OF LEARNING ANALYTICS AND WRITING ANALYTICS DATA

Applied appropriately and ethically, learning analytics and writing analytics tools have the potential to improve learning and student success (Junco & Clem, 2015; Pilgrim et al., 2017), teaching practices (Bronnimann et al., 2018; Wise et al., 2013), and courses and learning materials (Morse, 2014; Pardo et al., 2015). However, even a casual review of the sources of data about student behaviors in a course is likely to raise concerns from thoughtful readers about how we understand and support the teaching, learning, and success of our students. By relying too heavily on predictions based on student background and academic history, for example, we can adversely shape students' trajectory through a course of study (for instance, by advising them against pursuing a particular major). By monitoring student behaviors—both in the classroom and through multimodal sources of data such as connections to wireless networks and activity on social media—we are also likely to violate student expectations of privacy. In addition, but just as important, we might monitor and assess the performance and teaching effectiveness of our faculty in ways that are both reductive and, at many institutions, would violate faculty expectations about appropriately holistic assessment of teaching practices.

We must also be aware of the increasing danger posed by the collection of data through third parties. While educational institutions are bound by Federal FERPA requirements as well as a growing number of state laws (Noonoo, 2018), both educators and vendors find themselves faced with what might charitably be called a moving target: As new capabilities emerge in tools made available through educational technology vendors and publishers, so too do the potential misuses of data captured through those tools. Consider the use of public blogs in some writing and writing-intensive courses over the past two decades. In an effort to provide students with a real external audience, some instructors asked students to publish their work in public spaces. In some cases, unfortunately, this led to the exposure of personal information and to responses from readers that were both hostile and intimidating. Now consider the kind of information that might be collected about student reading, viewing, and surfing habits as well as other information that might prove valuable in marketing and political campaigns. Consider as well the large amount of student writing that might be collected for later analysis (as has been the case with Turnitin.com's growing database of student writing). As we work with vendors and publishers who are in a position to collect both student data and student writing, we should attend not only to the capabilities provided by the software tools but also to the uses to which the data they collect might be put.

Access to information made available through learning analytics and writing analytics tools also poses ethical questions about the choice to avoid using that information. Consider, for example, the use of predictive analytics to indicate the likelihood of success in a first-year calculus course. A WAC program leader might learn that particular groups of students are more likely than not to fail to complete the course—such as those who took pre-calculus in high school rather than after enrolling in college or those who attended particular high schools. Knowing that the use of writing assignments in the course is likely to improve the learning and success of those students, the program leader would likely feel ethically obligated to reach out to the course instructor in an effort to improve the situation. What, in short, are the ethical questions that WAC program leaders face as they gain greater access to information about students' likelihood of success in a course? What are the ethical questions associated with more detailed knowledge of student performance as the course is in progress? And what are the ethical questions associated with assessment of the effectiveness of WAC courses and programs?

THREE CAVEATS ABOUT LEARNING ANALYTICS

For all the discussion above about the potential uses of learning analytics tools to enhance teaching and learning in writing and writing-intensive courses, we need to recognize that effective use of these tools will require significant efforts by instructors. Simply put, if analytics tools are to make a contribution to our courses, we need to design our courses to use them effectively. Bolting on a new technology will not transform how we teach or how our students learn. "One of our biggest challenges is that we don't design our courses so that we can collect learning analytics data," said James Folkestad, director of the Center for the Analytics of Learning and Teaching at Colorado State University (personal communication, January 17, 2019). For example, learning analytics data can provide useful information about student learning and performance in the first four weeks of a course—but only if the course is designed so that at least one assignment is collected and evaluated in that time period. Instructors in many college courses wait until later in the academic term to collect student work. Faced with a low grade on a major assignment or examination in the middle of a course, some students will drop the course or reduce their level of effort because they perceive that they won't be able to achieve their initial goals for the course.

It's equally important to recognize differences in the kinds of information provided by learning analytics tools. A number of dashboards offer "zero-day" predictions of student success. These predictions, based on student demographic information and past academic performance, typically rely heavily on algorithms that are better suited to institutional analysis of trends in courses than to accurate predictions of the success of a given student. Information about the behaviors and performance of students in a course, in contrast, offers more accurate information about the progress of that student. When combined with demographic and academic information, it can be highly predictive. But it's important to recognize that many students either fail to live up to those predictions or significantly overperform the predictions. What students do in a course, in short, is far more important than the destiny painted by their demographic backgrounds.

Finally, it's important to recognize that learning analytics tools are only as useful as the information on which they are based. A tool that relies on the use of a particular learning management system's eReader for data about which students are reading an assignment and how much of the reading they've completed will not tell you anything of value about students who downloaded the reading to their phone or laptop. You would no doubt be warned that these students are not completing the reading assignment. That information would be inaccurate. Similarly, a student might log in to a learning management system and then leave to get lunch. The login data might indicate the length of time that the student was signed into the system—hours, in this case—and inaccurately indicate that the student was highly engaged in the course.

Writing and WAC scholars who might find it attractive to use the predictions available through learning analytics tools would be wise to keep these limitations in mind. To the extent that these tools allow us to see things we might otherwise miss, they can be useful. But even in those cases, we should interpret what these tools tell us through the lens of our experiences working with students in our classrooms.

CONCLUSIONS

Within the field of writing studies, journals are publishing work that draws fully or in part on learning analytics data and tools. *The Journal of Writing Analytics* published its second volume in December 2018 and a companion conference has been held since 2012. While learning analytics is still an emerging scholarly field (e.g., Siemens, 2013), it has important implications for the study of writing—not least of which is its characteristic use of multidisciplinary teams to carry out its work, a practice similar to the multidisciplinary approach often employed in WAC.

That said, there are certainly drawbacks associated with using tools and analytical techniques that are still in their infancy. As we explore the use of learning analytics and writing analytics, we should consider carefully the potential drawbacks—and even dangers—associated with current and potential tools and practices. We must understand thoroughly how they might be used in ways that can harm students and faculty, particularly in the areas of student and faculty privacy, commercialization of data, the use of predictive algorithms that might discourage students from pursuing their desired courses of study, and the use of data to inform (or, worse, constitute the bulk of evidence for) faculty evaluations. This latter concern is particularly important in a field in which a large percentage of faculty are employed in contingent positions.

For writing studies more generally—and within WAC more specifically—the use of learning analytics data holds a number of important implications for curriculum and program design and, most important, for the success of our students. We would be wise to attend to the kind of learning analytics data that might be drawn from courses that assign writing, to ethical issues associated with the use of this data, to issues related to privacy and surveillance, and to concerns about commercialization of data drawn from and about students. Exploring these issues will help us better understand and foster the conditions under which learning analytics tools—and, more specifically, writing analytics tools—might be used effectively and appropriately to enhance the learning and success of our students.

REFERENCES

Arthurs, N. (2018). Structural features of undergraduate writing: A computational approach. *The Journal of Writing Analytics, 2*. https://wac.colostate.edu/docs/jwa/vol2/arthurs.pdf.

Bronnimann, J., West, D., Huijser, H. & Heath, D. (2018). Applying learning analytics to the scholarship of teaching and learning. *Innovative Higher Education, 43*, 353–367. https://doi.org/10.1007/s10755-018-9431-5.

Carley, K. & Palmquist, M. (1992). Extracting, representing, and analyzing mental models. *Social Forces, 70*, 601–636. https://doi.org/10.2307/2579746.

Charles Sturt University. (2015). CSU learning analytics code of practice. http://www.csu.edu.au/__data/assets/pdf_file/0007/2160484/2016_CSU_LearningAnalyticsCodePractice.pdf.

Colorado State University Faculty Council Committee on Teaching and Learning. (2018). *Ethical principles of learning analytics at Colorado State University: A report created by the CoTL Task Force on the Ethics of Learning Analytics*. Fort Collins, CO. https://alt.colostate.edu/cotl-ethical-principles-la/.

Cormack, A. (2016). A data protection framework for learning analytics. *Journal of Learning Analytics, 3*(1), 91–106. https://doi.org/10.18608/jla.2016.31.6.

Crossley, S., Paquette, L., Dascalu, M., McNamara, D. S. & Baker, R. S. (2016). Combining click-stream data with NLP tools to better understand MOOC completion. In *Proceedings of the Sixth International Conference on Learning Analytics & Knowledge (LAK '16*; pp. 6–14). ACM. https://doi.org/10.1145/2883851.2883931.

Daniel, B. (2015). Big data and analytics in higher education: Opportunities and challenges. *British Journal of Educational Technology, 46*, 904–920. https://doi.org/10.1111/bjet.12230

Di Mitri, D., Schneider, J., Specht, M. & Drachsler, H. (2018). From signals to knowledge: A conceptual model for multimodal learning analytics. *Journal of Computer Assisted Learning, 34*, 338–349. https://doi.org/10.1111/jcal.12288.

Drachsler, H. & Greller, W. (2016). Privacy and analytics—it's a DELICATE issue: A checklist for trusted learning analytics. In *Proceedings of the Sixth International Conference on Learning Analytics & Knowledge* (pp. 89–98). ACM. https://doi.org/10.1145/2883851.2883893.

Ericsson, P. F. & Haswell, R. H. (2006). *Machine scoring of student essays: Truth and consequences*. Utah State University Press. https://doi.org/10.2307/j.ctt4cgq0p.

Flavin, M. (2016). Technology-enhanced learning and higher education. *Oxford Review of Economic Policy, 32*, 632–645. https://doi.org/10.1093/oxrep/grw028.

Fournier, H., Kop, R. & Sitlia, H. (2011). The value of learning analytics to networked learning on a personal learning environment. In *Proceedings of the 1st International Conference on Learning Analytics and Knowledge* (pp. 104–109). ACM. https://doi.org/10.1145/2090116.2090131

Gašević, D., Dawson, S. & Jovanović, J. (2016). Ethics and privacy as enablers of learning analytics. *Journal of Learning Analytics, 3*(1), 1–4. https://doi.org/10.18608/jla.2016.31.1.

Giaimo, G. N., Cheatle, J. J., Hastings, C. K. & Modey, C. (2018). It's all in the notes: What session notes can tell us about the work of writing centers. *The Journal of Writing Analytics, 2*. https://wac.colostate.edu/docs/jwa/vol2/giaimo.pdf.

Gursoy, M. E., Inan, A. Nergiz, M. E. & Saygin, Y. (2017). Privacy-preserving learning analytics: Challenges and techniques. *IEEE Transactions on Learning Technologies, 10*(1), 68–81. https://doi.org/10.1109/TLT.2016.2607747.

Howell, J. A., Roberts, L. D. & Mancini, V. O. (2018). Learning analytics messages: Impact of grade, sender, comparative information and message style on student affect and academic resilience. *Computers in Human Behavior, 89*, 8–15. https://doi.org/10.1016/j.chb.2018.07.021.

Jensen, L. & Roof, V. (2016.) *The ethical use of student data and analytics*. The Reinvention Center. Student Success/Learning Analytics Specialized Network. https://tilt.colostate.edu/files/pdi/986/File_D2C3EEE1-FE06-27F9-8CE26C707A9B65B7.pdf.

Jones, K. M. L. & Salo, D. (2018). Learning analytics and the academic library: Professional ethics commitments at a crossroads. *College & Research Libraries, 79*, 304–323. https://doi.org/org/10.5860/crl.79.3.304.

Junco, R. & Clem, C. (2015). Predicting course outcomes with digital textbook usage data. *Internet and Higher Education, 27*, 54–63. https://doi.org/10.1016/j.iheduc.2015.06.001.

Kagklis, V., Karatrantou, A., Tantoula, M., Panagiotakopoulos, C. & Verykios, V. S. (2016). A learning analytics methodology for detecting sentiment in student fora: A case study in distance education. *European Journal of Open, Distance and e-Learning, 18*(2), 74–94. https://doi.org/10.1515/eurodl-2015-0014.

Lang, S. (2018). Evolution of instructor response? Analysis of five years of feedback to students. *The Journal of Writing Analytics, 2*. https://wac.colostate.edu/docs/jwa/vol2/lang.pdf.

Lewkow, N., Zimmerman, N., Riedesel, M. & Essa, A. (2015, June 26–29). *Learning analytics platform, towards an open scalable streaming solution for education* [Paper presentation]. 8th International Conference on Educational Data Mining (EDM), Madrid, Spain.

Macfadyen, L. P., Dawson, S., Pardo, A. & Gašević, D. (2014). Embracing big data in complex educational systems: The learning analytics imperative and the policy challenge. *Research and Practice in Assessment, 9*, 17–28. http://www.rpajournal.com/embracing-big-data-in-complex-educational-systems-the-learning-analytics-imperative-and-the-policy-challenge/.

McNely, B. J., Gestwicki, P., Holden Hill, J., Parli-Horne, P. & Johnson, E. (2012). Learning analytics for collaborative writing: A prototype and case study. In S. B. Shum, D. Gašević & R. Ferguson (Eds.), *Proceedings of the 2nd International Conference on Learning Analytics and Knowledge* (pp. 222–225). ACM. https://dl.acm.org/citation.cfm?id=2330601 https://doi.org/10.1145/2330601.2330654.

Morse, R. K. (2014). Towards requirements for supporting course redesign with learning analytics. In *Proceedings of the 42nd annual ACM SIGUCCS Conference on User Services* (pp. 89–92). ACM. https://doi.org/10.1145/2330601.2330654.

Moxley, J. (2013). Big data, learning analytics, and social assessment. *The Journal of Writing Assessment, 6*(1), 1–10.

Moxley, J. & Walkup, K. (2016). Mapping writing analytics. In J. Rowe & E. Snow (Eds.), *Workshop and Tutorial Proceedings of EDM 2016* (pp. 1–5). SRI. http://ceur-ws.org/Vol-1633/ws2-paper1.pdf

Noonoo, S. (2018, Mar 12). States issue privacy ultimatums to education technology vendors. EdSurge. https://www.edsurge.com/news/2018-03-12-states-issue-privacy-ultimatums-to-education-technology-vendors.

Palmquist, M. E. (1990). *The lexicon of the classroom: Language and learning in writing classrooms* [Doctoral dissertation, Carnegie Mellon University]. ProQuest Dissertations & Theses Global (9033065).

Palmquist, M. (1993). Network-supported interaction in two writing classrooms. *Computers and Composition 10*(4), 25–57. http://candcblog.org/computersandcomposition/archives/v10/10_4_html/10_4_3_Palmquist.html.

Pardo, A., Ellis, R. A. & Calvo, R. A. (2015). Combining observational and experiential data to inform the redesign of learning activities. In *Proceedings of the Fifth International Conference on Learning Analytics and Knowledge* (pp. 305–309). ACM. https://doi.org/10.1145/2723576.2723625.

Pardo, A. & Siemens, G. (2014). Ethical and privacy principles for learning analytics. *British Journal of Educational Technology, 45*, 438–450. https://doi.org/10.1111/bjet.12152.

Peele, T. (2018). Is this too polite? The limited use of rhetorical moves in a first-year corpus. *The Journal of Writing Analytics, 2*. https://wac.colostate.edu/docs/jwa/vol2/peele.pdf.

Perelman, L. (2014). When "the state of the art" is counting words. *Assessing Writing, 21*, 104–111. https://doi.org/10.1016/j.asw.2014.05.001.

Pilgrim, M. E., Folkestad, J. E. & Sencindiver, B. (2017). Identifying non-regulators: Designing and deploying tools that detect self-regulation behaviors. In S. Shehata & J. P.-L. Tan (Eds.), *Practitioner track proceedings of the 7th International Learning Analytics & Knowledge Conference (LAK'17;* pp. 100–105). Simon Fraser University/SoLAR. https://solaresearch.org/wp-content/uploads/2017/02/Final-LAK17 -Practitioner-Track-Proceedings.pdf.

Rubel, A. & Jones, K. M. L. (2016). Student privacy in learning analytics: An information ethics perspective. *The Information Society, 32*, 143–159. https://doi.org/10.10 80/01972243.2016.1130502.

Sclater, N. (2014). *Code of practice for learning analytics: A literature review of the ethical and legal issues.* JISC. http://repository.jisc.ac.uk/5661/1/Learning_Analytics_A -_Literature_Review.pdf.

Sclater, N. & Bailey, P. (2015). *Code of practice for learning analytics* [Updated August 15, 2018. JISC. https://www.jisc.ac.uk/guides/code-of-practice-for-learning -analytics https://doi.org/10.18608/jla.2016.31.3.

Shoufan, A. (2018). Estimating the cognitive value of YouTube's educational videos: A learning analytics approach. *Computers in Human Behavior, 92*, 450–458. https:// doi.org/10.1016/j.chb.2018.03.036.

Shum, S. B. (2015, June 21). *Reflecting on reflective writing analytics.* http://simon .buckinghamshum.net/2015/06/reflecting-on-reflective-writing-analytics/.

Shum, S. B., Bektik, D., McNamara, D., Allen, L. & Crossley, S. (2016). Critical perspectives on writing analytics. In *Proceedings of the Sixth International Conference on Learning Analytics & Knowledge* (pp. 481–483). ACM. https://doi.org /10.1145/2883851.2883854.

Siemens, G. (2013). Learning analytics: The emergence of a discipline. *American Behavioral Scientist 57*, 1380–1400. https://doi.org/10.1177/0002764213498851.

Siemens, G. & Long, P. (2011). Penetrating the fog: Analytics in learning and education. *EDUCAUSE Review, 46*(5). https://doi.org/10.1177/0002764213498851.

Slade, S. & Prinsloo, P. (2013). Learning analytics: Ethical issues and dilemmas. *American Behavioral Scientist, 57*, 1510–1529. https://doi.org/10.1177/0002764213 479366.

Stephens, E. J. (2017). Doing big data: Considering the consequences of writing analytics. *The Journal of Writing Analytics, 1.* https://wac.colostate.edu/docs/jwa/vol1 /stephens.pdf.

University of Michigan. (2018). *Learning analytics guiding principles.* https://ai.umich .edu/learning-analytics-guiding-principles/.

Uttl, B., White, C. A. & Gonzalez, D. W. (2017). Meta-analysis of faculty's teaching effectiveness: Student evaluation of teaching ratings and student learning are not related. *Studies in Educational Evaluation, 54*, 22–42. https://doi.org/10.1016/j .stueduc.2016.08.007.

Viberg, O., Hatakka, M., Bälter, O. & Mavroudi, A. (2018). The current landscape of learning analytics in higher education. *Computers in Human Behavior, 89*, 98–110. https://doi.org/10.1016/j.chb.2018.07.027.

Wen, M., Yang, D. & Rosé, C. P. (2014). Sentiment analysis in MOOC discussion forums: What does it tell us? In J. Stamper, Z. Pardos, M. Mavrikis & B. M. McLaren (Eds.), *Proceedings of the 7th International Conference on Educational Data Mining (EDM 2014*; pp. 130–137). EDM. https://www.dropbox.com/s/crr6y6fx31 f36e0/EDM%202014%20Full%20Proceedings.pdf.

Wise, A. F., Zhao, Y. & Hausknecht, S. N. (2013). Learning analytics for online discussion: A pedagogical model for intervention with embedded and extracted analytics. In D. Suthers, K. Verbert, E. Duval & X. Ochoa (Eds.), *Proceedings of the Third International Conference on Learning Analytics and Knowledge Conference* (pp. 48–56). ACM. https://dl.acm.org/citation.cfm?id=2460296 https://doi.org/10 .1145/2460296.2460308.

Young, A. & Fulwiler, T. (1986). *Writing across the disciplines: Research into practice.* Boynton/Cook.

Yu, L. C., Lee, C. W., Pan, H. I., Chou, C. Y., Chao, P. Y., Chen, Z. H., Tseng, S. F., Chen, C. L. & Lai, K. R. (2018). Improving early prediction of academic failure using sentiment analysis on self-evaluated comments. *Journal of Computer Assisted Learning, 34*, 358–365. https://doi.org/10.1111/jcal.12247.

Zhang, J.-H., Zhang, Y.-X., Zou, Q. & Huang, S. (2018). What learning analytics tells us: Group behavior analysis and individual learning diagnosis based on long-term and large-scale data. *Educational Technology & Society, 21*, 245–258. https://drive.google.com/open?id=1zoW7a6VRNTQZwnJmRo1OxtDy9mPXn5dX.

PART 2. TEACHING AND LEARNING IN THE DISCIPLINES: DIVERSITY AND PARTICULARITY OF DISCIPLINARY PRACTICES AND GENRES

CHAPTER 5.

MAKING CONNECTIONS BETWEEN THEORY AND PRACTICE: PRE-SERVICE EDUCATOR DISCIPLINARY LITERACY COURSES AS SECONDARY WAC INITIATION

Christy Goldsmith

University of Missouri

In the absence of widespread Writing Across the Curriculum programming in secondary schools, the near-nationwide adoption of the Common Core State Standards—with their focus on disciplinary literacy—features a watershed moment for disciplinary writing instruction in teacher certification programs. Through required disciplinary literacy courses, pre-service teachers (PSTs) are initiated into the WAC/WID community. This chapter examines the context and development of a second disciplinary literacy course at one teacher certification institution, reviews the debate on the place of theory and practice in teacher education, and traces the ways PSTs' identity development occurs alongside their course learning. This chapter concludes by suggesting how discussions about reading can help to expand notions of disciplinary writing. Furthermore, the findings suggest that the PSTs' conversations around theory deepened their understanding of disciplinary writing characteristics and refined their identities as teachers of writing, leading to more skillful incorporation of writing strategies in their teaching.

Saying that disciplinary literacy is simply "how to read in a particular subject matter" is like saying learning to SCUBA dive is "learning to breath[e] in airless environments." It may be technically true, but it lacks the nuance to the point of being meaningless.

—Joe Foster, English education pre-service teacher

Although Writing Across the Curriculum (WAC) programs have existed at the secondary level for decades (see Childers & Lowry, 2012), the implementation

DOI: https://doi.org/10.37514/PER-B.2020.0360.2.05

of the Common Core State Standards (CCSS) in 2010 and, later, the Next Generation Science Standards (NGSS) "required a new level of buy-in and a new possibility for secondary WAC" (Lillge, 2012, p. 2). Eight years later, as states increasingly choose to opt out and write their own content standards, we find ourselves largely in a post-CCSS era; however, policymakers and administrators continue to set goals of measurable literacy achievement across the curriculum. As Michelle Cox and Phyllis Gimbel (2012) noted, the focus on measurable literacy outcomes "creates a mandate for schools to include more writing across the curriculum, but doesn't engage with the other pieces of a WAC program that would lead to a school-wide or district-wide culture of writing" (p. 2). In short, this push toward a quantifiable increase in students' writing skill leads to an increase in practical strategies disconnected from the theoretical support necessary for a sustained improvement in writing pedagogy.

Confirming these challenges for secondary WAC, Jacob Blumner and Pamela Childers (2015) cited the CCSS and the popularity of STEM education as catalysts for the rise in successful secondary/postsecondary WAC partnerships. And yet, beyond the stellar examples they cite in the volume, secondary WAC programming continues to be a challenge. We've not yet achieved the "futurist" notion of "an educational system that completely breaks down the barriers of moving from the K–12 system to higher education" that they imagined in their conclusion (Blumner & Childers, 2015, p. 173).

Perhaps secondary/postsecondary WAC partnerships are still rare because secondary WAC continues to feature unique considerations, namely, that "disciplines, as they are conceived in higher education, do not exist in secondary schools" (Lattimer, 2014, p. xi). The National Council of Teachers of English (2011) defined this distinction in their policy brief, *Literacies of Disciplines*, suggesting that school *subjects* function to "constrain or control how knowledge is presented" (p. 1), leading Heather Lattimer to label subjects as content-focused "silos" (2014, p. xi). In contrast, *disciplines* "emphasize the creation of knowledge" (National Council of Teachers of English, 2011, p. 1) and have "increasingly porous" boundaries (Lattimer, 2014, p. xi). Furthermore, secondary WAC initiatives ask teachers not only to reframe their conceptions *of* their disciplines but also their place within their disciplines. Whereas university instructors are recognized as experts in their disciplines through their educational experiences and publications (Fang, 2012; Shanahan & Shanahan, 2008), secondary teachers are often seen as subject-area teachers rather than disciplinary experts, which means that secondary teachers often feel unprepared to discuss—and teach—disciplinary discourses.

As a teacher educator at a public land-grant university, I have seen firsthand the ways pre-service education compounds these issues as students must learn to teach writing at the same time they are learning to teach. Not only are secondary pre-service teachers (PSTs) still college students who are novices in their disciplines, because they are learning to teach, they are also novices in pedagogy. Secondary PSTs are still learning the language of their disciplines while being expected to apprentice their own students to field-specific writing practices. Also, unlike university instructors, PSTs receive the bulk of their WAC/WID training prior to entering the profession (mostly through their methods of teaching coursework). This incongruity requires secondary school educators to reframe what it means to teach within their disciplines, and it led me to ask the question: How can we simultaneously develop secondary pre-service teachers' disciplinary literacy identities while also making them effective teachers of writing across the curriculum?

Specifically, my inquiry arose from the conflict between how teacher education courses have historically been taught on this research-intensive university campus—heavy in theory—and what pre-service teachers often see as most useful—practical applications. This disconnect, to me, seemed related to how PSTs characterize their own identities. As they are shifting from identifying as mere students to considering themselves teachers, their knowledge priorities also shift. In this chapter, I take up these questions through an exploration of the development and launch of a new disciplinary literacy course for pre-service educators in the teacher certification program. I overview the larger educational context which led to the course invention, consider the place of educator identities within this context, investigate the ways theory and practice converge through class discussion, and suggest findings about PSTs reshaped conceptions of disciplinary writing and pedagogy.

THE CONTEXT OF SECONDARY WAC AND INFLUENCES ON TEACHER EDUCATION PROGRAMS

American public education has, in many ways, been defined by a series of literacy crises. Perhaps the most significant literacy crisis arose in 1974 when the landmark National Assessment of Educational Progress (the NAEP or the Nation's Report Card) showed that writing proficiency had declined from the inaugural test in 1969. This crisis soon swept the public sphere when, in the now infamous 1975 *Newsweek* article "Why Johnny Can't Write," Merrill Sheils exclaimed, "Willy-nilly, the U.S. educational system is spawning a generation of semi-literates" (p. 58). Around this same time, Britton et al. (1975) noted how the burgeoning information age affected sentiments towards writing: "It is often enough claimed that in this telecommunication age the importance of writing is declining rapidly" (p. 201). Britton et al.'s study of "language across the curriculum" in British secondary schools paired with the process writing movement in America (Atwell, 1987; Calkins, 1983; Elbow, 1973; Emig, 1971, 1977; Graves, 1983;

Murray, 1980, 1982, 1985) and the advent of the National Writing Project in 1973 (Gray, 2000) led to a renewed focus on the process and manner of writing instruction in all content areas at the secondary level.

Although, as Pamela Childers and Michael Lowry (2012) remarked, secondary teachers have long been working across the hallway, pairing with teachers of other disciplines to create engaging cross-curricular lessons, in the burgeoning WAC moment of the late 1970s, we began to see individual teachers of various disciplines using writing to further learning. In the 1980s, secondary WAC programs shifted from "the individual classroom into the wider social arena of school, district, and state" (Farrell-Childers et al., 1994, p. 2). Like university WAC programs, these large-scale WAC initiatives in secondary contexts are as geographically, philosophically, and administratively diverse as the schools in which they reside.

With the rise of secondary WAC programs (e.g., the McCallie School in Tennessee, Minnetonka High School in Minnesota, and the Windward School in California), teacher education programs began to take note of the need to support disciplinary writing pedagogy (see Childers & Lowry, 2012, for more on exemplary secondary WAC programs). Childers and Lowry discussed how secondary WAC programs impacted teacher education:

> By [the 1980s], colleges' and universities' undergraduate and graduate secondary education departments were beginning to discuss WAC and writing process in their courses to reinforce what teachers brought to their own classrooms. The repercussions continued with these postsecondary institutions adding required courses in the teaching of writing for education majors across disciplines. (2012, p. 2)

Since the 1990s, most education programs have required at least one course in writing pedagogy—often in the form of a content area reading and writing course—for secondary pre-service teachers (Romine et al., 1996).

The twenty-first century features a continued concern for adolescents' writing abilities. Drawing from the data in the 2002 NAEP, the National Commission on Writing in America's Schools and Colleges (2003) released *The Neglected "R": The Need for a Writing Revolution*. Since the NAEP found that adolescents "cannot systematically produce writing at the high levels of skill, maturity, and sophistication required in a complex and modern economy" (National Commission, 2003, p. 16), the Commission made a series of recommendations to reform writing instruction. Namely, the report recommended that (1) writing be taught in all content areas and grade levels and that (2) pre-service educators of all disciplines take required coursework in writing pedagogy. At the same time, researchers such as Timothy Shanahan and Cynthia Shanahan (2008) tracked the development of teaching specialized writing practices starting in the 1990s when the global information age required more demanding writing tasks for all types of workers. And, finally, in 2009, in response to these perceived crises, the CCSS were developed as "a clear set of college- and career-ready standards for kindergarten through 12th grade in English language arts/literacy and mathematics" (Common Core State Standards Initiative, 2020). Specifically, the CCSS require non-English Language Arts teachers to have a role in writing instruction. They also require a variety of writing modes, lengths, and processes, including short and extended time frames for writing, and advocate for discipline-specific language use (Lillge, 2012).

DEVELOPING A DISCIPLINARY LITERACY COURSE: CONTEXT, PROCESS, AND PST IDENTITIES

The convergence of these three challenges—the subject position of pre-service secondary teachers as pedagogical and content area novices, the continued perceived writing crisis, the standards' insistence that all teachers be writing teachers—occurred around the same time my colleague (a writing program administrator) and I were tasked with developing and teaching a second disciplinary reading/writing course to be added to secondary teacher education coursework at our university.

Necessitating the creation of this new course, the State[1] Department of Elementary Secondary Education made a shift in focus, opting out of the CCSS in favor of developing and implementing their own learning standards. These newly created State Learning Standards (SLS), like the CCSS, placed an emphasis on college and career readiness. Even more than the CCSS, the SLS doubled-down on the necessity of disciplinary writing activities and support for struggling readers/writers, asking all content area teachers to support all students in reading complex disciplinary texts and writing evidence-supported arguments.

This second course in content area reading and writing would go beyond the first course's engagement with strategies to interrogate elements of disciplinary discourses. Following Judy Richardson, Raymond Morgan, and Charlene Fleener's (2009) findings that secondary pre-service teachers needed more training and disciplinary literacy knowledge to teach writing at a high level, this course would focus on moving all students to high levels of disciplinary writing. The new course would also be situated in the tensions Zhihui Fang (2014) raised for teacher education programs: "An emphasis on disciplinary literacy presents new challenges for teacher education because it requires deep understanding of both disciplinary content and disciplinary habits of mind" (p. 444). A further

---

1   To protect institutional and participant anonymity, I omit the state name and instead use State. This applies to acronyms as well.

challenge is the separation of disciplinary literacies—making a space for writing as a mode of instruction and moving beyond content area reading as the focus of such a course. Among other goals, as we developed this new class, we sought to highlight ways in which writing "can support a more complex kind of reasoning that is increasingly necessary for successful performance in our complex technological and information-based culture" (Langer & Applebee, 1987/2007).

The existing disciplinary literacy course—Reading and Writing in the Content Areas I (RWICA I)—provided PSTs with general reading and writing strategies to supplement their content teaching. This second course—Reading and Writing in the Content Areas II (RWICA II)—would involve disciplinary literacy as conceptualized by Shanahan and Shanahan (2008) and others (Fang, 2012; Lattimer, 2014; Moje, 2011; National Council of Teachers of English, 2011), focusing on writing as a discrete, disciplinary-related skill available to learners of all abilities. With the new requirement of a second disciplinary literacy course, our institution was able to seize the moment to work explicitly towards improvement of disciplinary writing instruction in secondary education.

However clear the task, course creation and implementation is fraught with challenges. The particular challenge of RWICA II was mostly owing to the historical debate regarding the place of theory and practice within teacher education. Educators and philosophers—Aristotle, David Hume, Immanuel Kant—have long written about the theory/practice dichotomy. Extending this discussion to teacher education, John Dewey advocated for a productive balance, viewing theory and practice as complementary rather than opposing (see Goodnaugh et al., 2016, for a more detailed discussion of theory/practice in teacher education). Dewey (1933) conceptualized theories as ideas—or "hypothetical possibilities" (p. 164)—that arise from the process of research and thinking. Therefore, as a pragmatist, Dewey (1974) argued "for the proper balance of theory and practice" (p. 314), considering the relationship between "reflective action" and "routine action" (1933). However, as Emily Remington Smith (2007) noted, teacher education researchers and practitioners are still interrogating the manner and method of achieving Dewey's desired balance. She pointed out a common reaction to theory-based discussions that is particularly applicable to the teaching context in this study: "Attempts to discuss the driving theories behind fundamental teaching practices, for example, are always met with questions from teacher candidates about when they are really going to start learning how to teach" (2007, p. 31).

IDENTITY AND PST EDUCATION

In addition to the theory/practice tensions, Leigh Hall (2005) found that identity affects the ways in which pre-service teachers interact with disciplinary literacies. Elizabeth Moje (2011) built on this idea, suggesting that disciplinary literacy is intricately connected to identity. For pre-service teachers, identity can be conceptualized as communal (O'Connor & Scanlon, 2005), contextual (McCarthey & Moje, 2002), and performative (Gee, 2000). John Smyth (2007) described identity—for teachers especially—as a "socially constructed 'production' which is never complete and always in process" (p. 409). And, as novices being inducted into the professional field, the pre-service teachers in this class are situated at the beginning of this recursive process.

Further, as PSTs work to become "disciplinary insiders" (Fang & Coatoam, 2013), and as they learn to teach the discipline to which they are apprenticed, their identities evolve. Their *becoming* highlights the "kind of person" (Gee, 2000)—or, as we'll discuss here, the "kind of teacher"—they become through their teaching. It only makes sense, then, to investigate the implementation of the RWICA II course alongside the PSTs' identity development to consider how their identity becoming affects their learning and teaching of disciplinary writing. These three overarching concepts—the tensions between theory and practice, the distinction of subjects versus disciplines, and the shifting nature of PST identities—became the foundation for my inquiry.

THE INQUIRY

Following Randy Bass' (1999) call to reframe the concept of a problem in teaching to more closely mirror how we consider problems in research or scholarship, I posited the above questions of identity development processes, the theory/practice dichotomy, and disciplinary writing pedagogy as "intellectual problems" inherent in the process of teaching a new course. In line with scholarship of teaching and learning philosophy (Bass, 1999; Hutchings, 2000), I invited my RWICA II students into this investigation of WAC teaching and learning, asking them to also engage in questioning and reflection during our semester together.

Teacher action research (an already established practice in many public school settings) asks for practitioners to do the work of investigating and theorizing—work previously left to academics. Because, as Marilyn Cochran-Smith and Susan Lytle (1999) stated, the most powerful new knowledge of teaching and learning comes from instructors investigating their own teaching practices and conducting inquiry in the courses they teach, educators are a powerful resource for improving teaching. Pat Hutchings (2000) extended this practice of instructor-led inquiry to the university level, tracing how the scholarship of teaching and learning can solve pragmatic questions of instruction, turning problems into "opportuni[ties] for purposeful experimentation and study" (p. 3). To this end, I placed "inquiry as stance" (Cochran-Smith & Lytle, 1999) at the forefront in my teaching of the inaugural RWICA II course. Grounding my teaching and inquiry in sociocultural notions of teaching and learning (Dewey, 1916; Vygotsky, 1978), I asked these questions:

- How do disciplinary PSTs view literacy acts—especially writing acts—within their disciplines?
- How do disciplinary PSTs characterize their roles as both disciplinary writers and teachers of writing?

DATA COLLECTION AND ANALYSIS

In Spring 2017, I taught this inaugural RWICA II class of 18 middle and high school PSTs from a variety of disciplines including English, social studies, science, and math. As second semester junior undergraduates, these PSTs were truly novices in pedagogy, content, and actual teaching experience. Though most were in their second field experience in local public school classrooms, few had the experience of teaching a lesson to "real" students.

Our course objectives were multifaceted. First, I hoped that by the end of the course, the PSTs would be able to identify and explain disciplinary literacy frameworks, including how disciplinary literacies interact with academic identities of the teacher and students (we might label this the *theoretical* aim). Perhaps more importantly, I hoped the PSTs would adapt and implement disciplinary writing strategies in their pre-service teaching (the *practical* aim). Of course, also implicit in these objectives was an exploration of the PSTs' disciplinary identities—or their perceived place within in their disciplines. Since this was the second course in the curriculum, these PSTs had an awareness of the many types of disciplinary literacies; therefore, it was my goal to move them from a place of disciplinary writing awareness to a place of disciplinary writing implementation.

This inquiry took place with these PSTs, and as we worked through the semester's assignments and teaching opportunities together, we embedded reflection into each class session. Therefore, the following findings are built from a diverse set of classroom data:[2]

- PSTs' informal post-class reflections
- my field notes from class discussions
- artifacts from in-class literacy building activities
- PSTs' formal essays with my written feedback
- rubrics from teaching experiences
- peer-to-peer feedback on these teaching experiences

---

2   I obtained IRB approval to collect the forms of data listed here on April 2, 2017.

After our semester was over, I analyzed the data using nominal and spatial thematic analysis (Riessman, 2008) to read both horizontally across individual participant data and vertically down all participants for a singular data point. Instead of isolating the course data into discrete categories, I employed narrative methods to approach the data set as a whole (Clandinin & Connelly, 2000; Riessman, 2008). The recursive process of analysis paired with engaging PSTs in classroom discussion about the data allowed me to establish themes that spoke to the PSTs' literacy development and the theoretical/practical WAC aims of the course. This form of analysis also allowed me to relate the themes to the larger context of the RWICA II sequence and the teacher education program. At the end of the process, I hoped to understand how the elements of inquiry interacted with and spoke to the larger question of WAC/WID teacher training at the postsecondary level.

FINDINGS

The semester of inquiry led to two distinct findings. These findings build on one another, contributing to our understanding of the theory/practice interaction of WAC pedagogy and teacher education. Most notably, the findings trace the participants' identity development as they work to become instructors of disciplinary writing. As one English PST wrote in his final synthesis essay, "As we moved deeper into the semester, it became apparent that disciplinary literacy moves beyond the ivory tower. After all, it is the responsibility of high schools to provide their students with a rounded education that prepares them for life in the real world—if the 'real world' requires a new kind of disciplinary literacy, teachers should step up and instruct it." Through our exploration of theory and application to practice, this future teacher—like many of his colleagues—came to recognize the necessity of disciplinary writing instruction to deepen secondary students' post-high school preparation.

FINDING #1: PSTs' READING/WRITING IDENTITIES AND THE PROCESS OF *BECOMING*

Recognizing how literacy performances contribute to identity development (McCarthey & Moje, 2002), in our course design sessions, my colleague and I created an introductory assignment we titled "Reading and Writing in My Discipline Essay." In this assignment creation and implementation, we considered the research on ways disciplinary experts read and write differently than do disciplinary novices (Shanahan & Shanahan, 2008) to ask students

- What does your reading look like?
- What does your writing practice look like?

- How has your discipline shaped how you think about text, knowledge, and the world?

My own essay concerning how English teachers read—a model I provided for the PSTs—included statements such as

- We read for subtext, at times neglecting plot for meaning.
- We find connections in reading and spend much time expressing those connections in writing.

Similarly, my model included an explanation of how those in the English discipline write, beginning with generalities like

- Voice matters.
- Mechanics are more than correctness.

And then it moved to more specific statements about field-specific discourses such as

- In my field, punctuation is more than a matter of correctness; it's a matter of impact.
- We use dashes to highlight interludes or to represent scatteredness.

This assignment was the first of the semester, and, when we created it, we assumed it would be a low-pressure way for students to begin to make the switch from being a student of their disciplines to *becoming* a teacher of their disciplines (with all the reflexivity that involves).

As with most best-laid plans, that did not turn out to be the case. On this assignment, 12 of the 18 PSTs wrote about their academic identities—who they are as readers, students, and writers—and how they handle general activities in the academic sphere. Most notably, the PSTs' discussion focused on the *reading* portion of their academic identity while a discussion of the *writing* portion of their identities was largely absent.

For example, one social studies pre-service teacher wrote, "I do not like reading . . . I love thinking and making connections while thinking." Similarly, a science PST wrote, "I wouldn't consider myself a good reader. I don't read for fun." The four PSTs who included mentions of writing in their essays expressed their love of writing in general or their disdain for it altogether. One middle school language arts teacher exclaimed, "My strength is creative writing. I love to tell stories!" In contrast, a physics secondary PST bluntly stated, "I do not like writing . . . I think [it] can become extremely overwhelming from time to time." Two social studies PSTs wrote, "I hate writing because I'm bad at grammar," and "Grammar makes writing less than enjoyable for me."

As I read these essays in the second week of the semester, it quickly became clear that these pre-service teachers viewed reading in a limited, traditional way—as connected to fiction books, enjoyed in their free time, or avoided altogether. Even more stark was their depiction of themselves as writers—focusing on missing the mark of one "correct" Standard English, noting how writing was difficult, and saying they rarely felt confident in the act. They did not, it seemed, view reading *or* writing as intimately connected to disciplinary ways of knowing and being. Both of these literacy activities were separated from the process of thinking. In fact, an English PST who, in one sentence celebrated his skill in writing, quickly followed up with the statement: "But thinking is a less focused/ developed skill at this point." Two questions emerged from this data analysis:

1. Why did the PSTs talk so much about reading while mostly neglecting writing?
2. And how might I access this existing knowledge to help the PSTs redefine the idea of reading and/or text to expand their disciplinary writing knowledge and pedagogy?

Regarding the first question, secondary disciplinary scholars focus most often on reading in the content areas rather than writing in the content areas (see Fang, 2014; Shanahan & Shanahan, 2008). For this population of PSTs, especially, it is notable that the textbook (Buehl, 2014) for the first course in the RWICA sequence focuses extensively on reading as the primary method for teaching disciplinary literacy. Finally, these undergraduate students were deeply immersed in the course content of their majors at the same time they were enrolled in the RWICA II course, so they were engaging with disciplinary texts nearly every day. However, these courses were also early in their major course sequence, so they also had less experience with disciplinary writing tasks as students.

Furthermore, as I considered ways to build on the PSTs' existing disciplinary knowledge to expand their conceptions of disciplinary writing, I considered ways disciplinary experts like faculty members learn and express disciplinary writing characteristics. In doing so, I echo Mary Lou Odom's (2013) assertion that "the ways faculty read—and learned to read—disciplinary texts are . . . transparent" (p. 3). Through making reading practices opaque, we are able to make disciplinary writing norms explicit. Alice Horning (2007) supported this assertion, noting the necessary connectedness of reading and writing instruction: "If teachers want students to produce solid academic prose, they must read such prose extensively and carefully in order for the 'din' of that language to get into their heads" (p. 9). So too, I would argue, must pre-service teachers absorb characteristics of disciplinary texts to effectively teach disciplinary writing to their own students.

Engaging in the "cycles of action" (Reason & Bradbury, 2008 p. 1) common in teacher research and the scholarship of teaching and learning, I sought to rectify misconceptions in my classroom. I decided to approach the discussion of disciplinary reading as a way into a discussion (and implementation) of disciplinary writing. After reading these essays, I revised my plans for the following week, and we spent the following class period working through definitions of *reading* and *text*. As the examples in Figure 5.1 demonstrate, most PSTs characterized reading as something done in English class or while writing a research paper.

Define Reading		
1a. "A way of gathering information"	2a. "Taking in images or information"	3a. "Observing a text and trying to make sense of it"
1b. "The observing of a text using the senses"	2b. "Being able to decipher a text"	3b. "Using the info and info you know to understand"
1c. "The ability to understand references"	2c. "Interpreting a text"	3c. "Making sense of the text and the world around you"

Figure 5.1. Pre-service teachers' definitions of reading in Week 2 (written on notecards in class). Entries 1a–2c have no shading; entries 3a–3b have light yellow shading; entry 3c has dark yellow shading.

Many PSTs (boxes 1a through 2c) viewed reading as "understanding" text, an act generalizable to all texts. A few (boxes 3a and 3b) moved toward viewing reading as a transaction (Rosenblatt, 1994), realizing that the reader's background knowledge and worldview affected the practice of reading. One PST (box 3c) connected reading to the world outside of the text, noting that reading is a complex "making sense" process.

Overall, most of these RWICA II pre-service teachers viewed reading as a one-directional, information-gleaning process. For them, reading involved little analysis. As we know, these missing elements are required for effective disciplinary reading (Fang, 2012; Shanahan & Shanahan, 2008) and, further, for disciplinary writing. They also conceptualized disciplinary writing in the same homogeneous way. In these early essays, PSTs often highlighted writing as adhering to one, correct Standard English, and there was little discussion of purpose, audience, or context—all elements integral to disciplinary writing tasks. To many of them, reading was simply gathering information, and writing was simply documenting information correctly. Through these discussions, it became clear that we had a lot more ground to cover in expanding understanding around writing than reading, and as we know, writing is often a more difficult endeavor.

Additionally, as I asked students to theorize what disciplinary writing *is* and *does*, they had first to feel like they had some element of disciplinary literacy expertise. This reading/text discussion allowed us to consider the PSTs' existing knowledge, broaden preconceived notions, and provide a way to grow their knowledge of disciplinary writing practices. This realization helped me understand why, when the PSTs were asked in the first assignment to write about their processes of disciplinary reading/writing, they defaulted to speaking about their academic identities. These academic identities were comfortable; as college juniors, many of these PSTs had been cultivating their academic identities for more than fifteen years. Their disciplinary expert identities, however, were in process. These PSTs knew the *what* of their disciplines; they were strong in content knowledge. But they didn't know the *how* of disciplinary literacy; they were unsure of how experts in their fields approached literacy acts. Though these pre-service teachers had completed one Reading and Writing in the Content Areas course and at least one Methods of Teaching course in their subject area, they still viewed themselves as novices both in their disciplines and in the teaching profession. Their identities-in-process meant that they were not qualified (or, at least they did not feel as though they were) to speak to the reading and writing practices of their discipline. This realization on their part (and also on mine) opened up space for an exploration of theory—a discussion that might have been less welcome had they not first done the identity work to reveal the necessity.

FINDING #2: THE INTERACTION OF DISCIPLINARY THEORY AND PRACTICE

In her study of the theory/practice balance in an English education methods course, Remington Smith (2007) found that when PSTs take ownership of theories, they are more likely to internalize them. She writes, "Perhaps one of the difficulties teacher candidates have with educational theories is that they belong to someone else" (2007, p. 34). The PSTs' responses to this RWICA II study confirm and extend Remington Smith's findings. Specifically, through theoretical readings, response essay writing, and small/large group discussion, the RWICA II pre-service educators were able to begin internalizing the theories.

In the early weeks of this course, we read discourse and identity theory (Gee, 2000), sociocultural learning theory (Gee, 2001; Vygotsky, 1978), theories about the specialization of disciplinary literacies (Moje, 2008; Shanahan & Shanahan, 2008), critical literacy theories (Beck, 2005; Lee, 2011; Morrell, 2012; Perry, 2012), and multimodal literacy theories (O'Byrne & Murrell, 2014). These texts are notoriously tough to parse and quite abstract in nature. Even though they found these texts difficult, according to their written and verbal reflections, the most useful element of the course was not—as PSTs often say —the practical activities. In fact, one English PST actively worked against this traditional paradigm, remarking that merely doing literacy activities was not enough. "Activities don't always imply learning," he wrote. Based on their early semester disdain for texts which "didn't directly transfer" to the classroom, I was surprised when these PSTs suggested it was the class discussions (often following a response paper engaging a theoretical text) which helped them decipher the difficult theory readings and try out new ideas. One high school math PST valued the discussions to help her "foster new questions and move the conversation [about literacy] along."

Early in the semester, these theoretical readings and discussions reshaped PSTs' conceptions of literacy and their place within the writing community. When discussing Fang's (2012) text on linguistic elements of challenging disciplinary texts, one social studies PST considered the role of nominalizations in history disciplinary texts. She discussed the ways these nominalizations cause readers of historical texts to "get caught up or focus on the words rather than the content," and she explored reasons why historical writers use these linguistic structures. Then she began to imagine ways to use writing in her classroom to dissect these nominalizations. She designed assignments for her students to work at the word, phrase, and sentence level to understand the linguistic structures of her discipline's texts, dissect the meaning within the structure, and transfer these nominalizations to their own writing when appropriate. In this way, the theory helped her understand how the language of disciplinary texts is connected to content, and it helped her overturn the one-size-fits-all conception of "correct" writing she had when she entered the course.

Other PSTs found the critical literacy texts to be the most novel and applicable theoretical readings. As they learned about critical literacy in multiple modes and genres, PSTs shifted their views of their role in teaching writing in their disciplines. Teaching writing was no longer just about extending what their students learned in elementary or middle school or teaching students how to write "correctly." Instead, they began to see their role as working from what students know about general writing practices to complicate the process and highlight nuanced disciplinary differences. After reading Ann Beck's (2005) and Cheu-jey Lee's (2011) texts, PSTs, in class discussion, expanded their view of critical writing practices from, as one English PST noted, "writing that demonstrates critical thinking" to "writing that requires students to be critically engaged with the content and also the larger world around them." In the same discussion, a social studies PST noted that the critical literacy theories highlighted, for her, the ways writing practices are changing for her twenty-first century students. Applying this to their practice, she and her social studies colleagues discussed ways to incorporate multimodal and multimedia writing opportunities into their classrooms to "show students how important writing is in our modern world." So, rather than desire to jump directly into my bag of literacy tricks, through engaging with theory, these PSTs realized their own gaps in knowledge regarding the learning and teaching of writing.

The importance of theory notwithstanding, the transfer to practice is always our ultimate goal, and it was within these whole class and small group discussions where the theory-practice transfer began. We saw a reconfiguring of what kind of knowledge is important to future teachers. After they had a chance to play with theory, to try it out via writing and class discussion, they were able to meaningfully incorporate practical and effective writing activities into their content instruction.

The final assessment in this RWICA II course was an interdisciplinary lesson plan and in-class teaching opportunity. In the last half of the semester, teachers from different content areas worked together to create a lesson around a theme common to both disciplines. They then taught this lesson to their RWICA II colleagues who acted as secondary students. The interdisciplinary nature of this lesson allowed PSTs to "negotiate the conflicts among motives" in different disciplines and "[learn] about interdisciplinarity, disciplinarity, and the role of writing in the disciplines" (Nowacek, 2012, p. 397). Within this lesson, PSTs were required to incorporate reading and writing to further students' disciplinary learning. These strategies needed to be appropriate to the lesson's goals and effective in the stated aim. In this cohort, PSTs' incorporation of disciplinary reading activities was 77.5% proficient[3] while their incorporation of disciplinary writing activities was 87.5% proficient. Within the 87.5% proficiency, PSTs included a variety of disciplinary writing activities to showcase their understanding of WAC/WID theory. One group comprised of a math and English PST used informal quick-writes to allow students to write-to-learn their way through a tough computational process, concluding their lesson with a formal argumentative paragraph where students had to use evidence to prove that their method was the most logical method. Other groups' writing-to-learn strategies included close-readings of short quotations, visual analysis of primary documents using sentence stems, and a write-around activity where students engaged in a pen-and-paper version of the old telephone game. Formal writing assignments asked students to construct graphs, blog posts, if/then statements, lab procedures, poetry, and formal letters.

It is important here to note that, in their shorter lessons earlier in the semester, the PSTs struggled with choosing the right strategy to pair with the content area objective. They often chose a strategy for strategy's sake, but, as these findings suggest, the continued theoretical reading and the corresponding classroom discussions helped PSTs to match the aim with the strategy, and their final teaching opportunity reflects this improvement. They moved beyond seeing writing activities as valueless and generic as they engaged more deeply in the linguistic

---

3   As scored by the instructor according to a two-part rubric provided to the PSTs ahead of the teaching opportunity.

practices (after reading/discussing Fang, 2012; Gee, 2001), organizational methods and modes (after reading/discussing O'Byrne & Murrell, 2014), and critical approaches (after reading/discussing Morrell, 2012; Perry, 2012) of disciplinary writing. Their writing assignments moved from asking students to display learning to asking students to interrogate disciplinary language, organization, and power structures through writing.

In a way, through our parsing of theory, PSTs considered and, perhaps, *re*considered what counts as knowledge in their disciplines. As they inquired *with* me on the best practices for supporting pre-service teachers' WAC/WID development, the line between theory and practice became permeable. Or, as Gerald Pine (2009) wrote regarding the act of teacher research, the "distinctions between formal and practical knowledge" (p. 51) began to disappear.

IMPLICATIONS FOR SECONDARY WAC/WID PROGRAMS AND TEACHER EDUCATION

As these findings demonstrate, pre-service teachers started to connect course theory to teaching practice when they began to view themselves as *becoming* experts in the discourses of their disciplines. By forefronting the ways in which their existing definitions of reading and writing neglected disciplinary distinctions, and by accessing their growing body of theoretical knowledge, PSTs were able to begin to see themselves as teachers of their disciplines rather than just teachers of their subjects. They began connecting what they learned in their methods course about how best to approach disciplinary content teaching to the theoretical readings about disciplinary literacy to choose the best mode of writing instruction for the task, context, text, and student need. In this way, they began to move away from a content-focused view of disciplinary education and toward a more literacy-focused view. Through interdisciplinary discussion with PSTs in other fields, they discarded subject "silos" for disciplines more broadly conceived. In doing so, they expanded their views of what counts as writing, and they included more discipline-specific writing in their courses (see Wardle et al. this volume for a similar impact of theoretical conversations on university faculty's writing pedagogy).

This inquiry opens up a space for theory in the RWICA II classroom. When they realized their narrow views of reading and writing, and when they engaged in rigorous reading, writing, and discussion practices themselves, the pre-service teachers were able to view the purpose behind the writing strategies I was advocating. This allowed the PSTs to see theory and practice as two sides of the same coin rather than as diametrically opposed foes, and as we saw in their interdisciplinary lessons, it allowed them to connect their writing assignments to the purpose, content, and aims of their disciplinary teaching. Most significantly, the transfer happened when they were able to do as students and then reflect as teachers, reinforcing Dewey's reflective thinking model (see Rodgers, 2002, for the article that the RWICA II PSTs read regarding reflective thinking).

LOOKING FORWARD

This study provides interesting starting points for further investigation. Most importantly, it encourages teacher educators to engage pre-service teachers in literacy identity work prior to the RWICA courses and subsequently throughout their time in teacher education. Just as disciplines are more than individual silos, and just as it takes a village to raise a child, so too is the education of postsecondary students. A campus culture which cultivates college students' disciplinary literacy identities from the moment they step into their math, science, literature, and history (and more) classrooms as freshmen produces stronger teachers which, in turn, produces stronger university students in the years to come. Therefore, these findings encourage the teacher education community and the larger WAC campus community to become allies in the education of postsecondary students.

Speaking to the power of the scholarship of teaching and learning, Bass (1999) suggested that inquiries such as this one "can begin to chart what is yet uncharted terrain, a landscape that will feature the convergence of disciplinary knowledge, pedagogical practice, evidence of learning, and theories of learning and cognition" (p. 8). This RWICA II inquiry, situated in the convergence of teacher education, disciplinary education, and WAC pedagogy, provides insights and raises more questions to add to the robust field of WAC/WID scholarship.

REFERENCES

Atwell, N. (1987). *In the middle: Writing, reading, and learning with adolescents.* Heinemann.

Bass, R. (1999). The scholarship of teaching: What's the problem? *Inventio: Creative Thinking About Learning and Teaching, 1*(1). https://my.vanderbilt.edu/sotl/files/2013/08/Bass-Problem1.pdf.

Beck, A. S. (2005). A place for critical literacy. *Journal of Adolescent and Adult Literacy, 48*(5), 392–400. https://doi.org/10.1598/JAAL.48.5.3.

Blumner, J. S. & Childers, P. B. (2015). What we have learned about WAC partnerships and their futures. In J. S. Blumner & P. B. Childers (Eds.), *WAC Partnerships Between Secondary and Postsecondary Institutions* (pp. 167–174). The WAC Clearinghouse; Parlor Press. https://wac.colostate.edu/books/perspectives/partnerships/.

Britton, J., Burgess, T., Martin, N., McLeod, A. & Rosen, H. (1975). *The development of writing ability (11–18).* Macmillan.

Buehl, D. (2014). *Classroom strategies for interactive learning* (4th ed.). International Reading Association.

Calkins, L. (1983). *Lessons from a child: On the teaching and learning of writing.* Heinemann Educational Books.

Childers, P. B. & Lowry, M. J. (2012). Introduction to Writing Across the Curriculum in Secondary Schools. *Across the Disciplines, 9*(3). https://wac.colostate.edu/docs/atd /k12/intro.pdf.

Clandinin, D. J. & Connelly, F. M. (2000). *Narrative inquiry: Experience and story in qualitative research.* Jossey-Bass.

Cochran-Smith, M. & Lytle, S. L. (1999). Relationships of knowledge and practice: Teacher learning in communities. *Review of Research in Education, 24*, 249–305. https://doi.org/10.2307/1167272.

Common Core State Standards Initiative. (2020). *Overview: Frequently asked questions.* Retrieved on February 4, 2020 from http://www.corestandards.org/about-the-stan dards/frequently-asked-questions/.

Cox, M. & Gimbel, P. (2012). Conversations among teachers on student writing: WAC/Secondary education partnerships at BSU. *Across the Disciplines 9*(3). https:// wac.colostate.edu/docs/atd/k12/cox_gimbel.pdf.

Dewey, J. (1916). *Democracy and education.* Free Press.

Dewey, J. (1933). *How we think.* Heath.

Dewey, J. (1974). The relation of theory to practice in education. In R. D. Archambault (Ed.), *John Dewey on education* (pp. 313–338). University of Chicago Press.

Elbow, P. (1973). *Writing without teachers.* Oxford University Press.

Emig, J. (1971). *The composing process of twelfth graders.* NCTE. https://doi.org /10.2307/356095.

Emig, J. (1977). Writing as a mode of learning. *College Composition and Communication, 28*(2), 122–128.

Fang, Z. (2012). The challenges of reading disciplinary texts. In T. L. Jetton & C. Shanahan (Eds.), *Adolescent literacy in the academic disciplines* (pp. 34–68). Guilford Press.

Fang, Z. (2014). Preparing content-area teachers for disciplinary literacy instruction: The role of literacy teacher educators. *Journal of Adolescent and Adult Literacy, 57*(6), 444–448. https://doi.org/10.1002/jaal.269.

Fang, Z. & Coatoam, S. (2013). Disciplinary literacy: What you want to know about it. *Journal of Adolescent & Adult Literacy, 56*, 627–632. https://doi.org/10.1002 /JAAL.190.

Farrell-Childers, P., Gere, A. R. & Young, A. (Eds.). (1994). *Programs and practices: Writing across the secondary school curriculum.* Boynton/Cook.

Gee, J. P. (2000). Identity as an analytic lens for research in education. *Review of Research in Education, 25*(1), 99–125. https://doi.org/10.2307/1167322.

Gee, J. P. (2001). Reading as situated language: A sociocognitive perspective. *Journal of Adolescent and Adult Literacy, 44*(8), 714. https://doi.org/10.1598/JAAL.44.8.3.

Goodnaugh, K., Falkenberg, T. & MacDonald, R. (2016). Examining the nature of theory-practice relationships in initial teacher education: A Canadian case study. *Canadian Journal of Education, 39*(1), 1–28.

Graves, D. H. (1983). *Writing: Teachers and children at work.* Heinemann Educational Books.

Gray, J. (2000). *Teachers at the center: A memoir of the early years of the National Writing Project.* National Writing Project.

Hall, L. A. (2005). Teachers and content-area reading: Attitudes, beliefs, and change. *Teacher and Teacher Education, 21,* 403–414. https://doi.org/10.1016/j.tate.2005.01.009.

Horning, A. S. (2007). Reading across the curriculum as the key to student success. *Across the Disciplines, 4.* https://wac.colostate.edu/docs/atd/articles/horning2007.pdf.

Hutchings, P. (2000). Introduction: Approaching the scholarship of teaching and learning. In P. Hutchings (Ed.), *Opening lines: Approaches to the scholarship of teaching and learning* (pp. 1–10). Carnegie.

Langer, J. A. & Applebee, A. N. (2007). *How writing shapes thinking: A study of teaching and learning.* https://wac.colostate.edu/books/landmarks/langer-applebee/ (Original work published 1987).

Lattimer, H. (2014). *Real-world literacies: Disciplinary teaching in the high school classroom.* National Council of Teachers of English.

Lillge, D. (2012). Illuminating possibilities: Secondary writing across the curriculum as a resource for navigating common core state standards. *Across the Disciplines, 9*(3). https://wac.colostate.edu/docs/atd/k12/lillge.pdf.

Lee, C. J. (2011). Myths about critical literacy: What teachers need to unlearn. *Journal of Language and Literacy Education, 7*(1), 95–102.

McCarthey, S. J. & Moje, E. B. (2002). Identity matters. *Reading Research Quarterly, 37,* 228–238. https://doi.org/10.1598/RRQ.37.2.6.

Moje, E. B. (2008). Foregrounding the disciplines in secondary literacy teaching and learning: A call for change. *Journal of Adolescent and Adult Literacy, 52*(2), 96–107. https://doi.org/10.1598/JAAL.52.2.1.

Moje, E. B. (2011). Developing disciplinary discourses, literacies, and identities: What's knowledge got to do with it? In G. Lopez Bonilla & K. Englander (Eds.), *Discourses and identities in the contexts of educational change: Contributions from the United States and Mexico* (pp. 49–74). Lang.

Morrell, E. (2012). 21st century literacies, critical media pedagogies, and language arts. *The Reading Teacher, 66,* 300–302. https://doi.org/10.1002/TRTR.01125.

Murray, D. M. (1980). Writing as process: How writing finds its own meaning. In T. R. Donovan & B. McClelland (Eds.), *Eight approaches to teaching composition* (pp. 3–20). National Council of Teachers of English.

Murray, D. M. (1982). *Learning by teaching.* Heinemann

Murray, D. M. (1985). *A writer teaches writing.* Houghton Mifflin.

National Commission on Writing in America's Schools and Colleges. (2003). *The neglected "R": The need for a writing revolution.* The College Board.

National Council of Teachers of English. (2011). *Literacies of disciplines: A policy research brief.* https://secure.ncte.org/library/NCTEFiles/Resources/Journals/CC/0211-sep2011/CC0211Policy.pdf.

Nowacek, R. S. (2012). Why is being interdisciplinary so very hard to do? Thoughts on the perils and promise of interdisciplinary pedagogy. In T. M. Zawacki & P. M. Rogers (Eds.), *Writing across the curriculum: A critical sourcebook* (pp. 380–398). Bedford.

O'Byrne, B. & Murrell, S. (2014). Evaluating multimodal literacies in student blogs. *British Journal of Educational Technology, 45*(5), 926–940. https://doi.org/10.1111/bjet.12093.

O'Connor, K. E. & Scanlon, L. (2005, July 4–5). *"What I do is who I am": Knowledge, skills, and teachers' professional identities.* Paper presented at the AARE Annual Conference, Cairns, Australia.

Odom, M. L. (2013). Not just for writing anymore: What WAC can teach us about reading to learn. *Across the Disciplines, 10*(4). https://wac.colostate.edu/docs/atd/reading/odom.pdf.

Perry, K. H. (2012). What is literacy? A critical overview of sociocultural perspectives. *Journal of Language and Literacy Education, 8*(1), 50–71.

Pine, G. J. (2009). Conducting teacher action research. In *Teacher action research: Building knowledge democracies* (pp. 234–263). Sage.

Reason, P. & Bradbury, H. (2008). Introduction. In P. Reason & H. Bradbury (Eds.), *The SAGE handbook of action research: Participative inquiry and practice* (2nd ed., pp. 1–14). Sage. https://doi.org/10.4135/9781848607934.

Remington Smith, E. (2007). Integrating theory and practice in an English methods course. In M. Gordon & T. O'Brien (Eds.), *Bridging theory and practice in teacher education* (pp. 31–45). Sense. https://doi.org/10.1163/9789087900991_004.

Richardson, J. S., Morgan, R. F. & Fleener, C. E. (2009). *Reading to learn in the content areas* (7th ed.). Wadsworth Thomson Learning.

Riessman, C. K. (2008). *Narrative methods for the human sciences.* State University of New York Press.

Rodgers, C. (2002). Defining reflection: Another look at John Dewey and reflective thinking. *Teachers College Record 104*(4), 842–866. https://doi.org/10.1111/1467-9620.00181.

Romine, B. G., McKenna, M. C. & Robinson, R. D. (1996). Reading coursework requirements for middle and high school content area teachers: A U.S. Survey. *Journal of Adolescent & Adult Literacy 40*(3), 194–198.

Rosenblatt, L. M. (1994). *The reader, the text, the poem: The transactional theory of the literary work.* Southern Illinois University Press.

Shanahan, T. & Shanahan, C. (2008). Teaching disciplinary literacy to adolescents: Rethinking content area literacy. *Harvard Educational Review 78*(1), 40–59. https://doi.org/10.17763/haer.78.1.v62444321p602101.

Sheils, M. (1975, December 8). Why Johnny can't write. *Newsweek, 92*(8), 58–65.

Smyth, J. (2007). Pedagogy, school culture and teacher learning: Towards more durable and resistant approaches to secondary school literacy. *Language & Education: An International Journal 21*(5), 406–419. https://doi.org/10.2167/le802.0.

Vygotsky, L. S. (1978). Mind and society: The development of higher psychological processes. Harvard University Press.

CHAPTER 6

WHAT IF IT'S *ALL* COMMON KNOWLEDGE? TEACHING ATTRIBUTION PRACTICES IN AN UNDERGRADUATE MATHEMATICS CLASSROOM

Malcah Effron

Massachusetts Institute of Technology

Current writing studies scholarship in attribution practice and instruction is underscored by two central questions: what needs attribution and how should sources and their attributions be incorporated? Professional practice generally answers these questions through systems designed to distinguish authors' original contributions from that of others and from shared/common knowledge in the field. Yet, in STEM classes, and in mathematics in particular, students are often asked to reproduce previously established results and communicate the same thesis and content as their classmates. Consequently, either they have no critical contributions and need to cite everything, or they only present common knowledge and need to cite nothing. Such attribution metrics are thus perplexing rather than clarifying. Using experiences in a mathematics WID classroom, this chapter outlines some challenges of teaching professional attribution strategies through classroom genres that ask students to reproduce common knowledge; it calls for further scholarship to understand and to develop pedagogy to address them.

Within the context of a given community of standards, plagiarism results from authors' failure to distinguish their own contributions sufficiently from the contributions of others. In studying why students plagiarize, Diane Pecorari (2013) distinguished between prototypical *plagiarism*—when writers intentionally deceive others about their original contributions—and *patchwriting*—when writers unintentionally pass off ideas or language as their own because they are unfamiliar with the rhetorical and generic signals of attribution (p. 28). The

DOI: https://doi.org/10.37514/PER-B.2020.0360.2.06

study of prototypical plagiarism revolves around why students cheat whereas the study of patchwriting tends toward questions about the barriers students face when learning to use professional source use practices. Since Rebecca Howard's (1992) eye-opening definition of patchwriting as source-use missteps during the learning process, the study of patchwriting—writing-centered (as opposed to cheating-centered) research into attribution practice—has developed two main strains of questions: What information needs attribution, and how are sources incorporated into a body of writing?

Studies of the latter question are generally interested in what happens when novices try to incorporate sources into their writing. Studies in WID and other upper-level contexts also assume students know they need to use attributions; they are just unsure, unskilled, or unpracticed in the mechanisms for effectively signaling what work is their original contribution and what work is taken from others (cf. Howard & Robillard, 2008; Pecorari & Shaw, 2019). Studies of upper level work (e.g., Jamieson, 2019; Serviss, 2016) tend to focus on this question, addressing upper level students' continued struggles with the means of incorporating others' work rather than what needs any attribution. Additionally, studies like the one in Misty Anne Winzenried's chapter in this collection engage with this line of inquiry; in understanding the geography literature review, the students in her study did not need to determine what needed to be cited but instead had to discover how to distinguish their own argument *about* the literature from their own argument *supported by* the literature. These students therefore needed to learn the rhetorical moves that signaled attributing ideas to sources rather than staking their own claims. As this example suggests, studies in this area of inquiry engage with how students learn the rhetorical techniques they need to distinguish their own contributions from those of others, creating awareness that different communities employ different techniques (see, e.g., Howard & Robillard, 2008).

Studies into the techniques that different communities use to distinguish authors' original contributions are closely related to the former question about what needs attribution. Whether about medium (e.g., Eisner & Vicinus, 2008) or discipline (e.g., Eckel, 2014; Jamieson, 2008), these studies are centered around what kind of information is considered collectively shared information, which can be used without attribution, and what is considered "owned" (Haviland & Mullins, 2009), which needs attribution. Style manuals and handbooks tend to refer to collectively shared information as common knowledge, which Amy England (2008) argued is often implicitly defined in these references as "an established, static set of facts" (p. 109). The shared nature of these facts relates to Kenneth Burke's (1973) parlor metaphor for academic discourse in which the student is a late arrival where everyone else is in the middle of a conversation.

Burke commented that "the discussion had already begun long before any of them [those already in the parlor] got there, so that no one present is qualified to retrace for you all the steps that had gone before" (1973, p. 110). This notion of "no one present [being] qualified" captures the space of what kinds of information pass into the realm of collectively shared knowledge in a community: it needs no attribution because it has lost its source and to attribute credit to anyone in particular is as misleading as attributing it to no one. Yet, students who have not yet been brought into Burke's parlor do not yet share this knowledge with the community and therefore often struggle to distinguish the content considered shared from the content still attributed to particular sources (Shaw & Pecorari, 2019, pp. 5–6). Studies into what needs to be attributed work to clarify such values and develop pedagogies to help introduce new arrivals to the conversation.

Studies in both what and how now attend to discipline- and genre-specific attribution practices, yet their responses coalesce around attribution practices' role in allowing authors to situate their interventions into a community of discussion or a body of knowledge. Distinguishing one's own contribution to a field is generally considered an important component of good academic practice, despite disagreements on what needs to be acknowledged and what forms attributions should take (Pecorari, 2013, p. 31). Such professional practice, however, becomes hard to emulate directly in writing classroom settings, especially in introductory STEM courses in which students are asked to replicate a field's well-known results. In mathematics proof-writing classes in particular, assignments do not generally enable students to express original contributions to the field, as students are primarily asked to re-prove established facts that form the basis of the field. Because attribution is not being used as in the profession, the line determining what does or does not need to be cited can often come across as arbitrary norms used to penalize students. If we ignore how this classroom genre induces perceived arbitrariness, our ignorance can exacerbate the perception of instructors as gatekeepers enforcing arbitrary norms around attribution (cf. Pecorari, 2013) and can impede students' abilities to transfer from classroom forms to professional practice (cf. Russell, 1995). Such assignments thus raise the following question: when solving problems that are already established examples (see Figure 6.1), what counts as common knowledge? And, if it is all common knowledge, how can we use these assignments to effectively teach values attached to professional attribution practices?

To explore these questions more concretely, this chapter considers the specific case of a class I teach at Massachusetts Institute of Technology (MIT), in which these problems acquired particular importance in writing assignment design and instruction. The chapter begins by exploring what counts as common knowledge, reviewing discussions both across the curriculum and specifically in STEM fields. In light of this background, the chapter introduces the mathematics writing classroom, in which the dominant form of argumentation is the formal proof, leading to the role of attribution in this space, especially in light of mathematical attribution practice and WID evaluation of peer review.

Prove the following claims:

(a) $\sum_{i=0}^{n} i^n = \frac{n(n+1)(2n+1)}{6}$.

(b) $(1 + x)^k \geq (1 + xk)$ for all $x \geq 1$ and all positive integers k.

(c) $\sqrt{2}$ is irrational. Furthermore, there exists irrational numbers x and y such that x^y is rational.

Figure 6.1. These are sample writing prompts for an assignment in MIT's Spring 2018 18.200, a communication-intensive discrete math course. Students were asked to prove that the (well-known and well-understood) claims listed above are correct.

As this chapter reflects on an experience, it does not offer data-driven arguments and recommendations, and its strategies are also less generalizable because they rely on field-specific attribution practices. Yet, this anecdotal experience brings attribution in the mathematics classroom into the writing studies conversations around attributions, from which it is currently absent. Moreover, I believe the questions raised both by the challenges and the strategies used to address them can be extended to other fields, particularly in STEM and other content-driven subjects. This chapter thus argues not for particular pedagogy but to recognize the transfer challenges created when we try to teach attribution strategies designed for original contributions through assignments asking students to reproduce common knowledge. Such recognition can lead writing studies to explore more fully the questions that classroom genres raise about the pedagogic goals of attribution instruction and how these goals can translate successfully into the WAC/WID classroom.

ATTRIBUTION AND COMMON KNOWLEDGE ACROSS THE CURRICULUM

Writing studies has recognized that students lack mastery of scholarly and professional attribution practices, and this lack is a primary cause of non-prototypical student plagiarism (see Howard, 1992; Howard & Robillard, 2008; Pecorari, 2013). Recognizing this educational (rather than ethical) challenge in students' source use, anti-plagiarism scholarship has worked to understand barriers to students' initiation into scholarly attribution practice. Such explorations have led some scholars to question whether enough commonality exists across attribution systems to teach generalizable, transferable concepts, with many concluding yes (Hayes et al., 2016; Pecorari, 2013).

However, the most generalized level of agreement—not passing off others' work as one's own—tends to form the basis of institutional plagiarism policies. For many academic and professional organizations, plagiarism means failing to attribute adequately (without defining *adequately*), and includes unacknowledged or unattributed use of another's words, ideas, data, or discoveries (see Table 6.1). For example, MIT defines plagiarism as the "use of another's words, ideas, assertions, data, or figures *[that does] not acknowledge that you have done so* [emphasis added]" (Brennecke, 2018, p. 5). As the italicized predicate emphasizes, the shared definition of plagiarism identifies the underlying problem as claiming the work of others as one's own.

Table 6.1: Plagiarism Definitions from Different Academic Organizations

Organization (field represented)	Definition
IEEE (electrical engineering)	"the reuse of someone else's prior processes, results, or words without explicitly acknowledging the original author and source" (IEEE, 2018)
MLA (language & literature)	"presenting another person's ideas, information, expressions, or entire work as one's own" (Modern Language Association, 2016, pp. 6–7)
AMS (mathematics)	"[t]he knowing presentation of another person's mathematical discovery as one's own constitutes plagiarism and is a serious violation of professional ethics" (American Mathematical Society, 2005)
NSF (natural sciences)	"the appropriation of another person's ideas, processes, results, or words without giving appropriate credit" (Fischer, 2011, p. 2)
APA (psychology and social sciences)	"Psychologists do not present portions of another's work or data as their own, even if the other work or data source is cited occasionally" (American Psychological Association, 2017).

In this regard, academics and other professionals do share an understanding of what needs attribution. However, writing studies and applied linguistics have shown we only agree on attribution at this high-level overview, and even this high-level overview quickly breaks down over what constitutes "claiming" and what constitutes "another's work." As early as 2001, Miguel Roig argued that university faculty across disciplines—and even within disciplines—did not share standards for distinguishing paraphrasing from plagiarizing because different fields accepted varying levels of textual appropriation (p. 321). More recently, Rebecca Howard and Amy Robillard (2008) called out many layers of differences in *Pluralizing Plagiarism,* and their contributor Sandra Jamieson (2008) noted that her university committee could only agree to prohibit deliberately passing off another's work as one's own, disagreeing about what counts as information that needs attribution and what mechanics are used to identify it (p. 77). She argued that such challenges result from the fact that disciplinary differences in attribution arise from different acknowledgment values.

For example, studies have shown that researchers in STEM are less concerned about word-for-word matches without quotation than in other fields (Buranen & Stephenson, 2009; Eckel, 2014), "plac[ing] a higher priority on the attribution of ideas than the attribution of words" (Eckel, 2014, p. 2). Such studies suggest that disciplinary distinctions often fall around the values of using one's own words and the importance of quotation; text-centered disciplines tend to value quotation in ways that other research forms do not. Jamieson (2008) pointed out that this difference often leads plagiarism policies based on humanities attribution systems to indict acceptable textual appropriation practice in other fields (pp. 77–78). Given such challenges on the level of faculty, it is not surprising that novices find it difficult to develop intuition about what information is considered usable without attribution and what needs attribution.

Intuition about what is usable without attribution is further complicated by the use of the term *common knowledge* to identify information that does not require attribution. MIT's definition of this term is fairly representative of issues around common knowledge (cf. England, 2008): "information that the average, educated reader would accept as reliable without having to look it up." But MIT adds a caveat: "What may be common knowledge in one culture, nation, academic discipline or peer group may not be common knowledge in another" (Brennecke, 2018, p. 8). Such caveats respond to England's (2008) argument that if common knowledge is introduced as highly contextualized, students will more readily internalize the boundaries in their own field and learn others as they enter new fields (p. 112). So while "the average, educated reader" is still an ambiguous construct, the caveat about the contextualized nature of common knowledge demonstrates attribution scholarship's positive influence, at least in the case of MIT's academic policy and pedagogy.

While these interventions work on the level of professional practice, *classroom genres* present complications beyond the mere process of professionalization.[1] In particular, many undergraduate classroom environments exist to teach

---

1   I define classroom genre by example: A term paper, while it may be related to an academic article, does not have identical needs and conventions to a publishable piece.

students the common knowledge of the field, and writing classrooms in these fields deliberately ask or expect students to reproduce common knowledge. Such challenges are particularly clear in light of England's (2008) explication of the implicit assumptions in writing manuals' definitions of common knowledge and its association with "*an established, static set of facts*" (p. 109). For instance, in mathematics writing classrooms, students are often asked to prove well-known claims already proved elsewhere. If students have learned that so-called common knowledge does not need to be cited, then they might not see any need for or value of attribution practice in the work they produce for class. Yet instructors want students to learn the value of attribution and to practice its forms of attribution while in these writing classrooms.

The difficulty, though, is that attribution needs in the rhetorical situation of classroom genres differ significantly from those of professional practice. As one example, students are not expected to possess the field's common knowledge being taught in the class, and they therefore are often expected to cite content that might be left unattributed in professional publications. Furthermore, professional attribution practices are based on the assumption that the authors can reasonably situate their interventions as a productive contribution to the field. Students in undergraduate writing classrooms rarely have the opportunity to generate truly original ideas for many reasons, including semester time constraints and access to materials. This disconnect between the content the students are writing up and the functionality of the tools they are being asked to use creates challenges in learning both the value and the practice of attribution, inhibiting the transfer of skills into professional practice. Classroom genres thus raise questions about how we can teach students to understand the values behind professional practice in the constructed conditions of the classroom.

THE MATHEMATICS WRITING CLASSROOM

Undergraduate mathematics classes generally teach students the mathematics discovered over the last several centuries. In particular, course instructors generally assign problems they already can prove. To *prove*, in mathematics, means to create "a logical argument that establishes the truth of a statement beyond any doubt. A proof consists of a finite chain of steps, each one of them a logical consequence of the previous one" (Cupillari, 2005, p. 3). Given that proofs are (typically) already known, students are neither expected nor anticipated to generate original interpretations. While students might follow multiple paths to the same answer, the scope of those paths is highly limited: students are expected to use the tools provided in class to arrive at an identical conclusion, namely the claim they have been asked to prove.

101

Humanities WAC Prompt:	Mathematics WID Prompt:
Using at least two examples from *The Newgate Calendar* in addition to this class' assigned reading, explain what types of evidence could be considered compelling to eighteenth-century readers. You may choose to answer this by considering the evolution—if any—from the presentation of evidence in earlier historical texts to the Neo-Classical texts, or you may choose to focus exclusively on the eighteenth century.	Write a formal expository paper (math article format) that explains the equivalence of the following five forms of the Completeness Property: **Statement [M] (Section 1.6 in Mattuck, 1999).** A bounded, monotone sequence converges. **Statement [N] (Theorem 6.1 in Mattuck, 1999).** Suppose $[a_n, b_n]$ is an infinite sequence of nested intervals, whose lengths tend to 0, i.e., $[b_n - a_n] = 0$. Then there is one and only one number L in all intervals; moreover, $a_n \to L$ and $b_n \to L$ as $n \to \infty$. **Statement [B] (Bolzano-Weierstrass theorem, Theorem 6.3 in Mattuck, 1999).** A bounded sequence has a convergent subsequence. **Statement [C] (Theorem 6.4 in Mattuck, 1999).** A Cauchy sequence converges. **Statement [S] (Theorem 6.5A in Mattuck, 1999).** If a subset of the real numbers is non-empty and bounded above, then it has a supremum.

Figure 6.2a. A prompt from a general education communication-intensive course

Figure 6.2b. A prompt from a communication-intensive mathematics course

Since students use the same tools to arrive at the same old conclusion, such assignments challenge traditional approaches to teaching attribution as a matter of orienting one's original insights within current critical conversations (Buranen & Stephenson, 2009, p. 71). The impracticality of this pedagogic goal becomes evident when comparing mathematics assignment prompts to other communication-intensive course assignments. Figure 6.2 compares a prompt from a general-education, communication-intensive humanities class I taught at Case Western Reserve University (Figure 6.2a) to one from a communication-intensive mathematics class I taught at MIT (Figure 6.2b). The prompt in Figure 6.2a asks students to perform a textual analysis and then draw socio-historical conclusions based on that analysis. The mathematics prompt (Figure 6.2b) asks students to prove the equivalence of five different ways of stating the completeness of the set of real numbers, a fundamental property that gives meaning to claims about limits and their behaviors. Once the equivalence of these statements is proven, mathematicians can use whichever form is more useful to them in any individual proof. To prove equivalence, one must show a connected path from any one of these statements to any of the others.

On a surface level, the math writing prompt (Figure 6.2b) has similar freedoms and constraints as the humanities prompt example (Figure 6.2a). Both prompts articulate basic conditions for acceptable submissions: responses to the humanities prompt need to discuss the assigned theme using two eighteenth-century texts and responses to the math prompt need to provide proofs for a complete path. Additionally, both assignments give the students several degrees of freedom for acceptable responses. For the humanities prompt, students may choose any number of acceptable combinations of primary texts. For the mathematics prompt, the student can choose any fully connected path they want. In both contexts, student responses are influenced by and are likely to reproduce class discussion. Instructors in both classes might therefore expect significant commonalities across submissions.

The significant difference between the nature of responses to these prompts, and by extension the difference between proof-based mathematics writing and writing in other fields, is the degrees of freedom allowed in the expression of ideas. In students' responses to the humanities prompt, an instructor would not expect to read linguistically similar and identically framed essays without direct collusion. However, a mathematics instructor would anticipate a high degree of textual overlap—and might be confused if there were not. As Susanna Epp (2003) explained, "mathematical language is required to be unambiguous, with each grammatical construct having exactly one meaning" (p. 888). Consequently, minor changes in expression can be the difference between a true statement (one that holds without exception) or a false one (one with even a single counterexample). Consider, for instance, the following statement:

$$\text{For all } x \in [0,1], \text{ we have } \frac{1}{x} > 1. \tag{1}$$

For most real numbers in the closed interval $[0,1]$, this inequality holds because 1 divided by a number between 0 and 1 (i.e., a fraction) is greater than 1; however, (1) is false because of two edge cases. First, when $x = 1$, the left side of the inequality simplifies to 1, but our statement claims the result should be strictly greater than 1. The difference between "greater than" and "greater than or equal to" is the difference between true and false. Second, when $x = 0$, the left side of the inequality becomes $1/0$, which does not exist and therefore has no definable relationship to 1. This simple example demonstrates the importance of precision in mathematical communication, and the arrangement and acknowledgment of quantifiers create this precision. Moreover, such language is used to provide a proof, an argument definitionally "beyond any doubt" (Cupillari, 2005, p. 3), so for the mathematics response, there are multiple correct paths to an answer but not multiple correct outcomes.

Such demands for linguistic precision likely cause mathematicians' different relationship with quotation, paraphrase, and textual appropriation from that typically taught in first-year composition (FYC) classes. This difference arises for two reasons: first, there might be only one (or only a few) correct ways to state a claim, and second, even minor rephrasing might introduce large error into the communication. These limits often lead students to assume that there is only one correct way to write a proof. Couple these (mis)conceptions to their awareness that their writing content is already common knowledge, it becomes easier to understand why it is difficult to teach students in a mathematics writing classroom not only the practice of attribution but also its value.

Additionally, the expected precision of mathematics writing underscores the challenges of applying traditional composition pedagogies in relation to the genre of proof writing. Sarah Bryant, Noreen Lape, and Jennifer Schaefer (2014) critiqued previous work on incorporating writing in mathematics and other quantitative subjects for suggesting composition strategies can be imported without attending to generic features of math writing (pp. 92–93; cf. Bahls, 2012; Sterrett, 1982). Moreover, they persuasively explain their interventions for modifying traditional communication pedagogy to meet the needs of the mathematics classroom. However, neither they, nor any of the sources they critique, make attribution practice a significant part of their discussion.

A potential reason for this absence is that undergraduate mathematics students are expected to be able to discover proofs for themselves using only their course materials. Students in proof-writing classes are not expected to do research in the first-year composition (FYC) sense of going out and finding sources to support one's claims. In MIT's proof-writing classes with explicit WID components, students are still not generally expected to find sources, but they are taught to acknowledge sources, like their textbooks, when they use them. Such citation practices closely follow other fields and styles, such as those taught in FYC courses.

WHEN TO ATTRIBUTE IN MATHEMATICS WRITING

In this regard, students in mathematics classes run the same risks as students in other fields—unless they misinterpret content that needs attribution as common knowledge. For example, while a theorem might be common knowledge, a specific proof of it might not be. However, textbooks often do not distinguish between facts in the field and the author's own interventions, so without additional guidance, students might reasonably expect that the proof strategy is as well-known as the rest of the book contents. From a generalist perspective, such failures to cite might be considered patchwriting, in that students "engag[e] in entry-level manipulation of new ideas and vocabulary" (Howard, 1992, p. 233) without sufficiently making it their own and without acknowledging their source(s). However, mathematical precision can lead students to perceive an author's manner of expression as a technical term—and they are not always wrong. Thus, with textbooks as their primary reading material, these students generally have only seen unattributed write-ups of common knowledge.

Moreover, students are encouraged to collaborate with each other to solve (mathematics) problems. Such collaboration on already-solved problems creates complications for using common knowledge as an attribution metric because not only are students not producing original results, they might be using approaches based on someone else's observations and discoveries. According to the American Mathematical Society (2005), "[t]he knowing presentation of another person's mathematical discovery as one's own constitutes plagiarism and is a serious violation of professional ethics." But what counts as another's mathematical discovery, when one is working collaboratively with classmates to re-prove statements that have been proven for over a century?

Such concerns first came to my attention in my first year as a communication instructor for WID mathematics classes at MIT. At MIT, WID classes pair instructors from specific departments with communication instructors from the Writing, Rhetoric and Professional Communication Program. In Spring 2017, I taught a communication-intensive Real Analysis class. We used two strategies to teach students professional mathematics attribution practice. First, we asked students to acknowledge collaboration: students name their collaborators on their submitted papers. This practice is a modified form of co-authorship; listing collaborators signals contributions at the level of invention but not arrangement. However, this practice does not account for the use of materials other than collaborators' insights.

Fortunately, mathematics as a professional field functions as collaboratively as students in a mathematics classroom, and the profession has already designated attribution practices for the students to follow. Though more mathematicians publish individually than is currently common in experimental STEM fields (Mihaljević-Brandt et al., 2016, pp. 2–3), they still frequently collaborate, even when this doesn't result in co-authorship. Because mathematicians' primary outputs are results (theorems) and validation(s) of those results (proofs), they value crediting the individual responsible for a given theorem or specific approach, so long as the ideas are not yet treated as common knowledge. To that end, they credit important contributions from discussions even when they do not constitute formal collaborations. Examples of such attributions appear in Figure 6.3, including one—example (1)—from an author who won a Fields medal, an analogous award to the Nobel Prize.

(1) "*As Alessio Corti explained to the author*, the fact that the dualizing sheaf of $\sum$ is trivial forces the quotient to be the sheaf of sections of the co-normal bundle of the diagonal in $P^1 \times P^{1}$"

(Donaldson 2018, p. 7; italics added)

(2) "enables us, with a little more effort, to prove existence of extremals on the sphere, by means of the following "renormalization" approach, *due to Karen Uhlenbeck*"

(Lee & Parker 1987, p. 55; italics added)

(3) "We begin with the following general result *which is kindly taught us by the referee*"

(Oguiso 2013, p. 11; italics added)

(4) "The example of this section is a Markov chain obtained by edge flipping on a line *and was suggested to us by Persi Diaconis*".

(Rhodes & Shilling 2018, p. 17; italics added)

Figure 6.3. Examples from papers published in arXiv

The italicized text in Figure 6.3 calls out how math colleagues acknowledge someone who provided a way of writing a proof. As the page numbers in my in-text citations demonstrate, these comments do not appear in prefatory acknowledgments but in the body of the text. The content surrounding the attributions in examples (3) and (4) in Figure 6.3 indicate that these passages are taken from the main text, not footnotes or endnotes. Viewing (1) and (2) in context will verify that I took those from the body of the papers as well. Such acknowledgments are common practice in mathematics. The examples in Figure 6.3 were kindly provided to me by Heather Macbeth within five hours of my query, indicating that she did not have to dig very far into the arXiv to find such forms of attribution. Her inclusion of example (c) in Figure 6.4 was inspired by this practice.

The text of your assignment must of course be in your own words, and should give appropriate and specific credit, for example:

(a) This proof is adapted from [6, Theorem 4.4].

(b) We recall [Mattuck, Theorem 6.2] that a real number K is a cluster point of a sequence if and only if it is the limit of some subsequence.

(c) I learned this argument from Sarah Smith.

Figure 6.4. Attribution instruction and template styles

To teach students such attribution practice, our writing assignment handouts included templates for attribution formatting, as shown in Figure 6.4. The introductory instruction incorporates language related to plagiarism policies to invoke students' prior experience with attribution, as they might have received during an FYC-style course. This introduction calls their attention to the similarities in methods and goals in the mathematics citation styles to those in other fields. The key difference in the mathematics style are related to the practice of numbering core statements (definitions, theorems, lemmas, etc.) for easy reference, as the citation system refers to numbered statements rather than numbered pages.

Figure 6.3 shows examples from papers published on arXiv, an online database housed at Cornell University in which mathematics (and other fields with arXivs) prepublish results. This database was developed to deal with the print publication backlog, allowing for faster dissemination of new information. Additionally, since mathematics gives priority to those who publish first, it creates greater egalitarianism in recognition rate, as mathematicians can post as soon as they have written up publishable results. Results published on arXiv are treated by the mathematics and other arXiv-using communities as credible—though not necessarily peer-reviewed—material.

Figure 6.4 presents the attribution instruction and template styles provided to students in an MIT communication-intensive Real Analysis class handout in Spring 2017. Heather Macbeth authored these model templates. The first number in (a) refers to a hypothetical sixth source in a hypothetical reference list (regardless of genre and medium). In (b), the author's name is used because the hypothetical reference list is alphabetical rather than enumerated.

In Spring 2017, my students tended most often to use templates (a) and (b) in Figure 6.4. This result was intuitively expected, as these forms of in-text citation are familiar from readings across the curriculum and should seem relatively familiar to students who arrive in WID classrooms with attribution experience from FYC-type courses. When students failed to apply attributions of forms (a) and (b) in Figure 6.4, their misunderstanding could easily be read as inaccurate assumptions about what constitutes common knowledge. However, sentences attributing components of one's results to others rarely appears in the body of a paper outside the field of mathematics, which might be a primary reason students struggled to include attributions following template (c) in their papers.

THE CHALLENGE OF PEER REVIEW

Our students' struggles with attributing the sources of their proof strategies was exacerbated through the process of peer review. Just as students do not generally arrive in a mathematics classroom familiar with acknowledging the ideas they learned through collaboration, they do not generally arrive in a mathematics class thinking about learning content from peer review, even if they have prior experience of peer review in FYC classes. Even though humanities professionals' publications sometimes acknowledge insights gained from reviewers or other discussants, in my experience, FYC students are rarely encouraged to make similar acknowledgments when revising term papers after a class peer review process. Moreover, while in FYC classes, the peer review process might provide helpful suggestions to improve the persuasiveness of an argument, the black-and-white nature of correcting information seems to occur most frequently in STEM contexts. Because another student could therefore be responsible for the author's correct result, not acknowledging peers' contributions would violate mathematics attribution values and practice.

In Spring 2017 in the Real Analysis class, we experienced this kind of attribution issue when a student's draft paper—submitted after peer review papers were made available to students—followed an almost identical structure of the review peer's argument, without acknowledging collaboration. From one perspective, this would clearly be plagiarism as defined by practices in mathematics, and potentially designated as cheating per MIT's academic integrity policies. Viewed through the lens of common knowledge, however, this ceases to be a case of malicious cheating and becomes instead a case of ignorance about what counts as others' ideas. It became our priority in the second iteration of the course to provide instruction to help students understand attribution values and practice for mathematics specifically, and in academia in general.

Potential incidents like the one we experienced are hinted at in the writing studies literature on mathematics, as well. For instance, one of Bryant et al.'s (2014) discussions around peer review called out students' abilities to improve their writing through peer observation and comment. The authors quote one of their subjects as noting that "it was extremely useful to see other's [sic] work and learn and share better ways of expressing solutions [emphasis deleted]" (2014, p. 100). The student's intent in "better ways of expressing solutions" remains ambiguous, but the student work I have seen leads me to believe this could refer to borrowing phrasing from other students without attributing the phrase to the peer source. So, while learning mathematical precision and correctness is indeed a benefit of peer review, without proper intervention, it can come at the cost of understanding attribution values and practice in mathematics.

In assessing students' (mis)understandings in relation to peer attribution, we recognized that without formal reflection such as that which Bryant et al. (2014) asked of their students, students might not recognize their content-learning that occurs during the review process. Our instructional team acknowledges the benefits of reflection, but our end goal was not simply to make the learning explicit, but to teach attribution practice. We wanted students to recognize their peers as sources, a value described in communication-intensive math curricula across levels (Day & Frost, 2009, p. 106). In light of this goal (and semester time constraints), we decided to make this implicit process explicit in the peer review assignment itself.

We revised our peer review handout so that it explicitly acknowledged the learning aspects of the review process and indicated ways for students to attribute these unfamiliar sources. New language in the handout, revised by Yu Pan and me, included the following directions:

> Now you have the opportunity to read your classmates' papers answering the question and responding to them. There are two main ways you might respond to them:
>
> (1) as a reader, looking for "new" information
>
> (2) as a writer, looking for ways to improve your own work
>
> . . . Do keep in mind that while stylistic changes are free for sharing (e.g., you like someone's use of sectioning), **if you modify your proofs based on your reviewee's work, you *must* acknowledge them in your paper**.

Students were thus explicitly asked to attend to how they use others' works in advancing their own understanding. Calling the students' attention to this role in their process provided space for them to think through the process of learning content through peer review.

In 2018, this approach was successful in that we had no more (recognized) instances of unacknowledged collaboration in our classroom,[2] and students employed a fuller range of attribution practice. Students more frequently included acknowledgments sections in their papers, thanking their peer reviewers for their contributions to the learning process.[3] Additionally, students would occasionally include remarks along the lines of "this proof was developed in collaboration with [peer]." Such attribution showed that students more fully understood what information is usable without attribution or that which needs attribution in this disciplinary context.

CALL FOR FURTHER RESEARCH

For me, this experience elucidated a specific challenge of using classroom genres to teach professional practices. While we can ask students to write "as if" they are in a professional context, when they don't have professional-level content to

---

2   As is always the case, there is a chance some work that should have been acknowledged passed by us unattributed but unrecognized as such.

3   Since this is the result of personal experience rather than formalized research, I do not have specific results I can share at this time.

use, such pretense becomes even more complicated for student implementation (Wardle 2009, p. 779–781). In particular, in courses where we ask students to reproduce common knowledge to help them join that community, writing assignments will not be geared toward pushing students to explore new ground. How, then, can we functionally use these courses and assignments to teach students professional practices built around introducing new information?

Our intervention of calling attention to where and when students learn has had some moderate success in the particular context of this class at MIT. Though motivated by personal experience, and not empirical research, the questions raised are expandable, as they call attention to areas left relatively unexplored in WAC/WID literature. In particular, it would be helpful to have more information about the impact on students from the mismatch between common knowledge contents students are asked to produce and the original contribution genres they are asked to perform. While this case study focused specifically on mathematics to illuminate these issues, it seems likely that other STEM fields would struggle with similar concerns and benefit from this data. This data could help the WID community develop discipline-specific instructional strategies and the WAC community develop generalizable pedagogy around determining what information is usable without attribution or that which needs attribution. This would make attribution instruction more transferable between and across communication contexts. I hope the perspective offered in this chapter helps the WAC/WID community develop better strategies, both in disciplinary and generalized contexts, for teaching students to distinguish between what information is usable without and that which needs attribution.

ACKNOWLEDGMENTS

The author acknowledges the generous intellectual support and sharing of intellectual property with course co-instructors, Dr. Heather Macbeth and Dr. Yu Pan, without whom the work undergirding this chapter would not have been possible. She wishes especially to thank Dr. Macbeth for her assistance in some of the research into mathematical attribution practices. Lastly, the author is grateful to the MIT School of Humanities and Social Sciences Dean's Fund for Professional Development for partial support of this project.

REFERENCES

American Mathematical Society. (2005). Mathematical research and its presentation. *Ethical guidelines of the American Mathematical Society.* https://www.ams.org/about -us/governance/policy-statements/sec-ethics.

American Psychological Association. (2017). Ethical principles of psychologists and code of conduct. *Apa.org*. https://www.apa.org/ethics/code/.

Bahls, P. (2012). *Student writing in the quantitative disciplines: A guide for college faculty.* San Francisco: Jossey-Bass.

Brennecke, P. (2018). *Academic integrity at MIT: A handbook for students.* https://integrity.mit.edu/sites/default/files/documents/AcademicIntegrityHandbook2018-grayscale.pdf.

Bryant, S., Lape, N. & Schaefer, J. (2014). Transfer and the transformation of writing pedagogies in a mathematics course. *The WAC journal, 25*. https://wac.colostate.edu/docs/journal/vol25/bryant.pdf.

Buranen, L. & Stephenson, D. (2009). Collaborative authorship in the sciences: Anti-ownership and citation practices in chemistry and biology. In C. P. Haviland & J. A. Mullins (Eds.), *Who owns this text? Plagiarism, authorship, and disciplinary cultures* (pp. 49–79). Utah State University Press. https://doi.org/10.2307/j.ctt4cgn56.5.

Burke, K. E. (1973). *The philosophy of literary form* (3rd ed.). University of California Press.

Cupillari, A. (2005). *The nuts and bolts of proofs* (3rd ed.) Elsevier Academic Press.

Day, K. & Frost, J. (2009). Sharing the WARMth: Writing and reading mathematics in a learning community. *Learning Communities Journal, 1*(1), 91–111.

Donaldson, S. K. (2018). A note on the -invariant of the Mukai-Umemura 3-fold. *arXiv*. https://arxiv.org/pdf/0711.4357.pdf.

Eckel, E. (2014). Textual appropriation and attribution in engineering theses and dissertations: An exploratory study. *University libraries faculty & staff publications, 37*. https://scholarworks.wmich.edu/library_pubs/37.

Eisner, C. & Vicinus, M. (Eds.). (2008). *Originality, imitation, and plagiarism: Teaching writing in the digital age.* University of Michigan Press. https://doi.org/10.3998/dcbooks.5653382.0001.001.

England, A. (2008). The dynamic nature of common knowledge. In C. Eisner & M. Vicinus (Eds.), *Originality, imitation, and plagiarism: Teaching writing in the digital age* (pp. 104–113). University of Michigan Press. https://doi.org/10.2307/j.ctv65sxk1.12.

Epp, S. (2003). The role of logic in teaching proof. *American Mathematical Monthly, 110*, 886–899. https://doi.org/10.1080/00029890.2003.11920029.

Fischer, P. (2011). *New research misconduct policies*. National Science Foundation. https://www.nsf.gov/oig/_pdf/presentations/session.pdf.

Haviland, C. P. & Mullins, J. A. (Eds.). (2009). *Who owns this text? Plagiarism, authorship, and disciplinary cultures.* Utah State University Press. https://doi.org/10.2307/j.ctt4cgn56.

Hayes, H., Ferris, D. R. & Whithaus, C. (2016). Dynamic transfer in first-year writing and "writing in the disciplines" settings. In C. M. Anson & J. L. Moore (Eds.), *Critical transitions: Writing and the question of transfer* (pp. 181–213). https://wac.colostate.edu/docs/books/ansonmoore/chapter7.pdf.

Howard, R. M. (1992). A plagiarism pentimento. *Journal of Teaching Writing, 11*(2), 233–245.

Howard, R. M. & Robillard, A. E. (Eds.). (2008). *Pluralizing plagiarism: Identities, contexts, pedagogies.* Boynton/Cook.

IEEE. (2018). *A plagiarism FAQ.* IEEE.org. https://www.ieee.org/publications/rights/plagiarism/plagiarism-faq.html.

Jamieson, S. (2008). One size does not fit all: Plagiarism across the curriculum. In R. M. Howard & A. E. Robillard (Eds.), *Pluralizing plagiarism: Identities, contexts, pedagogies* (pp. 77–91). Boynton/Cook.

Jamieson, S. (2019). Shouldn't our expectations of students' and academics' intertextuality practices differ? In D. Pecorari & P. Shaw (Eds.), *Student plagiarism in higher education: Reflections on teaching practice* (pp. 105–122). Routledge. https://doi.org/10.4324/9781315166148-8.

Lee, J. M. & Parker, T. H. (1987). The Yamabe problem. *Bulletin of the American Mathematical Society, 17,* 37–91. https://doi.org/10.1090/S0273-0979-1987-15514-5.

Mattuck, A. (1999). *Introduction to analysis.* Prentice Hall.

Mihaljević-Brandt, H., Santamaría, L. & Tullney, M. (2016). The effect of gender in the publication patterns in mathematics. *PLoS ONE, 11,* 1–23. https://doi.org/10.1371/journal.pone.0165367.

Modern Language Association. (2016). *MLA handbook* (8th ed.). Modern Language Association of America.

Oguiso, K. (2013). Automorphism groups of Calabi-Yau manifolds of Picard number two. *arXiv.* https://arxiv.org/pdf/1206.1649.pdf.

Pecorari, D. (2013). *Teaching to avoid plagiarism: How to promote good source use.* Open University Press.

Pecorari, D. & Shaw, P. (Eds.). (2019). *Student plagiarism in higher education: Reflections on teaching practice.* Routledge. https://doi.org/10.4324/9781315166148.

Rhodes, J. & Shilling, A. (2018). A unified theory for finite Markov chains. *arXiv.* https://arxiv.org/pdf/1711.10689.pdf.

Roig, M. (2001). Plagiarism and paraphrasing criteria of college and university professors. *Ethics & behavior, 11*(3), 307–323. https://doi.org/10.1207/S15327019EB1103_8.

Russell, D. (1995). Activity theory and its implications for writing instruction. In J. Petraglia (Ed.), *Reconceiving writing, rethinking writing instruction* (pp. 51–78). Lawrence Erlbaum.

Serviss, T. (2016, September 30). Using citation analysis heuristics to prepare TAs across the disciplines as teachers and writers. *Across the disciplines: A Journal of Language, Learning, and Academic Writing, 13*(3). https://wac.colostate.edu/docs/atd/wacta/serviss2016.pdf.

Shaw, P. & Pecorari, D. (2019). Why are there so many questions about plagiarism? In D. Pecorari & P. Shaw (Eds.), *Student plagiarism in higher education: Reflections on teaching practice* (pp. 1–11). Routledge. https://doi.org/10.4324/9781315166148-1.

Sterrett, A. (Ed.). (1982). *Using writing to teach mathematics.* Mathematical Association of America.

Wardle, E. (2009). "Mutt genres" and the goal of FYC: Can we help students write the genres of the university? *College Composition and Communication, 60*(4), 765–789.

CHAPTER 7.

QUANTIFICATION OF DISCIPLINARY DISCOURSE: AN APPROACH TO TEACHING ENGINEERING RÉSUMÉ WRITING

Mary McCall
North Dakota State University

Gracemarie Mike Fillenwarth
Rowan University

Catherine G. P. Berdanier
Pennsylvania State University

Through this chapter, the authors present a novel approach to quantifying Disciplinary Discourse Density in résumés. The authors demonstrate how, for an engineering context, disciplinary discourse in résumés can be analyzed using the American Association of Engineering Societies Engineering Competency Model, and they translate their research into a pedagogical approach that enables students to quantify disciplinary discourse in their own résumés. This approach facilitates students' ability to reflect on what their rhetorical choices mean for their disciplinary audience, working toward developing a disciplinary identity and communicating that identity via the résumé. The authors' positionality as experts in technical communication and engineering provides validity to the method, which has been employed across multiple contexts to date. The authors extend their approach to multiple pedagogical interventions and make recommendations for instructors teaching résumé writing as part of writing across the curriculum initiatives for any disciplinary community.

The résumé is a common assignment across the curriculum (Melzer, 2014) that presents an opportunity for students to learn how to frame their academic and professional experience according to the expectations of their discipline. Typi-

DOI: https://doi.org/10.37514/PER-B.2020.0360.2.07

cally part of a "job documents" or career unit that includes a range of deliver-
ables such as cover letters, personal websites, or portfolios, the résumé is also
frequently taught in introductory technical and professional communication
(TPC) courses (Francis, 2018; Melonçon, 2018) that often function as a "'service course'" to other departments (Melonçon & Henschel, 2013, p. 51). Faced
with this range of majors, writing instructors may not feel knowledgeable in—
nor have the time to learn—specific résumé guidelines of multiple disciplines.
Relying primarily on professional writing textbooks for résumé instruction may
not be ideal, as students often find this information to be outdated, generic, and
irrelevant to their field (Randazzo, 2016). Résumé writing is also a high-stakes
task as students often use this assignment to prepare for on-campus career fairs
for internships and post-graduate positions.

Despite these challenges, though, we argue that pedagogical approaches to
teaching résumés can move away from an adisciplinary focus on form over content (e.g., the use of parallel structure, action verbs, or bulleted lists) and instead
adopt writing across the curriculum (WAC) or "writing to learn" and writing in
the disciplines (WID) or "learning to write" practices. The latter corresponds to
David Russell's (2007) observation that the teaching of TPC courses is "always
already the teaching of writing in the disciplines" (p. 248), with instructors of
such courses needing to understand "writing to learn and learning to write in
a discipline or profession as two sides of the same pedagogical coin" (p. 250).
Likewise, in this chapter, we outline a pedagogical approach to résumé instruction that guides students in "learning to write" this genre in a way that models
disciplinary discourse and expectations while "writing to learn" how to craft
their professional identities.

This approach stems from prior research that studied how the quantification
and analysis of disciplinary discourse in engineering résumés can promote strong
résumé writing and further students' professional development (Berdanier et
al., 2016a, 2016b; Fillenwarth et al., 2018). By "professionalism," we mean
the "process whereby a person becomes a participant in conversations within
and about a defined discipline" (Pennell et al., 2018, p. 72). The emphasis on
"discipline" in this definition is an important one for two reasons. First, a discipline as a "field of practice" includes both "occupations" like medicine, law,
and engineering that require legal certification as well as "professions" that do
not (Carliner, 2012, p. 51). Second, the term corresponds to our definition of
engineering "disciplinary discourse" as "a tangible measure of an engineer's identification with the discipline of engineering" (Fillenwarth et al., 2018).

Saul Carliner (2012) also described professional organizations, bodies of
knowledge, education, professional activities, and certifications as common
components within the range of "infrastructure[s] of activities that support the

growth of a profession" (p. 51). We describe the résumé as one articulation of these components whose success depends in part on how well students can convey this range of knowledge and experience by adopting the language of their respective discipline. Specifically, we studied résumés in an engineering context both because of the nature of our interdisciplinary collaboration—two of us come from rhetoric and composition and specialize in TPC and the third is from mechanical engineering with an engineering education research expertise—and because engineering students often make up a significant portion of the TPC classes the first two authors teach. The latter point is largely correlated to technical communication's historical beginnings as being a specialized course (often separated from English departments) for engineering students in the early 1900s (Connors, 1982).

Although Russell (2007) stated that the integration of research and teaching within TPC and WID supports professional education through "showing (a) how disciplines and professions construct knowledge and know-how communicatively and (b) how students develop into professionals through communication" (p. 255), he adds that more research is needed in "examining the workplace communication of professionals and the development of students' ability to communicate as professionals" (p. 259). Such research should ideally be interdisciplinary and data-driven with a focus on collaboration between faculty and departments on curricular decisions pertaining to writing (Russell, 2007, p. 270). Our prior studies do not enact the global, departmental collaboration Russell called for, but they still stem from a cross-disciplinary partnership and are supported by empirical data. In this chapter, we focus on the pedagogical applications of this research by outlining classroom exercises involving résumé writing that facilitate undergraduate engineering students' understanding of engineering employers' disciplinary values. We also discuss ways in which these exercises can be adapted for other majors across the disciplines. Ultimately, we argue that such résumé activities can be instrumental in helping engineering and nonengineering students alike critically reflect on and engage in disciplinary discourse practices in the service of supporting their identity development as emerging professionals within their respective disciplines.

INTEGRATING PROFESSIONAL GENRE AND DISCIPLINARY KNOWLEDGE THROUGH RÉSUMÉS

Early research on résumés between the 1970s and 1990s largely focused on the preferences of students, instructors, and employers about résumé preparation and the organization of content (Bird & Puglisi, 1986; Culwell-Block & Sellers, 1994; Harcourt & Krizan, 1989; Hutchinson, 1984; Hutchinson & Brefka,

1997; Penrose, 1973, 1984; Stanley-Weigand, 1991). The rise of digital technologies and the Internet in the 2000s and 2010s precipitated an interest in scannable and electronic résumé writing practices (Barchilon, 1998; Diaz, 2013; Krause, 1997; Roever, 1997), but attention to the "regularities" of the résumé genre such as content, style, and delivery method remains prevalent (Blackburn-Brockman & Belanger, 2001; Martin-Lacroux & Lacroux, 2017; Schullery et al., 2009; Tillotson & Osborn, 2012; Wright et al., 2011). Rhetorical genre studies such as Carolyn Miller's seminal 1984 article, "Genre as Social Action," has also been a popular lens through which to study Web résumés and the rhetorical situations they create through the new exigences, audiences, and constraints of the ever-shifting Web environment (Killoran, 2006, 2009).[1]

Despite this range of research, few studies investigate the rhetorical use of disciplinary discourse within résumés and how such a practice can support the professional identity formation of undergraduate engineering students. Since a résumé is typically a synthesis of students' academic highlights (e.g., advanced courses in the major, senior projects, and academic honors) and workplace experiences (e.g., full-time jobs, part-time jobs, internships, and co-ops), it could be argued that this document *is* an embodiment of the university-to-workplace (and workplace-to university) transition often discussed in WAC literature (Anson & Forsberg, 1990/2003; Dias et al., 1999; Dias & Paré, 2000). By representing the accumulation of the student's noteworthy coursework and projects as well as her prior (and current) workplace responsibilities and tasks, the résumé can be seen as an amalgamation of both the "ingredients" of professional genre knowledge (Artemeva, 2009, p. 172) and the disciplinary expertise that she has acquired up to the present version. However, faced with a variety of more or less generic résumé resources (Randazzo, 2016), the student may feel at a loss to persuasively convey this expertise in her résumé. WAC consultants leading résumé workshops and/or visiting classes to support students writing in this genre and writing instructors, especially those teaching a communications course that is not linked to a content one, may also be unsure of how to teach discipline-specific résumé advice. This chapter articulates one approach to do so, which is based on empirical research addressing the gap of rhetorical, disciplinary language in engineering résumés (Berdanier et al., 2016a, 2016b; Fillenwarth et al., 2018). This approach can be integrated with other assignments that ask students to conduct primary and secondary research about résumé best practices (Randazzo, 2016) while encouraging students to participate in their disciplinary communities of practice (Wenger, 1998).

---

1   Other recent, comprehensive literature reviews of résumé scholarship include research from disciplines such as career development and applied psychology (Randazzo, 2016) and in technical and professional communication and STEM education journals (Fillenwarth et al., 2018).

METHODOLOGY OF CODING RÉSUMÉS
FOR DISCIPLINARY DISCOURSE

The pedagogical approach we present is based on the results of a mixed-methods study that sought to examine the characteristics of effective and ineffective engineering résumés, which we will briefly describe (for a more detailed discussion, see Fillenwarth et al., 2018). In this IRB-approved study, our team analyzed a corpus of résumés (undergraduate students, graduate students, and professionals) through both qualitative and quantitative means. The résumés in the corpus were collected from a national sample that ranged from first-year engineering students through retired professional engineers. After collection, 31 résumés were selected as part of the corpus (others were excluded based on non-conformity to résumé conventions, e.g., CVs). To validate our method and findings, we are currently working on analyzing a larger data set of more than 100 engineering web-résumés.

In the first stage of analysis, résumés were initially sorted qualitatively into *excellent, moderate,* and *poor* categories via an engineering rubric developed by the University of Iowa College of Engineering (2015), which was selected given its coverage of both discipline-specific and generalized aspects of résumé writing. For example, one of the excellent criteria on the rubric is "Use industry specific language and terminology," which would be unique to engineering.

After sorting, each résumé was then quantitatively analyzed according to the American Association of Engineering Societies' (AAES) Engineering Competency Model (see Figure 7.1). The Competency Model was published in 2015 through a collaboration between the AAES—an interdisciplinary engineering society comprised of engineers working in academic, government, and industry settings—and the U.S. Department of Labor. This Model is part of the larger Industry Competency Model Initiative from the U.S. Department of Labor's Employment and Training Administration, which collaborates with partners across multiple industries to develop and maintain dynamic models of the foundation and technical competencies that are necessary in economically vital industries and sectors of the American economy. The goal of the effort is to promote an understanding of the skill sets and competencies that are essential to "educate and train a globally competitive workforce" (CareerOneStop, 2018, para. 4).

To visualize these skill sets, each Industry Competency Model within the U.S. Department of Labor's Competency Model Clearinghouse (of which the AAES Engineering Competency Model is a part) is pyramid-shaped and composed of six tiers that showcase various competencies. These tiers are broadly divided into "Foundation Competencies" (Tiers 1–3) and "Industry Competencies" (Tiers 4–6). Each of the competencies within each tier are also called

"Building Blocks" (these are separated by a small vertical line in the original AAES Engineering Competency Model that we modified in Figure 7.1, giving the appearance of blocks).[2] Each Competency Model shares the same tiers (from bottom to top: Tier 1: Personal Effectiveness, Tier 2: Academic Competencies, Tier 3: Workplace Competencies, Tier 4: Industry-Wide Competencies, Tier 5: Industry/Sector Functional Areas, and Tier 6: Job-Specific Competencies). However, the Building Blocks, or specific competencies, that comprise each tier vary by industry. While Tiers 1 through 3 consist of broader competencies that may be applicable to a range of fields, there are differences between various Competency Models even at these levels. For example, both the Engineering and Cybersecurity Competency Models include "Interpersonal Skills" and "Integrity" as Building Blocks Tier 1. In Tier 2, however, the AAES Engineering Competency Model lists "Computer skills" while the Cybersecurity model lists "Fundamental IT User Skills." These competencies become more and more field specific in higher tiers.

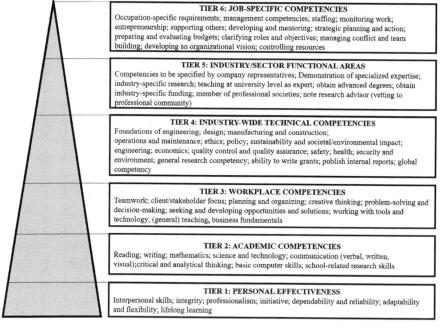

Figure 7.1. Modified AAES Competency Model, update with example competencies. Modified from AAES (2015), Berdanier et al. (2016a, 2016b), and Fillenwarth et al. (2018).

---

2   For this reason, we use competencies and Building Blocks interchangeably within this chapter.

The AAES Engineering Competency Model was chosen as a tool for analysis in this project because of its (1) clear articulation of engineering-specific competencies; (2) separation of these competencies into quantified tiers, with each higher tier representing more specialized competencies; and (3) development by industry representatives, rather than only academics. Using the AAES Engineering Competency Model for our résumé analysis, we coded résumé entries (individual units of meaning) by assigning the numerical score of the tier that the competency displayed in the entry. For example, in Figure 7.2, we coded "Graduate Student Instructor" as a Tier 5 because this entry demonstrates "teaching at university level as expert," which received a quantitative score of 5. A less specialized teaching experience, such as tutoring middle schoolers in algebra, would be coded as a Tier 3 and achieve a score of 3.

GENERAL ENGINEERING **GRADUATE STUDENT INSTRUCTOR (5)**

[Southeastern] University, [Location]   Spring 2014
Freshman and transfer students learn engineering fundamentals such as basic equations, unit conversions, and analysis techniques using Microsoft Excel software.
Single section of a three credit hour lecture course with **approximately 50 students (6)**
Presented (2) 50 minute lectures three times per week
Graded tests and projects (3) throughout the semester

Figure 7.2. Sample coding. Coded entries in bold.

One of the strengths of using the Industry Competency Models is their flexibility. During our initial research, we were able to easily code the vast majority of résumé entries. However, we found that some experiences in the corpus of résumés did not explicitly align with a block or tier of the AAES Model (e.g., proficiency in a second language). Rather than viewing this as a shortcoming of the Model or viewing linguistic proficiency as an item not worthy of inclusion, we used the Model's classification system to help us determine where the competency might fit within the Model. We determined that proficiency in a second language could potentially be categorized in a number of ways, perhaps as a Tier 1 Personal Effectiveness competency ("Lifelong Learning") or Tier 4 Industry-Wide Technical Competency. Because there was no mention of global competencies in the AAES Engineering Competency Model, we decided to code second language proficiency as Tier 4 by considering "Global Competency" to be a Building Block for this tier, based on calls in engineering education literature for globally competent engineers. While there are certainly viable arguments for why this competency could be placed elsewhere, we view the Model as an agile schema that gains its value in its ability to encompass a diversity of experiences.

As theorized in our prior work (Fillenwarth et al., 2018), members of disciplinary communities of practice display identification with that discipline not only through their activities, but also through their use of language. This use of language occurs at general levels, such as genre use, as well as at particular levels, such as lexicon. Building on our initial definition of "disciplinary discourse" from the introduction, we use this term to refer both to the lexical choices made by members of a discipline and to the use of such discourse, which is reflective of one's integration into that disciplinary community of practice. We posit that résumé entries can be analyzed quantitatively to produce a "score" reflective of one's use of disciplinary discourse, and that this score can be a useful tool in helping students revise their résumés and reflect on their professionalization.

After coding each entry in each résumé, we calculated the "Disciplinary Discourse Density" score, which is the sum of all the codes present in a résumé divided by the total number of codes (see Figure 7.3).

Overall Disciplinary Discourse Density =
Sum of Tier Codes / Total Number of Codes

Example: Disciplinary Discourse Density for Figure 2:
$(5 + 6 + 2 + 3) / 4 = 4$ (out of 6 maximum)

Figure 7.3. Calculation of Disciplinary Discourse Density.

After comparing Disciplinary Discourse Density scores across the qualitatively strong, moderate, and weak résumés, we observed statistically significantly higher levels of disciplinary discourse in "excellent" résumés than moderate résumés, and similarly statistically significantly higher scores in "moderate" résumés than "poor" résumés. Since higher tiers contain more specialized skills, the Disciplinary Discourse Density scores for résumés using more specific and relevant disciplinary language achieved higher scores when averaged.[3] However, professional-level engineers through undergraduate engineering students were all represented in the "excellent" category, which shows that crafting a persuasive résumé does not necessarily rest on the range and depth of one's engineering experiences or the adherence to generic résumé writing "rules" alone, but also on the writer's ability to describe their qualifications according to the values and needs of their disciplinary audience.

---

3   See Fillenwarth et al. (2018) for additional details and examples on coding.

This unique combination of qualitative and quantitative data suggests that disciplinary discourse may be a useful tool in the classroom to help students understand the actions, abilities, and characteristics that are sought in engineers (i.e., the "rules" and "expectations") and to display their identity as an engineer by using engineering discourse. The next sections of this chapter outline how we have adapted our research and the AAES Engineering Competency Model into classroom exercises that carry out these goals while teaching students both general and disciplinary résumé conventions.

QUANTIFICATION OF DISCIPLINARY DISCOURSE AS A PEDAGOGICAL TOOL IN THE WRITING CLASSROOM

Our classroom implementation seeks to take advantage of this clear delineation of engineering competencies in the AAES Engineering Competency Model and our findings on disciplinary discourse. We do so by encouraging engineering students to use the AAES Engineering Competency Model to consciously classify the various types of skills, experiences, and knowledge they acquire during their formal education and articulate their value. This tool can be particularly useful for helping students learn more about the field of engineering and its disciplinary expectations, ultimately guiding the development of their identity as engineers.

We have successfully used the AAES Engineering Competency Model to help students revise their résumés in two different courses: Sophomore Engineering Clinic at an East Coast research university (a hybrid first-year composition, technical writing, and design course for engineering students) and Writing in the Technical Professions at a Midwestern land-grant university (a TPC service course). For both courses, we spent two to three days covering the AAES Engineering Competency Model in our professionalization units, where we teach skills such as reading job ads and writing career documents (e.g., résumé and cover letter). While we largely review how we have adapted our résumé coding heuristic into pedagogical exercises for engineering students, we end this section with a discussion of how these exercises can be adapted for students in other disciplines.

INTRODUCTION TO DISCIPLINARY RÉSUMÉ CONVENTIONS

In our approach, we begin by talking with students about various ways to theorize résumés. One way of thinking about résumés, which the majority of students are familiar with, views résumé writing simply as an exercise in listing experiences

121

and putting them in a specified format (e.g., students' names in large type, sections with headings, short phrases and bullet points led by action verbs, etc.). In this view, the résumé essentially acts as a camera to capture students' experience in a presentable way. Next, we introduce the idea of disciplinary résumé conventions through the idea of discourse communities. After helping students grasp how different communities have different ways of acting, speaking, and writing that may be unique to that community, we explain that résumés, too, can be a sign of how connected a person is to a community. If an engineer communicates like an accountant, a teacher, or a historian, they are less likely to be perceived as having competency in engineering. One of the goals of a résumé, then, is to persuade readers of the candidate's competency as an engineer through a combination of content, style, and design—all of which can fall under the category of writing.

EXERCISE 1: INTRODUCTION TO AAES ENGINEERING COMPETENCY MODEL AND CODING

After providing theoretical context, we introduce students to the AAES Engineering Competency Model as a tool they can use to analyze their résumés and gain insight into how well their résumés might meet disciplinary expectations. We present the AAES Engineering Competency Model to students, provide them time to read through the categories and discuss them, and then show students how to code résumés using the Model. We provide several sample résumé entries to students in class (see Figure 7.4), and they assign codes to each of the entries. Next, we show students how we coded the résumés (see Figure 7.5), and we lead a discussion analyzing similarities and differences in the codes students assigned and those the instructor assigned.

Directions: Code the following underlined entries from the experience section of a résumé.

EXPERIENCE

BOLT Research Lab

- Gained valuable work experience in **operating** a **CNC Machine Developed research plan; directed team of interns to complete project**
- **Analyzed the assembly** within **ANSYS**, **ran simulations** using realistic forces and pressure by looking at **part strength** , **bolted flange separation** , and **contact pressure** .
- **Kept work area clean** and **organized**

Figure 7.4. Sample in-class coding exercise.

Through this discussion, we seek to highlight how the AAES Engineering Competency Model should be used as a guide rather than a strict set of rules, and that minor differences in coding are typically not problematic (e.g., coding an experience at Tier 3 versus Tier 4). When there are large discrepancies between students' coding and their peers' or instructor's coding, we use the discussion as an opportunity to think critically about the value of certain qualifications for engineering communities and how and why they may be viewed a particular way, depending on both the qualification and the language that is used to describe it (e.g., "Designed bottle rocket" vs. "Used parametric design to collaboratively develop and test bottle rocket to meet customer specifications").

Directions: Code the following underlined entries from the experience section of a résumé.

EXPERIENCE

BOLT Research Lab

- Gained valuable work experience in **operating (3)** a **CNC Machine** (3)
- **Developed research plan** (6); **directed team of interns to complete project** (6)
- **Analyzed the assembly** (4) within **ANSYS** (3), **ran simulations** (4) using realistic forces and pressure by looking at **part strength** (4), **bolted flange separation** (4), and **contact pressure** (4).
- **Kept work area clean** (1) and **organized** (1)

Figure 7.5. Sample in-class coding exercise with instructor codes.

EXERCISE 2: CALCULATING DISCIPLINARY DISCOURSE DENSITY

The second exercise we ask students to complete is calculating the Disciplinary Discourse Density of the sample they coded. Students add their codes together and divide by the total number of codes they assigned, which results in a score between 1 and 6. We discuss that this score is not a definitive score reflecting the strength of the résumé, but simply a numeric way to analyze how disciplinary discourse is at work in a résumé. We also relate the findings of our research that stronger résumés tend to have higher Disciplinary Discourse Density scores, regardless of the education level of the résumé writer.

EXERCISE 3: REVISING SAMPLE RÉSUMÉ ENTRIES

For a third and final exercise, we provide students with additional sample résumé entries that they are likely to score in Tiers 1–3. After asking students to code the entries, they rewrite the entries in order to raise the code to a higher tier, using the AAES Engineering Competency Model as a reference. For this exercise, the entries in the sample we provide are similar to projects students complete as part of their curriculum, ensuring students will be familiar enough with the experiences to understand what competencies each résumé entry might involve (see Figure 7.6). Figure 7.7 shows a possible revision of the action verbs and descriptions within Figure 7.6 that incorporates entries related to the "Foundations of Engineering" Building Block in Tier 4 such as "Designed" and "Conceptualized."

Directions: Rewrite the following résumé entries to incorporate a broader range of engineering competencies

Fundamentals of Electrical Design, Fall 2017
- Completed solar panel design project
- Participated in writing of technical report

Senior Design, Spring 2018
- Assisted with team guitar prototype

Figure 7.6. Sample in-class codes for students to rewrite.

Directions: Rewrite the following résumé entries to incorporate a broader range of engineering competencies

Fundamentals of Electrical Design, Fall 2017
- Designed a solar energy heating and electric system for Everson Ranch. Provided a link between the team and client by communicating effectively with both parties, as well as synthesized team members' contributions into a single report
- Researched solar technology, including materials, cost, and resilience and presented design proposals in technical reports

Senior Design, Spring 2018
- Conceptualized, designed, and built an autonomous player guitar with design team
- Led programming in both Python and Arduino
- Collaborated with team members in assembling the electrical system

---

Figure 7.7. Sample in-class codes for students to rewrite, with revisions.

EXERCISE 4: RÉSUMÉ REVISION AND PROFESSIONALIZATION GOALS REFLECTION

After these exercises, we provide students time to code their own résumés using the AAES Engineering Competency Model and calculate their Disciplinary Discourse Density. We then ask students to work on revising their résumés toward the goal of maximizing the tier code of their experiences. During this time, we encourage students to collaboratively work through concerns that arise, and we provide ample opportunity for one-on-one discussion with the instructor.

At the conclusion of this unit, we ask students to reflect on their professionalization goals for their remaining time in college based on the areas for growth they identified in their revision process (see Appendix). Students identify specific activities that will enable them to showcase competencies which they would like to add or increase. This reflective activity involves students in Etienne Wenger's (1998) "modes of belonging" (engagement, imagination, and alignment) redefined as "modes of identification" (Wenger, 2010, p. 184). Engagement refers to the relationships, interactions, and practices that one undertakes in the negotiation of meaning within community work. Imagination considers the images that members can have of themselves, their world, and their past and future. Alignment describes the synchronization of members' energies, actions, and practices to their respective communities of practice. These modes do not exist in isolation, but work together to balance each other's potential drawbacks (Wenger, 1998, pp. 173–174). Specifically, this activity encourages students to *imagine* their professional roles and contributions with their respective industry and thereby *align* their present and future academic and professional experiences to the expectations of this field. This reflection prompt also harks back to the central goal of this approach to résumé analysis—to *engage* students not only in learning to write in the conventions of résumés associated with their disciplines, but also in using writing to learn about disciplines and their professional expectations. Ultimately, the written reflection that occurs at the end of this project enables students to imagine their positions in the professional world and to help construct their professional identities.

POTENTIAL CHALLENGES OF IMPLEMENTATION

One challenge that inevitably occurs during implementation is that students, with their diverse backgrounds and experiences, often have résumé content that is not contained within one of the existing Competency Model tiers. In response, we explain to students that the Competency Models cannot reasonably contain every possible experience. We remind students that the key is to view the AAES Engineering Competency Model as a flexible, adaptable tool to filter one's experiences through the expectations and language of the discipline. The exact categorization of a single item matters less than the process of critically reflecting on how qualifications could be described in a way that aligns with a particular competency and how these will ultimately be perceived by professional audiences. As we work with students on revising their résumés, we encourage them to articulate the reasoning behind their classification of various achievements and competencies to keep this larger picture in mind.

Another challenge we have encountered during this unit is that students—especially at the freshmen and sophomore level—experience feelings of inadequacy as they calculate their Disciplinary Discourse Density scores. At this stage in their careers, the majority of students has had few leadership experiences that would earn scores in Tiers 4–6, resulting in Disciplinary Discourse Density scores they often perceive as lower than ideal. In response to these concerns, we facilitate a discussion regarding interpretation, writing, and experience. First, we remind students that the Disciplinary Discourse Density scores are only one way of interpreting the degree to which a résumé displays disciplinary identification, and that an audience would be aware of students' grade level when reading their résumé. We also explain that a range of competencies are essential for the profession of engineering, including Tier 1–3 competencies, and that these are still important to include. While students might perceive that their Disciplinary Discourse Density score should be as close to 6 as possible, a score in the 3–4 range could actually showcase a broader array of competencies.

Second, we discuss strategies for rewriting résumé entries to maximize the number of competencies that are showcased, talking with students about lexical choices and their impact on readers. We also incorporate a discussion of ethics, reminding students about the importance of using language responsibly so as not to misrepresent their abilities. Especially salient for freshman and sophomore students, though, is the opportunity to work with other departments and student development offices. This may be an opportunity to partner with offices that support co-ops or internships, undergraduate research opportunities, or service learning and study abroad experiences. At the very least, instructors can ask students to plan activities or desired experiences for the upcoming semester, using resources and websites available from their university. This can also be an effective "socialization" activity to get students at the freshmen and sophomore levels familiar with resources and opportunities available, and a method for engaging more senior students in the communities of practice that they will be joining soon.

RECOMMENDED ADAPTION OF CLASSROOM EXERCISES FOR STUDENTS ACROSS THE DISCIPLINES

While the AAES Competency Model caters specifically to engineering, we argue that it can still be adapted to other disciplines to support those students in computer science, agriculture, and other majors who enroll in TPC courses. Since many of these competencies are also valuable in workplaces across these fields, we encourage these students to think about how they can adapt "Foundations of Engineering" in Tier 4 to their own discipline. The AAES Competency Model is just one of the several examples the Competency Model Clearinghouse offers across a range of industries such as Fundamentals of Health Care, Bioscience, and Entrepreneurship. Whereas an engineering student might add coursework in thermodynamics and physics into his résumé to address the "Foundations of Engineering" Building Block in Tier 4, a computer science student might create a detailed list of programming languages she knows to speak to the "Fundamentals of Information Technology" Building Block equivalent in Tier 4 of the Information Technology Competency Model.

The Competency Model Clearinghouse also offers a Generic Building Blocks Competency Model that can be modified by students who do not see their specific discipline reflected in the current selection of Models. This Model includes competencies like "Teamwork," "Problem Solving," and "Communication" that a professional in any field should be proficient in that students can add to using resources like the Bureau of Labor Statistics (BLS). For instance, a student can search their preferred occupation (to use the BLS' terminology) in the BLS to learn more about what duties people in this position have, what skills they need to complete this work, and what educational degrees and certificates they need; then, students can turn this information into discipline-specific competencies to add to the Generic Building Blocks Competency Model or to an existing Model within their discipline (especially for Tiers 4 and 5, which are sometimes left blank).

When teaching the AAES Competency Model in introductory TPC courses that include non-engineering majors, we ask students to create their own tailored Competency Model using the BLS as an initial homework assignment. Engineering students also complete the assignment to find additional competencies not listed in the modified AAES Competency Model we give them (see Figure 7.1). Then, in class, students are encouraged to share the discipline-specific competencies they listed as a way to collaboratively build Models representing sub-disciplines in engineering as well as various, non-engineering disciplines. With the adaptation or creation of this Competency Model, students are then able to calculate their own Disciplinary Discourse Density scores with their résumés.

Further, this approach could be used for overarching writing competency assessment on a larger scale, turning it into an analytic method, calling to mind Mike Palmquist's chapter, "Learning Analytics in Writing Instruction: Implications for Writing Across the Curriculum," in this volume.

A classroom exercise like this one could be combined with an assignment like Chalice Randazzo's (2016), in which students interview disciplinary experts to learn about particular competencies for their field; such knowledge would be especially useful for freshman or sophomore-level students who might not have taken specialized courses in their major. In addition to referring to the BLS, students can mine the internet (e.g., job position announcements or social media) or arrange meetings with faculty or graduate students to gather "data" by which to populate tiers in the Generic Building Blocks Competency Model or their respective Industry Competency Model provided by the growing Competency Model Clearinghouse.[4] This work also has the potential to synthesize the student's disciplinary knowledge with the writing instructor's or WAC consultant's rhetorical expertise much in the same way that Randazzo's "reimagined" assignment asks students to conduct primary and secondary research about résumé best practices as they write up their job documents. In so doing, students are able to build professional networks, become better evaluators of conflicting résumé suggestions, and recognize the rhetorical expertise of their writing instructors in the process (Randazzo, 2016, p. 289).

Outside of direct classroom implementation, there is potential for the Competency Models and quantification of disciplinary discourse to be used as a tool in WAC workshops to help augment professionalization assignments across the curriculum and/or for faculty professional development. For example, a WAC Coordinator could teach and lead disciplinary faculty through the coding process to train them in how to help students use disciplinary discourse not only in résumé writing but in a range of writing assignments.

BENEFITS OF ADOPTING COMPETENCY MODELS AND QUANTIFICATION OF DISCIPLINARY DISCOURSE ACROSS THE CURRICULUM

Our disciplinary discourse-based approach to résumé pedagogy is not designed to replace lessons on rhetorical situation, genre, layout, content, and design that

---

4   The Competency Model Clearinghouse currently maintains Competency Models for the following industries: Accommodation and Food Service; Construction; Energy and Utilities; Entrepreneurship; Finance and Insurance; Health Care and Social Assistance; Information; Manufacturing; Professional, Scientific, and Technical Services; Retail Trade; and Transportation and Warehousing (see CareerOneStop, 2018, to view models online).

are traditionally incorporated into résumé instruction. Rather, we see it as a supplemental approach that offers a number of benefits to students in a range of cross-curricular writing contexts.

ACKNOWLEDGES STUDENTS' COMPETENCIES, NOT JUST EXPERIENCES

One benefit of the Competency Models provided by the Competency Model Clearinghouse combined with our approach to quantifying disciplinary discourse density is that they encourage students to think through potential résumé entries in terms of competencies, not just experiences. Students often have experiences and achievements that they have forgotten to include or that they have discounted as insignificant. By emphasizing competencies relevant to a particular industry, the Competency Models enable instructors and WAC consultants to help students think deeply about the competencies embedded in particular experiences. For example, a student with experience in retail work may not initially believe this experience is relevant to obtaining a job in Financial Services. By considering the Tier 1 Building Block of Integrity and Ethics in the Financial Services Competency Model, however, they may realize that they can include information on their résumé related to the responsible handling of large sums of money or performing store closing procedures. Similarly, a student can use the competencies as a heuristic for thinking through what they have accomplished. For instance, a student can see the competency "Teamwork" (present in a number of Industry Competency Models) and use this competency as a lens through which to view and characterize their backgrounds.

We also use this moment as an opportunity to emphasize the importance of additional professional development. As students work with these Competency Models, they identify gaps in their experience and expertise, and we work with them to develop concrete plans for building their competencies in the remainder of their career. As a result of these discussions, many students have approached us for assistance in applying for internships and research experiences, demonstrating that this focus on competencies motivates students to gain additional experiences that will provide them with the opportunity to develop new competencies.

ENCOURAGES REFLECTIVE THINKING ON PROFESSIONAL IDENTITY

The Competency Models provided by the Competency Model Clearinghouse provide opportunities for deep reflection by asking students to categorize each of their achievements according to industry and government standards. As students participate in exercises where they analyze their own disciplinary discourse in their résumés, they have the opportunity to think critically about how their experiences might be assessed from the perspective of various professional gatekeepers. Rather than simply listing every experience in which they've participated, students are encouraged to choose experiences that showcase an array of competencies and to write about these experiences in ways that emphasize their foundation and industry expertise. At its heart, this approach is a deeply rhetorical exercise, asking students to move beyond simply listing their previous experiences toward writing their résumés for a very particular disciplinary audience (e.g., not just a hiring manager, but the larger disciplinary community to which this manager belongs). This exercise also facilitates reflective practice, a competency which has been linked with development of expertise across contexts, including engineering (Adams et al., 2003; Atman et al., 2010).

INTRODUCES A NOVEL APPROACH

With its integration of coding and calculations, this approach introduces a novel quantitative aspect to résumé pedagogy. Our engineering students seemed to enjoy the quantitative approach to writing since students in STEM fields feel comfortable working with numbers. In student comments, many reported that they liked the novelty of approaching writing from a quantitative perspective and it was helpful in giving them a different view on their writing. Though it's possible that not all students across the disciplines would appreciate this quantified approach, the actual process of coding and calculating disciplinary discourse is accessible enough for any college-level student.

SUPPORTS FACULTY ACROSS THE CURRICULUM IN PROVIDING DISCIPLINARY RÉSUMÉ DEVELOPMENT

A final benefit of this approach is that it engages students in discipline-specific résumé development, regardless of the instructor or WAC consultant's expertise. Given the diverse makeup of U.S. higher education institutions and curricula, there is an array of configurations in which résumé writing is taught. Many courses that teach résumé writing enroll students from a range of disciplines and may be taught by instructors who do not share expertise in the students' respective areas. Similarly, faculty from different disciplinary backgrounds can use this method to assist students to hone their writing choice in their résumés.

CONCLUDING THOUGHTS

Overall, we see the quantitative disciplinary discourse approach to résumé writing as a tool that can supplement more traditional approaches, and can be extended from our experiences in engineering to other disciplines as well. While our approach here is centered particularly on engineering due to our own backgrounds and teaching experiences, we believe this approach could be successfully implemented in a range of disciplines to help students develop not only more rhetorically savvy résumés, but a greater understanding of their disciplines and their developing identities within them. The recommendations provided harness our experiences with our research-driven, cross-disciplinary model, and extend its usefulness to other instructors across the university curriculum in support of disciplinary professionalization.

ACKNOWLEDGMENTS

We thank our reviewers, Kristin Marie Bivens and Brian Hendrickson, and the editors for their comments that greatly improved this manuscript.

REFERENCES

Adams, R. S., Turns, J. & Atman, C. J. (2003). Educating effective engineering designers: The role of reflective practice. *Design Studies, 24*, 275–294. https://doi.org/10.1016/S0142-694X(02)00056-X.

American Association of Engineering Societies. (2015). *Engineering Competency Model.* https://www.careeronestop.org/competencymodel/competency-models/engineering.aspx.

Anson, C. M. & Forsberg, L. (2003). Moving beyond the academic community: Transitional stages in professional writing. In T. Peeples (Ed.), *Professional writing and rhetoric: Readings from the field* (pp. 388–410). Longman. (Reprinted from *Written Communication, 7,* 200–231, 1990) https://doi.org/10.1016/S0142-694X(02)00056-X.

Artemeva, N. (2009). Stories of becoming: A study of novice engineers learning genres of their profession. In C. Bazerman, A. Bonini & D. Figueiredo (Eds.), *Genre in a changing world* (pp. 158–178). The WAC Clearinghouse; Parlor Press. https://wac.colostate.edu/books/perspectives/genre/.

Atman, C. J., Sheppard, S. D., Turns, J., Adams, R. S., Fleming, L. N., Stevens, R., . . . Yasuhara, K. (2010). *Enabling engineering student success: The final report for the center for the advancement of engineering education* (CAEE-TR–10-02). Center for the Advancement of Engineering Education.

Barchilon, M. G. (Ed.). (1998). Technology's impact on online resumes. In *IPPC 98. Contemporary Renaissance: Changing the Way We Communicate. Proceedings of the 1998 IEEE International Professional Communication Conference, 2,* 83–187. IEEE. https://doi.org/10.1109/IPCC.1998.722095.

Berdanier, C. G. P., McCall, M. & Fillenwarth, G. M. (in press). *Capturing emerging activity: Comparing web and conventional engineering résumés through writing and genre research.*

Berdanier, C. G. P., McCall, M. & Mike, G. (2016a, October 12–15). A degree is not enough: Promoting engineering identity development and professional planning through the teaching of engineering résumé writing. In *Proceedings of the Frontiers in Engineering Education Conference.* Erie, PA. https://doi.org/10.1109/FIE.2016 .7757711.

Berdanier, C. G. P., McCall, M. & Mike, G. (2016b, October 2–5). Résumés in the development of undergraduate engineering identity: A genre analysis with teaching implications. In *Proceedings of the IEEE ProComm 2016: Communicating Entrepreneurship and Innovation.* Austin, TX. https://doi.org/10.1109/IPCC.2016.7740 488.

Bird, C. P. & Puglisi, D. D. (1986). Method of résumé reproduction and evaluations of employment suitability. *Journal of Business Communication, 23*(3), 31–39. https://doi.org/10.1177/002194368602300303.

Blackburn-Brockman, E. & Belanger, K. (2001). One page or two? A national study of CPA recruiters' preferences for résumé length. *Journal of Business Communication, 38*(1), 29–57. https://doi.org/10.1177/002194360103800104.

CareerOneStop. (2018). *About the Competency Model.* https://www.careeronestop.org /CompetencyModel/GetStarted/about-models-help.aspx.

Carliner, S. (2012). The three approaches to professionalization in technical communication. *Technical Communication, 59*(1), 49–65.

Connors, R. J. (1982). The rise of technical writing instruction in America. *Journal of Technical Writing and Communication, 12*, 329–352. https://doi.org/10.2190/793K -X49Q-XG7M-C1ED.

Culwell-Block, B. & Sellers, J. A. (1994). Résumé content and format—Do the authorities agree? *Business Communication Quarterly, 57*(4), 27–30. https://doi.org /10.1177/108056999405700405.

Dias, P., Freedman, A., Medway, P. & Paré, A. (1999). *Worlds apart: Acting and writing in academic and workplace contexts.* Lawrence Erlbaum.

Dias, P. & Paré, A. (Eds.). (2000). *Transitions: Writing in academic and workplace settings.* Hampton Press.

Diaz, C. S. (2013). Updating best practices: Applying on-screen reading strategies to résumé writing. *Business Communication Quarterly, 76*, 427–445. https://doi.org /10.1177/1080569913501860.

Fillenwarth, G. M., McCall, M. & Berdanier, C. G. P. (2018). Quantification of engineering disciplinary discourse in résumés: A novel genre analysis with teaching implications. *IEEE Transactions on Professional Communication, 61*(1), 48–64. https://doi.org/10.1109/TPC.2017.2747338.

Francis, A. M. (2018). A survey of assignment requirements in service technical and professional communication classes. *Programmatic Perspectives, 10*(1), 44–76.

Harcourt, J. & Krizan, A. C. (1989). A comparison of résumé content preferences of Fortune 500 personnel administrators and business communication instructors. *Journal of Business Communication, 26*, 177–190. https://doi.org/10.1177/002194 368902600206.

Hutchinson, K. L. (1984). Personnel administrators' preferences for résumé content: A survey and review of empirically based conclusions. *Journal of Business Communication, 21*, 5–14. https://doi.org/10.1177/002194368402100401.

Hutchinson, K. L. & Brefka, D. S. (1997). Personnel administrators' preferences for résumé content: Ten years after. *Business Communication Quarterly, 60*(2), 67–75. https://doi.org/10.1177/108056999706000206.

Killoran, J. B. (2006). Self-published Web résumés: Their purposes and their genre systems. *Journal of Business and Technical Communication, 20*, 425–459. https://doi.org/10.1177/1050651906290267.

Killoran, J. B. (2009). The rhetorical situations of Web résumés. *Journal of Technical Writing and Communication, 39*, 263–284. https://doi.org/10.2190/TW.39.3.d.

Krause, T. (1997). Preparing an online résumé. *Business Communication Quarterly, 60*(1), 159–161. https://doi.org/10.1177/108056999706000115.

Martin-Lacroux, C. & Lacroux, A. (2017). Do employees forgive applicants' bad spelling in résumés? *Business and Professional Communication Quarterly, 80*, 321–335. https://doi.org/10.1177/2329490616671310.

Melonçon, L. K. (2018). Critical postscript on the future of the service course in technical and professional communication. *Programmatic Perspectives, 10*(1), 202–230.

Melonçon, L. & Henschel, S. (2013). Current state of U.S. undergraduate degree programs in technical and professional communication. *Technical Communication, 60*(1), 45–64.

Melzer, D. (2014). *Assignments across the curriculum: A national study of college writing.* Utah State University Press. https://doi.org/10.7330/9780874219401.

Miller, C. R. (1984). Genre as social action. *Quarterly Journal of Speech, 70*, 151–167. https://doi.org/10.1080/00335638409383686.

Pennell, T. I., Frost, E. A. & Getto, G. (2018). Valuing contra-professionalization: Analyzing successful professionalization practices in technical and professional communication. *Programmatic Perspectives, 10*(2), 71–99.

Penrose, J. M. (1973). Does order make a difference in résumés? *International Journal of Business Communication, 10*(3), 15–19. https://doi.org/10.1177/002194367301000303.

Penrose, J. M. (1984). A discrepancy analysis of the job-getting process and a study of résumé techniques. *International Journal of Business Communication, 21*(3), 5–15. https://doi.org/10.1177/002194368402100301/

Randazzo, C. (2016). Where do they go? Students' sources of résumé advice, and implications for critically reimagining the résumé assignment. *Technical Communication Quarterly, 25*(4), 278–297. https://doi.org/10.1080/10572252.2016.1221142.

Roever, C. (1997). Preparing a scannable résumé. *Business Communication Quarterly, 60*(1), 156–159. https://doi.org/10.1080/10572252.2016.1221142.

Russell, D. R. (2007). Rethinking the articulation between business and technical communication and writing in the disciplines. *Journal of Business and Technical Communication, 21*, 248–277. https://doi.org/10.1177/1050651907300452.

Schullery, N. M., Ickes, L. & Schullery, S. E. (2009). Employer preferences for résumés and cover letters. *Business Communication Quarterly, 72*, 163–176. https://doi.org/10.1177/1080569909334015.

Stanley-Weigand, P. (1991). Organizing the writing of your résumé. *Bulletin of the Association for Business Communication, 54*(3), 11–12. https://doi.org/10.1177/108056999105400303.

Tillotson, K. & Osborn, D. (2012). Effect of a résumé-writing workshop on résumé-writing skills. *Journal of Employment Counseling, 49,* 110–117. https://doi.org/10.1002/j.2161-1920.2012.00011.x

University of Iowa College of Engineering. (2015). *Engineering professional development career resource manual.* https://tinyurl.com/uhlda8b

Wenger, E. (1998). *Communities of practice: Learning, meaning, and identity.* Cambridge University Press. https://doi.org/10.1017/CBO9780511803932.

Wenger, E. (2010). Communities of practice and social learning systems: The career of a concept. In C. Blackmore (Ed.), *Social learning systems and communities of practice* (pp. 179–198). Springer. https://doi.org/10.1007/978-1-84996-133-2_11.

Wright, E. W., Domagalski, T. A. & Collins, R. (2011). Improving employee selection with a revised résumé format. *Business Communication Quarterly, 74,* 272–286. https://doi.org/10.1177/1080569911413809.

APPENDIX: SAMPLE REFLECTION PROMPT

In this unit, you've learned about the AAES Engineering Competency Model, coded your résumé, calculated your Disciplinary Discourse Density scores, and revised your résumé. Now, it's time to think about how you can use what you've learned to strategically plan your professionalization activities over the next few years. Answer the following questions:

1. Which Tiers and/or Competencies do you have the most of?

2. Which Tiers and/or Competencies would you like to add before graduation?

3. What specific experiences will you seek out in this next few years? List at least three activities and the competencies you will gain from each (provide the numerical tier code as well). List at least one per academic year.

   a. Sophomore Year:

   b. Junior Year:

   c. Senior Year:

CHAPTER 8.

LEARNING TO ARGUE ABOUT THE LITERATURE: DISCOURSE CHOICES AND STUDENTS' ITERATIVE LEARNING OF LITERATURE REVIEWS IN GEOGRAPHY

Misty Anne Winzenried

The Seattle School of Theology & Psychology

This chapter illustrates the incremental processes by which undergraduate students in a geography class learned to write the social science literature review. Situated within a larger ethnographic study, this microanalysis examines students' process of genre learning as they discovered and then attempted the discourse choices that helped them successfully enact the genre. Through three cases, the chapter examines one student's interactions with teaching assistant comments that illuminated his need for attribution, another who discovered through a rubric that her paper should be an "argument," and a third who Googled model genres in order to understand the genre he was being assigned. The case studies reveal moments of insight during which essential discursive signposts became available to students and, as a result, they shifted their discourse choices. This deeper understanding of students' processes for learning new disciplinary genres suggests a number of possible pedagogical interventions to make clearer the connections between genre characteristics and discourse-level choices.

What does it mean to have learned a genre? Writers' success at achieving their rhetorical aims—an invitation to interview for a job, a request to revise and resubmit for a journal, a strong grade received on a paper—might be one clear indication of having learned and effectively performed a genre. However, the processes of learning, and the various pathways writers take to arrive at those successful performative moments, are often invisible in the final iteration of a particularly successful genre performance. The processes of revising through trial and error, producing drafts, examining genre models, and receiving feedback from others are essential to the genre learning that takes place—and a rich site of study for Writing in the Disciplines (WID) scholars. This chapter analyzes three case studies to illustrate the incremental processes by which students in a geography class learned to write a new genre—the social science literature review. The microanalytic approach used in this chapter enables readers to see students' process of genre learning as they discovered and then attempted the discourse choices that helped them successfully enact the genre. This deeper understanding of students' processes for learning new disciplinary genres suggests a number of possible pedagogical interventions to make clearer the connections between genre characteristics and discourse-level choices.

The instructor of the junior-level geography course at the heart of this chapter, Dr. Graham, made the common assumption that genre learning is demonstrated primarily through successful production of the genre, in this case the social science literature review. The instructor considered the literature review central to understanding the socially constructed nature of knowledge production, a core theme he sought to teach in his class. He measured students' progress in the class, and the adequacy of his own teaching practices, by whether students were able to successfully produce the primary genre of the course, and thus take on the necessary habits of mind and discursive practices of an emerging geography student.

As it turned out, Graham and the course teaching assistants (TAs) seemed to be looking for particular rhetorical moves and discourse choices that signaled to them that students conceptually "got" what it meant to take on the perspective of a geographer and write a social sciences literature review. As I will explore, these signposts tended to be discourse choices that were at times invisible to students, but essential to their being recognized as having successfully learned the genre. By analyzing student's learning processes, I was able to see when and how they discovered the discursive signposts their instructors expected to see in the genre. In this case, I examined students' interactions with TA comments, rubrics, and model genres to reveal moments of insight during which these signposts became available to them and understand how they shifted their discourse choices as a result.

SCHOLARLY CONTEXT

Learning a new genre is a complex process. The WAC and WID literatures have a long-standing body of scholarship articulating the challenges students experience as they encounter new disciplinary genres and move through university curriculum (Beaufort, 2007; Carroll, 2002; McCarthy, 1987; Russell & Yañez, 2003; Sternglass, 1993) and the complicated experience of writers acquiring new genres while immersed in internships, professions, and graduate programs (Artemeva, 2005; Dias et al., 1999; Dias & Paré, 2000; Prior, 1998). For example, we learn from Marilyn Sternglass (1993) that students' writing development is not straightforward but rather recursive and iterative, depending on the familiarity and complexity of the task. Similarly, Anne Beaufort (1999) defined genre learning as "iterative" rather than sequential and found that writers had to limit their attention to a few elements at once. The present chapter acknowledges the challenges that these scholars name, particularly as they pertain to students writing disciplinary genres for the first time. Furthermore, this chapter builds on existing scholarship to investigate students' learning processes in the moment, as they are first encountering those genres and interacting with the classroom artifacts. The microanalytic approach used in this chapter focuses on the moments of insight students experienced while writing a new genre and the discourse-level changes they made to their writing as a result of those insights. This approach enabled me to see how students interacted with course artifacts and examine how they discovered and practiced the discourse-level markers that signaled to their instructors successful genre performance.

This research study began with the theoretical lens of Rhetorical Genre Studies, using qualitative, ethnographic methods for studying the social interactions and sociocultural context as students learned the genre in question. The frame of Rhetorical Genre Studies, which privileges the view of "genre as social action" (Miller, 1984), allows an examination of genres not merely as forms but as actions doing work in particular social contexts, and in this case, as opportunities to practice disciplinary thinking and writing. In this study, it became clear that student participants were adept at understanding and describing the genre's goals and purposes. That is, students talked about the "non-linguistic" social situations that surrounded the genre as it existed in their discipline (Bawarshi & Reiff, 2010) in ways that mirrored their instructors' talk about the genre. However, students struggled with knowing how to enact those goals and purposes, and their struggle frequently occurred within their writing choices, on the sentence level.[1] By better understanding this disconnect, WAC/WID scholars can

---

1   Ann Johns (2008, 2011) made a distinction between genre learning and genre awareness, arguing that genre learning tends to focus on learning transferable text types, while genre awareness emphasizes the socio-rhetorical context of the genre and is often an approach advocated for in first-year composition courses (see Devitt, 2004). However, in disciplinary writing courses, instructors may not have the rhetorical training to teach specifically for genre awareness, and this is a pedagogical challenge of RSG acknowledged by Bawarshi & Reiff (2010).

help teachers become more aware of the discourse choices that signal successful genre production in order to draw students' attention to those choices.

Study of the linguistic choices used to enact academic genres is common practice in English for Specific Purposes (ESP) and systemic functional linguistics (SFL) approaches to genre. ESP and SFL have long histories of using applied linguistics and corpus-based studies to undertake linguistic analysis of published academic texts across a range of disciplinary fields (Hyland, 2004; Swales, 1990; for an overview, see Bawarshi & Reiff, 2010). These studies examine the linguistic features of published academic texts, and out of this research, student-facing textbooks and pedagogies have emerged, particularly for non-native English speaking graduate students aiming to publish in English (Feak & Swales, 2009; Hyland, 2009; Swales & Feak, 1994, 2000). However, these linguistic-focused approaches are largely absent from disciplinary writing courses taught by instructors within their academic fields.

Recently, scholars have engaged in similar methods to analyze student texts, highlighting some of the discursive features that show up in students' academic writing (Aull & Lancaster, 2014; Gere et al., 2013; Lancaster, 2014, 2016a, 2016b). In addition, Mary Soliday (2011) and Laura Wilder (2012) have examined student learning with regard to discourse choices within discipline-specific genres. Soliday and Wilder interviewed students and examined their writing in relation to particular discourse moves ("stance," for Soliday, and "literary topoi," for Wilder), with a focus on the discourse choices themselves, their emergence in student writing, and the supports that enabled students' successful genre performance.

My scholarship builds on the work of Soliday (2011) and Wilder (2012) by taking an ethnographic approach: in observing class sessions, interviewing students repeatedly throughout the course, and examining their papers with them, I was able to ask students to reflect on their understandings of the genre over time and examine their discourse choices during multiple attempts at the genre. While Soliday and Wilder interviewed students and examined their writing for particular rhetorical strategies, my focus was on students' learning processes, rather than on the discourse choices themselves. I analyzed students' learning in the moment, while students were encountering the rubric, submitting their papers, receiving feedback, and searching for model genres. Listening to students as they discovered and tried out discourse choices while reaching toward the genre of the literature review provided a window into the various ways instructors might better support students' learning processes.

If abstract descriptions of the genre's purpose, audience, and organization might be described as genre characteristics, then the patterned language choices at the sentence or paragraph level that help writers enact those genre characteristics might be described as discourse choices.[2] As I will demonstrate, the instructor's description of the genre of the literature review as an "argument" and as "about the literature" were successfully enacted at the sentence level through particular discourse choices—choices that were frequently invisible to students. Methodologically, by asking students to talk about their discourse choices in the midst of their learning process, I was able to document their moments of discovery and examine their learning processes as they tried out new discourse choices through their encounters with course artifacts.

James Gee's (2011) concept of "recognition" provides a helpful framework for thinking about what "counts" as successful genre production in classroom contexts:

> The key to Discourses is "recognition." If you put language, action, interaction, values, beliefs, symbols, objects, tools, and places together in such a way that others recognize you as a particular type of who (identity) engaged in a particular type of what (action), here and now, then you have pulled off a Discourse. . . . Whatever you have done must be similar enough to other performances to be recognizable. (p. 35)

Thus, the interplay of nonlinguistic and linguistic features is important, and links back to distinct Rhetorical Genre Studies, English for Specific Purposes, and Systemic Functional Linguistics approaches to genre (Bawarshi & Reiff, 2010). Recognition as a concept emphasizes the social interaction, such that when a person "pull[s] off a Discourse," there is a someone (in this case, an instructor or TA) doing the recognizing. There is power involved in recognizing (or not) students' attempts at genre production: when instructors are assigning and then grading student writing in disciplinary classrooms, Gee's conception of recognition is at play.

The students in the study I present here are working toward "pulling off" the genre and wrestling with understanding and then performing the specific discourse choices that were necessary in their texts in order for them to be recognized as having successfully enacted the genre. Like Peter Smagorinsky, Elizabeth Anne Daigle, Cindy O'Donnell-Allen, and Susan Bynum (2010), I view these attempts generously, as authentic and earnest movements toward the target genre, as evidence of partial and incremental learning and connection-making. As such, students' engagement with classroom artifacts became compelling opportunities for examining their learning and meaning making with regard to the disciplinary genre they were working to produce.

---

2   See Gere et al. (2013) for a discussion of "meso-level rhetorical actions"—levels of text smaller than the text but larger than a sentence.

RESEARCH QUESTION, STUDY CONTEXT, AND METHODOLOGY

The central driving research question for this study was "What are the processes by which students learn a new disciplinary genre?" For this chapter specifically, I was interested in these two subquestions:

- What discourse choices help students get recognized as successfully producing that disciplinary genre?
- How do students discover and learn to employ those discourse choices over the span of a course?

This qualitative research was conducted at a large research university in the West in the Spring of 2014 under an IRB-determined exemption. The course was a Junior-level disciplinary writing course required of all Geography majors, and approximately 80 students enrolled in the course. Participants included Dr. Graham, a lecturer-level instructor, two graduate-student TAs, and seven undergraduate student participants who volunteered to participate in the research. The course was an introduction to research methods and writing in Geography, with an emphasis on epistemology. Students met three times per week in lecture, and again in small group "quiz" sections led by graduate-level TAs. The primary course genre was a literature review, and Graham taught this genre explicitly and had worked with the campus center for teaching to build scaffolding assignments into the paper sequence. The students first completed annotated bibliographies from instructor-provided articles, and then wrote a "mini" literature review about HIV/AIDS in Africa from those same articles before choosing their own topics to write an expanded literature review.

The study was part of a larger qualitative ethnographic case study that involved in-depth interviews, classroom observations, and collection of artifacts throughout a complete quarter. Though I offer examples from many of the seven students, the analysis for this chapter arises from the second of three semi-structured interviews with three of the student participants. Kyle[3] was a white male student studying linguistics and geography; he was in his sophomore year. Hope was a multilingual Korean American; she was a sophomore business major exploring the option of declaring geography as a second major. Finally, Roberto was a multilingual first-generation college student from Mexican immigrant parents; he was a junior majoring in geography. Together Kyle, Hope, and Roberto were typical among the seven student participants in terms of their development of genre knowledge over the course of the term. They were selected as comparative cases here because their second interviews illustrate the range of ways students were understanding

---

3   All pseudonyms. Students' identities are self-described.

the literature review mid-quarter and serve to highlight how students used their interactions with course artifacts to clarify their genre knowledge.

At the time of these interviews, Kyle, Hope, and Roberto had just received feedback on their first "mini" literature review. The interview protocol for the second interview involved describing their process for writing the paper, reading TA comments on their submitted papers—some of them for the first time—and then reflecting aloud on the sense they made of their TA comments. Thus, data collection for the findings represented here included a combination of semi-structured interviewing, stimulated elicitation interviewing, and analysis of student texts (Prior, 2004). This in-depth micro-analysis allows an examination of something instructors rarely see: students' meaning-making processes across time, in retrospect, as they draw connections between their prior understandings and their new learning. Through witnessing students' interactions with TA feedback on their papers, an assignment rubric, and the resources they sought out to better understand a new and difficult genre, readers are able to see how students wrestled with the discourse choices that helped them get recognized by their instructor and TAs as successfully performing the genre.

FINDINGS

In teaching the literature review, Graham spent an entire week of the course introducing the literature review: what it was, how it was used in the field of geography (and social sciences broadly), and its overarching genre characteristics. He emphasized a number of characteristics in class talk, rubrics, and other course documents—or what Janet Giltrow (2002) called "meta-genres." For the purposes of this chapter, I focus on students' interactions around two of these salient genre characteristics: a literature review is an "argument" and it is "about the literature." Graham defined an argument as "beyond a summary, involving both synthesis and evaluation" and contrasted the literature review to "a book report," saying to students in class, "Don't tell me about the topic. . . . Tell me what the authors are writing about the topic." This particular genre characteristic—that a literature review is "about the literature"—was identified by Graham as one of the most challenging aspects of the writing project for students, but also the most important for students' grasp of the socially constructed nature of knowledge in geography.

Throughout their interviews, all the students in the study generally talked about the literature review using language indicating that their understanding of the genres' salient characteristics matched their instructor's. All but one student called out the literature review as an argument, and every single student talked about the literature review being "about the literature." Yet despite their capacity to describe the genre of the literature review in ways that mirrored Graham's talk, students struggled with moving from articulating the genre's characteristics to enacting them, and they expressed hesitation about their confidence in producing the genre.

READING TA COMMENTS

I present Kyle's case first as the clearest example of a student's engagement with a discourse choice that signaled to their instructor and TAs successful enactment of the genre. For the larger group, some of the rhetorical characteristics of the literature review were invisible to students, even when they were earnestly trying to enact the genre. Kyle was among a number of students in the class who felt like he understood the primary purpose and characteristics of the genre of the literature review as Graham described it—but struggled enact the genre and get recognized by TAs as having done so. Kyle's case study is particularly illuminating because of the connections he made right in the interview that furthered his understanding. Kyle thought he was writing "about the literature" and claimed he understood that the paper was supposed to be about the literature, but his TA, Miles, highlighted particular sentences or phrases in Kyle's paper and requested that he write about the literature. Here I illustrate that although the discourse choices that would have signaled this genre knowledge to his instructor were at first invisible to Kyle, his interaction with the TAs comments demonstrate his ongoing, incremental learning process.

The last sentence of the introduction to Kyle's first literature review read as follows:

> This paper seeks to understand how underdeveloped countries in sub-Saharan Africa are seeking to expand efforts to help not only spread knowledge of the HIV/AIDS virus and protection from it among youth populations but also how these countries involve the adult population in this process through a review of five different current articles discussing the various topics surrounding this issue.

Miles highlighted this last sentence—a common student move to use the last sentence of the introduction to provide a roadmap rather than articulate an explicit argument—and made this comment: "Good, but for a lit review, rather than making an argument about HIV/AIDS itself, try to frame your argument around what the *authors* are saying about HIV/AIDS. Focus on the articles over their subject matter!" Here, Miles explicitly reminded Kyle that the literature review was "about the literature."

In his verbal response to me about this comment, Kyle said, "Mmm. This is like saying I was trying to use the paper to talk about HIV and AIDS itself. Which I guess I can understand, but at the same time, I was mostly just summarizing [the articles], and most of the articles were about like—they introduce some sort of program to teach the local population, and then they tracked it over time." The sentence in Kyle's text was tagged by Miles as an argument, but here, Kyle said he saw the work he was doing in this sentence as summarizing the articles. To him, this summarization was indeed writing "about the literature," but it was not recognized by Miles in the same way.

Kyle had similar insights when he read the last sentence of his paper: "In terms of the youth population of all of the areas analyzed throughout these five articles, it appears that they are ahead of the general knowledge, care, protection and prevention curve, and it should rather be their adult population counterparts that should perhaps a greater focus so that they can in turn ensure that the youth population stay on their current path to relative healthiness from the HIV/AIDS epidemic [TA highlighting preserved]." Kyle read part of this sentence aloud to me, then said: "Yeah. [Reading sentence] That was kind of the conclusion I drew." Here, the comment that Miles made on this sentence, which he had highlighted, was "Not your job to say what 'ought' to be done. Is this what the authors think should be done?"

In reading this comment, Kyle responded in the interview: "But it was because I said 'should' rather than just format it in sort of like an observational way. . . . And I think I should've phrased it like, 'Based on these articles, it appears that the youth populations in the test areas show less of a, um, improvement in terms of HIV and AIDS knowledge as opposed to their adult counterparts.'" That is, Kyle revoiced in his interview with me what his sentence would have sounded like with the appropriate attributive phrase.

Attributive phrasing, while it might seem like a simple discursive move, became a key to students being recognized by Graham and Miles as successfully writing "about the literature." Students were aware of their need to write "about the literature," but not always aware of the discourse choices that they needed to produce to do so, and attribution was not something that Graham ever spoke explicitly about in class. However, in an interview with me, Graham described an office hour appointment with another student from the class, in which he had prompted the student to revoice his talk about the paper to be not about the topic but about the literature. Such talk, with attribution, demonstrated to Graham that the student had taken up this important genre characteristic. Despite this, for many students, the move that signaled this important discourse choice—the attributive phrases—was invisible until someone explicitly pointed it out on their papers.

Kyle's case was interesting because his initial self-assessment was that he had indeed been writing about the literature: he was summarizing the literature, and he knew—and knew his TA knew—he did not do this research himself. On the first round of this paper, he did not realize that there was a particular rhetorical signal that Miles was looking for to indicate that he had taken up this particular genre feature appropriately. Attribution seemed to be what Miles was looking for as the discourse marker for the paper being "about the literature." When Kyle realized this, he was quickly able to revoice the sentence he originally wrote and include the attribution. Throughout the rest of this interview, in other places where he received similar comments from Miles, he re-worded his sentences aloud for me: "So I should've just said, 'Author's Name.'. . . ." Together, his talk, his writing, and his verbal response to TA comments show the process of his learning in the moment. In his final paper, Kyle included much more attribution throughout when referencing findings from articles, demonstrating his movement toward understanding the importance of this discourse choice in successfully producing the genre of the literature review in this class.

Discovering the Rubric

While Kyle's case illustrates one moment of insight through feedback on writing, in any given course there are a range of other opportunities for students to make the kinds of discoveries that Kyle made through TA comments. As I will show, Hope was a student whose insight came when she read the rubric right before submitting her paper, demonstrating that teachers may not always know how various classroom supports will resonate with students, and when, during their learning process.

Throughout my first, second, and third interviews with students, I asked them to talk both about the genre of the literature review in their class and about their writing and learning processes. Like many students in the study, Hope was grappling with an apparent contradiction in her instructors' genre descriptions: the literature review was simultaneously an argument, and it was "about the literature." For example, another student, Samantha, talked about how she imagined engaging the literature in her paper and put it this way: "Cause I was really thinking about the idea that the argument should be your own, but *it shouldn't seem like your own that much.* . . ." Generally, students in the study had difficulty conceiving how to craft an argument that was not an opinion while simultaneously integrating literature—and focusing their paper on the literature itself rather than the topic. Through iterative practice with the genre and her grappling with this apparent contradiction, Hope's conception of the literature review evolved—but not always in expected ways.

In her first interview, Hope articulated that she understood the literature review she was preparing to write as entirely source based, and excluding her ideas or her opinion altogether—in fact, she was concerned how the paper would look if it were all citations. However, during the second interview, Hope told me the story of a new understanding that came through writing and submitting her first "mini" literature review. Right as she was getting ready to submit the paper, she discovered the rubric provided online by Graham, where she realized for the first time that the literature review was actually supposed to be an argument. "Yeah, the rubric. And I did not see that until like 30 minutes before I was gonna submit my paper. So for the 15 minutes, I went through and tried to make it more, like, argument style because I didn't know we had to have an argument at all. . . . So I started going back and putting in certain sentences there that really made it seem like I'm focused on one side versus the other."

The rubric described an "excellent" literature review in this way: "Paper has a clear argument or research question; both the 'summary' and 'analysis' aspects of the lit review are present; literature is organized to support the argument." Upon reading the rubric, Hope had to first recognize that she did not previously have an argument in her paper, and second, she had to have some sense of what to do about that. Interestingly, it was at least two of these "added last minute" sentences that solicited comments by her TA, Miles.

One prominent example of this occurred at the end of the paper's first paragraph. In her first draft, she had ended her paragraph, "The two main focuses, including the similarities and differences between the articles, will be the topics/issues researched along with the methodological approach of the research conducted." Again, this common student move at the end of the introduction provided a "roadmap" for what followed but was not necessarily an argument. Hope added these sentences before submitting the paper:

> The *theories of the articles* [emphasis added] largely target the prevention of this disease as well as the future outcome due to HIV/AIDS, but also lack efforts for those already infected by this disease. *The concern here is* [emphasis added] not to focus on just the preventative efforts, but the underlying issues that come as a result of HIV/AIDS spreading and how to effectively implement ideas to aid those with AIDS.

The comment Miles made, pointed with an electronic flag at the end of this paragraph, was "Good, concise argument that focuses on the articles (rather than the virus itself)." Here, Miles highlighted what Hope had done well—she both made an argument and had written "about the literature" instead of about the topic. Indeed, her sentence's subject is "the theories of the articles"—

indicating to Miles that she understood she was supposed to write "about the literature."

When we arrived at this comment in the interview, Hope said to me, "Cause this is what I think I added, kind of last minute, saying that instead of just focusing on the preventative efforts, we should also work on the treatment. I think that's what he's saying—it's not just the virus itself. It's like the argument that I'm trying to have. And then this [the original roadmap sentence] is like the two things I'm focusing on. It's similarities and differences. And then methodological approach." Hope's phrase "The concern here is . . ." emphasizes the contrast between her contribution and the synthesis of the articles' findings in her previous sentence.

While Hope's approach of tacking on "argument-style" sentences throughout her paper might not have led to a fully developed argument, her awareness that something was missing and her move to add "argument style" sentences demonstrated some interesting last-minute, incremental learning. Hope had a sense, first, that arguments could be enacted (at least in part) at the sentence level, and second, that there were particular sorts of rhetorical moves made in "argument style" sentences. As she encountered the rubric after writing her own paper, her understanding evolved, and she made a pointed revision by adding sentences throughout her paper to make it more of an argument.

By the third interview, the idea of a literature review being both about the literature and an argument was central to her understanding: there, she emphasized argumentative nature of a literature review and spent time describing the shift she had made from thinking about the literature review as being "just talking about, this article's this, and this author said this" to "what I'll be arguing about or what I'll be saying." We can see that her facility with argument and her ability to integrate "argument style" sentences became more sophisticated between her first and second paper. For example, in her introduction to her final paper on global poverty, she writes: "Most academics agree that estimates produce different results and emphasize why and how that occurs[;] however, an important concept lacking within this perspective is the overlooked lack of published analysis that target improved human and health development." Here, Hope uses attribution to synthesize a consensus among the articles she read and uses "however" to contrast her argument as an insight about what was overlooked in the studies: one conventional articulation of a "gap" in many social science research studies (Swales, 1990).

GOOGLING FOR MODEL TEXTS

The cases of Kyle and Hope illustrate their interactions with classroom artifacts and their iterative attempts to learn and perform the genre in their class.

Throughout my interviews, I also asked students to identify any resources they sought out themselves that were useful to their learning. In general, students were eager to find genre samples as part of their learning process. When they did not feel that the class materials they had been provided were sufficient, they sought out additional resources on their own but, in doing so, were left alone to make sense of how close the "literature reviews" they found through Google searches matched the genre as it emerged in their classroom.

Four of the seven students in the study took the initiative to find a sample paper on their own. Samantha found a published literature review in geography through the library guides, and Thomas, Roberto, and Jun Googled to find sample papers on the Web. Jun was able to find a sample paper from another university that also had some instruction and annotation, and Thomas used the empirical articles he was reading for his research as a model.

Roberto's search was particularly interesting because it surfaced an iterative meaning-making process as he wrestled with the samples in a more complex way. Like his classmates, Roberto also Googled for sample papers, but he had a keen awareness that the samples he found when he Googled "Literature Review" weren't necessarily the same genre his teacher was looking for:

> I went online, and I looked at other lit reviews that had been done, and a lot of them are these peer-reviewed academic lit reviews that had been published. And they are—though they're similar in what the objective is, learning what's already been done, kind of assessing the conversations between academics on subject, I saw that they were very, very specific to like a case. They were more, like, scientific in terms of . . . not necessarily talking about how it's looked at, but more talking about the actual issue itself and . . . so, I was like, OK, this is one way of doing a literature review. But this is not really how I'm being taught to do it. So I'm kind of confused. This is a really good lit review. It makes, you know, good, strong points. But it's just kind of—I just saw—it wasn't necessarily the same as I would've thought.

This quote provides a window into Roberto's meaning making around the sample genre he sought out. First, he quickly became aware that the genre samples he found online did not exactly match the genre as it was presented in his class. In fact, his observation of the peer-reviewed published literature reviews, even though they made "good, strong points," was that they were "more talking about the actual issue itself"—something Graham regularly reminded students to avoid. In this quote, Roberto articulated that he made sense of this contradiction by concluding that there might be more than one way to write a literature review and that what Graham was asking was particular and nuanced: "So I was like, OK, this is one way of doing a literature review. But this is not really how I'm being taught to do it." His desire for more samples, which he sought out on his own, was linked to his hope that samples might help him "understand the structure of them."

Roberto had an easier time than other students navigating the conceptual tension between the genre characteristics. Instead, his struggle was wondering what exactly his argument was supposed to be about. In his interviews, Roberto posed the question that troubled him: What do we argue about? At the end of his first interview, he said, "I understand that we're arguing about other people's arguments and that we're kind of linking them together and saying, OK, this is how this person looks at it. . . . But in the conclusion part, I'm still wondering how—like, what, essentially, we're going to be discussing. Like do we just continue talking about how different they are . . . or do we try to propose our own way of going about studying this now that we know all the different approaches that have been taken?"

A comparison between Roberto's discourse choices in his thesis statements in Paper 1 and Paper 2 illustrate both a decision to focus his argument on methodology and a growing comfort with taking an argumentative stance (see Table 8.1).

Table 8.1. Comparison of Roberto's discourse choices in his thesis statements between Paper 1 and Paper 2

Roberto's Paper 1 Thesis	Roberto's Paper 2 Thesis
This review will focus on how five geographic studies outline the impact of HIV/AIDS in sub-Saharan Africa (or a particular sub-Saharan area) in order to understand the type of responses that have derived from strictly geographic perspectives on the HIV/AIDS epidemic and most importantly how data quality affect the stigma of HIV/AIDS.	However, I assert in this paper that among these studies, the measurement of food security among participants is not thoroughly being considered as having an association to understanding the high obesity rates in the US. I think some research attention to the quality of work lives and household income that are typical of food insecurity and obesity interventions is needed.

In his first paper, Roberto's thesis was clearly focused on the literature but went beyond that to say something about the literature: that data quality affects how people understand HIV/AIDS. His argument on articles' data quality was present but subtle. However, by his third interview, Roberto had determined that his argument should actually be about the methods themselves: "The thesis [in my second paper] is kind of like, what is driving all these research methods and all these studies." His second paper's thesis illustrates more comfort with the discourse choices that emphasize an argument: "However, I assert in this paper . . ." Moreover, Roberto foregrounded a methodological argument early and as the subject of his thesis sentence: "The *measurement* [emphasis added] of food security among participants is not thoroughly being considered." Roberto's case illustrates movement over time toward more sophisticated enactments of the discourse choices that helped him get recognized as producing a literature review that was both an argument and about the literature.

DISCUSSION AND IMPLICATIONS

The cases of Kyle, Hope, and Roberto give readers three snapshots of learning moments that occurred between students' first encounter with the genre and their final papers. Together, the cases illuminate insights students had as they interacted with course artifacts and talked with me about their writing. These insights illustrate students' discovery of the discourse choices that were not made explicit in the class but that were key to getting recognized as successfully enacting the genre of the literature review in their geography class. By taking a microanalytic approach, I was able to trace students' discovery of those discourse choices and attempts to practice them, giving us a picture of their learning processes and movements toward the genre at key moments.

For instructors and WAC/WID directors who work with faculty, this research supports a large and long-standing body of scholarship in the field advocating for faculty development around increased awareness of the rhetorical moves and discourse choices used to enact their disciplinary genres (McLeod, 2001; McLeod et al., 2001; Thaiss & Zawacki, 2006). As Angela Glotfelter, Ann Updike, and Elizabeth Wardle (this volume) demonstrate, faculty who engage in WAC/WID development often become aware of the tacit assumptions they have about writing, and the ways those assumptions are linked to disciplinary understandings.

Even in classrooms like this one, where Graham was working to scaffold students' learning, illuminate the disciplinary thinking behind disciplinary genres, and give students multiple opportunities to practice, more can be done to connect discourse-level choices to the general genre characteristics instructors use to talk about genres. Instructors' clarity about the discourse choices they are looking for in disciplinary genres—those choices that, whether explicitly or implicitly, give students the ability to be recognized as successfully performing the genre—is central to providing students access to disciplinary genre knowledge. Scholarship by Zak Lancaster and Laura Aull examines some of the linguistic features that are valued in academic writing (Aull, 2015; Aull & Lancaster, 2014; Lancaster, 2014, 2016a, 2016b; see also, Hyland, 2004), and this kind of linguistics or corpus-based research is valuable for unmasking the particularities of academic discourse for new students. This chapter demonstrates that classroom artifacts such as instructor and TA feedback, assignment rubrics, and model genres might be productive sites for highlighting the particular discourse choices instructors are looking for students to emulate.

One key finding of this research is that in students' talk with me, they articulated increasing understanding about the genre and how to go about performing it successfully, though sometimes this learning occurred after the paper had been submitted and graded. WAC and WID scholars, faculty, and advocates are well positioned to help instructors across their campuses not only be more effective in supporting students' learning of disciplinary genres—and identifying the particular discourse choices that are used to enact those genres—but also more aware of the iterative processes that students are engaged in as they learn new genres.

Moreover, this research suggests that scholars too might benefit from expanding studies to examine incremental yet imperfect movement toward target genres. In this chapter, I focused on three moments of insight that allow readers to see students' learning processes unfold. My microanalysis of students' texts and talk about their interactions with TA feedback, assignment rubrics, and genre models gives readers a window into student learning that interviews or analyses of student writing alone do not. Students' iterative meaning-making processes across time, and in retrospect, illustrate their "reaches" toward, their attempts at enacting a new genre, their genre knowledge becoming more precise, complex, and nuanced. This view of their process—how they went about learning the genres through interaction with course artifacts and concrete discourse choices across drafts—offers WAC/WID instructors and scholars both ways of identifying and supporting those key learning moments before the "aha" happens and ways of valuing students' movement toward a target genre, even if their genre knowledge and the writing they produce are still emerging.

REFERENCES

Artemeva, N. (2005). A time to speak, a time to act: A rhetorical genre analysis of novice engineer's calculated risk taking. *Journal of Business and Technical Communication 19*, 389–421. https://doi.org/10.1177/1050651905278309.

Aull, L. (2015). *First-year university writing: A corpus-based study with implications for pedagogy.* Palgrave Macmillan. https://doi.org/10.1057/9781137350466.

Aull, L. & Lancaster, Z. (2014). Linguistic markers of stance in early and advanced academic writing: A corpus-based comparison. *Written Communication, 31*, 151–183. https://doi.org/10.1177/0741088314527055.

Bawarshi, A. & Reiff, M. J. (2010). *Genre: An introduction to history, theory, research, and pedagogy.* Parlor Press; The WAC Clearinghouse. https://wac.colostate.edu /books/perspectives/genre/.

Beaufort, A. (1999). *Writing in the real world: Making the transition from school to work.* Teachers College Press.

Beaufort, A. (2007). *College writing and beyond: A new framework for university writing instruction.* Utah State University Press. https://doi.org/10.2307/j.ctt4cgnk0.

Carroll, L. A. (2002). *Rehearsing new roles: How college students develop as writers.* Southern Illinois University Press.

Devitt, A. J. (2004). *Writing genres.* Southern Illinois University Press.

Dias, P., Freedman, A., Medway, P. & Paré, A. (1999). *Worlds apart: Acting and writing in academic and workplace contexts.* Lawrence Erlbaum.

Dias, P. & Paré, A. (2000). *Transitions: Writing in academic and workplace settings.* Hampton.

Feak, C. B. & Swales, J. M. (2009). *Telling a research story: Writing a literature review.* University of Michigan Press. https://doi.org/10.3998/mpub.309338.

Gee, J. P. (2011). *An introduction to discourse analysis: Theory and method.* Routledge. https://doi.org/10.4324/9780203847886.

Gere, A. R., Aull, L., Perales Escudero, M. D., Lancaster, Z. & Vander Lei, E. (2013). Local assessment: Using genre analysis to validate directed self-placement. *College Composition and Communication, 64,* 605–633.

Giltrow, J. (2002). Meta-genre. In R. Coe, L. Lingard & T. Teslenko (Eds.), *The rhetoric and ideology of genre: Strategies for stability and change* (pp. 187–205). Hampton.

Hyland, K. (2004). *Disciplinary discourses: Social interactions in academic writing* (Michigan Classics Edition). University of Michigan Press. https://doi.org/10.3998 /mpub.6719.

Hyland, K. (2009). *Academic discourse: English in a global context.* Continuum International Publishing Group.

Johns, A. M. (2008). The future of genre in L2 writing: Fundamental, but contested, instructional decision. *Journal of Second Language Writing, 20,* 56–88. https://doi .org/10.1016/j.jslw.2010.12.003.

Johns, A. M. (2011). Genre awareness for the novice academic student: An ongoing quest. *Language Teaching, 41,* 237–252. https://doi.org/10.1017/S02614448070 04892.

Lancaster, Z. (2014). Exploring valued patterns of stance in upper-level student writing in the disciplines. *Written Communication, 31,* 27–57. https://doi.org/10.1177 /0741088313515170.

Lancaster, Z. (2016a). Do academics really write this way? A corpus investigation of moves and templates in "They say/I say." *College Composition and Communication, 67,* 437–464.

Lancaster, Z. (2016b). Using corpus results to guide the discourse-based interview: A study of one student's awareness of stance in academic writing in philosophy. *Journal of Writing Research, 8*(1), 119–148. https://doi.org/10.17239/jowr-2016.08 .01.04.

McCarthy, L. P. (1987). A stranger in strange lands: A college student writing across the curriculum. *Research in the Teaching of English, 21*, 233–265.

McLeod, S. (2001). The pedagogy of writing across the curriculum. In G. Tate, A. Rupiper & K. Schick (Eds.), *A guide to composition pedagogies* (pp. 149–164). Oxford University Press.

McLeod, S., Miraglia, E., Soven, M. & Thaiss, C. (Eds.). (2001). *WAC for a new millennium: Strategies for continuing Writing-Across-the-Curriculum programs.* National Council of Teachers of English. https://wac.colostate.edu/books/landmarks/millennium/.

Miller, C. (1984). Genre as social action. In A. Freedman & P. Medway (Eds.), *Genre and the new rhetoric* (pp. 23–42). Taylor and Francis. https://doi.org/10.1080/00335638409383686.

Prior, P. (1998). *Writing/disciplinarity: A sociohistoric account of literate activity in the academy.* Lawrence Erlbaum.

Prior, P. (2004). Tracing process: How texts come into being. In C. Bazerman & P. Prior (Eds.), *What writing is and how it does it: An introduction to analyzing texts and textual Practices* (pp. 167–200). Lawrence Erlbaum.

Russell, D. R. & Yañez, A. (2003). "Big picture people rarely become historians": Genre systems and the contradictions of general education. In C. Bazerman & D. R. Russell (Eds.), *Writing selves/writing societies* (pp. 331–362). The WAC Clearinghouse; Mind, Culture, and Activity. https://wac.colostate.edu/books/perspectives/selves-societies/.

Smagorinksy, P., Daigle, E. A., O'Donnell-Allen, C. & Bynum, S. (2010). Bullshit in academic writing: A protocol analysis of a high school senior's process of interpreting *Much ado about nothing*. *Research in the Teaching of English, 44*, 368–405.

Soliday, M. (2011). *Everyday genres: Writing assignments across the disciplines.* Southern Illinois University Press.

Sternglass, M. (1993). Writing development as seen through longitudinal research: A case study. *Written Communication, 10*, 231–261. https://doi.org/10.1177/0741088393010002004.

Swales, J. M. (1990). *Genre analysis: English in academic and research settings.* Cambridge University Press.

Swales, J. M. & Feak, C. B. (1994). *Academic writing for graduate students: Essential tasks and skills.* University of Michigan Press.

Swales, J. M. & Feak, C. B. (2000). *English in today's research world: A writing guide.* University of Michigan Press. https://doi.org/10.3998/mpub.9059.

Thaiss, C. J. & Zawacki, T. M. (2006). *Engaged writers and dynamic disciplines: Research on the academic writing life.* Boynton/Cook.

Wilder, L. (2012). *Rhetorical strategies and genre conventions in literary studies: Teaching and writing in the disciplines.* Southern Illinois University Press.

CHAPTER 9.

USING GENRE TO TEACH THE PUBLICATION-BASED THESIS

Rachael Cayley

University of Toronto

One key contemporary shift in doctoral writing is the growing preva-
lence of the publication-based thesis (PBT). A PBT refers to a broad
category of theses that involve the publication of component articles
during the thesis writing process. As students are increasingly encour-
aged to publish during the doctorate, the PBT is becoming an increas-
ingly attractive option for many writers. Doctoral writers who choose
this style of thesis will produce publishable articles while also crafting
additional texts that transform those articles into an acceptable thesis.
In this chapter, I will argue that doctoral writers who are undertaking
this form of thesis will benefit from clear genre-based instruction to
help them meet the unique challenges of the PBT.

An increased emphasis on publishing during doctoral study is leading to an increased prevalence of the publication-based thesis (Aitchison et al., 2010; Nethsinghe & Southcott, 2015; Sharmini, 2018). A publication-based thesis (PBT) is composed of some number of publishable articles, supplemented with linking texts. This type of thesis, increasingly prevalent in North America, has been common for much longer in European doctoral study (Guerin, 2016). The prevalence of this type of thesis can be generally explained by the need for speed in the communication of scientific results and the fact that many fields do not communicate research findings in book form. Given that the research community as a whole tends to benefit from the expeditious communication of results in scholarly article form (Jackson, 2013; Nethsinghe & Southcott, 2015), it is unsurprising that some doctoral writers are being encouraged to publish as part of their doctoral thesis writing process. While this move towards the PBT may sound natural and advantageous, the transition is not without challenges for doctoral writers (Robins & Kanowski, 2008). When a thesis is based on ongoing publication, decisions will need to be made about a structure for the full thesis that ultimately emerges from those publications. Those decisions will consider a range of factors: internal demands of the topic, supervisory preferences, doctoral writer assumptions, and

DOI: https://doi.org/10.37514/PER-B.2020.0360.2.09

disciplinary and geographic culture. However, even with guidance, the inherent challenges of this thesis structure mean that doctoral writers may be uncertain about how to manage the writing task (Autry & Carter, 2015; Pretorius, 2017).

This uncertainty is exacerbated by the way that discussions of thesis writing often pay less attention to variant forms. Since treatments of thesis writing often assume—implicitly or explicitly—a more traditional thesis form, the issues connected to the unique features of a PBT may be ignored. As a result, the support that is available for thesis writers may still be failing to offer insight into the specific challenges faced by PBT writers. While the PBT is not novel, particularly in many scientific fields, it is not common in the humanities fields in which most North American writing specialists have themselves been trained. Much of the conversation, especially within the thesis advice genre (Kamler & Thomson, 2008), tends to assume the traditional thesis as its model. This assumption, however, can seem problematic in light of the growing prevalence of the PBT; it is crucial that those who provide writing support to graduate students are able to provide advice to doctoral writers preparing to write PBTs. In this chapter, I will discuss how situating the PBT within the broader thesis genre can facilitate teaching this form of thesis. I will begin by characterizing the PBT and its relationship to other thesis patterns before going on to discuss the benefits of employing a genre approach to confront the unique challenges of the PBT. Throughout, I will argue that a clear understanding of the generic workings of the PBT is essential for doctoral writers seeking to undertake this increasingly widespread form of thesis.

DEFINING THE PUBLICATION-BASED THESIS

To understand the PBT, it may be helpful to picture it in the middle of a continuum with the traditional thesis at one end and the portfolio thesis at the other (see Figure 9.1).

Figure 9.1: Continuum from Traditional Thesis to Portfolio Thesis. Three interlocking circles with overlap between traditional thesis and publication-based thesis and overlap between publication-based thesis and portfolio thesis.

At one extreme, we have the traditional thesis, also known as a monograph or big-book thesis, which is essentially a book-length text with a single, coherent narrative; this type of thesis is entirely integrated with each chapter providing additional development of a project set out in the introduction and resolved in the conclusion. In all likelihood, such a thesis will be publishable only in significantly altered form: either transformed into a monograph or even more transformed into an article or series of articles. At the other extreme is the portfolio thesis, a form of thesis in which a certain amount of publishing will "equal" a thesis, without requiring a separate text to be written. This type of thesis is also known as a stapler thesis, an evocative name that illustrates the mechanism by which the papers become a thesis. This process is sometimes called a Ph.D. by publication, a name that highlights the absence of an actual thesis: the Ph.D. is achieved by amassing a certain amount of publication without requiring that any additional text be generated. Between these two poles, we find the PBT, also known as the article-based thesis, paper-style thesis, or manuscript thesis. Since this terminology involves a lot of overlapping terms and since it is absolutely used differently by different people, I want to be clear that I am making a distinction between a thesis that is replaced by sufficient publication—what I am here calling a portfolio thesis—and a PBT. My decision to use the term publication-based thesis is deliberate: a PBT is a thesis that is based on publication, not a thesis that is replaced by publication. From a writing perspective, this distinction is crucial because a portfolio thesis can be a much more transparent writing task. The composite articles will need to be crafted according to disciplinary norms and journal specifications, both of which provide the doctoral writer with relatively accessible guidance. The PBT, on the other hand, challenges doctoral writers by requiring that the articles be supplemented with a novel type of text, one that is rarely discussed in pedagogical terms.

Presenting the PBT as part of a continuum is a useful way to help doctoral writers manage the extreme variability that exists within this model of thesis writing. In all PBTs, writers are being asked to produce published or publishable articles and then to write linking texts unifying those articles. Those linking texts generally include an introduction and conclusion as well as discussions of scholarly literature, methods, and results. The extent and placement of those linking texts can vary widely. It is easy to find examples in which the published papers are greatly transformed to become part of a highly integrated thesis; similarly, it is easy to find examples in which the published papers are completely untouched and only loosely yoked by the unifying thesis texts. The extent of this variability means that situating the PBT within a continuum can be instructive for a writer who is in the process of establishing the optimal structure for their own amalgamation of published material and linking texts.

To properly grasp the diversity of the PBT requires a discussion of both disciplinary and geographic difference. The prevalence of the PBT varies from field to field and does so in a predictable manner. In the sciences, where speed of publication in research article form is crucial, the notion of a thesis that builds on publishable articles has long made sense. In the humanities, where speed is less prized and where scholarly monographs are still a valuable currency, the traditional thesis remains central. In the social sciences, where scholarly communication has been moving more towards research articles, we see some growth of the PBT as well as continued replication of the traditional thesis. This disciplinary variation and the fact that practices are in flux in many fields make it vital that the PBT be conceptualized from a pedagogical perspective. Thesis structures also vary decisively along geographic lines; it can be hard enough to establish thesis-writing practices at a single institution, let alone across institutions or across countries. It is well beyond the scope of this paper to give an empirical overview of thesis-writing practices; my investigation of this issue within my own university has shown me that practices of thesis writing are highly local and often poorly supported by institutional discourses (Starke-Meyerring et al., 2014). The value of a continuum is that it opens a pedagogical space to talk about the model of the PBT without needing to specify the particular arrangement that any one writer might use to organize their work. Thesis writers need to design PBTs that meet institutional requirements and satisfy supervisory preference; both of those demands will naturally be influenced by disciplinary and geographic trends. Most thesis writers need pedagogical insights about the thesis that can then be adapted and shaped according to dictates of their particular writing situation; this need is particularly acute for those working in the relatively indeterminate space created by the variable forms of PBTs found across the continuum.

UNDERSTANDING THE THESIS AS A GENRE

Once this continuum has been presented, the idea of thesis as a genre (Autry & Carter, 2015; Carter, 2011; Cheng, 2018; Swales, 2004; Tardy, 2009) can be used to explain the rhetorical goals and constraints of the PBT. Using genre to teach advanced academic writing means alerting writers to the ways in which texts are designed to act in particular situations (Artemeva, 2004; Bawarshi & Reiff, 2010; Miller, 1984; Paré, 2014). In order to broaden the teaching of thesis writing to include the PBT, it is crucial to see the structural patterns of the PBT against the backdrop of the broader genre of a doctoral thesis. A doctoral thesis can be seen as having two key imperatives: communicating research and displaying expertise. In a traditional thesis, these two elements are intertwined; in order to have the research findings taken seriously, a thesis writer must go beyond research communication to demonstrate their own expertise. The explicit performance of expertise can be seen as the defining aspect of the doctoral thesis: the goal of the thesis is the dissemination of novel research but that dissemination must be lodged within a broader framework of expertise. That scholarly display work is what ultimately allows the committee (on behalf of the department, faculty, and institution) to aver that the candidate's research has met the requirements of the Ph.D. In a portfolio thesis, on the other hand, the work of communicating research and displaying expertise are completely coextensive: the publications communicate the research while also, through the gatekeeping function of scholarly publishing, vouching for the expertise of the writer. In contrast to these two models, the PBT rests on a notable disaggregation of the communication of research and the display of expertise.

This disaggregation highlights why the PBT can be challenging to a doctoral writer. The doctoral writer has already communicated their research via the scholarly apparatus of a research article, a process that has been implicitly validated through the peer review process. The need to produce additional texts—ones which primarily exist to display expertise—may be puzzling. However, once the doctoral writer grasps the dual imperatives of the thesis genre, it is much easier to elaborate what the PBT requires of a writer. The basic form of the PBT is, of course, fairly straightforward: doctoral writers will readily understand that they must combine publishable articles with new texts that will transform that collection of articles into a thesis. The prevalence of this form of thesis means that many doctoral writers will expect to write one and will thus see doing so as natural. As time goes on, more and more doctoral writers are sure to be writing with supervisors who themselves wrote a PBT, which will presumably further increase their prevalence. For some doctoral writers, depending on discipline, the choice to write a PBT may be more daring; in some cases, those writers may need to convince their committee of the advisability of this form of thesis. Regardless of the route to the PBT, all doctoral writers undertaking this form of thesis will be entirely clear on its basic form. However, that superficial clarity can readily give way to a sense of puzzlement about the structure and purposes of the linking texts. In a PBT, the author has to demonstrate their expertise even though the research in question has already been shaped and presented in article form. To do so requires that the writer understand that there are rhetorical functions of the thesis that have not been exhausted by the published articles. That is, the writer needs to understand that they may need to demonstrate their expertise with a substantial literature review, with an extended discussion of methods and methodological rationale, and with a fuller account of their data. In order to provide this essential display work, the author has to create an infrastructure for the thesis: a surrounding set of texts doing the thesis work that the articles were not built to do.

To teach the PBT, we need to teach doctoral writers about the overarching genre of the thesis and then help them to understand how their linking texts must meet those generic demands. As Misty Anne Winzenried argues in "Learning to Argue about the Literature: Discourse Choices and Students' Iterative Learning of Literature Reviews in Geography" (this volume), having genre awareness is not necessarily sufficient for the satisfactory production of the type of text in question; however, the introduction of genre raises the potential that a doctoral writer may be able to reframe their writing challenges in generic terms. The PBT has to do the same work as any thesis, but do so without the generic reassurance of a more integrated thesis. To help a doctoral writer find a more comfortable place from which to write, the challenges of the PBT need to be reframed as a by-product of a particular manifestation of the thesis genre. This reframing means, first, characterizing the challenges of the PBT as inherent to its disaggregation of research communication and expertise display and, second, treating the linking texts of the PBT as having distinct generic features. Grasping these features of the linking texts will allow doctoral writers to move beyond the idea that such texts are an arbitrary imposition, a kind of institutional busywork imposed on the writer even though they have already done the work of preparing their research for scholarly publication. Crucially, in my experience, exploring the justification for these linking texts helps doctoral writers to see that the difficulties of the PBT may be more in conception than in execution. In truth, writing the linking texts need not be as difficult as writing the articles; however, the degree of uncertainty attending those texts may mean that the writer finds them significantly more challenging.

CHALLENGES OF THE PUBLICATION-BASED THESIS

The most common challenges facing PBT writers are managing repetition and establishing coherence. Managing repetition is an issue since the publishable papers will already exist as standalone texts; when the writer tries to link the articles, they often struggle to write linking texts without simply repeating what has already been said. This concern about repetition needs to be seen within the broader context of thesis writing: the thesis writing process is already fraught with worries about repetition. Managing a book-length project inevitably involves anxiety about undue repetition. As writers live with a research project over a number of years, they can become so habituated to its fundamental dimensions that they naturally lose the ability to accurately conceptualize the needs of the reader; what the reader would experience as a healthy amount of repetition can start to feel, to the thesis writer, like a problematic degree of repetition. If this is, as I believe, a basic condition of thesis writing, it is exacerbated for the writer of a PBT, who will need to engage in some fairly explicit repetition. Establishing coherence is also challenging because the writer must introduce and situate a collection of papers that may not blend seamlessly. To bring together an assemblage of papers that may have been written at different points in time within an evolving research agenda requires a degree of higher-order thinking that may tax a thesis writer, especially one who is deeply engaged with the current minutiae of their project. While it is entirely possible to advise doctoral writers on how to manage repetition and cohesion in their particular PBT, these writers could benefit from a better understanding of the overarching generic features of a PBT; indeed, the struggles of PBT writers may be best understood as a lack of familiarity with the purposes of the linking texts. By using the notion of the thesis genre to elaborate on the purposes of the linking texts, instructors could guide doctoral writers to a deeper engagement with these texts. The very notion of undue repetition and insufficient coherence arguably comes from a misconception of the thesis genre. Once its rhetorical features are laid bare, the work of the linking texts starts to make sense: they are the locus for crucial display work. The perceived challenges of repetitiveness and incoherence can be reframed through an elaboration of the purpose of these moves.

In practice, reframing these challenges means showing how the PBT works to meet its generic demands by displaying common subgeneric patterns of the linking texts. In my work with doctoral writers in the classroom, I identify three such patterns: isolated scholarly display, strong authorial presence, and mediated repetition. The scholarly display work of the PBT is isolated in that it must appear outside the bounds of the research article. These linking texts will generally include a distinct literature review that is either a standalone chapter or a significant part of the introduction. Similarly, extensive discussions of methods, technical details, or raw data—all of which were necessarily excluded from the published articles—may appear in a PBT either in the linking texts or in appendices. Drawing attention to the isolated display work of a PBT allows me to highlight the rhetorical value of these linking texts; while the published articles may have done the work of research communication, the thesis itself requires something more from the writer. Isolating that display of expertise may not feel natural to a writer, but the presentation of that expertise will feel requisite for the thesis reader. Not understanding the rhetorical value of this isolated scholarly display can have an inhibiting effect on the writer: even when a writer has a great deal to say on a particular topic, concerns about the aptness of their communication can undermine a writer's confidence. Taking a generic approach to the linking texts can give the writer the confidence to elaborate on crucial material that might otherwise have felt awkward alongside the familiar rhythm of the research articles.

A strong authorial presence can also be discerned across the linking texts of the PBT; indeed, authorial voice is necessary since the overall thesis will have a unique structure. Each PBT is put together in a singular manner, reflective of the way the composite articles work together; authors must assert themselves to guide the reader through that singular structure. It is common to see a real difference between the authorial voice employed in the articles and that found in the linking texts. This authorial framing tends to appear in the introduction and the conclusion; it may also appear in prefatory remarks or in comments attached to the published articles. Since doctoral writers often manifest a certain reticence about placing themselves explicitly in the text as the author, these linking texts can place unwelcome authorial demands. The essential dynamic of these texts is to provide the authorial framing that will bring potentially dissimilar elements together in a manner that guides the reader and provides an adequate conceptualization of the whole research project. Drawing attention to the authorial voice required in a PBT allows me to highlight the legitimacy of the authority claimed by the writer who uses these linking texts to explain the coherence of their overall research project.

Finally, a close examination of PBT linking texts shows mediated repetition: material that is notably similar to that found in the articles must appear with significantly different framing. This mediated repetition can be offered unapologetically by the writer because it is expected by the reader. Drawing attention to repetition as an expected and desirable feature of the linking texts allows me to highlight a more nuanced understanding of repetition. For the reader, expertly managed repetition is their only route to understanding the overarching narrative of the full research project; when a thesis writer hesitates to use the linking texts to reiterate their project from a broader perspective, the thesis reader may struggle to see the project in sufficient breadth. An understanding of these three sub-generic features—isolated scholarly display, strong authorial presence, and mediated repetition—can help guide a thesis writer to produce linking texts that meet the demands of the broader thesis genre.

VALUE OF A GENRE-BASED APPROACH

Teaching the PBT as a particular manifestation of the thesis genre provides a way to guide doctoral writers before they start writing; using genre to reframe the challenges experienced by the writer makes it possible to give guidance that anticipates writing challenges rather than just responding to them once the writer is already struggling. Elaborating these patterns can save writers both time and frustration by acknowledging generic anomalies and then providing strategic guidance. Teaching the PBT in this way has also convinced me of its inherent value. By undertaking a PBT, doctoral writers are engaging with the pedagogical as well as the professional benefits of thesis writing (Aitchison et al., 2010). The traditional thesis is a highly pedagogical text, one that seeks to benefit the writer while requiring additional effort to arrive at publishable material for professional benefit (Paré, 2017). On the other hand, a true portfolio thesis can move the needle entirely in the direction of professional benefit without necessarily giving the writer the pedagogical benefits of thesis writing (Frick, 2019). Arguably, the PBT affords a doctoral writer the professional benefit of publishing while still requiring the development of crucial academic skills: the ability to articulate a sustained research agenda and the formation of an identity as an academic writer to communicate that research. As we saw above, the linking texts give the thesis writer space to articulate how the whole project coheres, even in cases when that coherence may feel elusive to the researcher. In a similar manner, the linking texts are an opportunity for the thesis writer to take explicit authorial responsibility for the text. Seen in this manner, the linking texts framed as crucial to the generic tasks of the thesis can potentially move from an unwelcome and arbitrary burden to an opportunity to build capacity in the realm of scholarly communication.

These intriguing benefits of the PBT mean that a doctoral writer undertaking this task may be getting a desirable blend of pedagogical and professional benefit from the thesis writing process. Given this possible benefit and the undeniable prevalence of the PBT model, supporting thesis writers by presenting its generic challenges and patterns is a worthwhile project. Doctoral researchers who are writing a PBT, even if they are doing so by choice, often express frustration at having to do anything beyond the already exacting task of publishing their research within a competitive scholarly communication context. Supporting these writers with an understanding of the generic challenges and patterns of the PBT can give them the ability to approach the linking texts with a sense of commitment to the value of those texts and a confidence in their own capacity to manage the challenges.

ACKNOWLEDGMENTS

I would like to thank the volume editors, Lesley Erin Bartlett, Sandra L. Tarabochia, Andrea R. Olinger, and Margaret J. Marshall, for their encouragement and insightful feedback. I'd also like to thank the reviewers for their helpful suggestions. When I presented this work to my colleagues at the University of Toronto's Graduate Centre for Academic Communication, they asked excellent questions that helped me to improve this chapter. Lastly, I'd like to thank the many U of T graduate students who have talked to me about their theses; those conversations inspired this work and continue to help me to understand the challenges associated with writing a publication-based thesis.

REFERENCES

Aitchison, C., Kamler, B. & Lee, A. (Eds.) (2010). *Publishing pedagogies for the doctorate and beyond.* Routledge. https://doi.org/10.4324/9780203860960.

Artemeva, N. (2004). Key concepts in rhetorical genre studies: An overview. *Technostyle, 20*(1), 3–38. https://doi.org/10.31468/cjsdwr.524.

Autry, M. K. & Carter, M. (2015). Unblocking occluded genres in graduate writing. *Composition Forum, 31*, n.p.

Bawarshi, A. S. & Reiff, M. J. (2010). *Genre: An introduction to history, theory, research, and pedagogy.* Parlor Press; The WAC Clearinghouse. https://wac.colostate.edu/books/perspectives/genre/.

Carter, S. (2011). Doctorate as genre: Supporting thesis writing across campus. *Higher Education Research & Development, 30*(6), 725–736. https://doi.org/10.1080/07294360.2011.554388.

Cheng, A. (2018). *Genre and graduate-level research writing.* University of Michigan Press. https://doi.org/10.3998/mpub.9558175.

Frick, L. (2019). PhD by publication: Panacea or paralysis? *Africa Education Review,* 1–13. https://doi.org/10.1080/18146627.2017.1340802.

Guerin, C. (2016). Connecting the dots: Writing a doctoral thesis by publication. In C. Badenhorst & C. Guerin (Eds.), *Research literacies and writing pedagogies for masters and doctoral writers* (pp. 31–50). Brill. https://doi.org/10.1163/9789004304338_003.

Jackson, D. (2013). Completing a Ph.D. by publication: A review of Australian policy and implications for practice. *Higher Education Research & Development, 32*(3), 355–368. https://doi.org/10.1080/07294360.2012.692666.

Kamler, B. & Thomson, P. (2008). The failure of dissertation advice books: Toward alternative pedagogies for doctoral writing. *Educational Researcher, 37*(8), 507–514. https://doi.org/10.3102/0013189X08327390.

Miller, C. R. (1984) Genre as social action. *Quarterly Journal of Speech, 70*(2), 151–167. https://doi.org/10.1080/00335638409383686.

Nethsinghe, R. & Southcott, J. (2015). A juggling act: Supervisor/candidate partnership in a doctoral thesis by publication. *International Journal of Doctoral Studies, 10,* 167. https://doi.org/10.28945/2256.

Paré, A. (2014). Rhetorical genre theory and academic literacy. *Association for Academic Language and Learning, 8*(1), A83-A94.

Paré, A. (2017). Re-thinking the dissertation and doctoral supervision/Reflexiones sobre la tesis doctoral y su supervisión. *Infancia y Aprendizaje, 40,* 407–428. https://doi.org/10.1080/02103702.2017.1341102.

Pretorius, M. (2017). Paper-based theses as the silver bullet for increased research outputs: First hear my story as a supervisor. *Higher Education Research & Development, 36*(4), 823–837. https://doi.org/10.1080/07294360.2016.1208639.

Robins, L. & Kanowski, P. (2008). Ph.D. by publication: A student's perspective. *Journal of Research Practice, 4*(2), 1–20.

Sharmini, S. (2018). Supervising a thesis that includes publications. In S. Carter & D. Laurs (Eds.), *Developing research writing: A handbook for supervisors and advisors* (pp. 140–143). Routledge. https://doi.org/10.4324/9781315541983-26.

Starke-Meyerring, D., Paré, A., Sun, K. Y. & El-Bezre, N. (2014). Probing normalized institutional discourses about writing: The case of the doctoral thesis. *Journal of Academic Language and Learning, 8*(2), A13-A27.

Swales, J. M. (2004). *Research genres: Explorations and applications.* Cambridge University Press. https://doi.org/10.1017/CBO9781139524827.

Tardy, C. M. (2009). *Building genre knowledge.* Parlor Press.

PART 3. APPROACHING DIFFERENCE TOGETHER: CREATIVE COLLABORATIONS ACROSS UNITS, DISCIPLINES, LANGUAGES, AND EXPERTISE

CHAPTER 10.

"SOMETHING INVISIBLE . . . HAS BEEN MADE VISIBLE FOR ME": AN EXPERTISE-BASED WAC SEMINAR MODEL GROUNDED IN THEORY AND (CROSS) DISCIPLINARY DIALOGUE

Angela Glotfelter
Miami University

Ann Updike
Miami University

Elizabeth Wardle
Miami University

In this chapter, we describe a theory- and expertise-based model of a WAC seminar we have developed in the Howe Center for Writing Excellence (HCWE) at Miami University (Ohio) called the Howe Faculty Writing Fellows Program. We describe our rationale for developing such a seminar, outline the components of the model, describe some of the work faculty have engaged in as a result of participating, and overview some of what we have learned thus far in our program assessment about faculty response to the model. The program is designed to change conceptions of writing as tied to disciplinary expertise, and our program assessment seems to be demonstrating success in achieving this goal. While there is still much to be learned from the data we have collected, we so far see evidence that the program is resulting in changed and expanded conceptions of writing, a greater recognition that disciplinary writing is inseparable from disciplinary threshold concepts, and a wide variety of changed teaching practices. Participants themselves, when asked what accounts for change in thinking and practice, point to the disciplinary teams and cross-disciplinary dialogues, while we

DOI: https://doi.org/10.37514/PER-B.2020.0360.2.10

also observe that many of the changes they report entail applications of particular theoretical lenses to which they were exposed.

Many WAC programs seek to promote institutional, long-term, sustainable changes around writing across campuses (Cox et al., 2018; Wilhoit, 2013). One-time workshops designed for individuals struggle to achieve such change or to alter faculty members' "view of the relationship between student writing and learning in their disciplines" (Wilhoit, 2013, p. 125). There are a variety of reasons for this, including the fact that enacting change in organizations requires groups rather than individuals, and that changing (mis)conceptions of writing and what it means to "teach writing" takes time. Semester- or year-long faculty learning communities have proven more successful in changing teaching practices than one-time workshops (Beach & Cox, 2009; Desrochers, 2010). Both Pamela Flash (2016) and Chris Anson and Deanna Dannels (2009) have worked to enact group-based changes by facilitating projects at the departmental level, relying on disciplinary faculty and their expertise to revise outcomes and curricula. They have had great success at their respective institutions, enabling departments to explore practices and outcomes around student writing and to create faculty-driven goals and plans for improving student writing. As Flash (2016) noted, however, helping faculty recognize what they implicitly know about writing and how their disciplinary discourses differ from others can be difficult. As Brad Hughes and Elisabeth Miller (2018) have recently discovered, simply having faculty from different disciplines in the same room is not enough to overcome this difficulty. Combining the opportunity for cross-disciplinary conversations provided by the Faculty Learning Community (FLC) model with an explicitly theory-based frame for departmental team-based WAC programs might be one way to facilitate the process of helping faculty "see" what they only know implicitly and examine their conceptions of writing in order to encourage ground-up change at a department level.

In this chapter we describe a WAC program that relies on disciplinary teams participating in a semester-long, cross-disciplinary seminar rooted in theories of threshold concepts, writing studies, and applied linguistics. Like Christy Goldsmith in "Making Connections Between Theory and Practice: Pre-Service Educator Disciplinary Literacy Courses as Secondary WAC Initiation" (this volume), we have discovered that learners find a theory-based approach rooted in their own expertise compelling, generative, and practical. Asking faculty to consider their underlying disciplinary assumptions and research-based ideas about writing, as embodied in threshold concepts, offers a means by which they can examine and, when necessary, change their conceptions about writing and how it works in disciplinary contexts. In addition, an expertise-based approach positions faculty as experts who can improve student writing in their disciplines in ways that outsiders to their discipline cannot. Their own expertise is more readily visible and nameable when they can compare their practices with those of other disciplines. Our Faculty Writing Fellows Program has been designed to change conceptions of writing as tied to disciplinary expertise, and our program assessment seems to be demonstrating success in this area. However, moving from changes in individual faculty conceptions of writing to larger changes in conceptions held by entire departments proves to be a more elusive goal.

FOREFRONTING THEORY IN A WAC MODEL OF FACULTY DEVELOPMENT

Rolf Norgaard (1999) argued that WAC staff may struggle to reach faculty in varied disciplines if we cannot find ways to value the expertise of those faculty—including ways to help them name what they implicitly know and do as experts in their fields (pp. 44–45). In a special issue of *Across the Disciplines*, scholars argued for expanding the European notion of Integrating Content and Language (ICL) or Content and Language Integrated Learning (CLIL) in order to foster "the exchange of knowledge and experience regarding collaboration between content . . . and language [specialists] in higher education contexts" (Gustafsson et al., 2011, n.p.). They suggested creating "productive institutional discursive spaces" that transgressed "disciplinary boundaries [with] the potential to bridge the distance between communication specialists and disciplinary specialists" (2011, n.p.). They argued that, in these spaces, faculty can "reflect on what they are doing differently and theorize [about] why they are doing it differently" (2011, n.p.). The focus in such spaces is not on workshops where writing faculty teach what Walvoord et al. (2011) called "WAC strategies" (p. 1) but rather "on disciplinary discourse as access to disciplinary content knowledge" (Gustafsson et al., 2011, n.p.).

What might such a discursive space look like in practice? When Elizabeth was newly appointed as the director of the Howe Center for Writing Excellence (HCWE) at Miami University (Ohio) in 2016, she hoped to design a WAC model that forefronted theory on writing and learning from writing studies, threshold concepts, and applied linguistics. A similar impetus has guided previous scholarship on first-year composition (Wardle, 2004, 2009, 2013) and led to a "writing about writing" approach (Wardle & Downs, 2007, 2012, 2014, 2016). There has been subsequent success, providing students the lenses, tools, and language to understand for themselves how writing works in order to empower them to make their own decisions about effective rhetorical responses. The same could be true for faculty enrolled in WAC seminars.

169

In considering how to design such a WAC program, University of Minnesota's Writing Enriched Curriculum (WEC) (Flash, 2016) and North Carolina State's Communication Across the Curriculum (CAC) program (Anson & Dannels, 2009) served as models. Both emphasize the autonomy and expertise of faculty members and departments rather than the expertise and strategies to be imparted by the writing specialists, who instead serve as facilitators and consultants. While both models were helpful to our planning in many ways, neither included an interdisciplinary discursive space (as both center around intensive work within one department) or an explicit theoretical frame (though both, clearly, are guided *by* theory).

Threshold concepts can provide a framework for a faculty WAC seminar, as Chris Anson (2015) suggested in his chapter in *Naming What We Know*. Erik Meyer and Ray Land (2003) noted that faculty in various disciplines identified what Meyer and Land began to call "threshold concepts"—concepts critical for epistemological participation in a discipline. They identified several characteristics of such concepts: they are troublesome, transformational, and integrative; they illustrate the boundaries of disciplinary territory and enact both ways of knowing and ways of practicing in a particular field. Learning them also requires recursive time in a liminal space—time that can't be rushed.

Ian Kinchin, Lyndon Cabot, and David Hay (2010) have argued that the threshold concept framework provides an "expertise-based model" of teaching and thus, implicitly, of professional development, that places "subject specialists at the centre of pedagogic developments" (p. 81). The expertise-based model "places [faculty] development within the disciplines, using familiar discourse" (Meyer et al., 2010, p. 91). In this model,

> not all teaching has to change. . . . Rather than dictating to
> academics how they *should* [emphasis added] act, part of the
> reason for visualizing the hidden processes of expertise is
> to make explicit how they already *do* [emphasis added] act.
> The strength of the pedagogy of expertise therefore lies not
> in its prescriptive ability, but rather in its descriptive ability.
> (Kinchin et al., 2010, pp. 91–92)

The threshold concepts framework can help disciplinary experts examine what they already know about writing and how they use writing in their disciplines. With such implicit knowledge and assumptions made explicit, they can make informed and expertise-based decisions about writing in their classrooms—and also make the values and beliefs behind such decisions visible to their students.

THE SEMINAR DESIGN

The threshold concepts-based WAC seminar, Howe Faculty Writing Fellows, that we began offering at Miami in Spring 2017 was designed to attempt to enact all of these ideas (see Wardle, 2019).[1] To participate, faculty must come in programmatic teams in order to better name and draw on their expertise (and have a greater likelihood of making change when they return to their departments). Teams from multiple disciplines participate at the same time so that they can see similarities and differences across their communities of practice. Participants meet one and a half hours a week for a full semester or three hours a day each day for a two- to three-week intensive summer program. Participants spend the first three-quarters of the seminar thinking about theory and naming their expert practices; then they engage in a change-making project of their choosing. Participants receive $2,000 in professional development funds.

The program proceeds in the following segments (for a sample schedule, see Appendix A):

- Introducing the threshold concepts framework (Cousin, 2006; Meyer & Land, 2003);
- Having teams identify threshold concepts of their disciplines/subdisciplines;
- Having teams work with threshold concepts of writing and test them against their own experiences and knowledge (Adler-Kassner & Wardle, 2015);
- Considering the idea of disciplinary values and ideologies and examining how those are enacted in their writing (Hyland, 2000; Swales, 1990);
- Reading about theories of learning, prior knowledge, and transfer (Ambrose et al., 2010);
- Surveying ideas for teaching and responding to writing (Bean, 2011); and
- Working on team projects and presenting them in a final showcase.

Nearly every day is spent with teams and individuals engaging in activities to test and better understand the theories. After learning about the threshold concepts framework (Cousin, 2006; Meyer & Land, 2003), for example, participants spend time identifying some of the troublesome threshold concepts of their own disciplines or subdisciplines, which they then teach to the teams from

---

1   This seminar is only one piece of our larger WAC program. Other elements include stand-alone workshops and lunches, one-on-one consulting, writing groups and writing hours, an assignment review service, and oversight of the university's "advanced writing" requirement (see http://miamioh.edu/hcwe/hwac/about/index.html).

other departments. The purpose is to help faculty get explicit about the practices and processes that inform their expectations and conventions around writing and disciplinary knowledge and epistemology. The teams engage enthusiastically in this activity, naming threshold concepts such as these:

- gerontology: aging, a social and cultural construction of a biological phenomenon; intersectionality
- anthropology: ethnocentrism, cultural relativism; holism; biocultural change
- family science and social work: empowerment, dignity, unconditional positive regard
- philosophy: appearance/reality distinction, condition for possibility, mental geography, for the sake of argument

Next they read the first four sections of *Naming What We Know* (Adler-Kassner & Wardle, 2015) and, with their teams, interrogate some of those writing-related threshold concepts in light of their own practices, uncovering what they already know about writing based on how they use writing as experts and in their daily lives. The goal is to give them language and a framework for considering what they already do with and know about writing and how that might then inform how they use writing in their classrooms. For example, when they consider the idea that writing mediates activity and gets things done, they fill the whiteboards with all the purposes for which they use writing and the various forms that writing takes. Through this activity they illustrate that they write daily for many purposes, that purposes take many forms, and that form follows function—yet in classrooms, forms may tend to be rigid and purposes may tend to be limited. In other words, by interrogating their own practices, they come to understand some of the basic tenets of rhetorical genre theory.

After several weeks, participants interrogate how their disciplinary values and social goals are enacted in their discipline's textual conventions. They read excerpts from John Swales (1990) and Ken Hyland (2000) to acquire some language and lenses for this linguistic analysis. Each participant brings an article from their field, trades with a partner from a different discipline, and asks questions such as: What's familiar and strange here? What counts as evidence? What theories frame the work? Who is cited and how? Here participants are trying to identify their often buried and unstated assumptions about what they think constitutes "good writing."

By this point in the seminar, participants have collected enough information, reflected extensively about writing and their own experiences with writing, and made explicit enough of their implicit knowledge to try to explain what they think counts as "good writing" in ways that the other disciplinary groups might understand well enough to try to operationalize. The philosophy faculty,[2] for example, wrote the following:

"Good" writing in philosophy
- is a clearly articulated motivated problem or question that has not been considered or considered in this way before
- situates itself within the scholarly conversation on this topic
- allows the reader to see something in a new way
- provides and follows a conceptual map articulated at the beginning
- doesn't get caught up in jargon but understands its significance

Teams often see some similarities across disciplines but notice in their article exchanges that particular conventions or "moves" are enacted quite differently in different disciplines (for example, what constitutes effective and expected "organization" differs; what counts as "jargon" or "common knowledge" is quite different across disciplines, and not immediately obvious to newcomers or outsiders). At times, participants realize that expectations for writing that seem obvious to them are not easily understood by other teams—or that other disciplines would not accept particular conventions (for example, whether narrative and storytelling is expected or unacceptable is often a source of discussion). Faculty teams then draw on everything they have done so far to complete a "Mad Libs"[3] (see Appendix B) activity where they try to operationalize their ideas about writing by filling in incomplete sentences (like: "we tend to write in genres such as _____.") They present these to the other teams to test whether or not they are able to describe their work and discourse in ways that are accessible to outsiders and, particularly, to students (see, for example, Figure 10.1).

Finally, team members then work on a team project of their choosing. Sometimes, those final projects entail turning their Mad Libs and other ideas into writing resources that are accessible to students. For example, Philosophy turned their Mad Libs into a document directly for students, titled "So . . . you're taking a philosophy course" (see https://www.miamioh.edu/hcwe/hwac/teaching-support/disciplinary-writing-hwac/philosophy/index.html). In this document, they not only named and operationalized some "essential methods and tools" for writing in philosophy, but linked to examples of each (e.g., "distinguishing between conceptual and empirical" links students to a fuller description of what that means and looks like in writing). The philosophers then annotated a student paper to further illustrate where and how the moves and ideas outlined in that previous explanation play out in writing.

---

2   Philosophy team members: Keith Fennen, Elaine Miller, and Gaile Polhaus, Jr.

3   Thanks to Linda Adler-Kassner and Heidi Estrem, who use similar activities and have enhanced our thinking about the "Mad Libs" activity.

Our field of <u>Philosophy</u> is rooted in the study of <u>the nature of anything and every-</u><u>thing.</u> The goals for our work <u>are contestable but nonetheless include understand-</u><u>ing being (including possible being), articulating what it means to know, and how</u><u>to live well individually, with others, and with nature.</u> We have some fundamental ways of <u>looking at reality or doing conceptual analysis.</u> Sometimes outsiders or newcomers misunderstand or are confused or surprised <u>by the lack of agreement on</u><u>anything in our field.</u> Some "threshold concepts" that have grown up around our work and are central to being able to do work in this field include <u>distinguishing</u><u>between the conceptual and the empirical, making conceptual distinctions and</u><u>connections, logical validity, and tracing the genealogy of ideas.</u> Our field tends to value <u>critique and often or usually empirical data is not as valued or forefronted.</u> Our values and threshold concepts are embodied in how and what we write. We tend to write in genres such as <u>argumentative essays.</u> We rarely write <u>reports or sur-</u><u>veys.</u> We find writers to be credible when they <u>situate themselves within a scholarly</u><u>debate and when they use conceptual analysis, present a logically valid argument,</u><u>and charitably consider opposing positions.</u> Effective writing in our field tends to <u>walk you through a sequence of thoughts about a question or problem, and may</u><u>consider multiple sides, even those the author disagrees with.</u> Ultimately the goal is to <u>draw you in and transform your thinking.</u> Our citation practices embody and help enact our values and goals. You can see this in how we <u>commonly make</u><u>reference to other philosophers with whom we are in dialogue, including dead ones.</u><u>Names are foregrounded in our citations, and, without necessarily documenting it,</u><u>reference is often made to classical problems without further explanation.</u> Cita-tions are rarely used <u>simply to establish authority.</u> Thus, our advice to you when you write in our classes is to <u>imagine yourself in dialogue with the texts you are</u><u>discussing, rather than simply reporting on them (the authors of the texts are also</u><u>not simply reporting facts to you).</u>

Figure 10.1. The Mad Libs statement drafted by the philosophy team.

Other teams have redesigned courses or assignments, designed new courses, created resources for faculty in their departments, and designed workshops for their departments, among other projects. Some of their projects are described on our website: http://miamioh.edu/hcwe/hwac/about/miami-writing-spotlight/index.html (Miami Writing Spotlight, 2018).

AFTER THE SEMINAR: FACULTY-GENERATED DISCIPLINARY WRITING RESOURCES

Faculty members are not required to complete any additional work after the seminar ends. However, many of them regularly attend our other WAC events, and we have been designing follow-up events and activities solely for Fellows graduates. After the seminar ends, our staff members follow up in order to assist

Fellows if they wish to revise the seminar materials to create disciplinary writing resources for students and writing center consultants. The purpose of these disciplinary writing resources is to provide an introduction to writing within particular disciplines through the lens of threshold concepts. These resources build on the theoretical explorations and naming that Fellows began during the program but include concrete examples of specific values or conventions. Such concrete examples are important in helping writers try to distinguish among what teachers from varied disciplines are asking them to do and in assisting students who are asked to write in new ways. Students need examples of how writing "a logical, organized, evidence-based argument that is written clearly and directly" differs across disciplines, especially when quite different conventions are referred to by the same name across disciplinary classrooms. The Mad Libs activity often serves as an effective "roadmap" as faculty decide what writing values and conventions—including common genres, citation practices, and expectations—they would like to illustrate for students.

The Mad Libs statement is also useful for students as they learn how to write and think and practice like a gerontologist, historian, biologist, etc. Many Fellows have annotated scholarly articles or shared exemplary pieces of student writing, pointing out places where writers are making moves common in their fields. Faculty have also provided other examples that are helpful for students, including visualizations of complex concepts, lists of vocabulary or jargon, videos discussing writing conventions or citation style, and more. HCWE staff compile these pieces into a cohesive disciplinary resource that is shared on our website and can be used by a wide range of audiences including faculty, students, and writing consultants. These resources look different by discipline, but they generally include

- an explanation of threshold concepts in the discipline
- the naming of writing conventions/values in the discipline
- examples that help illustrate those writing conventions/values

To illustrate, we detail one disciplinary writing resource developed for the discipline of gerontology (Glotfelter et al., 2018).[4] The gerontology resource begins with an adaptation of their Mad Libs statement:

> Being a Gerontologist means more than just studying later life
> and applying methods to solve problems. It means having a
> "Gerontological voice. . . ." Writers are seen as credible when
> they present a conceptual context that draws from multiple

---

4   All the guides are available at https://www.miamioh.edu/hcwe/hwac/teaching-support
/disciplinary-writing-hwac/index.html.

disciplinary areas and demonstrate methodological sophistication and rigor. Papers should represent a "dialogue." The field's citations practices embody these values, and you can see that in the breadth of sources used, with specific citations from Gerontology sources. Citations should be purposeful, strategic, and support the writer's argument/claim and avoid overgeneralizations, oversimplifications, and unfounded opinions. Effective writing in Social Gerontology does the following:

- presents logical, parsimonious argument with neutral language
- uses standard signposts and structure
- avoids absolutes
- demonstrates respectful authority

This gerontology resource also includes graphics to visually depict the interdisciplinary nature of the field (see Figure 10.2), as well as a word cloud showing scholars who are widely cited (see Figure 10.3).

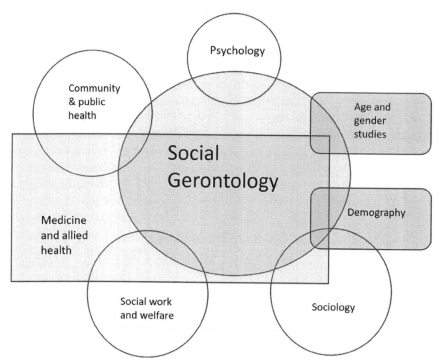

Figure 10.2. Visual representation of the interdisciplinary nature of the field of gerontology

In Figure 10.2, the interdisciplinary nature of the field of gerontology is represented using a Venn diagram. "Social Gerontology" appears in a beige circle in the middle of the figure. The names of other fields appear in shapes that surround and overlap with Social Gerontology. Starting at the top and moving clockwise are the following fields: psychology, age and gender studies (also overlaps with medicine and allied health), demography (also overlaps with sociology and medicine and allied health), sociology (also overlaps with demography and medicine and allied health), social work and welfare (also overlaps with medicine and allied health), medicine and allied health (also overlaps with age and gender studies, demography, sociology, social work and welfare, and community and public health), and community and public health (also overlaps with medicine and allied health).

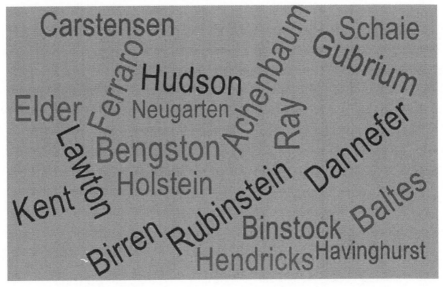

Figure 10.3. Word cloud of widely cited scholars in gerontology.

In Figure 10.3, the names of influential theorists/researchers are stacked on top of each other. The names (from top to bottom: Lawton, Kent, Bengston, Dannefer, Ferraro, Rubinstein, Cole, Hudson, Elder, Baltes, Achenbaum, Ray, Holstein, Binstock, Settersten, Gubrium, Birren, Schaie, Hendricks, Carstensen, Havinghurst, and Neugartenare) appear in different colors over a black background.

The guide concludes with an annotated journal article that illustrates how particular writing conventions are enacted in that article. The conventions they highlight include the following:

- "respectful authority"
- signposting
- descriptive headings
- diverse sources from relevant disciplines

This resource presents readers with both a theoretical explanation of how writing happens in the field of Gerontology and practical examples of how the field's values and characteristics appear in writing. All of the disciplinary writing resources faculty have created are flexible enough to be used in a variety of contexts, including writing center consultations, faculty/student conferences, and for student reference.

While we understand these resources as flexible, we have wondered whether articulating and writing about the conventions of a field might suggest that these conventions are rigid and stable across time. In other words, can naming conventions run the risk of reifying calcified beliefs that may be problematic or even inequitable? Clearly, faculty must introduce the materials to students in ways that carefully frame and contextualize. We encourage teams to explain when there are conflicts or multiple means of achieving a writing goal or to explain why some conventions are as they are. Faculty in some fields have found that they dislike or disagree with commonly accepted conventions, and they subsequently have the language to explain conflicts to students rather than reinforce them or suggest that they are universally accepted.[5]

ASSESSING THE WRITING FELLOWS THUS FAR

We began offering the Fellows seminar in the Spring 2017 semester and have run a total of six seminars, graduating 71 alumni representing 19 departments/programs and five of Miami's six divisions. The response to our invitations to participate has been positive with very little advertising or recruiting needed, at least for these first cohorts. There are several likely reasons for this. One is that the program aligns well with the values Miami has long embodied. Teaching is deeply valued and supported in myriad ways, and Miami is regularly listed in *US News and World Report* as among the best institutions nationally for undergraduate teaching. The Faculty Learning Community model originated at Miami and continues to be popular through the Center for Teaching Excellence. Thus, the Fellows program as we have been enacting it is dispositionally suited for our

---

5   There is much more to be said about how discourse enacts and entrenches oppressive practices (see Prendergast, 1998; Green & Condon, this volume) and what the WAC Fellows seminar can do to help faculty recognize such practices. However, space does not allow us to adequately elaborate in this chapter; we will do so in a future publication.

local academic environment. Another likely reason we have good response to the program is that Elizabeth's arrival at Miami coincided with a new general education writing requirement ("advanced writing") that required her to consult immediately with many departments and faculty across campus. These relationships and conversations also made it possible for the HCWE and its new director to gain credibility and for the new Fellows program to attract some attention across campus.

We have assessed the Fellows program in a number of ways. The primary goal of all our assessments is to learn what the impact of the program has been on how faculty think about writing and teaching writing, with the assumption that these changes, coupled with their own expertise, will lead to changes in both individual and, perhaps, departmental teaching practices. It has not been our goal to assess faculty members' teaching directly or to assess their students' writing; we consider those to be assessments and research projects that faculty members and departments should initiate, though we do ask them to self-report on how their teaching has changed since the Fellows seminar. Our assessments thus far include administering an anonymous survey at the end of each semester's program, one anonymous follow-up survey of all previous participants (35 at the time), and holding one focus group with four faculty members representing four departments and three colleges. The graduate assistants and associate director also take notes as they observe each seminar session. In addition, our graduate assistants (Angela Glotfelter and Caitlin Martin) have conducted interviews with former participants intended to learn more about people, programs, or practices that we can describe in our Miami Writing Spotlight (2018) feature. We have received IRB approval to use all of this assessment and interview data for research purposes. All the survey responses and interview and focus group transcripts were uploaded to Atlas.ti, and the three of us plus Caitlin Martin, who joined our team after the IWAC presentation, read it together for recurring themes which helped us develop codes. While there is still a great deal to be learned from the data we have collected, faculty members frequently describe changed and expanded conceptions of writing after completing the program, pointing to how the invisible is now visible to them. In their explanations of how they understand writing, they frequently illustrate an understanding that writing in their disciplines is inseparable from its disciplinary threshold concepts. Faculty members frequently talk about changes in their teaching.

Fellows often point to both extended conversations within their disciplinary teams plus the ability to see differences across the disciplinary teams as one reason they came to the insights they did. We also surmise that being exposed to relevant theories and then using those to immediately interrogate their ideas within and across disciplines aids movement toward change.

EXPANDING CONCEPTIONS OF WRITING

Surveys, interviews, and focus groups all suggest that faculty members' conceptions of writing shift in fairly dramatic ways during the program. For some participants, this means that their ideas of what "counts" as writing shifted and expanded. For example, an economist said during the focus group, "My perception of what constitutes writing has changed a lot. . . . Because if you'd asked me before we started, 'Do your Intro to Econ students write?' I would have said, 'No. They don't write; they just solve this equation; they graph it. And they might explain the implications of that a little bit.' But having our discussions . . . [in Fellows] . . . showed me that when I ask them to do that on the exam, they're actually writing."

For others, expanding conceptions of writing has meant more deeply inhabiting some of the threshold concepts about writing that we discussed during the program. As an example, a social work faculty member stated, "Writing is not natural. I think that I repeat that now way more now than I used to. I think I knew it, but now I really *know* it. And I say it to students and I mean it in a way that I don't think I did before. So it's not natural. . . . [I]t is a skill [and] you can get better at it. [T]hat takes practice. And these are going to be the opportunities to practice."

Faculty also recognize that writing differs across disciplines and that students cannot be expected to understand writing in their discipline unless faculty explicitly teach it. As one historian put it, "I was just so struck by . . . how different our norms of good writing are from our colleagues *in this building* (the gerontologists)—to say nothing of the [business] people . . . [I]t was really striking . . . and . . . the disciplinary cultures, of course, are inculcated in our student population." An anthropologist noted, "When we saw what another discipline valued, we realized how we do things differently, that we value different things." We have found that faculty expressed realizations about disciplinarity and disciplinary writing that were similar to the way that Goldsmith (this volume) describes what pre-service teachers learned when constructing an interdisciplinary lesson plan. These pre-service teachers were able to use their evolving sense of themselves as disciplinary experts and their recognition of interdisciplinary literacies to explicitly teach their students disciplinary writing conventions. So, too, Faculty Fellows come to realize that differences in disciplinary literacy practices are not transparent to students and must be taught explicitly. Instead of siloing disciplines further, articulating disciplinary differences can actually allow faculty to see more clearly and communicate across disciplinary lines.

By the end of the program, faculty tend not to assume that students should have learned their disciplinary conceptions of "good writing" in first-year composition or another writing course taught by English faculty. They recognize the challenges students face writing across the curriculum and into their chosen discipline and the responsibility this places on them to teach writing themselves. As one faculty member noted: "They can't learn what you don't teach."

INSEPARABILITY OF DISCIPLINARY WRITING AND THRESHOLD CONCEPTS

Another frequent trend in our assessment data is that faculty often acquire an understanding of how disciplinary writing is inseparable from disciplinary content and threshold concepts. While faculty might come into the program believing that they have to "make room" for writing in their syllabi, many leave with the realization that writing and disciplinary content are inseparable and that students learn the values and content of their discipline through writing about it and practicing disciplinary genres. A faculty member from history commented that he had realized "how many assumptions about writing in history are wrapped up in assumptions about the discipline itself. . . . It was really useful to think about how difficult it is to teach writing apart from these other deeper disciplinary assumptions." This history faculty member left the program with a deep understanding of how connected their ways of writing are to their ways of thinking and practicing in history.

Some faculty came to understand themselves to be writing like a "philosopher," "historian," or "biologist" and to recognize the implications for their scholarly work and interdisciplinary collaborations. A faculty member from gerontology described her emerging awareness of why writing with and for scholars from other fields is difficult:

> I've been working with philosophers . . . and [the Fellows program] makes me now more aware of the fact that I'm writing for philosophers: . . . What might their threshold concepts be? How are they going to interpret—how can I tell my story in their voice when it's not a language that I necessarily speak? So [Fellows] makes me more aware of the differences . . . we're talking about aging, but even our fundamental starting point is just completely different. I never cite Aristotle for anything. Just how . . . arguments are built—[Fellows] has made me very aware of thinking about how other people approach their arguments, and it's not a one size fits all.

Participants come to recognize, then, that all aspects of writing, from what is cited to how much is cited to how much of an argument is made explicit, are tied to disciplinary conventions, beliefs, and knowledge.

CHANGES IN TEACHING PRACTICES

We asked faculty in the survey of 35 graduates, as well as in the interviews and focus group, to describe any changes they have made in teaching. We did not ask about any specific teaching practices or activities in the Fellows program, as we cover very few except in passing discussions and as examples of particular ideas (although faculty are given a copy of *Engaging Ideas*, by Bean, 2011, and *How Learning Works*, by Ambrose et al., 2010, and they share their own teaching practices quite frequently). Rather, we hope to learn what *they* have innovated as a result of their changes in thinking about writing itself. In their responses, faculty frequently talk about providing more scaffolding, breaking large writing assignments down into smaller parts, and allowing more time for writing. For example, one anonymous survey respondent said, "While I used scaffolded writing in the past, I have increased the number of low-stakes assignments, and become more deliberate in tailoring them to specific, initially limited objectives."

Faculty also describe an increased awareness of the need to explicitly tell students what they expect and why they are giving particular writing assignments, as well as providing students written examples. One survey respondent said they do more "modeling [of] processes," while another said they "use far more examples so students can first 'mimic' what they read and write and move on from there." (Mimicry is frequently discussed in the literature as expected and necessary when students are in the liminal space of learning new threshold concepts.)

Faculty also talked about specific activities and practices that changed, but these varied widely and there seemed to be no one common activity or practice that changed for a majority of the graduates. Fellows mentioned changing when and how they responded to writing (earlier rather than later in the drafting process), teaching about citation and source use more explicitly, moving large assignments from the end of the semester to the middle, moving more toward writing and away from exams. Faculty members and teams also designed new assignments and even courses, but, again, what they did and why has varied widely—as we expected and imagined it would, given the philosophy of the program. Some of these changes are described on our website at https://miamioh .edu/hcwe/hwac/about/miami-writing-spotlight/.

WHAT ACCOUNTS FOR CHANGES?

So far, our program assessments have suggested that faculty who complete the program have experienced changes in both their thinking about writing and in their classroom practices. What might account for these changes? Participants themselves, when asked, point to the disciplinary teams and cross-disciplinary dialogues, while we also observe that many of the changes that they report entail applications of particular theoretical lenses to which participants were exposed.

Disciplinary and Cross-Disciplinary Dialogue

Repeatedly, seminar participants pointed to having extended time to talk with their own disciplinary colleagues, combined with comparing their experiences to those of other disciplines, as the reason for many of their insights. In terms of time with their own colleagues, participants noted that space for talking about ideas and teaching within their departments is lacking in their daily work lives, so simply having extended space to talk was important to their thinking. In an interview, the philosophers emphasized the importance of having time to talk with one another about teaching and writing in their own discipline, recognizing that even this extended time will not be enough, and then also being able to see how what they are doing does or doesn't align with teaching and learning in other departments:

> It was the combination of having two of my colleagues
> with me *and* colleagues from other departments . . . now I
> understand my own students when they [ask] "What kind
> of bibliographic style do you want?" [Because] I don't care.
> And then when I heard people from international studies say,
> "Oh my god, I care, I really care." And then to ask them why.
> [N]ow I can . . . see where my students are coming from a
> little bit better. But to have also [the other two philosophers]
> along . . . [T]he balance of having people who do understand
> me and people who don't understand me at the same time was
> . . . immensely helpful.

Thus, spending time with colleagues but also noticing differences and connections across disciplines helped make the invisible visible. As one philosopher explained, "Now I feel like there's something invisible that has been made visible for me, and now I can make it visible for my students as well."

This idea of cross-disciplinary dialogue as catalyst for making the invisible visible is a thread we have seen throughout the interviews and surveys. For example, an economist made this observation:

> That was probably the most eye-opening thing for me . . .
> you got to see how different fields emphasized different kinds
> of writing styles . . . taking a step back and [asking], "Well,
> why aren't they writing the way that I write?" . . . Having that
> perspective . . . helped in terms of shaping the writing instruc-
> tions and pointing out examples.

Once faculty recognize their own invisible assumptions and conventions, they then move to a realization of how difficult it must be for their students to learn diverse discourses at once—and they resolve to be more explicit in their teaching.

Learning and Applying Theories

The initial, underlying assumption of the Fellows program was that providing theoretical lenses and tools for faculty rather than "how-tos" or lists of best practices would be useful and potentially transformative. While threshold concepts provided the main lens, we also relied on linguistic theories from John Swales (1990) and Ken Hyland (2000). Additionally, we implicitly covered theories as embodied in the writing threshold concepts that we discussed; genre theory, in particular, was referenced many times during the program to explain and frame ideas and activities. Repeatedly in the assessment data we see these theories frame ideas that faculty members describe as having changed. For example, the way graduates talk about source use and citation changed fairly radically as a result of the Hyland and Swales readings, which were coupled with analysis of articles across disciplines. Faculty from across the cohorts stopped talking about citation as following rules, and began talking about citation as socially motivated and achieving goals and conventions of their disciplines. A social work faculty member gave this explanation in the focus group:

> It wasn't until after the workshop that I had language to talk about, What does it mean to say, "So-and-so and so-and-so, paren., date," as opposed to a little footnote and what that conveys? . . . [T]hat has been . . . a great way to not only talk about citations, but the whys behind and the importance of it, and that's . . . changed the plagiarism conversation. . . . I'm talking about honoring the ancients, if you will. And *that* students get.

Faculty members also talk about genre conventions and genres themselves as specific to disciplines and socially motivated. The theoretical frames seem to have taken hold and continue to influence faculty members' thinking long after the program ended.

CONCLUSION

The Faculty Fellows program values faculty and disciplinary expertise, providing a theoretical framework that empowers faculty members, recognizes them as experts already in disciplinary writing, and allows them to make their own innovations and choices about teaching writing. Some faculty noticed and explicitly commented on the design of the program in its effort to value and forefront faculty expertise and a theoretical frame. An anthropologist pulled one of us aside after the last day of the seminar to share his appreciation for an approach that valued his own expertise:

> This workshop was so refreshing because we weren't treated like children, which has been my experience at so many other workshops. I mean, you did not have the attitude of "I'm the expert in this area and I'm going to tell you everything you need to know and do." [You] allowed faculty to come to their own realizations, define their own outcomes within the framework.

These and other similar responses suggest that Kinchin et al.'s (2010) recognition of the need to value what faculty already know and to provide them a theoretical lens and vocabulary for coming up with their own ideas for teaching are important and effective components of a WAC model.

Our programmatic assessment suggests there is value in forefronting theory over practice—and that faculty enjoy and are engaged by this approach. We've learned that faculty are most engaged when they are acting from and examining their own expert practice (instead of being lectured to about ours). And they are better able to visualize and name their own expert practices when they can compare and contrast across disciplinary boundaries. The cross-disciplinary contact zones that Norgaard (1999) argued for can be extremely productive sites for faculty to reflect on what they are doing differently and why.

When faculty are able to recognize and name accurate conceptions of writing, they are then empowered to innovate assignments and practices appropriate to their goals and contexts—something we could not do for them as disciplinary outsiders. If we agree that writing and content are truly inseparable, then faculty must be empowered in this way to design innovative writing tasks and assignments that enact and help students learn about (and even critique) their disciplinary values, goals, methodologies, and threshold concepts. What needs to change are faculty conceptions of what writing is and how writing works. If we design assignments and activities for them, this change in conception and the enactment of that change is never realized. We have now seen in action that once faculty conceptions about writing truly shift, they don't call us in panic or frustration very much, because they know what to do and when and how it works or doesn't—and they generally have a better sense of why something might be going wrong.

Where Faculty Writing Fellows graduates do need support is in returning to their departments and helping enact department-wide change. While their conceptions of writing have changed, their colleagues' have not. And there is little space in the daily interactions and work of an academic department to tackle that problem. So this year we are piloting various "Phase 2" follow ups: we have helped lead discussions with three full departments, held follow up "high-impact happy hours" with all graduates to share experiences and generate ideas for further support, and are planning a three-day intensive course on assignment redesign for graduates. In moving from departmental teams to full-department conversations, we can look to the examples of Anson and Dannels and Flash. In fact, we might imagine the Fellows seminar as a gateway to the larger departmental work that Anson and Flash have developed.

ACKNOWLEDGMENTS

We are grateful to Roger and Joyce Howe, who provided the resources to make the work of the Howe Center possible. We also appreciate all of the Howe Faculty Writing Fellows who have participated in our programming and generously participated in follow-up interviews and focus groups. Finally, we want to acknowledge the ideas and generosity of Caitlin Martin, a graduate student assistant director who joined our team after this article was in progress, but whose work has in many ways influenced the final draft of what we've written here.

REFERENCES

Adler-Kassner, L. & Wardle, E. (Eds.). (2015). *Naming what we know: Threshold concepts of writing studies*. Utah State University Press. https://doi.org/10.7330/9780874219906.

Ambrose, S. A., Bridges, M. W., DiPietro, M., Lovett, M. C. & Norman, M. K. (2010). *How learning works: Seven research-based principles for smart teaching*. Jossey-Bass.

Anson, C. M. (2015). Crossing thresholds: What's to know about writing across the curriculum. In L. Adler-Kassner & E. Wardle. (Eds.), *Naming what we know: Threshold concepts of writing studies* (pp. 203–219). Utah State University Press. https://doi.org/10.7330/9780874219906.c0013.

Anson, C. M. & Dannels, D. (2009). Profiling programs: Formative uses of departmental consultations in the assessment of communication across the curriculum. *Across the Disciplines, 6*, 1–15. https://wac.colostate.edu/docs/atd/assessment/anson_dannels.pdf.

Beach, A. L. & Cox, M. (2009). The impact of faculty learning communities on teaching and learning. *Learning Communities Journal, 1*(1), 7–27.

Bean, J. (2011). *Engaging ideas: The professor's guide to integrating writing, critical thinking, and active learning in the classroom* (2nd ed.). Jossey-Bass.

Cousin, G. (2006). An introduction to threshold concepts. *Planet, 17*, 4–5. https://doi.org/10.11120/plan.2006.00170004.

Cox, M., Galin, J. & Melzer, D. (2018). *Sustainable WAC: A whole systems approach to launching and developing writing across the curriculum programs.* National Council of Teachers of English.

Desrochers, C. G. (2010). Faculty learning communities as catalysts for implementing successful small-group learning. In J. Cooper & P. Robinson (Eds.), *Small group learning in higher education: Research and practice* (pp. 1–17). New Forums Press.

Flash, P. (2016). From apprised to revised: Faculty in the disciplines change what they never knew they knew. In K. B. Yancey (Ed.), *A rhetoric of reflection* (pp. 227–249). Utah State University Press. https://doi.org/10.7330/9781607325161.c011.

Glotfelter, A., Kunkel, S., de Medeiros, K. & Kinney, J. (2018). *Writing in gerontology.* http://miamioh.edu/hcwe/disciplinary-writing/gerontology/index.html.

Gustafsson, M., Eriksson, A., Räisänen, C., Stenberg, A.-C., Jacobs, C., Wright, J., . . . Winberg, C. (2011). Collaborating for content and language integrated learning: The situated character of faculty collaboration and student learning. *Across the Disciplines: A Journal of Language, Learning, and Academic Writing, 8*(3). https://wac.colostate.edu/docs/atd/clil/gustafssonetal.pdf.

Hughes, B. & Miller, E. L. (2018). WAC seminar participants as surrogate WAC consultants: Disciplinary faculty developing and deploying WAC expertise. *WAC Journal, 29,* 7–41. https://wac.colostate.edu/docs/journal/vol29/hughes_miller.pdf.

Hyland, K. (2000). *Disciplinary discourses: Social interactions in academic writing.* Longman.

Kinchin, I. M., Cabot, L. B. & Hay, D. B. (2010). Visualizing expertise: Revealing the nature of a threshold concept in the development of an authentic pedagogy for clinical education. In J. H. F. Meyer, R. Land & C. Baillie (Eds.), *Threshold concepts and transformational learning* (pp. 81–96). Sense. https://doi.org/10.1163/9789460912078_006.

Meyer, J. H. F. & Land, R. (2003). Threshold concepts and troublesome knowledge: Linkages to ways of thinking and practicing. In C. Rust (Ed.), *Improving student learning—Theory and practice ten years on* (pp. 412–424). Oxford Centre for Staff and Learning Development.

Meyer, J. H. F., Land, R. & Baillie, C. (2010). *Threshold concepts and transformational learning.* Sense. https://doi.org/10.1163/9789460912078.

Miami Writing Spotlight. (2018). http://miamioh.edu/hcwe/hwac/about/miami-writing-spotlight/index.html.

Norgaard, R. (1999). Negotiating expertise in disciplinary "Contact Zones." *Language and Learning Across the Disciplines, 3*(2), 44–62. https://wac.colostate.edu/llad/v3n2/norgaard.pdf.

Prendergast, C. (1998). Race: The absent presence in composition studies. *College Composition and Communication, 50*(1), 36–53. https://doi.org/10.2307/358351.

Swales, J. M. (1990). *Genre analysis: English in academic and research settings.* Cambridge University Press.

Walvoord, B., Hunt, L. L., Dowling, H. F., Jr. & McMahon, J. D., with contributions by V. Slachman & L. Udel. (2011). *In the long run: A study of faculty in three*

Writing-Across-the-Curriculum programs. National Council of Teachers of English. https://wac.colostate.edu/books/walvoord/.

Wardle, E. (2004). Can cross-disciplinary links help us teach "academic discourse" in FYC? *Across the Disciplines, 1.* https://wac.colostate.edu/docs/atd/articles /wardle2004.pdf.

Wardle, E. (2009). "Mutt genres" and the goal of FYC: How can we help students write the genres of the university? *College Composition and Communication, 60,* 765–88.

Wardle, E. (2013). Intractable writing program problems, kairos, and writing about writing: A profile of the University of Central Florida's First-Year Composition program. *Composition Forum, 27.*

Wardle, E. (2019). Using a threshold concepts framework to facilitate an expertise-based WAC model for faculty development. In L. Adler-Kassner & E. Wardle, *(Re)considering what we know: Learning thresholds in writing, composition, rhetoric, and literacy.* Utah State University Press.

Wardle, E. & Downs, D. (2007). Teaching about writing, righting misconceptions: (Re)envisioning FYC as Intro to Writing Studies. *College Composition and Communication, 58,* 552–584.

Wardle, E. & Downs, D. (2012). Reimagining the nature of FYC: Trends in writing-about-writing pedagogies. In K. Ritter & P. K. Matsuda (Eds.), *Exploring Composition Studies: Sites, issues, and perspectives* (pp. 123–144). Utah State University Press.

Wardle, E. & Downs, D. (2014). Looking into writing about writing classrooms. In D. Coxwell Teague & R. Lunsford (Eds.), *First-Year composition: From theory to practice* (pp. 276–320). Parlor Press.

Wardle, E. & Downs, D. (2016). *Writing about writing: A college reader* (3rd ed.). Bedford/St. Martin's.

Wilhoit, S. (2013). Achieving a lasting impact on faculty teaching: Using the WPA outcomes statement to develop an extended WID seminar. In N. N. Behm, G. R. Glau, D. H. Holdstein, D. Roen & E. M. White (Eds.), *The WPA outcomes statement a decade later* (pp. 124–135). Parlor Press.

APPENDIX A: SAMPLE FELLOWS SCHEDULE

Date	Topic	Activities During Seminar	Reading Prior to Seminar
Week 1:	Threshold Concepts Framework What are threshold concepts of your disciplines?	Set up Google Drive folders and begin taking/keeping notes and records there each week Identify threshold concepts of your discipline(s)/fields	*How People Learn* Chapter 2: "How Experts Differ from Novices" Meyer and Land "Threshold Concepts and Troublesome Knowledge" "Threshold Concepts and Troublesome Knowledge: Issues of Liminality" Cousin, "An Introduction to Threshold Concepts"
Week 2:	Threshold concepts of writing Where are threshold concepts enacted in your syllabi and assignments?	Teach one of your threshold concepts to another team if we did not get there last week. Begin investigating how you are enacting conceptions of writing you read about in your own professional lives & how these can inform classrooms	Adler-Kassner and Wardle, *Naming What We Know*, classroom edition —Metaconcept and Concepts 1 & 2 (pages 15–47)
Week 3:	Threshold concepts of writing Where are threshold concepts enacted in your syllabi and assignments?	Begin investigating how you are enacting conceptions of writing you read about in your own professional lives & how these can inform classrooms	Adler-Kassner and Wardle, *Naming What We Know*, classroom edition —Concepts 3 & 4 (pages 48–70)

continued on next page

Date	Topic	Activities During Seminar	Reading Prior to Seminar
Week 4:	How does your disciplinary discourse enact your discipline's values and ideologies?	Exchange one article across disciplines and examine the conventions, values, and ideologies being enacted.	Hyland, *Disciplinary Discourses: Social Interactions in Academic Writing* "Disciplinary Cultures, Texts, and Interactions" "Academic attribution: Interaction Through Citation" John Swales, summary of CARS model of research introductions Optional: Swales, "Research articles in English"
Week 5:	How can you explain conventions of writing to students?	Extrapolate from last week: how can you provide students with frames and questions to help them interrogate the kinds of writing you assign? Write a statement for students that conveys explicit guidance about writing in your discipline (the "mad libs")	Read <u>Miami Writing Spotlights for Gerontology, Psychology, Philosophy, and History</u> (all short) to see how they are helping students understand writing differently.
Week 6:		Creating disciplinary writing guides Consider how Ambrose and your "mad libs" descriptions might lead you to revise an assignment or a course	Look at disciplinary writing guides created by other Fellows, particularly the philosophy guide Ambrose et al., *How Learning Works*. **Skim:** –Chapter 1: How Does Students' Prior Knowledge Affect Their Learning? –Chapter 4: How Do Students Develop Mastery? –Chapter 5: What Kinds of Practice and Feedback Enhance Learning? –Chapter 7: How Do Students Become Self-Directed Learners?

Date	Topic	Activities During Seminar	Reading Prior to Seminar
Week 7:	Learning, prior knowledge, mastery, and transfer Applying ideas from Bean to your classroom	Consider how Ambrose, Bean, and your "mad libs" descriptions might lead you to revise an assignment or a course	Bean, *Engaging Ideas*. **Skim:** –Chapter 4: Teaching a Variety of Genres –Chapter 7: Writing to Learn –Chapter 6: Formal Writing, Writing to Communicate
Week 8:	Applying ideas from Bean to your classroom Planning for team projects		Bean, *Engaging Ideas*. **Skim:** –Chapter 10: Using Small Groups to Coach Thinking and Teach Disciplinary Argument –Chapter 15: Writing Process and Paper Load –Chapter 16: Writing Comments
Week 9:	Work on team projects		
Week 10:	Work on team projects		
Week 11:	Work on team projects		
Week 12:	Work on team projects		Plan for next week
Week 13:	Present team projects	Ways HCWE can support you: -Embedded consulting -Department liaisons -Assignment review -Faculty workshops -GA training	Make a short presentation to the large group of your plans for returning to the classroom and your department

APPENDIX B: WRITING "MAD LIB"

Note of Caution: Participants do not draft this until Week 5, drawing on all of the reflection, activities, and reading they have completed in prior weeks. Asking faculty to complete this without the prior groundwork is unlikely to be successful.

Our field of _____ is rooted in the study of _____ and goals for our work include _____ [what are you trying to accomplish]. We have some fundamental ways of looking at _____ [the object of your study] or doing _____ [your work, your methods]. Sometimes outsiders or newcomers misunderstand or are confused or surprised by _____ about our field.

Some "threshold concepts" that have grown up around our work and are central to being able to do work in this field include _____ [list TCs you identified earlier].

Our field tends to value _____ and often or usually _____ is not as valued or forefronted. Our values and threshold concepts are embodied in how and what we write.

We tend to write in genres such as _____ [reports, policy analysis, narratives, IMRD articles, etc.]. We rarely write _____ [a particular genre or in a particular way].

We find writers to be credible when they do _____ and when they use _____ [options here include the kinds of theories and methodologies that are appropriate, the way centrality is established, the way the author presents her/himself and addresses the reader and others in the field, the kinds of evidence they use, etc. Hyland & Swales can help].

Effective writing in our field tends to look like/do _____ .

Our citation practices embody and help enact our values and goals. You can see this in how we _____ [think about citation practices such as quoting vs. summarizing, how many citations are used, what kind of work tends to get cited, what is forefronted in citations—year, person, etc. See Hyland and Swales].

Thus, our advice to you when you write in our classes is: _____ .
- Undergraduates in general education courses in our program are expected to do/understand _____ when they write in our courses.
- Undergraduates in our major are expected to do/understand _____ when they write in our courses.
- Graduate students in our field are expected to do/understand _____ when they write in our courses.

CHAPTER 11.

ATTEMPTING TO CONNECT DISCIPLINARY PRINCIPLES OF "EFFECTIVE WRITING" WITH STUDENTS' PRIOR WRITING EXPERIENCES IN FOUR DISCIPLINES

James Croft

St. John's University

Phyllis Conn

St. John's University

Joseph Serafin

St. John's University

Rebecca Wiseheart

St. John's University

WAC theory supports the idea that faculty can better teach disciplinary principles of effective writing to students by attempting to connect disciplinary writing with students' prior writing experiences. WAC theory also supports the idea that writing experiences are more meaningful to students if such experiences are personal to them. This chapter reports the efforts of faculty in four disciplines to implement these theories and to better teach disciplinary writing to their students by asking their students to connect disciplinary principles of "effective writing" with the students' thoughts on "effective writing" and the students' prior writing experiences. These IRB-approved activities took place at St. John's University in New York and involved a first-year legal writing course, a second-year history seminar, a third-year chemistry laboratory and a third- or fourth-

year clinical and research writing course. Different methods were used to connect disciplinary principles of effective writing with the students' thoughts on effective writing in each course. In all of the courses, the faculty found that their efforts to connect disciplinary principles of effective writing with students' thoughts on effective writing revealed the complexity of students' relationships to writing and disconnects between the instructors' thoughts on effective writing and their students' thoughts about effective writing. Each of the faculty also valued this collaboration. Among other things, this collaboration across disciplines helped the faculty contextualize disciplinary conventions of effective writing relative to conventions of effective writing in other disciplines.

WAC theory supports the idea that faculty can better teach disciplinary principles of effective writing to students by attempting to connect disciplinary writing with students' prior writing experiences. For example, in *Naming What We Know*, Andrea Lunsford stated that "when writers can identify how elements of one writing situation are similar to elements of another, their prior knowledge helps them out in analyzing the current rhetorical situation" (cited in Adler-Kassner, 2015, p. 55). Similarly, in *Engaged Writers and Dynamic Disciplines*, Chris Thaiss and Terry Meyers Zawacki (2006) noted the importance of reflecting on the "connections and distinctions" between writing experiences and the development of students' writing abilities (p. 140). Similarly, WAC theory supports the idea that writing experiences are more meaningful to students if such experiences are personal to them (Eodice et al., this volume; Eodice et al., 2017; Kells, 2018).

We teach at St. John's University in New York, a private Catholic university in New York City with a diverse student population and a total enrollment of roughly 20,000 students. We teach disciplinary writing in our respective courses: a first-year legal writing course, a second-year history seminar, a third-year chemistry laboratory, and a third- or fourth-year clinical and research writing course. The four of us have been working together for several years on ways to implement in our classrooms what we have learned through participating in International Writing Across the Curriculum (IWAC) conferences, reading WAC literature, participating in WAC workshops and programs, and from each other. Through this work we have learned about how we each carry distinct identities as writers—identities as writers within our disciplines as well as identities as writers in other aspects of our lives—and how these identities, culturally shaped and contested, often encompass ideas and practices that carry over from one writing context to another.

Based on our knowledge of WAC theory, our experiences in our past collaborations and our experiences in the classroom, we decided to attempt to help students connect their prior writing experiences with their writing in our disciplines—as a means of helping them learn disciplinary writing. This chapter reports our reflections on our IRB-approved attempts to implement that practice in our classrooms. As faculty on the ground in the disciplines, we are simultaneously working to learn to become better teachers of writing and to teach our students to write. In that respect, we are similar to the Pre-Service Educator students discussed by Christy Goldsmith (this volume), who are asked to simultaneously develop in their disciplines and develop as teachers of writing. We're hoping to contribute to WAC discourse by offering that perspective— the perspective of faculty in dramatically different disciplines collaborating and struggling to implement WAC theory.

In our courses, we each used different methods to try to help our students connect disciplinary principles of effective writing with writing outside of our disciplines, but we each used some combination of the following activities:

- asking students what they think "effective writing" is
- asking students to bring us samples of "effective writing" in and outside of our disciplines and asking students to discuss why they think that the samples that they chose are effective
- asking students to use unmodified versions of the American Association of Colleges & Universities (AACU) Written Communication VALUE Rubric (hereafter "AACU Rubric") to evaluate samples of writing
- asking students to evaluate writing, including the writing of other students, using locally developed course rubrics
- asking students to write about nondisciplinary topics using disciplinary writing styles

In working with our students, we used the term *effective* writing instead of terms like *good* or *standard* writing because the term effective writing seemed to us to better dovetail with the purposes for which our students are writing in our disciplines—to inform, to analyze or to persuade. We note that the term "effective" is sometimes used in the literature to discuss purposeful writing. For example, in *Naming What We Know*, Kevin Roozen stated that "if teachers can help students consider their potential audiences and purposes, they can better help them understand what makes a text effective or not, what it accomplishes and what it falls short of accomplishing" (cited in Adler-Kassner, 2015, p. 18). The position statement on writing assessment from the National Council of Teachers of English (2014) discusses "assessing writing on the basis of effectiveness for readers." The term *effective* is also commonly used in style manuals such as *The Elements of Style* (Strunk & White, 2007) and *The Sense of Style: The Thinking Person's Guide to Writing in the 21st Century* (Pinker, 2015). We are aware that the terms *good* and *standard* writing are also used in the literature. Putting our disciplinary differences aside, at a high level of generality, we each expect our students' effective writing to have the qualities of "standard academic writing" that Thaiss and Zawacki (2006) identified in *Engaged Writers and Dynamic Disciplines*: (a) "clear evidence in writing that the writer(s) have been persistent, open-minded, and disciplined in study"; (b) "the dominance of reason over emotion or sensual perception"; and (c) "an imagined reader who is coolly rational, reading for information, and intending to formulate a reasoned response" (pp. 5–7).

We are also aware of the controversy around AACU VALUE Rubrics. We agree with Anson and others that these rubrics are not the best way to assess student writing or the best way to communicate instructor expectations to students (Anson et al., 2012). But we do think that these rubrics can be a useful way to *begin* conversations with students about what instructors expect from student writing and what is expected of writers in our disciplines, generally. We think, for example, that discussing these rubrics with our students can be a useful way to begin applying Thaiss and Zawacki's (2006) Seventh Practice of "teaching students . . . the general academic principles that all majors share and how to distinguish between these principles and variations" (p. 155) from these principles in different rhetorical contexts. In many of our courses, we essentially used the AACU Rubric as a statement of "general academic principles" of writing—a bridge to help our students connect their thoughts on writing with the "variations" from those principles in our disciplines. We also want to be clear that we—as instructors—did not use the AACU Rubric in assessing student writing. As advocated in WAC Clearinghouse's (2014) statement of the principles and practices of WAC and the National Council of Teachers of English's (2014) statement of its position on writing assessment, among other places, we agree that assessment should be tailored to the context and purpose of the assignment being assessed.

Our attempts to help students connect their thoughts on effective writing with disciplinary conventions of effective writing were, at bottom, about us as teachers of disciplinary writing. We agree with the WAC principle that writing is highly situated and tied to a field's discourse and ways of knowing and therefore that writing in the disciplines (WID) is most effectively taught by faculty in the disciplines (WAC Clearinghouse, 2014). We are aware of our roles as teachers of disciplinary writing. We value our discourse across our disciplines as a way of increasing our teaching effectiveness (WAC Statement of Principles) and as a means of providing us, as teachers, with "multiple opportunities to articulate, interrogate, and communicate [our] assumptions and expectations" about student writing (WEC Model, 2019). And, we value reflecting on our own teaching with writing practices as a means of improving those practices (Thaiss & Zawacki, 2006). The efforts that we discuss here were part of that process of continuous reflective improvement for us.

Below, we discuss each of our respective courses in turn—from the course that students take earliest at St. John's to the course that students take the latest at St. John's. In doing so, we will cover

- What each of our courses is, including the objective(s) of the course, and how the course fits into our respective disciplines and majors.
- What activities we added into our courses to attempt to help our students connect their thoughts on effective writing, generally, with disciplinary principles of effective writing.
- The extent to which we perceived these activities to be useful to our teaching.
- The extent to which our students perceived these activities to be useful to their learning. We each asked our students about this in similar end-of-the semester surveys.
- How and whether we intend to continue using these activities going forward in our respective courses.

After discussing each of our courses in turn, we will close with some modest common observations across our courses.

LEGAL RESEARCH AND WRITING I—JAMES CROFT

Legal Research and Writing I is a required course in the undergraduate Legal Studies major at St. John's, an undergraduate law major. In the Legal Studies major, the purpose of the Legal Research and Writing I course is to teach students to communicate a legal analysis in writing in a way that is customary in the legal profession. Ideally, students take this course in the second semester of their first year, after taking an introductory course in legal analysis in their first semester. I primarily taught this course by collaboratively writing a large legal research memorandum with the students over the course of the semester. This semester, we wrote about hypothetical murders committed by our hypothetical defendant's buddy with our hypothetical defendant's rifle. Most of the work in the course was directly related to this semester-long assignment. But, I also asked the class to do a small legal writing assignment on the second day of class to facilitate a discussion about the qualities that we value in legal writing. And, throughout the semester, I also asked the class to respond to and reflect on several readings on legal writing.

In addition to the assignments mentioned above, this semester I also asked my students to do several assignments connecting legal and nonlegal writing. For example, in the beginning of the semester, I asked the students to give me a sample of nonlegal writing that has the qualities that we value in legal writing—makes a clear and concrete assertion, makes that assertion up front (at the beginning of the writing), supports that assertion with evidence and does so concisely—and to discuss the extent to which the samples have these qualities. And, at the end of the semester, I asked the students to give me a sample of nonlegal writing that they think is effective but that does *not* have the qualities that we value in legal writing. I asked the students to discuss why they thought that the piece was effective and to discuss the extent to which the samples have/ do not have the qualities that we value in legal writing.

When I asked the students to complete these assignments, my goal was to get the students thinking about how the writing that we were doing in my class was similar to and different from their prior writing experiences. My hope was that helping the students to make these connections would help them become better writers. But, looking back on these assignments, I don't think that they had the desired effect. Like many instructors, I realized that I did not effectively communicate my expectations regarding these assignments to my students. When I asked the students to give me a piece that makes an "assertion," for example, I meant something like a litigation position—a position on something debatable. The fact that many students gave me news articles reporting facts or song lyrics reporting feelings suggests that many students didn't understand "assertion" the way that I meant. Similarly, the students seemed to understand "evidence" differently from me. When I asked for "evidence," I wanted support for debatable positions, but a lot of students gave me reports of perceptions or feelings. In hindsight, I should have seen this disconnect coming. When I modeled the activities described above for my students, I connected legal writing to song lyrics and essays. By pointing out the similarities between legal writing and those very different genres of writing, I may have inadvertently invited my students to identify similarities between those genres that do not exist.

In end-of-the semester surveys, my students reported a similarly tepid feeling toward these activities. While a small minority of students reported that they thought that the activities connecting legal and nonlegal writing were the most effective activities in the course and a small minority of students reported that they thought that these activities were the least effective activities in the course, a majority of the students thought that these activities contributed to their learning—but not as much as the course activities that involved direct instruction in effective legal writing.

In hindsight, I think that these activities were more valuable to me as an instructor than they were to the students. Asking the students to connect legal and nonlegal writing showed me how the students think about writing and how I can better communicate my expectations about legal writing to them. Similarly, I think that this collaboration with my colleagues has also helped me understand what is expected of my students when they are taking courses in other disciplines, which has also helped me communicate to my students how the writing we are doing in my class is similar to and dissimilar from writing that they do in other courses. In class, discussing the qualities that I value in legal writing, I find myself saying things like (a) This is like science. Your goal is to communicate your analysis in a way that can be understood and replicated by others. (b) This isn't like philosophy or theology where you build up to your point. Here, you make your point first and then support it. And (c) Here our goal is to write as simply and directly as possible. This isn't like some of your humanities courses where simplicity is viewed as a sign of lack of rigor.

Going forward, I do not plan to keep using the course activities that asked the students to connect legal and nonlegal writing. I found that more students were misled by those activities than were helped by those activities. But, as discussed above, I valued working through these activities with my students and working through this project with my colleagues because those processes helped me better understand how my students think about writing and understand what qualities are valued in writing in their other courses. That understanding helps me better directly communicate to my students how the writing that we are doing in my class is similar to and different from some of their other writing experiences—which was the goal of the project in the first place.

HISTORY SEMINAR—PHYLLIS CONN

The sophomore history seminar is a required three-credit course for history majors and minors designed to introduce students to foundational practices in historical methods, analysis, and research. It addresses how to read historical sources and prepares students for historical writing in future courses. I organized this section around the theme of immigration to New York City, particularly in the nineteenth and twentieth centuries.

Early in the semester, I asked students to think about effective historical writing through three prisms: a definition I provided; the AACU Rubric; and their own prior writing and reading. My definition stated that effective historical writing is the result of analysis and synthesis of appropriate research, is clearly sourced and contextualized, centers on a strong thesis or argument, and follows general conventions about mechanics and grammar. I asked them to select a piece of historical writing or any other writing they believed was effective and to rate it using the AACU Rubric, then write a few paragraphs about why they thought the piece was effective. Students identified these terms as the most important aspects of effective historical writing: well-organized, strong use of appropriate evidence (preferably primary sources), engaging style, follows disciplinary conventions, meaningful content, and clear syntax and mechanics.

During our semester-long discussion of these characteristics, there were moments when students clearly had diverse ideas of how to interpret these criteria, as well as moments when student perceptions of criteria diverged somewhat from common disciplinary interpretations. For example, the question of "engaging style" arose during student responses to complex journal articles, with some students questioning whether a dense text represented ineffective historical writing, while others stated that "engaging style" was not an appropriate criterion for historical writing after all. Student perceptions also varied about what constitutes "appropriate evidence" and what constitutes its "strong use," and in many cases their definitions would not have met common standards in the field. For example, one student suggested that encyclopedia articles would be appropriate evidence. We had a class discussion about how their previous history professors had responded to that type of use and when it might be appropriate to cite encyclopedia articles.

The discrepancy between common student perceptions and common disciplinary conventions is not surprising, since these students were enrolled in their first seminar on disciplinary writing. Our ongoing discussions about effective historical writing returned most frequently to using evidence, the research question, the thesis, and the argument—of which only one (use of evidence) was clearly stated in all three definitions: my definition, the AACU Rubric, and the class-defined characteristics of effective historical writing.

Based on student responses to a survey at the end of the semester, our work on effective writing was clearly significant for their learning. I also learned a great deal about writing pedagogy in history. One conclusion I reached is that student historical writing develops through multiple methods of discussing, performing and evaluating all types of writing—students' own writing, course readings, primary sources, other students' writing, and readings from outside the course. When we repeatedly asked a set of questions about pieces of writing (what is the main argument, what are the sources, how is the piece contextualized, is it clear to the reader), our perspective on these questions evolved through the semester.

Secondly, I began to understand how ineffective my attempts were to make connections between students' prior writing experiences and writing in my course, and perhaps how difficult it is to do so. Instead of "looking backward," as one student said, several students were most interested in becoming stronger historical writers. Third, I noticed that students can develop their understanding and perception of effective historical writing and effective writing practices before they master historical content, a conclusion that would probably not surprise WAC scholars. Before this project, I believed that effective historical writing developed first through mastering content, analysis and synthesis, then afterwards working on aspects such as organization, logic, the thesis statement, and related matters. Now I understand that just as it might take me several months or years to master a historical topic, students need more than fifteen weeks to develop historical understanding, analysis and synthesis for a selected topic. Thus, even though students cannot master a historical topic in one semester, students can improve their historical writing in one semester through practices such as developing more effective thesis statements, stronger use of appropriate evidence, and improved application of historical conventions. Indeed, as students learn some of the conventions of writing in history, these new ways of writing help develop new ways of thinking that promote mastery of content. For future iterations of the history sophomore seminar, these practices are where I intend to focus my efforts. I plan to reduce the course attention on some aspects of historical writing (such as how to choose a research topic) and focus more on writing thesis statements and strong use of appropriate evidence.

EXPERIMENTAL PHYSICAL CHEMISTRY—JOSEPH SERAFIN

Experimental Physical Chemistry (EPC) is a required third-year, second-semester course in the traditional chemistry course sequence. The chemistry program is externally accredited by the American Chemical Society. These students have been introduced to technical communication in the form of laboratory reports in their first, second, and third years. This aspect of the course is different from the two previously discussed introductory courses. This course has a significantly more extensive writing component than their previous chemistry courses. I wanted to see what the students brought with them from their previous courses in the hope that I would better be able to use that prior understanding to assist the students in becoming more effective communicators.

A "formal" laboratory report mirrors the format used in the chemical literature. The Committee on Professional Training of the American Chemical Society

(2015) offers a description of a research report that is an excellent launching point for the disciplinary novice. In addition to the normal laboratory reports, I added a new series of assignments to the course this semester to help unpack the students' ideas of effectiveness at the start and end of the semester:

- In assignment 1 (A1), the students provided samples of an "effective" nontechnical writing and were given the following prompts: 1. Why do you consider this work to be effective? 2. Are there any elements you could adopt for your technical communications (lab reports)?
- In assignment 2 (A2), the AACU rubric was used as a lens to reflect on a piece of technical writing that the students perceived to be effective, and the students were given the following prompts: 1. Why do you consider this work to be effective? 2. Please rate the article using this rubric.
- Assignment 3 (A3) was a blind peer evaluation of a student report using the internal rubric designed for this course. This was a course rubric for the written reports, based on the needs of this group of students at this point in their academic careers.
- The fourth and final assignment (A4) was the end of semester student survey on student perception of effectiveness. Many of these questions are closely related to survey questions from the other authors in this study.

The biggest finding for me as the instructor was that I did not have sufficient information either about the students' understanding of effective writing before this course or how that understanding has evolved in this course. My initial questions at the start of the semester and final questions at the end were not specific enough to require the students to identify specific elements of their writing for analysis.

In retrospect, instead of asking broadly about what effective writing is, I should have narrowed that down to what was effective writing in their previous chemistry courses. And then, as pointed out above by James, a more meaningful task would be identifying how and why this course has different standards for effective writing. This is not to imply a higher or more demanding standard, but to recognize different aspects are given more attention and may have different formats in different chemistry courses, one size does not fit all—nor should it. Five contexts have been identified that shape individuals' expectations when they read/evaluate writing: the general academic, the disciplinary, the subdisciplinary, the local/institutional, and the personal/idiosyncratic (Thaiss & Zawacki, 2006).

While the student surveys provide useful information, a perception of improvement may not correlate with actual improvement. A better approach would be to have the students critically reflect and evaluate how elements in later reports are different from previous reports. Having the students perform this reflective analysis is far more useful than the instructor performing the task because it is a) a formative assessment of learning for the student, and b) it provides actionable insight into how the student perceives the evolution of effective writing during the semester when corrections or discussions can occur.

I view this project as a success not because I can now identify what elements are best at making student writing more effective, but rather I have a better idea of what kinds of information I will need in order to assess that improvement in the future.

In the next iteration of the course, new assignments would be a discussion of how and why the grading rubrics for the various chemistry written reports are different, and why those differences are important. A critical student self-assessment analysis of their improvement (or lack) over the course of the semester will be performed by the student in consultation with the faculty.

In terms of the specific assignments, I would still keep A1 because it provides a useful introduction to the topic and serves as a good ice-breaker to meet the students. For A2, I would use the specifically created internal course rubric because any advantage from looking at effectiveness from another viewpoint (a "standard" writing rubric) is probably outweighed by reinforcing a common theme throughout the semester to the students. A3 remains a useful exercise, if for no other reason than for the student to look at the internal rubric from the perspective of the reader.

RESEARCH & CLINICAL WRITING—REBECCA WISEHEART

Research and Clinical Writing teaches discipline specific writing forms in Communication Sciences and Disorders with special emphasis on organization, clarity, and use of evidence. For this analysis, I focused on students' understanding of the use of evidence as being a critical component or marker of effective writing. Evidence-based practice is a cornerstone of preprofessional training in speech-language pathology and audiology and in this course, I review ways in which empirical evidence is used in both research and clinical writing. For example, a course objective for research writing is for students to master APA format for citing sources and reporting experimental findings. For clinical writing, students learn how and where to report objective data in diagnostic reports and in clinical (SOAP) notes. Students learn that such data is the evidence clinicians use to support decisions about diagnosis and treatment. The Association of American Colleges & Universities Written Communication VALUE Rubric also includes evidence as a separate component, defined as "use of high-quality, credible, relevant sources." Using this broad definition as a starting point, and assuming students had been exposed to this (or a similar) rubric in other classes, I hoped to gain some insight into students' general, "adisciplinary" view of evidence before coming into the class and to gauge what types of teaching or writing activities might impact that view.

In an attempt to bridge prior writing experiences with discipline specific forms, I added two assignments. For Assignment 1, students selected a nonresearch article and rated it according to the AACU Rubric with an explanation for their ratings. Though not instructed to do so, all students selected articles from electronic (online) platforms. Regarding sources and evidence, substantially more students (21/28) gave their pieces high marks (i.e., ratings of 3 or 4) than gave their pieces low marks (i.e., ratings of 1 or 2; n = 8/28), indicating a general trust in the sources of evidence of work published online. Overall, students demonstrated a solid understanding that multiple sources of evidence are necessary for any type of effective writing. However, students are not yet able to critically evaluate the quality of such evidence within a piece. This concept is summed up by a student's comments on a piece on the gender pay gap: "The writer uses a multitude of linked sources throughout her article. Where some of her information may have been lacking, she supplemented it with other articles on the topic to give a deeper understanding to the reader." Other students were more critical: "If I wanted to try to verify the information . . . I would have to look into more research."

For Assignment 2, students were asked to rate an assigned article from the popular magazine *Scientific American Mind* about the history of autism which I considered to be very interesting and well-written, but objectively lacking in terms of sources or evidence as there was no accompanying references or citations. Most students picked up on this: using the AACU Rubric, a majority of the students (17/28) gave the piece low marks (1 or 2) for the category "sources of evidence." Yet, when asked whether they considered the writing to be effective, only four students indicated that it was *not*, three of whom specifically stated this was because it did not include sources or evidence. Examining open-ended explanations for why students felt the writing *was* effective, many students (16/28) described either an organizational structure that "flowed" or a specific writing style that was "elegant" or "accessible."

Overall, despite demonstrating effective use of the AACU Rubric in rating evidence, students continued to define effective writing as that which is clear, concise and generally convincing, but not necessarily evidence-based. In this way, use of the AACU Rubric did not achieve the goal of helping students adopt the use of evidence as a necessary component or hallmark of effective writing. Nevertheless, students found the use of rubrics, both the AACU Rubric and course-specific rubrics, as valuable, based on results of the end-of semester surveys. When asked to indicate the extent to which various learning activities contributed to learning, students valued most the assignments that will impact their immediate futures rather than those that might be more challenging in terms of critical analysis. Their top two picks were writing assignments related to graduate school applications and 1:1 writing conferences whereas the effective writing assignments came in second to last, followed by diagnostic report writing.

Because the student workload is already so high in this course, I will not likely use these particular effective writing assignments again; however, this project revealed to me the importance of devoting more time to class discussion and guidance on topics related to information literacy in general and on quality or levels of evidence, in particular, as defined within my discipline. Reading, evaluating, and reflecting on both good and bad examples of clinical and research writing may provide students more opportunities to critically evaluate arguments and evidence (and not just rhetorical style) of nondisciplinary writing, as well, which, in my view, is an important endeavor. Rubrics for clinical writing may in fact help guide students through these types of reflective practices. In this class, for example, students prepare documents for their graduate school applications. This includes a resume, a personal statement, and practice essays for the GRE. While I have routinely scheduled these assignments at the beginning of the course—under the assumption that this writing practice serves as a bridge between "adisciplinary" and discipline-specific forms—it would be interesting in the future to see if practicing clinical and research writing first might lead students to write essays and resumes that are more richly supported by evidence. In this way, rubrics for clinical and research writing might provide students with a new structure or heuristic through which previous writing habits are revised.

COMMON OBSERVATIONS

While we each used different methods to attempt to connect principles of effective disciplinary writing with our students' prior writing experiences, and while we each had different experiences with our students, we are able to make some modest common observations.

First, attempting to connect disciplinary principles of effective writing with students' prior writing experiences is hard. It was hard for the students because we were asking them to transfer writing skills from their prior experiences and classes to new or different rhetorical situations and to know when to transfer similarities from those past experiences and when to draw distinctions between such experiences. We were asking students to draw distinctions between disciplinary writing and to apply principles of effective writing in our own discipline while they were also doing disciplinary writing in their other courses—in other disciplines. We were surprised by how difficult this transfer was for the students. In hindsight, we realize that we could have done a better job articulating to the students when to transfer prior experiences to writing in our courses and when to distinguish their prior writing experiences from the writing in our courses. We also found ourselves remembering that our students are undergraduates who exist in multiple disciplines at once. They are not experienced professionals (or even graduate students) who have the luxury of focusing on writing in one discipline. In fact, we experienced similar challenges working and writing across our diverse disciplines for this research. We realize, in reflection, that much of the value of our WID/WAC work stems from the very act of facing the same challenges our undergraduate students face within the cross-disciplinary microcosm we have created in this group.

Second, going through this process, we each noticed disconnects with, or had miscommunications with, our students about our expectations for assignments or about disciplinary principles of effective writing. For example, when James asked his students to bring him pieces that made "assertions," it was clear that what James meant and what many of his students understood were two different things. Similarly, discussing "evidence" with her students, Rebecca noted that she had a different expectation regarding the "quality" of appropriate "evidence" than her students. Joseph noted that many students failed to include important pieces of evidence to support their claims in their submitted work, despite the fact that he went over the course rubric with the students. Phyllis found that many of her students would have applied the AACU Rubric to an assigned blog post on immigration very differently than she would have, seemingly allowing their thoughts on the political content of the post to affect their thoughts on the quality of its content and its use of evidence. These kinds of disconnects are consistent with findings in the literature. Thaiss and Zawacki (2006), for example, point out that it is understandable for students to be confused by faculty use of common terms like "evidence," "organization," and "clarity" because, although such terms are common across disciplines, the way that those terms are applied in the disciplines is different. Reading our respective sections of this article for the purpose of drafting these common observations, we see that we too all use common terms like "evidence," "clarity," "concision," and "organization" with our students, but that we each mean different things by these terms—these terms are applied differently in our respective disciplines. Again, in reflection, we realize that talking through these disconnects in our WID/WAC group discussions forced us as instructors to explicitly define terms or parameters to one another, which will hopefully transfer to our students. In demanding clarification from our colleagues, we ask hard questions that our students might not know, or might not have the confidence, to ask. Without the extra layer of scrutiny from our colleagues, we could have easily attributed student-teacher disconnects entirely to the student. Essentially, this collaboration provided us, as teachers, "multiple opportunities to articulate, interrogate, and communicate [our] assumptions and expectations" about writing and writing instruction (WEC Model, 2019).

And, third, we see some potential benefits for teaching and learning in explicitly attempting to connect disciplinary principles of effective writing with students' prior writing experiences. We recognize the complex and diverse array of experiences that inform students' relationships to writing in our disciplines and to their understanding of the connections between their own learning and writing. Having completed these course activities from an action research perspective, we see a more intentional and measured path forward for this research. In addition to being more aware of our students' complex relationships to writing, and to many disciplines, we also uncovered many subtle and nuanced disconnects between our ideas of effective writing and our students' ideas of effective writing. We see an opportunity to collaborate with our WAC colleagues to accommodate these complexities and disconnects—by, for example, working with our WAC colleagues to clarify aspects of our assignments or by devoting additional time to explicitly discussing disciplinary conventions of effective writing with our students.

In "Making Connections Between Theory and Practice: Pre-Service Educator Disciplinary Literacy Courses as Secondary WAC Initiation" (this volume), Christy Goldsmith notes that the difficult, seemingly contradictory task of teaching siloed, discipline-specific writing while also maintaining porous boundaries across disciplines is often abandoned because secondary teachers are novices of both discipline and pedagogy. This rings true for us as college professors, as well, because, while we all have established expertise in our specific disciplines, we too began our WID/WAC research as novices of pedagogy. Over the past six years, our research group, which came together as alumni of a well-established WAC Fellows program, has managed to present writing research at nine conferences and produce two full-length manuscripts for well-respected writing journals. We still consider ourselves novices of writing pedagogy, but the success of our cross-disciplinary collaboration provides at least one model for how this type of work, which is slow, but steady, can begin.

ACKNOWLEDGMENT

The authors would like to thank Anne Ellen Geller for bringing us together and for her mentorship and support.

REFERENCES

Adler-Kassner, L. & Wardle, E. (Eds.). (2015). *Naming what we know: Threshold concepts in writing studies.* Utah State University Press. https://doi.org/10.7330 /9780874219906.

American Chemical Society. (2015). *Preparing a Research Report.* Committee on Professional Training. https://www.acs.org/content/dam/acsorg/about/governance /committees/training/acsapproved/degreeprogram/preparing-a-research-report.pdf.

Anson, C. M., Dannels, D. P., Flash, P. & Gaffney, A. L. H. (2012). Big rubrics and weird genres: The futility of using generic assessment tools across diverse instructional contexts. *Journal of Writing Assessment, 5*(1). http://journalofwritingassess ment.org/article.php?article=57

Association of American Colleges and Universities (AAC&U). (2009). *Written communication VALUE rubric.* Retrieved from https://www.aacu.org/value/rubrics/written -communication.

Eodice, M., Geller, A. E. & Lerner, N. (2017). *The meaningful writing project: Learning, teaching and writing in higher education.* University Press of Colorado. https:// doi.org/10.7330/9781607325802.

Kells, M. H. (2018). Writing across communities. In J. I. Liontas & M. DelliCarpini (Eds.), *The TESOL encyclopedia of English language teaching* (pp. 4438–4445). Wiley. https://doi.org/10.1002/9781118784235.eelt0152.

National Council of Teachers of English. (2014, November 30). *Writing assessment: Position statement.* http://www.ncte.org/cccc/resources/positions/writingassessment.

Pinker, S. (2015). *The sense of style: The thinking person's guide to writing in the 21st century.* Penguin Books.

Strunk, W. & White, E. B. (2007). *The elements of style.* Penguin Books.

Thaiss, C. & Zawacki, T. M. (2006). *Engaged writers and dynamic disciplines: Research on the academic writing life.* Boynton/Cook.

WAC Clearinghouse. (2014). *Statement of WAC Principles and Practices.* https://wac .colostate.edu/principles/.

WEC Model. (2019). University of Minnesota. https://wec.umn.edu/wec-model.

CHAPTER 12.

EMBRACE THE MESSINESS: LIBRARIES, WRITING CENTERS, AND ENCOURAGING RESEARCH AS INQUIRY ACROSS THE CURRICULUM

Jaena Alabi
Auburn University

James C. W. Truman
Auburn University

Bridget Farrell
University of Denver

Jennifer Price Mahoney
Indiana University-Purdue University Indianapolis

As educators, how do we clarify the concept of research into a manageable form so it's communicated effectively while still creating space for the complexity inherent across different academic disciplines, different classroom settings, at different levels from first-year students to graduate students? How do we look at this work of meaning-making appropriately so we can build an engaged pedagogy that can move across disciplines? This chapter will explore and attempt to define the challenging "mess" that comes with teaching research and writing in the disciplines; it will provide strategies for and examples of embracing the complexity of information literacy, scholarly inquiry and research writing. Finally, it will articulate the experiences of writing center staff and librarians who collaborate to embrace the messiness of research and writing to empower students.

Helping students become better writers, researchers, and thinkers across all disciplines is hard. This isn't news to anyone in higher education, but it's the

DOI: https://doi.org/10.37514/PER-B.2020.0360.2.12

everyday work of writing centers and libraries across institutions as we work with students in different disciplines outside the classroom. For educators, these challenges can seem overwhelming; how do we clarify the concept of "research" into a manageable form so it's communicated effectively, while still creating space for the complexity inherent across different academic disciplines, different classroom settings, at different levels from first-year students to graduate students? How do we look at this work of meaning-making appropriately so we can build an engaged pedagogy that can move across disciplines? This is a question not of abstract theory or institutional restructuring, but of building a culture of collaborative praxis. Such collaborations only operate if individuals—librarians and writing administrators who work with disciplinary faculty—have the freedom to collaborate creatively in their everyday work; as the authors of "English Across the Curriculum Collaborative Projects: A Flexible Community of Practice Model at the Chinese University of Hong Kong" (this volume) work toward broad cross-disciplinary communities of practice, we likewise emphasize not a fixed structure of implementation, but an engagement of student learners in the messy process of library research.

One challenge that writing center staff, librarians, and disciplinary faculty face is how to creatively engage with the static, fixed assumptions behind the generic research paper, elegantly deconstructed by scholars such as Jackie Grutsch McKinney (2002), Robert Davis and Mark Shadle (2000), Sarah Marshall (2015), and Rebecca Moore Howard and Sandra Jamieson (2014). Writing centers and libraries have been on the front lines of this struggle and in the past 10 years have been working to collaborate in "Learning Commons" to do this work, both with institutional changes and attempts at cross-training between staffs (Elmborg & Hook, 2005).

But despite some institutional shifts that recognize the complexity of disciplinary research and writing, institutions are not inherently equipped to tackle the intense complexity and fundamental "messiness" of scholarly research across disciplines in a collaborative way. To encourage the necessary adaptability to engage with this messiness, you need individuals—administrators, reference librarians, and writing consultants—willing to collaborate creatively to maintain a culture of flexibility that creates a space where students can develop creative research skills across disciplines. This chapter will explore and attempt to define the challenging "mess" that comes with teaching research and writing in the disciplines; it will provide strategies for and examples of embracing the complexity of information literacy, scholarly inquiry and research writing. Finally, it will articulate the experiences of writing center staff and librarians who collaborate to embrace the messiness of research and writing to empower students.

LIMITATIONS OF THE LINEAR

Imagine that a first-year composition student working on a research project has two plastic storage bins that she uses to organize her knowledge and skills related to research and writing. She's labeled one bin *Research* and the other *Writing*. Within the bins, she has divided her knowledge further with the use of folders. For instance, within her research bin, she has folders marked *Step 2: search for articles* and *Step 6: cite sources*; in her writing bin, folder three is labeled *revise*. Her teacher has asked her to co-mingle the contents of the bins and folders. This would require her to disrupt her nice, neat structure in order to experience a more authentic research and writing experience; she grows frustrated with the messiness of this process. Students do this not only in their composition courses, but also with any writing project in any discipline, be it their history paper on the Civil Rights Movement, their literature review for a biology lab report, or their economics paper on the Great Recession.

This student's actions mirror the conventional habits of educational institutions, which also make use of labeled bins; in the research bin, libraries support scholarly research, while writing programs and writing centers exist in the writing bin to support writers. When students work on assignments, they often employ this compartmentalized, linear approach; they access the research bin first, then return it to storage, even though the writing and research processes are intertwined and cannot be fully detached from one another. Even Wayne Booth, Gregory Colomb, and Joseph Williams' (2008) nuanced and complicated *The Craft of Research* can't avoid this sequenced approach. The authors title an early section of their book "Asking Questions, Finding Answers" (2008, p. 29). This section, like most of the first half, focuses on finding sources. It takes more than 140 pages before the authors arrive at "Planning, Drafting, and Revision" (2008, p. 173). This structure is repeated in writer's guides, composition textbooks, and syllabi across academia. For example, the University of Wisconsin–Madison Writing Center's (2018) online *Writer's Handbook* breaks "Writing a Research Paper" into eight steps—the first three on the research process and the next five on the writing process.

Despite these linear models, research and writing thrive as one recursive process. The teleology that focuses on the product (the current traditional rhetoric model, for example) has been displaced in writing studies by a recognition of the creative and recursive process, popularized by scholars like Elbow (1973) and Murray (1972) throughout the 1960s and 1970s (see Hairston, 1982); that is, to become a more effective writer, you need to work on developing an effective writing process that is recursive and embraces discovery. This paradigm shift paralleled both the emergence of WAC programs, which embraced a similarly fluid and contextual understanding of meaning making, and the emergence of the modern, collaborative writing center with its student-centered approach to learning (Mullin, 2001). Likewise, librarians recognize that research is a process of inquiry that—similar to writing—requires a nonlinear, iterative and creative process (Association of College and Research Libraries, 2015). For librarians, information literacy (the process of finding, evaluating, and using information effectively) cannot be the sole responsibility of libraries, but requires engagement from stakeholders across campus (Grafstein, 2002).

Librarians wrestle with the problem of how to introduce information literacy to novice learners in a way that embraces complexity, but acknowledges that there also exists a dimension of information literacy that focuses on acquiring rote skills. As with writing, information literacy as a concept can be approached from a multitude of perspectives (Hall et al., 2018). Mandy Lupton and Christine Bruce (2010) detailed three distinct windows through which practitioners can examine information literacy as a literacy: generic, situated, and transformative perspectives. These lenses approach information literacy with increasing degrees of complexity, from the rote skills mindset of the generic window to the critical perspective of the transformative window.

Through the lens of the generic window, information literacy is approached from a skills-based mindset where students are taught the processes necessary to find information through the use of tools and the evaluation of information is carried out through checklists, such as the CRAAP test (Blakeslee, 2004), with limited discussion of disciplinary differences in evaluation. With a situated perspective on information literacy, the context through which information items are produced becomes inseparable from the teaching of information literacy, as students are asked to think about information as a practice that varies by discipline, community, occupation, or level of expertise (from first-year students to graduate students and beyond). There is a movement from the linear to a more complex and nuanced focus on evaluation, where students do not consider a text independent of other works, and information itself is more broadly defined to include, "opinions, ideas, text, images and aural, visual, affective, kinesthetic, and embodied stimuli" (Lupton & Bruce, 2010, p. 15).

This complexity increases when approaching information literacy with a transformative lens. In the transformative window, information is no longer viewed as static or unchangeable, but instead as an empowering force that is capable of provoking change in oneself and society, including questioning structures and institutions that contribute to the creation and dissemination of information. With this lens, students are no longer seen as simple consumers of information, but creators in their own right who are complicit in supporting oppressive systems and empowered to provoke change.

Librarians are often called upon only to speak about information from a generic perspective, which may be taught linearly with a discussion of how to search and evaluate in tidy, bullet-pointed lists. Teaching information literacy from situated and transformative perspectives, however, defies this orderly approach. When information is viewed in context, it is impossible to ignore the messiness of authentic evaluation practices and the non-linearity of the publication process. To have the opportunity to cover information literacy topics from a situated or transformative perspective requires work, collaboration with disciplinary faculty, and time—all things that can often be in short supply.

As librarians and writing center/writing program faculty, we are aware of the complexity of the subject we teach. Underlying both disciplines is the goal that students will develop as deep critical thinkers, to think actively as they process, examine, employ, and engage with knowledge in their field (Bruffee, 1993; Detmering & Johnson, 2011; Weiler, 2005). Why then, do we discuss the writing process and information literacy in linear and generic ways? There's clearly a practical reason for this reductiveness—clear communication of complex practices often requires tactical simplification. (The University of Wisconsin-Madison Writing Center includes a disclaimer that "the actual process of writing a research paper is often a messy and recursive one, so please use this outline as a flexible guide.") The scale of the messiness is too large. So how do we "scale down" the messiness of the process to make it manageable, while introducing students to complexity in a manner that will not overwhelm or discourage them? This requires partnerships, reflective thought, and a commitment to rejecting the oversimplification of these processes and embracing the messiness.

THE RIGHT WAY IS THE HARD WAY: RESEARCH AS INQUIRY

How do we embrace messiness in the real world, where students want to put things in clearly labeled, carefully collated bins? Of course, this is hard. Many writing assignments, such as lab reports, policy papers, and business plans, ask students to locate, evaluate, and synthesize a variety of outside sources in order to support their arguments. To many students' chagrin, these types of assignments do not equate to a linear process and require students to tolerate ambiguity. It involves locating sources, reading and evaluating them, saving the relevant ones, identifying new questions from their reading, searching again, and so on.

To muddy the waters, different disciplines have different expectations, and the instructors within those disciplines will have their own idiosyncratic experiences that produce a wide range of conceptions of how to teach research and writing. Librarians and writing center consultants help students navigate this complex terrain, working across disciplinary differences and with disciplinary faculty to clarify expectations. For example, in a business course, peer-reviewed sources might not be the only sources students are asked to use. They might need to look at demographic data, analyze market research, and cite industry reports. Using these sources requires creative thinking with citations and evaluation. Because of the messiness of source evaluation and the broad pedagogical interpretations, librarians and instructors have tended toward simplifying the process for students.

Over the past few years, the academic library profession has undergone a shift away from a generic, product-based approach to teaching. This shift, to balance the different perspectives on information literacy, is reflected in the evolution of the disciplinary documents that define what information literacy is and methods through which it can be taught. In 2015, the Association of College and Research Libraries (ACRL) adopted the *Framework for Information Literacy for Higher Education* as a new guiding document for information literacy instructors. A year after its adoption, the ACRL announced the sunsetting of the previous guiding document, the *Information Literacy Competency Standards for Higher Education* (ACRL, 2000), leaving the *Framework* as the document of record for librarians. The adoption of the *Framework* and the sunsetting of the *Standards* has led to an increased focus on teaching the context that surrounds the creation and dissemination of information. Considerable thought has been given to the reality of research within our current state of information production and dissemination. Perhaps students don't leave the classroom knowing how to search a specific database but instead leave with a new or different way of thinking about searching.

COMING TOGETHER

In 2003, Rolf Norgaard recommended that the fields of information literacy and writing form a partnership of "intellectual engagement" (p. 124). He argued that writing's transformation from the current traditional model to a process-based approach could be replicated in the information literacy field; in particular, this shift in thinking could promote research as a process, rather than merely a mastery of skills (Norgaard, 2003).

With the publication of *Framework for Success in Postsecondary Writing* by the Council of Writing Program Administrators (CWPA), National Council of Teachers of English (NCTE), and National Writing Project (NWP) in 2011, the field of writing signaled its embrace of the process in its most dynamic and pluralistic form. The document contains a section titled "Developing Flexible Writing Processes," in which the first sentence of the second paragraph states that "writing processes are not linear" (CWPA et al., 2011, p. 8). About five years later, when the academic library profession adopted its own "framework," the authors used the word "process" 30 times (ACRL, 2015).

Barry Maid and Barbara D'Angelo (2016) discussed similarities between the two documents, including parallels in how each addresses the affective aspects of learning. The writing document refers to the affective qualities of a writer as "habits of mind," and describes specific habits using one word and a statement (CWPA et al., 2011). Written broadly, the habits refer to all parts of the writing process. The information literacy document, on the other hand, focuses its affective learning—or, "dispositions"—on specific parts of the research process. When displayed side-by-side, the similarities are difficult to miss (ACRL, 2015; see Figure 12.1).

ACRL Research as Inquiry Dispositions	WPA Habits of Mind
"Learners value *intellectual curiosity* in developing questions and learning new investigative methods"	*Curiosity*: "The desire to know more about the world"
"Learners value *persistence*, adaptability, and flexibility and recognize that ambiguity can benefit the research process"	*Persistence*: "The ability to sustain interest in and attention to short- and long-term projects"
"Learners maintain an *open mind* and a critical stance"	*Openness*: "The willingness to consider new ways of being and thinking in the world"
"Learners consider research as open-ended exploration and *engagement* with information"	*Engagement*: "A sense of investment and involvement in learning"
"Learners value persistence, adaptability, and *flexibility* and recognize that ambiguity can benefit the research process"	*Flexibility*: "The ability to adapt to situations, expectations, or demands."

Figure 12.1. Comparison of the ACRL (2015) and WPA (Council of WPA et al., 2011) frameworks.

Why does this matter? The congruent and overarching goals that writing and information literacy share form the theoretical underpinnings for a partnership of "intellectual engagement" (Norgaard, 2003, p. 124), which could result in strategies to address the messiness of the combined processes rather than going it alone.

HARD THINGS ARE HARD: PRACTICAL STRATEGIES FOR COLLABORATION

Writing programs, like libraries and writing centers, have tried a number of ways to help undergraduates navigate this messy process. At Indiana University—

Purdue University Indianapolis (IUPUI) one of the strategies involves scaling down the research/writing mess into two smaller messes, "closed" research and "open" research.[1] Beginning in the 1990s, some writing programs in the United States introduced a two-semester writing course sequence (Hood, 2010). The first semester uses a "closed" research approach; faculty provide sources for the students to incorporate into their writing projects. Collaborating with librarians, faculty use articles and non-fiction readers. For example, a student might be able to choose between curated articles on current topics as diverse as Bitcoin, marijuana legalization, or rising healthcare costs from nonscholarly sources, like *Vanity Fair, Newsweek,* or *The Atlantic.* Since the students do not have to find their own articles, they can focus on the *why* of scholarly inquiry: Why do students need to read critically? Why do they need to integrate source materials in to their arguments? Why do they need to worry about attribution and citation?

In the second semester, students progress to an open research approach. They start getting into the *how* of scholarly inquiry. How do students formulate good research questions? How do students find authoritative sources? How do they practice information literacy? Students are asked to identify a real-world problem (for example, an issue in the local business community) and their writing is scaffolded from developing their question, to finding keywords for database searches, to evaluating the resources they find, to using their sources to develop and build support for their proposal. As they draft and revise, students are encouraged to revisit their sources and consider their individual contributions to an ongoing conversation, as Kenneth Burke (1974) posited in his parlor metaphor.

This approach (sequenced research writing) could also be applied in disciplinary gateway courses. For instance, in a history course, maybe the first assignments would focus on analyzing and writing about primary sources provided by the instructor, while later assignments might require students to find their own primary sources. In a statistics class, perhaps students would initially be given datasets to analyze and then later would need to find their own datasets. In the latter part of a chemistry course, students might be expected to incorporate a limited literature review into their lab report to frame the experiment. As students grow and become more experienced with these complex processes, the instructors can begin to remove the scaffolding, encouraging the students to develop their own strategies for tackling the research-writing relationship.

By breaking the big, messy process of research into two smaller messes, students may start to appreciate the messy, but symbiotic relationship between

---

1   Several faculty at IUPUI have tried to track down their notes from the late 1980s/early 1990s when the program made its shift to the closed-open research model, but no one can find a clear genesis. The model is mentioned in the Allyn and Bacon Guide to Writing (Ramage & Bean, 1997), but it was not the first textbook to do it.

research and writing. Ideally, librarians, writing center consultants, and writing faculty can model the types of collaboration needed to navigate these processes and to develop a worthy final product.

COLLABORATION OF LIBRARY AND WRITING CENTER

Partnerships between writing centers and libraries have been a goal for the last 15 years; many institutions have moved their writing center to the library to become part of a "learning commons"—open space that fosters collaborative learning between students while bringing together a variety of campus centers to support student learning. Because of the "complementary practices" of writing centers and libraries, this collaboration seems natural (Hook, 2005). In our experience at Auburn University, however, proximity does not necessarily result in productive collaborations; simply having similar practices and goals does not guarantee that separate units coordinate their activities. Rather, an increased intentionality is necessary to connect and integrate the practices of writing center consultants and librarians.

Several librarians with different disciplinary responsibilities worked with the writing center director to "scale down" the messiness of the research and writing processes by highlighting the similarities of everyday practice by both groups, similar to what Lea Currie and Michele Eodice (2005) described in "Roots Entwined: Growing a Sustainable Collaboration" (2005). Of particular emphasis was the classic non-directive premises of Stephen North's (1982) "better writers, not just better writing" (p. 439) and the active listening strategies of the librarian's "reference interview" (North, 1982, p. 439; Ross et al., 2009). Both of these practices embrace the messy collaborative learning in Lev Vygotsky's Zone of Proximal Development, in which writers or researchers work to build upon already developed skills, with support. It is in their messy, interpersonal character that the power of these moments emerges (Elmborg, 2002; Nordlof, 2014). This interpersonal approach has been part of Auburn's writing center training for years, as it is a fundamental principle of writing center pedagogy following the work of Elizabeth Boquet, Anne Ellen Geller, Michele Eodice, Frankie Condon, and Meg Carroll (Boquet, 2002; Geller et al., 2007).

At Auburn, our more focused, intentional collaboration between the library and the writing center began with the writing center consultants' first training sessions and continued throughout their monthly professional development series. The training's goals included (a) to illuminate the parallels in practice between the reference interview and the writing consultation, (b) to have consultants connect their thinking about the writing process to the research process, (c) to integrate scholarly readings into the consultants' ongoing professional development practicum, and most important, (d) to build a culture of collaboration between consultants and librarians. The training also had an underlying, broader goal of developing consultants' confidence in their own research skills.

To achieve these goals, librarians were invited to a training session for the consultants, where they demonstrated the reference interview. For librarians, the reference interview is a particular kind of conversation—one in which the librarian must gather from the user what they're looking for and why. This must be done in a non-threatening way so that the user does not feel that they're being interrogated or judged, lest they withdraw from the interaction without receiving the support they need. Open-ended questions and reflective listening are often employed in the reference interview to ensure that the librarian understands the user's need so they can direct them appropriately (American Library Association, 2008).

After watching a re-enactment of a typical reference interview, writing consultants were asked to connect the tactics and strategies they saw in the skit to their own practice in one-on-one consultations. Consultants were invited to share their observations with the group. In particular, consultants noted that they, like the librarians, attempted to show the writer that they were interested and invested in the exchange by adopting an open body posture and asking reflective questions. Additionally, the writing consultants resisted the impulse to be directive, and instead let the writer take the lead.

In a subsequent semester, consultants were introduced to a scholarly article that connected research and writing in a more substantive way—the first year the article was Joseph Bizup's (2008) "BEAM: A Rhetorical Vocabulary for Teaching Research-Based Writing;" the second year the reading was Rebecca Moore Howard and Sandra Jamieson's (2014) "Researched Writing." The librarians returned to discuss the article with the consultants, who had discussed the articles in smaller groups, focusing on how the readings could enrich their practice. This allowed for more reflective discussion regarding the similarities between the work of librarians and consultants. The consultants responded very positively to Bizup's call to disrupt the oversimplified vision of sources as simply "primary" and "secondary," and to see the source assessment as a fundamental to the construction of meaning, rather than the mere gathering of information. This discussion shed light on the nebulous nature of classifying sources as primary or secondary, as disciplines define these terms differently.

This squared very well with the consultants' writer-centered approach, where the core question "what are you trying to say?" would drive discussions with clients, rather than a simplistic categorizing of "what kind of sources are you supposed to use?" In fact, the consultants were initially somewhat resistant to

Bizup's new model because they first saw it as a new set of "rules" that they'd have to impose on writers—an approach they have been trained to resist. The discussions with the librarians helped to refocus the consultants to see Bizup's approach as a new tool to use to help writers make more active choices about how they utilize sources in their writing.

From a librarian's perspective, the writing center consultant is in a unique position to ensure a smooth, anxiety-free introduction between the writer-researcher and the librarian because they have already established a connection and built rapport with the writer-researcher. At Auburn University, although our writing center has no walls around it, we saw that our consultants were often stopped from approaching the librarians by an invisible barrier. Our joint training sessions sought to remove this barrier. But we also want more than for consultants to merely handoff a writer to the librarian. We want the consultants, when research questions emerge in their discussions, to feel confident in beginning a conversation about how to find sources, and when a consultant feels the conversation has moved beyond her comfort level, we want her to feel confident moving to the reference desk and continuing that session with the reference librarian, "dovetailing" the reference interview and writing consultation. Focusing on these shared practices in the everyday experience of writers, consultants, and librarians, helps refocus away from a linear narrative to the productive and empowering messiness of the individual writer's choices as they work on a project and build their skills through collaboration.

We've seen many moments when this empowerment emerges in a session; consultants, again and again, see students (especially from introductory courses in disciplines from Human Development and Family Studies to Crop, Soil, and Environmental Sciences) looking to find sources to support a point they've already established, or (even more dramatically) completely at a loss for what to say about a complex issue which they've read extensively about and on which they need to take a position. Embracing the messiness of this moment, for those students, is about finding their voice within a broad conversation. For example, one student came to a consultant with a project for their introductory Crop Soils class, in which they had to take a position on a current controversy—the student had chosen to write on the weed killer Roundup and recent revelations that it is a significant carcinogen. The student had read multiple sources, but they were struggling to find a position—they were looking for the "right answer," and were uncomfortable with the messiness of their indeterminate research. At that moment, the consultant reassured them that it was okay that what they saw was messy, and that they should feel empowered to find their own understanding within that messiness—that recognition of indeterminacy let that writer find a clarity from which they could build their meaning, based on their reading and research.

Sometimes, that empowerment can come from much smaller gestures. For example, a student came looking for help with her English composition paper on her chosen topic, the hip-hop artist Gucci Mane, but had run into a roadblock as she attempted to find sources. At this moment, it was gratifying to see the creative, process-oriented thinking of the consultant kick in, as she wasn't looking for the "right way" to look for sources—she was not intimidated, but saw working creatively with library resources as fun, internalizing the work we'd done in the training to empower her as a researcher, and in turn help her share that knowledge with other students. It turned out, the writer had been in the wrong search box on the library's website—she'd been searching the library's catalog instead of an article database. She went from not being able to find any sources on her topic to retrieving over 100 sources, including Gucci Mane's autobiography.

This is a powerful moment because it illustrates the liberation of an emerging writer from a rigid, linear process to engage in a scaled down version of a messier research/writing process, which reflects a more authentic research and writing experience. What resonates most is the positive energy the consultant and writer brought to this creative moment, an array of over 100 different sources became an opportunity not a challenge. The consultant was confident enough in her research skills to help the writer navigate the stumbling block they faced in identifying where to search for their topic, but it was also clear that, following our training, had the issues become more complicated, the consultant could move the discussion to the reference desk to continue the conversation. In the past several years, the reference librarians at Auburn have seen an increase in these kinds of conversations where writing center consultants have introduced writer-researchers to the reference desk for help in finding sources related to accounting (comparison of U.S. and international accounting standards), education (impact of school dress codes), psychology (test anxiety and academic outcomes for homeschooled adolescents), and biology (the population effect of warfare on men's life expectancy in the nineteenth century South).

This positive energy, finally, is the power of the interpersonal engagement of the writing consultation and the reference interview. The empowerment of the student to find their creative place in an ongoing conversation. The writer-researcher can discover the affirmation to navigate the messiness, to make choices and build their thinking (and writing) skills. Those moves can be as simple as using a different search box—or searching in a different bin. But without an active and engaged perspective on the empowering messiness of research, writing consultants will be less likely to create moments like this for writers—so we want to continue to build environments that will empower students in these moments.

CONCLUSION

The research process and the writing process are not mutually exclusive, and the overlaps between them are fraught and messy. However, in trying to simplify the complex processes of research and writing, painting them as linear or sequential does our students no favors. If they embrace this simplistic approach, students will think they have mastered research and writing when they are, in fact, merely performing at a superficial level; when they do encounter a complex research writing situation, they will be frustrated and overwhelmed. This is increasingly more likely as students move into their disciplinary courses, and begin to unpack what research and writing looks like in different disciplines.

Disciplinary faculty, writing center staff, and librarians can use the messy overlaps between research and writing to our advantage. Through collaboration among our disciplines, we can model best practices for students who are struggling. Just as we encourage students to engage in a creative, recursive process that transfers beyond the composition classroom and library into their courses across campus, so must faculty, librarians and writing center consultants be willing to cede some "turf." Such collaborations can be uncomfortable; they are unpredictable, non-linear, and iterative, just like the writing and research processes themselves. It is in our students' best interests, and ultimately our own, to partner with our colleagues across campus and across disciplines to pursue the many shared skills and experiences we value and want students to develop in their research and writing throughout their academic careers. By embracing the messiness of collaboration, research, and writing, we will help our students recognize the tremendous value in all three processes.

ACKNOWLEDGMENT

Special thanks to Toni Carter for her contributions to the earlier versions of this manuscript and the accompanying panel session at IWAC 2018.

REFERENCES

American Library Association (ALA). (2008). *Guidelines for behavioral performance of reference and information service providers*. http://www.ala.org/rusa/resources/guidelines/guidelinesbehavioral.

Association of College and Research Libraries (ACRL). (2000). *Information literacy competency standards for higher education: Standards, performance indicators and outcomes*. https://alair.ala.org/handle/11213/7668.

Association of College and Research Libraries (ACRL). (2015). *Framework for information literacy for higher education*. http://www.ala.org/acrl/standards/ilframework.

Bizup, J. (2008). BEAM: A rhetorical vocabulary for teaching research-based writing. *Rhetoric Review, 27*(1), 72–86. https://doi.org/10.1080/07350190701738858.

Blakeslee, S. (2004). The CRAAP test. *LOEX Quarterly, 31*(3), 4.

Booth, W. C., Colomb, G. G. & Williams, J. M. (2008). *The craft of research.* University of Chicago Press. https://doi.org/10.7208/chicago/9780226062648.001.0001.

Boquet, E. H. (2002). *Noise from the writing center.* Utah State University Press. https://doi.org/10.2307/j.ctt46nwjt.

Bruffee, K. A. (1993). *Collaborative learning: Higher education, interdependence, and the authority of knowledge.* Johns Hopkins University Press.

Burke, K. (1974). *The philosophy of literary form: Studies in symbolic action.* University of California Press.

Council of Writing Program Administrators (CWPA), National Council of Teachers of English (NCTE) & National Writing Project (NWP). (2011). *Framework for success in postsecondary writing.* https://ncte.org/statement/collwritingframework/.

Currie, L. & Eodice, M. (2005). Roots entwined: Growing a sustainable collaboration. In J. K. Elmborg & S. Hook (Eds.), *Centers for learning: Writing centers and libraries in collaboration* (pp. 42–60). Association of College and Research Libraries.

Davis, R. & Shadle, M. (2000). "Building a mystery": Alternative research writing and the academic act of seeking. *College Composition and Communication, 51*(3), 417–446. https://doi.org/10.2307/358743.

Detmering, R. & Johnson, A. M. (2011). Focusing on the thinking, not the tools: Incorporating critical thinking into an information literacy module for an introduction to business course. *Journal of Business & Finance Librarianship, 16*(2), 101–107. https://doi.org/10.1080/08963568.2011.554771.

Elbow, P. (1973). *Writing without teachers.* Oxford University Press.

Elmborg, J. K. (2002). Teaching at the desk: Toward a reference pedagogy. *portal: Libraries and the Academy, 2,* 455–464. https://doi.org/10.1353/pla.2002.0050.

Elmborg, J. K. & Hook, S. (Eds.). (2005). *Centers for learning: Writing centers and libraries in collaboration* (No. 58). Association of College & Research Libraries.

Geller, A. E., Eodice, M., Condon, F., Carroll, M. & Boquet, E. (2007). *Everyday writing center: A community of practice.* Utah State University Press. https://doi.org/10.2307/j.ctt4cgmkj.

Grafstein, A. (2002). A discipline-based approach to information literacy. *The Journal of Academic Librarianship, 28*(4), 197–204. https://doi.org/10.1016/S0099-1333(02)00283-5

Hairston, M. (1982). The winds of change: Thomas Kuhn and the revolution in the teaching of writing. *College Composition and Communication, 33*(1), 76–88. https://doi.org/10.2307/357846.

Hall, R. M., Romo, M. & Wardle, E. (2018). Teaching and learning threshold concepts in a writing major: Liminality, Dispositions, and Program Design. *Composition Forum, 38.*

Hood, C. L. (2010). Ways of research: The status of the traditional research paper assignment in first-year writing/composition courses. *Composition Forum, 22.* http://compositionforum.com/issue/22/ways-of-research.php.

Hook, S. (2005). Teaching librarians and writing center professionals in collaboration: Complementary practices. In J. K. Elmborg & S. Hook (Eds.), *Centers for learning: Writing centers and libraries in collaboration* (pp. 21–41). Association of College and Research Libraries.

Howard, R. M. & Jamieson, S. (2014). Researched writing. In G. Tate, A. Rupiper & K. Schick (Eds.), *A guide to composition pedagogies* (pp. 231–247). Oxford University Press.

Lupton, M. & Bruce, C. (2010). Windows on information literacy worlds: Generic, situated and transformative perspectives. In A. Lloyd & S. Talja (Eds.), *Practising information literacy: Bringing theories of learning, practice and information literacy together* (pp. 3–27). Centre for Information Studies. https://doi.org/10.1016/B978-1-876938-79-6.50001-7.

Maid, B. M. & D'Angelo, B. J. (2016). Threshold concepts: Integrating and applying information literacy and writing instruction. In B. J. D'Angelo, S. Jamieson, B. M. Maid & J. Walker, (Eds.), *Information literacy: Research and collaboration across disciplines*. The WAC Clearinghouse; Parlor Press. https://wac.colostate.edu/books/perspectives/infolit/.

Marshall, S. (2015). *Negotiating genre: Emergence and development of "the research paper" in first-year composition, 1912–1962* [Doctoral dissertation, Florida State University]. Proquest Dissertations & Theses Global (1600065).

McKinney, J. G. (2002). The American scholar writes the "new" research essay. *Journal of Teaching Writing, 20*(1 & 2), 71–86.

Mullin, J. (2001). Response: We will find a way to work together. *Journal of College Reading and Learning, 31*, 244–250. https://doi.org/10.1080/10790195.2001.10850119.

Murray, D. (1972). Teach writing as a process not product. *The Leaflet, 71*(3), 11–14.

Nordlof, J. (2014). Vygotsky, scaffolding, and the role of theory in writing center work. *The Writing Center Journal, 34*(1), 45–64.

Norgaard, R. (2003). "Writing information literacy: Contributions to a concept." *Reference and User Services Quarterly, 43*, 124–130.

North, S. M. (1982). "Training tutors to talk about writing." *College Composition and Communication, 33*, 434–441. https://doi.org/10.2307/357958.

Ramage, J. D. & Bean, J. C. (1997). *The Allyn and Bacon guide to writing*. Allyn and Bacon.

Ross, C. S., Radford, M. L. & Nilsen, K. (2009). *Conducting the reference interview: A how-to-do-it-manual for librarians*. Neal-Schuman.

University of Wisconsin-Madison Writing Center. (n.d.). "Writing a research paper." https://writing.wisc.edu/handbook/assignments/planresearchpaper/.

Weiler, A. (2005). Information-seeking behavior in Generation Y students: Motivation, critical thinking, and learning theory. *Journal of Academic Librarianship, 31*(1), 46–53. https://doi.org/10.1016/j.acalib.2004.09.009.

CHAPTER 13.

ENGLISH ACROSS THE CURRICULUM COLLABORATIVE PROJECTS: A FLEXIBLE COMMUNITY OF PRACTICE MODEL AT THE CHINESE UNIVERSITY OF HONG KONG

Jose Lai
The Chinese University of Hong Kong

Elaine Ng
The Chinese University of Hong Kong

Laura Man
The Chinese University of Hong Kong

Chris Rozendaal
The Chinese University of Hong Kong

While Writing Across the Curriculum (WAC) initiatives have a history stretching back several decades in the West, their development in Asia has been more recent. This paper discusses the development and implementation of an institutionalized initiative, the English Across the Curriculum (EAC) project at The Chinese University of Hong Kong. This campus-wide movement differs from many Western initiatives in that it utilizes Community of Practice (CoP) collaborative projects which include applied linguists and ESL specialists as well as content specialists. Additionally, due to student diversity and the unique language policy of the university, the project has eschewed adopting a fixed implementation model, instead allowing alternative forms of collaboration and implementation approaches to emerge based on needs and specific domains. This paper specifically explores

DOI: https://doi.org/10.37514/PER-B.2020.0360.2.13

225

the similarities, differences, challenges, and keys to success of four CoP projects that have been implemented in four departments: statistics, information engineering, music, and psychology.

Writing Across the Curriculum (WAC) initiatives have been prevalent for decades at institutions throughout the United States and the United Kingdom (Jones & Comprone, 1993; McConlogue et al., 2012; Wingate, 2016; Zawacki & Cox, 2014; Zawacki & Rogers, 2012), where the majority of students use English as a first language (L1), and in Europe (Boch & Frier, 2012; Dalton-Puffer, 2007; Zuckermann et al., 2012), where English is generally a second language (L2). In recent years, WAC has also gained popularity in Asia (Wu, 2013), notably in Hong Kong, where English L2 students commonly face English as the medium of instruction (Braine & McNaught, 2007; Lughmani et al., 2016).

At The Chinese University of Hong Kong (CUHK), an institution-wide language enhancement English Across the Curriculum (EAC) initiative has been implemented over the past two years with government funding. This initiative extends the WAC tradition and previous WAC implementations at CUHK, which exclusively focused on academic writing (Braine & McNaught, 2007), to include all language modalities in an L2 setting, allowing English acquisition for students to proceed beyond traditional English as a Second Language (ESL) courses directly into their chosen disciplines.

The EAC project at CUHK differs from traditional implementations in several ways. Unlike WAC administrators in the US who are often composition specialists for L1 writers, EAC supervisors at CUHK are either applied linguists or ESL specialists dealing almost exclusively with L2 learners. Furthermore, the EAC team not only works closely with content teachers, but also directly with students, who are mostly L2 learners in need of assistance in both higher- and lower order concerns. In other words, assumption of monolingual learners with L1 proficiency simply does not hold, and, as a result, EAC interventions can neither ignore lower-order concerns nor allow them to overwhelm higher-order concerns. As universities in the West increasingly address multilingualism, a situation described by Hebbard and Hernández in "Becoming *Transfronterizo* Collaborators: A Transdisciplinary Framework for Developing Translingual Pedagogies in WAC/WID" (this volume), approaches implemented in multilingual environments may be of interest. In this paper, we will first introduce the setting in which this EAC project has been implemented. Then, we will justify the adoption of a flexible model for developing Community of Practice (CoP) collaborative projects, four of which were selected for further explanation due to their unique requirements. Based on the experiences and insights gained, we will discuss the similarities, differences, challenges, and keys to success of the four

CoP projects with four departments in question: statistics, information engineering, music, and psychology. We hope that this discussion can not only show the diversity of situations into which EAC interventions are being introduced, but can also highlight some of the commonalities found across these projects.

The EAC movement at CUHK owes much to the WAC scholarship despite its predominant focus on L1 settings. In return, it is our humble hope that, by sharing our experience in this article, our implementation of EAC in an L2 setting would be seen as a practical implementation of the "mutually transformative model of ESL/WAC collaboration," advocated by researchers within the L2 writing field (see Matsuda & Jablonski, 2000) and by WAC advocates such as Cox (2011), Ferris and Thaiss (2011), and Zawacki and Cox (2014).

SETTING

Since 2012, all universities in Hong Kong have adopted a four-year undergraduate curriculum, and local students are admitted based on the Hong Kong Diploma of Secondary Education (HKDSE) Examination results, a public university entrance examination administered to students upon the completion of a six-year secondary schooling. This is to replace the former Hong Kong Certificate of Education Examination (HKCEE) and the Hong Kong Advanced Level Examination (HKALE) (Hong Kong Examinations and Assessment Authority, 2015). Due to this territory-wide educational reform, all freshmen are now admitted with one less year of advanced English language training, which has adversely affected the linguistic landscape of CUHK, as students are less able to communicate in English at the levels required by various departments.

The Chinese University of Hong Kong (CUHK) is a comprehensive research university that has eight faculties (equivalent to a "college" at most U.S. universities) with an annual intake of over 4,000 undergraduate students. It is the only local university to adopt a biliterate (Chinese and English) and trilingual (Cantonese, Mandarin, and English) language education policy, which allows departments flexibility in determining their language of instruction. The proportion of Chinese and English used in an individual department is then based on the nature of their academic subject, student activities and available course materials (Chinese University of Hong Kong, 2006). Regardless of their discipline, all students, except English majors, are required to take credit-bearing English language courses for graduation requirements.

The English Language Teaching Unit (ELTU), where the EAC project team comes from, is tasked with the responsibility of developing and offering credit-bearing English language courses to undergraduates across the university. A nine-credit ELTU curriculum spanning three years has been in place since 2012, covering courses on English for Academic Purposes (EAP), English for Specific Purposes (ESP), English for Professional Purposes (EPP), as well as interest-based courses. However, some credit-bearing courses cannot adequately prepare students for genre-specific/domain-specific disciplinary requirements necessitated by different departments, resulting in a gap between what students are expected to do and what they are able to do. Hence, additional language enhancement funding from the University Grants Committee (UGC) in Hong Kong is often made available through pedagogical projects.

The University Grants Committee (UGC) under the Hong Kong Government provides both recurrent grants and capital grants to eight universities in Hong Kong, including The Chinese University of Hong Kong (University Grants Committee, 2017a). Teaching Development and Language Enhancement Grant (TDLEG) is one of the capital grants to encourage innovative language enhancement activities, with a total of $512.8 million allocated in the 2016–2019 triennium (University Grants Committee, 2017b). Universities have the autonomy to decide on the use of the funding according to their institutional needs. At CUHK, the need to bridge the gap between expected outcomes and actual student abilities, especially in terms of developing disciplinary literacies in English, became apparent due to the replacement of HKALE by HKDSE, which resulted in students receiving one less year of advanced English language input. This gap was further confirmed by the one-year pilot project titled "EAC at CUHK (2015–2016)" funded by the University's Community of Practice (CoP) Grant. To address this specific need, ELTU further proposed to launch a large-scale English Across the Curriculum (EAC) initiative, comprising collaborative Communities of Practice (CoPs) on campus.

ENGLISH ACROSS THE CURRICULUM (EAC)

With the support of the Teaching Development and Language Enhancement Grant (TDLEG), a three-year institutionalized EAC project (2016–2019) was launched by the English Language Teaching Unit (ELTU) at CUHK to complement the existing curriculum by extending the acquisition and use of English from traditional language course settings to other disciplines, beyond ESL classes. Consistent with the ELTU mission statement of "seeking out opportunities to work with departments and faculties across the university to address the specific English language learning needs of their students" (ELTU, 2018) and modeled on U.K. "disciplinary literacy" (Lea & Street, 1998; Wingate, 2012, 2016; Wingate & Tribble, 2012) and U.S. WAC practice (Anson, 2002; Zawacki & Rogers, 2012) whereby subject specialists collaborate with language specialists to empower students in their use of English within their discipline, the aims of the EAC project at CUHK have been to further enhance students' academic literacies beyond formal ESL class settings and to help content professors and students develop a heightened awareness of disciplinary literacy. It is hoped that students will acquire language and knowledge transfer skills (Graff, 2010) by incorporating what they have learned from the EAC interventions into their respective disciplines.

The EAC project also hopes to encourage content professors to see beyond their disciplinary specialization to assume stronger ownership in fostering language education. To this end, the EAC team has invited disciplinary specialists and language specialists to cooperate in establishing collaborative Community of Practice (CoP) projects (after Wenger, 1998). According to social anthropologists Etienne C. Wenger, Richard McDermott and Williams C. Snyder (2002), CoPs are "groups of people who share a concern, a set of problems, or a passion about a topic, and who deepen their knowledge and expertise in this area by interacting on an ongoing basis" (p. 4). This definition has been subsequently characterized by three key coexisting elements—the domain, the community, and the practice (E. Wenger-Trayner & B. Wenger-Trayner, 2015)—which keep the CoP together. When translated into our setting, content teachers and language teachers are collaborators of CoP who share a common domain (a shared problem of students' limited academic literacy), form a community (in which constant interactions and negotiations take place), and establish a practice (from which shared resources, outcomes, and repertoire are found).

Given the widely diverse contexts within which each CoP is operating, as Jaena Alabi and colleagues note in "Embrace the Messiness: Libraries, Writing Centers, and Encouraging Research as Inquiry Across the Curriculum" (this volume), we have chosen not to employ a single top-down, fixed-model approach. Instead, we have adopted a flexible approach, where each individual CoP is encouraged to develop any type of intervention that would be most appropriate and useful within the context in which it is being implemented. This was decided largely because of the diversity in academic backgrounds of our partnering content professors, as well as the diverse levels of English proficiency among the students in different departments. As a result of these differences, the language needs being addressed by the EAC team are also diverse, and highly genre-specific/domain-specific. To account for this diversity, the EAC project has been supportive of a variety of alternative forms of collaboration and approaches in implementing CoP projects.

The EAC team is currently working with all eight faculties at the university, including collaborations with more than 40 professors in the development of more than 16 collaborative CoP projects. In the following sections, four of these collaborative CoP projects—statistics, information engineering, music, and psychology—will be described and then discussed in terms of similarities, differences, challenges, and coping strategies shared amongst them. The four projects presented here were chosen primarily because they represent well the diversity of contexts faced by different collaborators. By highlighting this diversity, we hope to show the value and necessity of maintaining a flexible model. Tables 13.1 and 13.2 highlight these diversities, including differences in subject domain, student proficiency and motivation, linguistic contexts, and motivations for intervention.

Table 13.1. Summary of four communities of practice: Characteristics

Community of Practice	Proficiency	Motivation	Medium of Instruction	Target Language Output
Statistics	Low	Low	English	Evaluative Report
Information Engineering	Low	Low	English	Final Year Project Report
Psychology	High	High	Mixed	Web Discussions
Music	Mixed	High	Mixed	Examination Writing & Reflective Writing

Table 13.2. Summary of four communities of practice: Interventions

Community of Practice	Intervention Type	Scheduling	Content Professor Attendance
Statistics	Classroom Workshops, Debriefing Sessions	During class hours	Yes
Information Engineering	Lecture-style Workshop, TA Training	Outside class hours	No
Psychology	Lecture-style Workshop	During class hours	Yes
Music	Classroom Workshops	During class hours	Partial

STATISTICS

The Department of Statistics, which uses English as its medium of instruction, was one of the earliest to show interest in the EAC initiative, which was piloted with full support of a content professor who was also a member of the university's senior management team. She had learned from ELTU about the previous attempt of WAC at CUHK (Braine & McNaught, 2007) and was pleased that the unit would like to rekindle and expand this good practice through implementing EAC as an institutional movement. This professor was interested not only in improving outcomes in an individual course, but more broadly in exploring the practicality, effectiveness, and sustainability of EAC at CUHK. The course identified for a pilot intervention was STAT3005: Applied Nonparametric Statistics, which is taken by year two and three students who are generally considered to have low motivation for language learning and relatively weak English language skills. The aims of this intervention were (a) to enhance the level of language awareness and language use among the students in writing an evaluative report; and (b) to enhance the competence and confidence of the content teaching assistant (TA) in awarding language marks for the reports. The evaluative report was chosen for the intervention because it is a commonly used genre but often poorly handled by statisticians in the workplace. Despite the students' competence as statisticians, they were having difficulty communicating research findings or recommendations to non-specialists in their reports.

Noting the importance of written communication skills both in the academic and professional settings, the professor agreed to adopt a writing-to-learn pedagogy (Gere, 1985; Herrington, 1981) by incorporating short writing tasks in class and including several more substantive writing tasks as part of higher stakes assessments. She also agreed to allocate 10 percent of the marks for each of these assessment tasks to language use.

To emphasize the importance of language training, all workshops and debriefing sessions were conducted during content lecture hours, with the content professor present. The initial step was taken by the professor who asked her students to discuss in class what constitutes an effective briefing paper, in order to raise students' awareness of the genre. Their written responses based on these discussions were collected and subsequently collated for comparison. Interestingly, the criteria and relative weightings produced by the students were surprisingly similar to those devised by the EAC team based on genre features, reducing the need to create student "buy-in" for the language-related intervention in subsequent meetings.

To obtain a baseline understanding of students' needs and to prepare for the intervention workshop, the EAC team and the content TA from the Statistics department cooperated to analyze the mid-term examination papers of all the students in the class (around 60), using certain pre-defined criteria and weighting. At the same time, textual analysis was conducted by the EAC team to identify specific areas of improvement to be highlighted in the training workshops. It was determined that the focus of training would be on the structural and language features of the evaluative report.

To deepen students' understanding of the genre, interactive in-class activities were designed, with salient features exemplified in a model text developed by the EAC team with the concurrence of the content professor. The training also included authentic student samples being shown on the screen, which seemed to capture the students' interest especially effectively, and a concise one-page handout outlining the most important structural and language features of an evaluative report (see Appendix A). Student uptake was tracked by including a similar question on the final examination, which was marked using the same set of assessment criteria. Results of this showed a statistically significant improvement in the students' final evaluative report outcomes.

Pleased with the results of this collaboration, the content professor and the EAC team decided to continue the collaboration for a second academic year. In this second iteration, in addition to the workshop on writing an evaluative report, the professor requested a workshop on writing a briefing paper, which is a proposal intended for non-specialists. The needs analysis for the briefing paper was done using take-home assignments from the previous semester, in which students were asked to explain technical statistical concepts to a nontechnical audience. The students were each given 15 briefing papers from this pool and asked to rank them for quality, and they were then asked to articulate the assessment criteria they had used in the exercise. This exercise allowed the students to infer connections between content knowledge and language use. At the same time, the EAC team and the content TA assessed the entire pool of briefing papers using a standardized rubric.

Materials for the briefing paper workshop were designed based on the findings of the needs analysis, and included a model text and student work presented with annotations. Although the workshop was initially scheduled for 45 minutes, the content professor spontaneously requested that it be extended to 90 minutes, noting students' active engagement with the learning tasks and the useful materials developed.

For the third academic year, student feedback was starting to imply that, while the workshops were helpful, the writing load for the class was becoming excessive. Thus, the intervention was limited to a single text type, the briefing paper. This genre was preferred as it requires both evaluative skills and business communication skills. Two workshops were conducted on this topic (rather than one, as in previous years), and students were again provided feedback on assignments and examination writing.

Results of this intervention were shared with students during a debriefing session in the language they knew best: statistics. In addition to descriptive statistics and evidence of improvement, in the same debriefing meeting, the team also shared key observations about student writing in terms of formality, structure, and quality of analysis. Finally, the team showcased examples of excellent work on screen, demonstrating to students that language improvement is something achievable, even for students with lower proficiency.

According to post-workshop surveys, students found the intervention practical and relevant. It was noted especially that the use of students' own writing samples during the workshops contributed much to their success. In addition, the content TA also found the exercise very valuable. Not only has he become more competent in assessing students' written language, he also found his own disciplinary literacy enhanced as a result. Invariably over the years, the success of this CoP hinges upon the continuous interplay between the content professor and the EAC specialist throughout the process, with each party assuming an active and key role at different stages of collaboration. Based on the successful experiences, continued collaboration between the Statistics Department and the EAC team is already being planned.

INFORMATION ENGINEERING

The Faculty of Engineering was targeted because English is the official medium of instruction for the faculty but, ironically, these students tend to have the weakest language proficiency. A professor in the Information Engineering (IE) department responded to the EAC team's call for collaboration in order to address language shortcomings in written reports produced by fourth-year students as part of their *IERG 4998: Final Year Project* (FYP) course. The FYP is a required, two-semester capstone project that each student completes under the guidance of a faculty advisor. The grading guidelines for the project, derived from the department's accrediting engineering body, include the requirement that students display an "ability to communicate effectively" (Department of Information Engineering, 2018). As the Faculty of Engineering is an English-medium faculty, this requires that the communication be done in English.

To help students improve their written reports, the team analyzed past student work, while also completing a genre analysis of published work in the IE field (Wingate, 2012) to observe conventions of structure, language, and reference (Linton et al., 1994). Input from the IE department indicated their preference that interventions focus primarily on conventions of structure. One of the challenges faced was that the written guidance being given to students by the department for writing their FYP reports was limited, and seemed designed to provide flexibility rather than structure. This makes sense, as genre analysis confirmed that published articles followed multiple organizational patterns. However, student samples showed that this flexibility was leading to the omission of certain critical information, information that was present in all published articles, regardless of their exact organization.

The team initially designed two interventions to provide students with more direction. The first was a one-off student workshop delivered by a member of

233

the EAC team to around 90 students early in the semester. The workshop was held in a lecture theatre and was mandatory for all students enrolled in the FYP course. The primary goal for this workshop was to present a framework that students could use for writing their FYP reports, without imposing a rigid structure or overwhelming them with advice.

This framework was presented to students by organizing the workshop around "Seven Questions That Need an Answer" (see Appendix B). These seven questions were devised such that the answer to each would present critical information necessary for a complete, understandable report. The workshop emphasized the flexibility as to where this information could be included, depending on the organizational pattern agreed upon with the advisors, but also emphasized that all questions needed to be answered somewhere in their reports.

The second intervention was possible because the department agreed to allocate 10 percent of the final course grade to language issues and to provide three graduate student teaching assistants (TAs) to mark and provide feedback on student work, including preliminary drafts. Although these TAs were fluent L2 English speakers, their expertise was in engineering, with no prior experience marking for language issues.

Thus, the EAC team was left with a number of challenges: to come up with a scheme for determining how the 10 percent language mark for each report could be calculated; to find a way to train the TAs effectively; and to maintain a high level of transparency in order to dispel any possible confusion among students and advisors as to how language scores were being calculated. These challenges were addressed by creating a detailed rubric (see Appendix C), with criteria focusing not only on language, but also on whether language was used appropriately to further content goals. In order to provide necessary support to the TAs, detailed descriptors for each level were provided as well. Descriptors for the content goals were carefully worded to correspond to the stated learning outcomes of the course. This rubric provided a measure of objectivity and standardization to the TAs' marking, as well as a support structure to assist them as first-time language markers, and elucidated expectations clearly for students and advisors.

TAs were trained by an EAC team member (an ESL specialist) to use the rubric for marking in an hour-long session and were given further instruction about providing students with limited, concrete, positive advice about improving subsequent drafts. The TAs also attended a standardization meeting led by the same EAC team member when the first draft of student work was submitted, as well as a moderation meeting at the end of the semester before final grades were submitted.

Student feedback obtained through a post-workshop survey was generally positive, with some even requesting that the workshop be longer. The TAs were also positive about their work, believing that their role was "necessary," but also noting with disappointment that some students seemed to ignore their advice. The TAs added that the experience caused them to reconsider aspects of their own writing process, and that they had gained content knowledge from their marking as well. Despite the heavy marking load, all three expressed interest in serving as TAs for the course again in the future. Finally, the FYP course professor was also positive about the collaboration. He believed that the collaborative efforts led to real improvement, and further noted that the Faculty of Engineering considers this collaboration as a possible model for future EAC collaborations with other departments within the faculty.

The experience of this collaboration has left us with several takeaways. First, to really help students with their disciplinary literacy, it is imperative that EAC team members for each project familiarize themselves with both the standards of that discipline and the reality of what students are producing. The diversity of situations being encountered demands that this be done afresh for each new project. Second, when dealing with such a large group of diverse stakeholders (100+ students working with 15+ advisors, in addition to the course teacher and TAs), transparency is vital. By designing the rubric carefully to make expectations and grading policies as clear as possible, everyone involved knew up front what would be happening, and we were able to avoid surprises.

Music

Similar to how the other CoP projects have started, this CoP project in music was another result of the EAC team's effort in reaching out to content professors. A professor in musicology and western music history from Department of Music who is a native speaker of English requested specifically a workshop on language awareness, grammar, and writing concise paragraphs for examinations on music history. Needs analysis, which involved a series of textual analyses, was conducted based on students' previous writing samples collected by an EAC teaching assistant (TA) and with the input of the music professor. Based on these student samples and outcomes generated by the needs analysis, the music professor and the language specialist agreed that these music majors are highly motivated learners well-focused on their instruments but not on English and writing. When given a writing task, most students would formulate ideas quickly based on whatever came to mind, and record these on paper quickly with limited organization. Some did not revise these initial texts at all. Some also paid little attention to grammatical accuracy or word choice, as long as they considered the texts to be comprehensible. Consequently, it was determined that the students would benefit little from basic skills, such as sentence structure, but instead needed explicit guidance on organization, and on musical and academic literacies with sample texts that they could learn from. Students with a lower level of writing proficiency could also learn by adapting their writing directly from the model texts given.

A series of three workshops, conducted during regular lecture hours, were given to year two and three music majors. These 45-minute workshops, which involved mini-lectures, group discussions, reading activities and writing activities, were developed with an aim of helping students with the written component of the course MUSC 3233: History of Western Music II. This first workshop that focused on language awareness and examination writing was requested specifically by the music professor. English has become a de facto requirement in classes where professors are not Chinese speakers. Consequently, even though students might benefit little from basic skills, being able to write effectively in English in an exam situation was still critical.

Part one of the first workshop required students to identify a series of common grammatical errors in sentences and correct them, while part two involved a teacher-demonstration and then a student activity on organizing and formulating concise written paragraphs. In this activity, students received a reading text and an accompanying question, as well as a sample written response to learn from. After this, students were given a new writing question to work on, and were asked to generate their own written responses based on the texts provided. According to feedback from students, these writing workshops were interactive, engaging, focused and effective, despite their limited scale and short duration.

In contrast to the first workshop, the foci of workshops two and three were completely different—reflective writing. Writing reflective texts such as reflective journals has been an ongoing assignment for these music students. Workshop two involved a mini-lecture on "why do musicians reflect" and the different types, functions and organizations of reflective texts, followed by a reading and writing activity in groups on analyzing the structure and language features of a theatre review of the Broadway musical *The Lion King*. Workshop three was a feedback session on the actual reflective journals that students produced during the semester.

As mentioned, students generally enjoyed these workshops and found them useful, because they were highly contextualized and relevant to their major and assessments. However, students have also expressed the need for more or longer workshops in the future. Because the sessions were only 45 minutes, structures and language features introduced were somewhat limited. Moreover, it was difficult for students to see depth in what they did in the workshops when the language specialist was pressed for time. There was also no time for students to understand clearly how learning, knowledge and language were transferable between the workshops and other parts of their major.

Many of these challenges will be addressed in future collaborations between the EAC project and the Department of Music. The content professor has been supportive of the project, making it likely that the project will be sustainable. Future plans include collecting further student writing samples and continuing to develop and offer writing workshops where students can continue to develop their English language and content knowledge in music at the same time. It is our hope that language components such as grammar and vocabulary use can be included in future assessment rubrics used by the department.

PSYCHOLOGY

The CoP project with the Psychology Department is relatively new, having been implemented for just one semester. The Psychology Department uses English as the primary medium of instruction in student assignments and assessments, and follows the APA citation guidelines (Department of Psychology, n.d.). Although psychology majors have relatively high English proficiency, needs analysis of student samples indicated that they lack training in articulating content knowledge concisely in writing. Therefore, the main aim of the collaboration was to improve the students' English writing in a specific course assignment: interactive web discussions.

The students targeted for intervention were 140 first-year students in PSYC1050/UGEB1570: Consciousness, a class containing both psychology majors and students from other departments. The class was made up of two sections, taught by the same content professor with identical learning topics and assignments. Student language proficiency and motivation varied but were generally medium to high relative to CUHK students in general.

Students from these two classes were asked to answer six web-discussion questions spread throughout the term, accounting for 80 percent of the final course grade. Students were expected to answer each discussion question with concise answers of 50 to 100 words containing high levels of language precision, assessing their understanding and application of concepts taught in class. According to the content professor, students were usually unaware of strategies that could be used to create a strong impression in a short piece of writing, as well as documentation skills for direct quotes.

Needs analysis was conducted using student samples across a range of grades from the previous year in order to identify common linguistic pitfalls in answering the questions. Initial findings were shared with the content professor, who concurred with them. However, discovering the reasons behind each individual grade was more difficult, as there was little in the way of a formalized assessment rubric. Thus, much of the EAC team's task was to try to piece together how exactly the grades were being given. This was done largely through back-and-forth email communications with the content professor.

The intervention for this project took the form of a workshop held before the students' first assignment submission. The aims of the workshop were to teach students (a) how to write precisely, concisely, and professionally; (b) how to tackle the course assignments, namely web discussion questions, effectively; and (c) how to avoid plagiarism. Given the 90-minute, one-off nature of the workshop, the EAC team had to distill the workshop content down to most salient language issues that repeatedly emerged during the needs analysis. Due to the relatively strong linguistic profiles of the target students, the workshop centered on advanced linguistic elements such as academic writing style and sentence patterns rather than fundamental grammar.

The size of the workshop was another challenge, as over 100 students attended. To avoid turning the workshop into a one-way lecture, the EAC team decided to adopt a student-centered approach, allowing the learners to discover effective writing strategies by themselves. This was done by pairing carefully-selected strong and weak samples, and allowing students to discuss what they felt were strong and weak features of each. Each pair of samples focused on a single target element, and the workshop teacher constantly asked questions, provided immediate feedback on the students' findings and offering additional advice when necessary. A video was also used when recapping main points.

The feedback from the students was positive. A paper-form post-workshop questionnaire was administered immediately after the workshop, indicating that students greatly appreciated the organization of the workshop, the explanations of the teacher, and the use of authentic student samples. However, they also hoped for even more student samples, as well as greater transparency about how they were being graded.

Feedback from the content professor was positive as well. During a post-workshop meeting, he commented that most of the students who had received C-range grades and lodged grade appeals were those who had chosen not to attend the workshop, implying the effectiveness of the workshop in helping students better meet course requirements and enhance their performance.

Overall, the workshop has brought out the importance of using authentic student samples to facilitate teaching and learning in WAC-related workshops. Although future collaboration has not yet been finalized, it is hoped that it could involve two workshops during the semester, arranged before and after the students' first assignment, so that the learners could receive both guidance before the assignment and feedback afterwards. This kind of arrangement would also allow the EAC team to track students' performance over time to better ascertain the effectiveness of the intervention.

DISCUSSION

The above reports on four CoP projects with Statistics, IE, Music, and Psychology seem to validate the approach of adopting flexible CoP models for the implementation of EAC at CUHK. It is evident that each CoP collaborator had unique support requirements based on the students' language profile, expected learning outcomes, and practical considerations. Some requests from departments greatly exceeded expectations, leaving the team impressed by the readiness of these professors to go the extra mile for enhancing their students' disciplinary literacy. While it is true that we have learned unique lessons from each CoP (Table 13.1), some insights gained can be applicable to all cases and are worth spreading across the disciplines and across contexts. First and foremost, the importance of interplay between content professors and the EAC team is crucial to helping students bridge the perceived gap between content learning and language enhancement activities. In cases where the student population is large and diverse, transparency of practice should be observed to avoid unnecessary confusion. In all cases, relevance to student assessments in the context of content subject knowledge and the use of authentic student samples are key to motivation of learning. To further elaborate our findings, we will discuss the similarities, differences, challenges and coping strategies in greater detail in the following sections.

SIMILARITIES

Although the EAC team's "no-fixed model" approach led to considerable diversity in the types of interventions undertaken, some commonalities can be observed, illustrating aspect of the interventions which seem to be useful across contexts. The most important of these was that the key to a successful collaboration was the "sustained mutual relationships" with content professors, with consensus on appropriate "actions and products" (Wenger, 1998, p. 125) throughout the process. To that end, once potential CoP collaborators were identified, initial meetings were aimed not at "solving problems," but at cultivating mutual understanding of the joint venture to make it a shared enterprise. Establishing a shared vision early in the process almost invariably laid the groundwork for the success of the interventions.

For each of these projects, the mutual trust and respect that were fostered with partner departments allowed the EAC team to benefit from the rich resources these content teachers were able to provide: relevant course documents such as course outlines and schedules; assessment tasks, including guidelines and rubrics; and samples of past student work, when available. These documents formed the basis for conducting needs analyses and preparing the interventions, which again relied on honest discussion and mutual agreement with the CoP collaborators. As trust continued to develop, collaborators were often willing to build language marks into their assessment rubrics, helping to bridge students' perceived gap between language acquisition and content knowledge building.

As relationships with CoP partners deepened, so did levels of collaboration. For example, after three years of interaction, the EAC team for Statistics was invited to comment on the program's examination and assignment prompts. Similarly, after two years of collaboration, the IE team was asked to assist in writing a new student assignment sheet and has broadened their focus beyond student writing to preparing students for oral poster presentations as well. The Music team was unexpectedly asked to expand their collaboration from examination question writing to reflective writing. Finally, although the Psychology intervention was a one-off collaboration, initial feedback implies that content professors would be quite interested in future collaboration as well. In all cases, taking the time to establish a shared vision was found to be extremely worthwhile not only because it can help ensure a smooth implementation of a particular CoP but also because it is necessary for sustainability.

Another common feature found analogous in all contexts is the use of student samples as learning materials. As reported in all CoPs, student samples were used not only for analyzing learning needs; they were used as learning materials during the interventions to engage students and motivate learning. This practice was greatly appreciated by students from different CoPs, as reflected in the post-intervention surveys.

A final commonality among these projects was that all included evaluative measures to determine the possible impact of interventions on student learning and to improve practice in future attempts. These included post-intervention student surveys, feedback interviews with content professors and TAs, and tracking of student learning over time. Assessment rubrics or frameworks, developed by the EAC team with input from content teachers, have proved useful for tracking student learning objectively.

Differences

Major differences between these collaborative projects seemed largely the result of the diversity in language abilities and attitudes among students, as well as the diverse requirements and expectations of partnering departments. These differences naturally led to very different types of requests, which were very specific and had compelling reasons behind them. For example, although IE and Statistics students have similarly weak language proficiency, the IE department wanted help with a technical report written for an audience of engineers, while the Statistics department preferred a focus on workplace communication skills, especially in conveying statistical concepts to a nontechnical audience. Thus, even with similarities between students, EAC practitioners need to consider language and disciplinary needs alongside each other rather than either set of needs alone when implementing an intervention.

Psychology students, on the other hand, tend to have much higher language proficiency, and the professor viewed improved conciseness and language precision as ways to enhance student content knowledge. This required training in advanced linguistic skills and criticality. For the Music department, where both English and Chinese are official languages of instruction, it is crucial that students continue to master their written and spoken communication in English. Being able to produce written and spoken products effectively in assessments conducted in English becomes particularly important in subjects where professors teach in English and do not know Chinese.

In addressing students' diverse needs, the EAC team has had to handle a wide range of cognitive and linguistic tasks, from higher-order concerns, such as macro organizational skills to lower-order concerns, such as mechanical language issues. The successful implementation of these tailored interventions within disciplinary settings confirms not only the necessity of a flexible CoP model in implementing EAC, but also, and more importantly, the positive impact of having applied linguists/TESOL teachers to support WAC/EAC initiatives. It is believed that our experience lends strong support to what Zawacki and Cox (2011) underscored in their "Introduction to WAC and Second Language Writing": the importance of establishing a seamless relationship between WAC administrators and ESL program directors whose disciplinary boundaries rarely cross in North America.

CHALLENGES

Although these projects met with success, there were a number of challenges that were faced by the teams, some surmountable, and some less so. One of the key constraints was time. Almost all the interventions involved contact with students, meaning that the content professor needed to give up some portion of their scheduled contact hours, or that workshops outside of class had to be made compulsory. Given the difficulties of both of these options, various EAC subteams were generally forced to design and deliver a very condensed workshop, with the hope that it would be memorable enough to have a sustained impact on student learning. This challenge was obviously much greater in interventions involving large classes.

Another challenge is the bilingual language policy at CUHK, which is a double-edged sword. While the policy has important cultural and linguistic advantages, it nevertheless complicates second language learning by resulting in a student body with extremely diverse English language proficiencies. It also results in a de-emphasis of language features in the standardized assessment guidelines and rubrics, which often ignore language components altogether. Some students exhibit a general lack of motivation for English study, and poor competence as a result. Unfortunately, those who need the most help are often the least likely to desire it. The EAC team has no effective solution for dealing with this issue systematically. The approach thus far has been to reach out to all departments, and to simply give priority to those who respond first.

A final challenge that these projects faced is this: How can these projects be sustained?

STRATEGIES FOR SUSTAINABILITY

The issue of sustainability has been part of the EAC project's thinking from its inception. As noted earlier, having strong mutual engagement with content teacher partners is key. Sustainability has been enhanced in concrete ways with the assistance/collaboration of content teachers in training content TAs, writing assessment guides and rubrics, incorporating language marks, and sharing teaching materials. Holding purposeful and focused post-intervention review meetings has also proved useful for sustaining and extending collaborative projects.

To pass resources on for future use, share them with content teachers, and make them available to students for independent study, an EAC repository of learning and teaching resources has been set up within the university's Blackboard LMS, providing access to the EAC team, collaborators and students. Potential EAC teachers can make use of the lesson plans, PowerPoint files, activity sheets, student samples, assessment guides and rubrics to run or re-run workshops in the future. Additionally, students and TAs can gain access to all relevant materials for independent learning, including discipline-specific handouts, annotated student samples, assessment rubrics, videos, and micro-modules for independent learning.

Although the impact of these cases has been encouraging, the EAC initiative is still in its infancy. It is hoped that these related initiatives can serve as impetus for a greater integration between language learning and acquisition of content knowledge (McLeod & Miraglia, 2001).

CONCLUSION

Through close collaboration with disciplinary specialists, the project team has explored the academic literacies of multiple fields and helped to develop among both content teachers and students a heightened awareness of language use within their discipline using a genre-based approach underpinned by a sound linguistic theory. The EAC project at CUHK should be seen as a demonstration of a practical implementation of the "mutually transformative model of ESL/WAC collaboration," (Matsuda & Jablonski, 2000), where EAC is being applied not only in an L2 context but also in diverse situations that include both L1 and L2 instruction.

The EAC project at CUHK differs from many similar initiatives in several ways. First, it is being implemented in English L2 settings, within departments that use English as a medium of instruction, as well as in departments that use Chinese as a medium of instruction. Second, although the cases mentioned above all involve written output, the EAC project has also extended the WAC model to include oral output. Third, the CoP model being used includes applied linguists/TESOL specialists interacting directly with students, rather than behind-the-scenes collaborations between writing and content instructors which may involve students only indirectly. Finally, the EAC project has been careful to avoid following a fixed model of implementation, opting instead to afford CoPs flexibility to enact the most appropriate type of intervention for their specific context.

The team has concluded that proactively reaching out to share vision and spending time with collaborators on trust-building is an indispensable first step to launch any CoP project. Engaging in dialogue with content teachers throughout the collaboration process invariably adds value and strength to the joint venture. By far, the "flexible CoP model" approach to implementing EAC within the bilingual setting has been one of the keys to success, as it has allowed genre-specific/domain-specific needs to be met and has also encouraged content teachers to assume stronger ownership of fostering language education.

ACKNOWLEDGMENTS

The authors would like to acknowledge the funding support of The Teaching Development and Language Enhancement Grant (TDLEG) of The Chinese University of Hong Kong. Additionally, we would also like to thank the following CoP Collaborators and their students for their support: Professor Isabella Wai-Yin Poon, Department of Statistics; Professor Sidharth Jaggi, Department of Information Engineering; Professor Jeffrey Levenberg, Department of Music;

and Professor Wong Alan Chun-Nang, Department of Psychology. The authors would also like to thank Mr. Paul Pan, Research Assistant, for his support of the Statistics CoP, and Ms. Arlynn Gutierrez Alarcon, Teaching Assistant, for her support of the Music CoP.

REFERENCES

Anson, C. S. (2002). *The WAC casebook: Scenes for faculty reflection and program development*. Oxford University Press.

Boch, F. & Frier, C. (2012). The teaching of writing skills in French universities: The case of the Université Stendhal, Grenoble III. In C. Thaiss, G. Bräuer, P. Carlino, L. Ganobcsik-Williams & A. Sinha (Eds.), *Writing programs worldwide: Profiles of academic writing in many places* (pp. 213–223). The WAC Clearinghouse; Parlor Press. https://wac.colostate.edu/books/perspectives/wpww/.

Braine, G. & McNaught, C. (2007). Adaptation of the "Writing Across Curriculum" model to the Hong Kong context. In J. Liu (Ed.), *English language teaching in China: New approaches, perspectives and standards* (pp. 311–328). Continuum.

Chinese University of Hong Kong. (2006, September 7). *CUHK upholds bilingual education* [Press release]. http://www.cuhk.edu.hk/cpr/pressrelease/060907e2.htm.

Cox, M. (2011). WAC: Closing doors or opening doors for second language writers? *Across the Disciplines, 8*(4), 1–20. https://wac.colostate.edu/docs/atd/ell/cox.pdf.

Dalton-Puffer, C. (2007). *Discourse in content and language integrated learning (CLIL) classrooms*. Benjamins.

Department of Information Engineering, The Chinese University of Hong Kong (2018). *Programme outcomes*. https://www.ie.cuhk.edu.hk/programmes/ierg_overview.shtml.

Department of Psychology, The Chinese University of Hong Kong. (n.d.). *Grand theme*. https://www.psy.cuhk.edu.hk/index.php/en/undergraduate/grand-theme.

English Language Teaching Unit. (2018). *Our mission*. http://eltu.cuhk.edu.hk/about-us/our-mission/.

Ferris, D. & Thaiss, C. (2011). Writing at UC Davis: Addressing the needs of second language writers. *Across the Disciplines, 8*(4), 1–25. https://wac.colostate.edu/docs/atd/ell/ferristhaiss.pdf.

Gere, A. (1985). *Roots in the sawdust: Writing to learn across the disciplines*. National Council of Teachers of English.

Graff, N. (2010). Teaching rhetorical analysis to promote transfer of learning. *Journal of Adolescent & Adult Literacy, 53*(5), 376–385.

Herrington, A. J. (1981). Writing to learn: Writing across the disciplines. *College English, 43*(4), 379–387. https://doi.org/10.2307/377126.

Hong Kong Examinations and Assessment Authority. (2015). *Recognition of HKEAA's exams*. http://www.hkeaa.edu.hk/en/recognition/introduction/.

Jones, R. & Comprone, J. (1993). Where do we go next in writing across the curriculum? *College Composition and Communication, 44*(1), 59–68.

Lea, M. R. & Street, B. V. (1998). Student writing in higher education: An academic literacies approach. *Studies in Higher Education, 23*(2), 157–172. https://doi.org/10.1080/03075079812331380364.

Linton, P., Madigan, R. & Johnson, S. (1994). Introducing students to disciplinary genres: The role of the general composition course. *Language and Learning Across the Disciplines, 1*(2), 63–78. https://wac.colostate.edu/llad/v1n2/linton.pdf.

Lughmani, S., Gardner, S., Chen, J., Wong, H. & Chan, L. (2016). English across the curriculum: Fostering collaboration. In Y. S. Fong & M. Brooke (Eds.), *ELTWO: Special issue on 5th CELC symposium proceedings* (pp. 19–33). https://pureportal.coventry.ac.uk/en/publications/english-across-the-curriculum-fostering-collaboration-2.

Matsuda, P. K. & Jablonksi, J. (2000). Beyond the L2 metaphor: Towards a mutually transformative model of ESL/WAC collaboration. *Academic Writing: Interdisciplinary Perspectives on Communication Across the Curriculum.* https://wac.colostate.edu/aw/articles/matsuda_jablonski2000.htm.

McConlogue, T., Mitchell, S. & Peake, K. (2012). Thinking writing at Queen Mary, University of London. In C. Thaiss, G. Bräuer, P. Carlino, L. Ganobcsik-Williams & A. Sinha (Eds.), *Writing programs worldwide: Profiles of academic writing in many places* (pp. 203–211). The WAC Clearinghouse; Parlor Press. https://wac.colostate.edu/books/perspectives/wpww/ .

McLeod, S. H. & Miraglia, E. (2001). Writing across the curriculum in a time of change. In S. H. McLeod, E. Miraglia, M. Soven & C. Thaiss (Eds.), *WAC for the new millennium: Strategies for continuing writing-across-the-curriculum programs* (pp. 1–27). National Council of Teachers of English.

University Grants Committee. (2017a). *UGC-funded universities.* https://www.ugc.edu.hk/eng/ugc/site/fund_inst.html.

University Grants Committee. (2017b). *Teaching development and language enhancement grant.* https://www.ugc.edu.hk/eng/ugc/activity/teach_learn/tdg.html

Wenger, E. (1998). *Communities of practice: Learning, meaning, and identity.* Cambridge University Press.

Wenger, E., McDermott, E. & Snyder, W. (2002). *Cultivating communities of practice: A guide to managing knowledge.* Harvard Business School Press.

Wenger-Trayner, E. & Wenger-Trayner, B. (2015). *Communities of practice: A brief introduction.* http://wenger-trayner.com/wp-content/uploads/2015/04/07-Brief-introduction-to-communities-of-practice.pdf .

Wingate, U. (2012). Using academic literacies and genre-based models for academic writing instruction: A "literacy" journey. *Journal of English for Academic Purposes, 11*(1), 26–37. https://doi.org/10.1016/j.jeap.2011.11.006.

Wingate, U. (2016). Academic literacy across the curriculum: Towards a collaborative instructional approach. *Language Teaching, 51*(3), 1–16. https://doi.org/10.1017/S0261444816000264.

Wingate, U. & Tribble, C. (2012). The best of both worlds? *Studies in Higher Education, 37*(4), 481–495. https://doi.org/10.1080/03075079.2010.525630.

Wu, D. (2013). *Introducing writing across the curriculum into China: Feasibility and adaptation*. Springer. https://doi.org/10.1007/978-3-642-33096-4.

Zawacki, T. M. & Cox, M. (2011). Introduction to WAC and second language writing. *Across the Disciplines, 8*(4). https://wac.colostate.edu/docs/atd/ell/zawacki-cox.pdf.

Zawacki, T. M. & Cox, M. (Eds.). (2014). *WAC and second language writers: Research towards linguistically and culturally inclusive programs and practices*. The WAC Clearinghouse; Parlor Press. https://wac.colostate.edu/books/perspectives/l2/ .

Zawacki, T. M. & Rogers, P. M. (Eds.). (2012). *Writing across the curriculum: A critical sourcebook*. Bedford/St. Martin's.

Zuckermann, R., Rubin, B. & Perpignan, H. (2012). New writing in an old land. In C. Thaiss, G. Bräuer, P. Carlino, L. Ganobcsik-Williams & A. Sinha (Eds.), *Writing programs worldwide: Profiles of academic writing in many places* (pp. 271–292). The WAC Clearinghouse; Parlor Press. https://wac.colostate.edu/books/perspectives/wpww/.

APPENDIX A: STRUCTURAL AND LANGUAGE FEATURES OF AN EVALUATIVE REPORT (STATISTICS)

Title: Noun Phrase (*Evaluation of . . .*)

	Structure	Language
Introduction	Motivation/aim	To-Infinitive (*to evaluate*)
	Background	Past tense (*were*)
	Claim	Present tense (*is*)
Approach	The adopted approach	Past tense, passive voice (*was used / adopted*)
	Justification for the approach	Present tense (*requires*)
	Purposes of procedures	Parallel structure (*to determine . . . to estimate . . . to calculate . . .*)
Results and Discussions	Reference to the appendix	Present tense, passive voice (*is shown*)
	Statistical results	Past tense (*was found*)
	Interpretation of results	Interpretive verbs in present tense (*shows/means . . .*)
Conclusion	Summary of statistical results	Present tense (is)
	Claim	Present tense (is)
Appendix	Statistical calculation	

APPENDIX B: STUDENT WORKSHOP STRUCTURE (INFORMATION ENGINEERING)

Seven Questions the Final-Year Project Report should answer:

1. What problem am I trying to solve?
2. How have other researchers tried to solve this problem?
3. What did I do/make/build/design to solve this problem?
4. How did I try to test what I did/made/built/designed?
5. What did I find when I tested what I did/made/built/designed?
6. What does this mean? (Is there an application of what I found?)
7. What should be studied next?

APPENDIX C: RUBRIC FOR ASSIGNING LANGUAGE SCORES FOR ENGINEERING FINAL-YEAR PROJECT REPORTS

Use of Language in Achieving Content Goals

Introduction & Background

<5 points	5–6 points	7–8 points	9–10 points
No engineering problem/gap in existing processes is evident to the reader; no attempt made to present past work	Engineering problem/gap in existing processes is not stated and must be inferred by reader; past work on the problem was mentioned in only a precursory way	Engineering problem/gap in existing processes is identified but explanation is not thorough; past work on the problem was identified and explained but source quality may be questionable	Engineering problem/gap in existing processes is clearly identified and explained; past work on the problem was identified and explained well, with references including high-quality, scholarly sources

Methodology

<5 points	5–6 points	7–8 points	9–10 points
Prototype/design is not explained in any systematic way, and cannot be understood by the reader	Prototype/design is explained but is missing critical information, thus leaving the reader confused	Prototype/design is explained but leaves the reader with questions	Prototype/design is explained clearly and thoroughly

Testing & Results

<5 points	5–6 points	7–8 points	9–10 points
Testing procedures and benchmarks are not explained in any systematic way; results cannot be understood by the reader	Testing procedures and benchmarks are explained but are missing critical information, leaving the reader confused; results are thus confusing at points and/ or poorly presented	Testing procedures and benchmarks are explained but leave the reader with questions; results are shown adequately but could be presented better	Testing procedures and benchmarks are clearly explained; results are clearly shown with appropriate presentation

Conclusion & Future Direction

<5 points	5–6 points	7–8 points	9–10 points
Implications are unclear to the reader; future research possibilities are not mentioned	Implications are not stated and must be inferred by the reader; future research possibilities are mentioned only precursorily	Implications are noted but not well explained; future research possibilities are mentioned but may be disconnected from the project	Implications are clearly identified and explained; future research possibilities are thoughtful

Referencing

<5 points	5–6 points	7–8 points	9–10 points
Citations and references are completely non-functional and of no use to the reader in connecting information to its source	An attempt has been made at referencing but is inadequate for the reader to locate some of the information	Citation and references are generally functional but may contain errors or provide some incomplete information	Citations and references appear to conform well to a commonly used system and are complete

Language Usage and Accuracy

Overall Organization

<5 points	5–6 points	7–8 points	9–10 points
Organizational strategy is unclear, making it difficult or impossible for the reader to follow the flow of ideas	Organizational strategy is not well implemented, with relationships between sections and paragraphs often unclear	Good organization overall, but flow of ideas in not always smooth, and information may be out of place	Clear organization with smooth flow of ideas and relevant information placed appropriately

Grammar

<5 points	5–6 points	7–8 points	9–10 points
Grammar errors can be seen regularly throughout the essay, including some that are severe enough to obscure meaning	Grammar errors can be seen regularly throughout the essay but generally do not interfere with meaning	Simple grammar structures are generally error-free, but complex structures are not always correct	Complex grammar structures are used skillfully and appropriately with errors observed only rarely

Paragraph Organization and Cohesion

<5 points	5–6 points	7–8 points	9–10 points
Paragraphs appear to be randomly constructed with no logical connections between sentences	Paragraphs do not always contain obvious topics and cohesive devices are regularly omitted or used poorly	Paragraphs are generally on topic but may contain unrelated information; ideas within paragraphs are not always well-connected	Paragraphs contain clear topics and are constructed logically with adept use of cohesive devices

Language and vocabulary choices

<5 points	5–6 points	7–8 points	9–10 points
Vocabulary and language choices are largely inappropriate leading to confusion on the part of the reader	Vocabulary and language choices are poor and may obscure meaning at points	Vocabulary and language is adequate to convey meaning but contains marked expressions; language may contain informal elements	Sophisticated vocabulary is used appropriately, and language is well-chosen and appropriately formal

Spelling and punctuation

<5 points	5–6 points	7–8 points	9–10 points
Spelling and punctuation errors are obvious and distracting to the reader, evidencing a lack of proofreading	Minor spelling and punctuation errors are common within the text	Minor spelling and punctuation errors are rare within the text	Spelling and punctuation are error-free

© Prepared by the EAC team, English Language Teaching Unit

CHAPTER 14.

BECOMING *TRANSFRONTERIZO* COLLABORATORS: A TRANSDISCIPLINARY FRAMEWORK FOR DEVELOPING TRANSLINGUAL PEDAGOGIES IN WAC/WID

Marcela Hebbard

The University of Texas Rio Grande Valley

Yanina Hernández

The University of Texas Rio Grande Valley

Given that pedagogical approaches that challenge dominant language ideologies are not yet well represented in WAC/WID scholarship, this chapter outlines a transdisciplinary framework for developing translingual pedagogies. The framework is built around the notion of transfronterizo/a collaborators because before instructors can engage their students in exploring and challenging their views toward language, instructors must first critically interrogate their own. This interrogation must consider the unique political, social, economic, and linguistic exigencies of where an institution is located. The chapter concludes by showing that a transdisciplinary and translingual collaboration that is mutually transformative changes faculty collaborators in how they perceive their linguistic histories and abilities, challenges/enriches their instructional practices, and expands/complicates their scholarly knowledge. This chapter seeks to assist WAC/WID faculty interested in developing translingual and transdisciplinary collaborations in institutions where no professional development opportunities that focus on language difference exist or as an addition to a workshop setting.

Cognizant of an increasingly linguistically diverse student population in U.S. higher education institutions, the globalization of education, and the internationalization of English (Cox, 2011; Hall, 2009; Johns, 2001; Matsuda, 2012),

DOI: https://doi.org/10.37514/PER-B.2020.0360.2.14

WAC/WID research on multilingual and second language (L2) writing has worked to develop more linguistically and culturally inclusive WAC/WID programs and practices (Cox & Zawacki, 2011; Ferris & Thaiss, 2011; Zawacki & Cox, 2014). Studies have focused on learning with and from L2 students (Harklau & Siegal, 2009; Zamel & Spack, 2004), exploring faculty concerns and expectations of L2 writers (Fishman & McCarthy, 2001; Ives et al., 2014), and more recently, calling faculty to change their attitudes toward multilingual writers by adapting their pedagogies to serve these students' needs (Fredericksen & Mangelsdorf, 2014; Jordan & Kedrowicz, 2011; Siczek & Shapiro, 2014). Despite the serious progress in WAC/WID scholarship in multilingual writing, we are still in the relatively early stages of developing WAC-based language-oriented pedagogical approaches that address the needs of students with a wide variety of linguistic backgrounds, including monolingual ones (Hall, 2014a). The seemingly slow progress in developing pedagogies that consider language difference is due in large part to the subtle bias against any language but standardized English in the academy (Geller, 2011), the assumptions of perceiving mainstream students as monolingual, and/or trying to assimilate multilingual students to a monolingual norm by excluding their written and spoken languages or language variations (Hall, 2009; Horner & Hall, 2018). In addition to these assumptions, there is the challenge to persuade faculty across disciplines to experiment with alternate pedagogical practices that consider language difference (Hall, 2014b).

Given that pedagogical approaches that challenge dominant language ideologies are not yet well represented in WAC/WID scholarship, in this chapter, we outline a transdisciplinary framework for developing translingual pedagogies because exploring issues of language calls for transdisciplinary efforts "despite the challenges and problems of engaging in such work" (Hall, 2018a, p. 6). We build our framework around the notion of *transfronterizo/a* collaborators (De la Piedra & Guerra, 2012; Zentella, 2009, 2016) because before we can engage our students in exploring and challenging their views toward language, we must first critically interrogate our own (Parra, 2016). This interrogation must consider the unique political, social, economic, and linguistic exigencies of where an institution is located. Thus, we hope that the example of our transdisciplinary and translinguistic collaboration, while rooted in our unique context, resonates with WAC/WID scholars and educators in other contexts. We conclude by showing that a transdisciplinary and translingual collaboration that is mutually transformative (Matsuda & Jablonski, 2000) changes collaborators in how they perceive their linguistic histories and abilities, challenges and enriches their instructional practices, and expands and complicates their scholarly knowledge. We hope this framework assists WAC/WID faculty interested in developing translingual and transdisciplinary collaborations in institutions where no professional development opportunities that focus on language difference exist or where it might be used in addition to a workshop setting.

LOCAL CONTEXT: STRIVING TO BECOME A BILINGUAL UNIVERSITY

Every scholarly work is constrained by and reflects a unique sociocultural and linguistic context (Gentil, 2018). For us, our context is The University of Texas Rio Grande Valley (UTRGV), a mid-size Hispanic-Serving Institution located on the southmost area along the Mexico/US border. Upon its establishment in Fall 2015, a merger between the University of Texas at Brownsville and the University of Texas-Pan American, the Department of English and the Department of Modern and Classical Languages consolidated into the Department of Writing and Language Studies (WLS). WLS includes the following units: modern languages, applied linguistics, and rhetoric and composition. Marcela teaches first-year writing (FYW) in the rhetoric and composition unit and Yanina teaches Spanish as a Heritage Language (SHL) courses in the modern languages unit.

Because of our location, UTRGV has the mission of becoming a "highly engaged bilingual university" and, as a department, we are currently at the beginning stages of determining what this means. With this mission in mind, WLS has engaged TAs and faculty in rhetoric and composition with Spanish TAs and faculty in rhetoric and composition with Spanish TAs and faculty in conversations about how our region and the transdisciplinary realities of our respective disciplines influence the teaching of writing and languages. The ideas that ultimately led us to develop the framework we propose in this chapter originated when we participated in a department-sponsored initiative in the fall 2016 semester (see Cavazos et al., 2018).

DEFINING *TRANSFRONTERIZO* COLLABORATORS

The concept of *transfronterizos* from cultural studies informs our framework. In its original conceptualization, *transfronterizo* refers to the continuous linguistic and cultural practices that children and young adults who traverse the Tijuana/San Diego border maintain daily across both sides (Zentella, 2009). *Transfronterizos* tend to be U.S. citizens, either by birth or naturalization, and have the flexibility to reside on both sides of the border (Relaño Pastor, 2007). Yet, despite their proficient bilingualism and identity as border-crossers, *transfronterizo* students struggle with language and identity (Zentella, 2016) and resist forging allegiances with social groups at school based on nationality, citizenship, language and social class (Relaño Pastor, 2007). We find the concepts of struggle with language and identity, the border-crossing action, and the resistance to forge social allegiances with others very useful to help illustrate and understand the complexities and challenges faculty face when engaging in transdisciplinary and translingual collaborative activities within WAC/WID contexts.

While most *transfronterizo* studies have focused on youth residing on the Tijuana/San Diego border, recently, scholars like María E. Fránquiz and Alba A. Ortiz (2017) have begun to include other border regions and populations. They claim that not only students, but also teachers and researchers in institutions and communities located in the U.S./Mexico *frontera* (borderland), are *transfronterizos*. For them, being *transfronterizo* means to be fluent in different types of border crossings. These multiple crossings, whether physical or metaphorical, shape their identities, lives, perspectives, and actions (Fránquiz & Ortiz, 2017, p. 111). *Transfronterizos* forge transnational identities and multiliteracies by a constant negotiation on-the-move between two nation-states (Ceballos, 2012; Smith & Murillo, 2012). Our definition of *transfronterizos* moves beyond being bilingual, bicultural, and binational; it also includes self-identified monolinguals and monocultural faculty across the curriculum, willing to engage in transdisciplinary collaborations to critically and consciously interrogate their language ideologies.

Becoming *transfronterizo* collaborators demands learning to traverse across disciplinary and linguistic borders in order to develop what we call *transborder thinking,* the intellectual openness that considers that perspectives and methods in one's discipline have come from and/or been influenced by perspectives and methods outside one's discipline (Bazerman, 2012; Hendricks, 2018; Horner, 2018; Sandford, 2015). Engaging in these types of border crossings, like *transfronterizos,* might leave WAC/WID practitioners struggling with language and academic identity, resisting social allegiances with other disciplines, and/or becoming fluent in disciplinary crossings. Whichever the case, one thing is certain, partaking in transdisciplinary and translingual collaborations will challenge and change participants' identities, lives, perspectives, actions, and pedagogies.

TRANSDISCIPLINARITY: AN EXISTING BUT UNDERUSED FORCE IN WAC/WID

Historically, WAC/WID has been considered an inherently transdisciplinary field where WAC/WID scholars have called for reciprocal exchanges between composition and other disciplines in order to expand our understanding on how students use writing to move across academic and non-academic contexts (Hendricks, 2018). A transdisciplinary collaboration, unlike a multi-disciplinary collaboration or an interdisciplinary collaboration, requires participants to "push the methodological and conceptual bounds of their own respective disciplines, making collaborations both participatory and problem-centered in place of disciplinary allegiance" (Rademaekers, 2015, p. 1). Jonathan Hall (2018a) noted that transdisciplinarity is "an existing force that has already been driving widely diverse intellectual endeavors for several decades" (p. 3). He explained that in the humanities and social sciences transdisciplinarity has functioned more as "theory" whereas in STEM fields it has been more "pragmatic" in that it "concentrates on [social problems] that are too large for any one discipline to tackle alone" (2018a, p. 3) such as climate change, poverty, and hunger. Viewed from this perspective, to tackle issues about language, writing, learning, and teaching, issues central to WAC/WID, we need both transdisciplinary theory and practice.

However, in WAC/WID developing transdisciplinary collaborations has been challenging and at times even resisted (Russell, 2012). Reasons for this include the disciplinary division of labor (Matsuda, 1998), a lack of skills for negotiating working partnerships with disciplinary faculty (Jablonski, 2006), having narrow attitudes toward the role of writing and language in pedagogy (Cox, 2010, 2011), an intellectual fear of internal displacement of one's discipline by another (Mercier, 2015), and being trained to function within the parameters of one discipline (Rademaekers, 2015). A discipline is defined as a bordered and hierarchically organized intellectual community of practice formed by a complex network of individuals (e.g., predecessors, mentors, peers, colleagues, collaborators, students at all levels) whose membership is determined by their acceptance of certain ideas, methods, procedures, habits of mind, epistemological assumptions, rhetorical conventions, genre practices, and publication/dissemination procedures (Hall, 2018a; Osborne, 2015). From this perspective, when disciplines are understood mostly in terms of territorial epistemologies (Mignolo, 2000) and specializations (Hendricks, 2018), and observed as discreet histories of thought and intellectual practices (Osborne, 2015), cultivating transborder thinking might not obtain. That is, when we decide not to engage in transdisciplinary collaborations, we are not fulfilling a WAC/WID mission that calls us "to examine the ways that students manage multiple languages and disciplines in the course of their education" (Hall, 2018a, p. 4) because in order to do this, we must develop an intellectual openness that transcends disciplinary perspectives and methods.

Developing transborder thinking calls for WAC/WID practitioners to engage in epistemological disciplinary disobedience (Mignolo, 2000). For our purpose, we define disciplinary disobedience as the willingness to radically question our conceptualization about/around language and its relation to writing, teaching, and learning which requires we traverse physical, intellectual, and metaphorical borders and lines that divide/unite disciplines. Here it is important to emphasize that an institution does not need to be located on a geographical border for its faculty (and students) to experience being "linguistically bordered" by others. Anne Ellen Geller's (2011) study on 64 self-identified multilingual faculty from across the disciplines who teach with writing in English noted the deeply ingrained institutionalized assumption to see faculty as monolingual. She writes about multilingual faculty colleagues at St. John's University who "feel (and/or have been made to feel) as if their spoken and written English is not standardized enough for their colleagues in the American academy to think of their linguistic ability in English as anything other than still deficient" (2011, p. 5). Engaging in epistemological disciplinary disobedience can take many forms such as participating in interdisciplinary learning communities or workshops focused on language (Cavazos et al., 2018), engaging in formal and/or informal conversation with colleagues from other disciplines about their views on language diversity and teaching (Matsuda & Jablonski, 2000), and/or reading scholarship from other disciplines about language issues (Horner, NeCamp et al., 2011).

TRANSLINGUALISM: A HELPFUL THEORETICAL LENS IN/FOR TRANSDISCIPLINARY WORK

In addition to engaging in transdisciplinary collaborations that focus on/around language and its relation to writing, teaching, and learning, it is important to consider scholarship that discusses language ideologies. Translinguality refers to a growing body of scholarly work from disciplines such as composition, sociolinguistics, second language acquisition, linguistic anthropology, cross-cultural studies, literary study, and multilingual education that calls into radical question the tenets of the monolingual ideology (Horner, 2018), and its use of the monolingual native speaker as the reference when teaching and learning writing and languages to multilingual students in school contexts (Cenoz & Gorter, 2015; Garcia & Kleyn, 2016; Horner, Lu et al., 2011; May, 2014). Because the conception of languages as stable, discreet, and uniform excludes other languages and varieties (Kachru, 1994), ignores the diverse language practices of most people around the world (Block, 2003), and imposes a view of the writer, reader, and speaker of other languages and varieties as deficient (Horner, Lu, et al., 2011), translinguality scholars have articulated language approaches and methods of knowledge-making and teaching as alternatives to monolingualism.

Out of all the different articulations within translinguality, we find the notion of transligualism the most useful in assisting faculty transdisciplinary collaborations in exploring and/or challenging their beliefs about language. The term was first introduced in 2011 in the field of U.S. composition to counter the monolingual ideology that dominates the teaching of writing (Horner, Lu, et al., 2011). Unlike other translinguality terms such as "metrolingualism" (Pennycook, 2010), "contemporary urban vernacular" (Rampton, 2011), "code-meshing" (Canagarajah, 2011), "lingua franca multilingualism" (Makoni & Pennycook, 2012), and "translanguaging" (Garcia, 2009), translingualism is not rooted in a monolingual ideology or the traditional additive model of multilingualism (Horner, NeCamp, et al., 2011). Translingualism has called for a reorientation of what error or language difference might mean (Trimbur, 2016), to treat difference not as a deviation but as a norm (Bawarshi, 2016), to change our own and our students' disposition toward language practices by engaging in composing practices less familiar to us (Shipka, 2016), to include in writing curricula and programs the knowledge multilingual writers bring and how they negotiate language ideologies (Canagarajah, 2016), to confront the structuring of monolingualism into writing assessment (Dryer, 2016), to cultivate rhetorical sensibility to language difference (Guerra, 2016), and to position writers of any linguistic background as active and purposeful negotiators of meaning (Lu & Horner, 2013).

Although the notion of translingualism has created tension mostly with the field of second language writing over disciplinary territory, theoretical development, and practical pedagogical applicability (Atkinson et al., 2015; Schreiber & Watson, 2018), we find it helpful for transdisciplinary work. As a pedagogical approach, translingualism sees difference in language not as a problem to eradicate, but as a resource "to be preserved, developed, and utilized" (Horner, Lu, et al., 2011, p. 304). However, a pedagogy is translingual not because it merely exposes students to language diversity, reconsiders what "errors" in grammar or usage are, or allows students to use their full linguistic repertoires in their writing, but because it asks "students to investigate/consider how language standards emerge, how and by whom they are enforced, and to whose benefit" (Schreiber & Watson, 2018, p. 95). Jonathan Hall (2018b) noted that at a minimum, a translingual pedagogy should help students become aware that on a global and historical basis monolingualism is the exception rather than the norm, see their multiple languages as a resource and receive encouragement to explore that resource, and understand that Standard English is a social construct, thus, it can be un-made and changed by groups of people through rhetorical and linguistic negotiations. As a theory, translingualism challenges the monolingual orientation "that contains languages from contact with each other, associating language mixing with contamination and lack of proficiency" (Lee, 2016, p. 177). From this perspective, "siloed" disciplines are seen as functioning from a monolingual orientation in that they train their professionals within specific parameters both discursively and methodologically resulting in the acquisition of disciplinary knowledge through the critical investigation of disciplinary language, which has been a foundational goal of WAC/WID curricula (Rademaekers, 2015).

Helping students develop disciplinary expertise and disciplinary epistemological understanding through language instruction aligns with the WAC/WID premise to see writing as highly situated and tied to a field's discourse. However, this view of language and writing is limited when it comes to transdisciplinary collaborations. In transdisciplinary work, inevitably a participant's disciplinary discourse would come into contact with the other participant's disciplinary discourse and in the process of cooperating with one another, both collaborators' discourses would be altered and changed in different ways. This disciplinary discursive encounter could result in either "linguistic and conceptual divides" (Eigenbrode et al. as cited in Rademaekers, 2015), defined as "disagreements regarding the specialist terminology used in varying disciplines and the different connotations for the same terms across disciplines" (p. 6), or "new disciplinarity" (Markovitch & Shinn as cited in Gere, Knutson & McCarthy, 2018), which acknowledges the ongoing existence of the disciplines and of elasticity, the capacity of collaborators to move temporarily to the dynamic borderlands that exist outside disciplines in order to carry out projects of their own devising. As said earlier, a goal of transdisciplinary collaborations is that participants think far outside the boundaries of their own disciplinary discourses to form situated, problem-centered, and early-integrated methods for problem solving (Rademaekers, 2015).

Thinking and moving temporarily far outside the confines of our respective disciplines to explore language difference can assist WAC/WID faculty in becoming conscious of our linguistic beliefs because they make "'the language question' essentially unavoidable in ways that can productively lead to a new disciplinary partnership or at least to mutually respectful growth" (Donahue, 2018, p. 132) through rhetorical and linguistic negotiations. Enacting these negotiations can inspire new conversations and invite us not to "other" fields that might inform language discussion in our own disciplines. Christiane Donahue (2018) noted that "as language questions move disciplines to engage in dialogue, [we will] (re)discover the other we have been thinking was alien to us" (p. 133) and "the experience of the Other always determines the perception of the self" (Gentz & Kramer as cited in Donahue, 2018, p. 133). Hence, engaging in transdisciplinary and translingual collaborations allows us to gain a perspective of ourselves by relating to all that is other (Bakhtin, 1986), even as we continue to operate within the persisting power of a monolingual ideology, because together we can begin to think of ourselves as agents making active choices in real rhetorical situations about language difference as we write and teach (Hall, 2018a).

BECOMING *TRANSFRONTERIZO* COLLABORATORS: A TRANSLINGUAL AND TRANSDISCIPLINARY FRAMEWORK TO DEVELOP TRANSLINGUAL PEDAGOGIES

In the context of a transdisciplinary faculty-led project that seeks to develop translingual student-centered activities, becoming *transfronterizo* collaborators requires engaging in epistemological disobedience in order to foster transborder thinking, adopting a collaborative multilingual scholarly practice, and identifying possible connectors-for-teaching. Figure 14.1 depicts the components of our proposed framework. In the rest of this chapter, we will explain each component and provide examples from our own collaboration to illustrate each element.

Components	Description
Engage in epistemological disobedience in order to foster transborder thinking.	Get involved in translingual, transcultural, and transdisciplinary conversations to learn the personal, linguistic and cultural, and disciplinary background of each collaborator.
Adopt a collaborative translingual scholarly practice.	Take time/initiative to read scholarship in English and across languages about translinguality and important disciplinary theoretical concepts while at the same time ensure intellectual accountability.
Identify possible connectors-for-teaching.	*Connectors-for-teaching* refers to the moment collaborators are able to pinpoint an area where both disciplinary expertise can converge regarding language and writing issues.
Develop student-centered translingual activities.	Classroom activities should allow students to see their languages as resources, investigate/consider how language standards work and are sustained, and be aligned to Student Learning Outcomes (SLOs) and assessments goals, appropriate reading material, and delivery format.

Figure 14.1. Transfonterizo/a collaborator framework.

ENGAGE IN EPISTEMOLOGICAL DISOBEDIENCE TO FOSTER TRANSBORDER THINKING

To become *transfronterizo* collaborators, faculty should move out from their disciplinary territories by crossing physical, intellectual, and/or metaphorical borders that divide/unite disciplines in order to radically question conceptualizations of language. The goal of moving out is to engage in meaningful and rich cross-disciplinary conversations and share translinguistic histories. Motha et al. (2012) claimed that all teachers, monolingual and multilingual alike, have "translinguistic histories" which means that our teaching practices are informed by our life histories, including our linguistic and social identities, and that our identities impact our pedagogies (p. 14). Hence, exploring and acknowledging our language experiences and beliefs beyond the classroom is crucial to uncover (un)seen linguistic ideologies.

For us, this moving out began when we participated in the Multilingual Pedagogies Professional Development (MPPD) in our institution in fall 2016 (see Cavazos et al., 2018). The goal of the series was to engage TAs and faculty in rhetoric and composition in conversations with Spanish TAs and faculty about disciplinary realities and their repercussions in the teaching of writing and languages in our region. In addition to attending the series, we met several times during the semester to talk about our translinguistic histories. Some meetings took place outside campus in a relaxed and informal environment. Looking back at these meetings, we now see that we engaged in reflexive practice, the deliberate way of systematically recalling experiences, values, and assumptions in relation to new or even counterintuitive ideas and situations (Taczak & Robertson, 2017; Tarabochia, 2017). The more we talked, the more we became aware of our own backgrounds as users of the languages we speak and teach (Lacorte, 2016) and our own linguistic, social, and cultural biases toward others, including our students (Parra, 2016) and shockingly also ourselves, the authors, since the two of us learned English as a second language. We include short vignettes of our translinguistic histories that reflect our linguistic experiences and beliefs at the time of our participation in the MPPD series and our conversations to illustrate this point:

> Marcela was born and raised in Mexico City where she began learning English at the age of 13. At the age of 23, she migrated to the United States to attend university. After graduating with a degree in education, she returned to Mexico to work as a teacher for two years. She migrated again to the United States to pursue a master's degree. While in graduate school, she married an Anglo man from Pennsylvania and became a naturalized citizen. Upon graduation, they moved to South Texas where the two work in higher education. She has taught in higher education for over 15 years. Since she is the only one in her family residing in the States, she traverses across linguistic (and physical) borders every day through the multiple interactions with her diverse social networks. At home, she speaks English with her Anglo husband and Spanish with their Mexi-White daughter.[1] Through technology, she maintains daily contact in Spanish with family and friends in Mexico City. At work, she intentionally divides her language system, speaking and writing only English since she believes that is what her discipline requires and because, based on her experiences and struggles as

---

1   Mexi-White is the term Marcela's daughter uses when someone asks her about her ethnic/racial background.

a language learner in higher education, she wants to equip her students to succeed in English. She speaks Spanish only when students and colleagues initiate the conversation.

Yanina identifies herself as Mexican American. She was born and raised in Mexico and immigrated to the US as a young adult. She feels deep ties to Mexico because her parents and siblings are still there and because that is the place where she grew up. Her profession in the teaching of language also allows her to maintain an active, daily use of her heritage language. She has taught Spanish courses in higher education for about 17 years and has lived in the Rio Grande Valley for more than 12 years. However, she also perceives herself as an American after living in the United States most of her life. She is bilingual, and Spanish is still the language she uses more at home, at work, and in her daily exchanges in the community. For her, living in a border region creates multiple contexts and opportunities to speak Spanish with her family, friends, colleagues, and people around the community.

Listening to translinguistic histories can make faculty appreciate others' and their own backgrounds, raise their awareness on how they use language, and show them common concerns and questions about language and writing (Cavazos et al., 2018). This activity paved the way for our collaboration because it made visible how our previous experiences (personal and professional) have shaped our assumptions about pedagogy, language, disciplinarity, and writing. These kinds of interactions that mixed the "personal and professional dimension of work/life" (Jablonski, 2006) are an important aspect to forge transdisciplinary and translingual collaborations in WAC/WID contexts because they serve as sites where prospective collaborators can (un)consciously begin negotiating roles and assumptions.

Adopt a Collaborative Translingual Scholarly Practice

Dorothy Worden (2013) asserted that a goal in reimagining writing research and teaching is to connect communities and classrooms, "but we cannot connect what we do not understand" (p. 238). Therefore, in addition to sharing translinguistic histories, *transfronterizo* collaborators should adopt a collaborative translingual scholarly practice in which participants take time to read and discuss scholarship on important transdisciplinary and translinguistic theoretical concepts in English, but also across languages, rhetorical traditions and contexts. Horner, NeCamp, et al. (2011) claimed that the "dominance . . . by English monolingualism is manifested not only simply in the language(s) of the scholarship produced but the language(s) of scholarship cited, the bibliographic resources on which . . . scholars rely, the forums in which the scholarship circulates, and the arguments it makes" (p. 273). They call for scholarship to engage with non-English-medium scholarship published outside the United States despite the intense objections and challenges in doing so. Adding to their call, we include non-English-medium scholarship published within the United States in fields such as Spanish-as-a-Heritage Language. Doing this can help the teaching of writing in the US "develop an appreciation and respect for discourse practices that are different" (Matsuda, 2002, p. 194) as well as help increase linguistically diverse scholarship in WAC/WID work.

We emphasize here that the goal of adopting a collaborative translingual scholarship practice is not to become experts in each other's disciplines, but to ensure what Matsuda (2013) called "intellectual accountability," which avoids borrowing or critiquing terms from another disciplinary context without first defining them carefully and reflecting an awareness of the origin and history of the term as well as its variations (p. 135). Doing this will assist collaborators in acquiring a better understanding of each other's disciplinary languages, and personal and professional ways of knowing (Ede & Lunsford, 1990; Jablonski, 2006; McCarthy & Fishman, 1991).

For us, adopting a collaborative translingual scholarly practice began when we found ourselves theoretically lost after we were introduced to the term *translingualism* and were asked to design a linguistically inclusive student assignment in a workshop session. As a starting point to fill this theoretical gap, we selected articles from the list of suggested readings provided by the organizers of the professional development series. Most of the listed articles were from the field of composition, therefore, for Marcela, understanding and developing theoretical connections with these readings was "easier" than for Yanina who experienced a linguistic and conceptual divide, an internal disagreement regarding the terminology about language difference used in her discipline and the different articulations found across disciplines (Rademaekers, 2015). Despite feeling a theoretical dissonance, Yanina decided to continue engaging in epistemological disobedience and dwelling temporarily in the discipline of composition to carry out our collaborative project.

Recognizing we were reading scholarship mainly from Marcela's discipline, we turned our attention and read scholarship in the field of Spanish as a Heritage Language (SHL) and bilingual education. Bilingual scholars claim U.S. border regions are considered areas of stable bilingualism, but "in the official worlds of the schools and universities [. . .], English is the dominant language, and every day practices and policies are often contradictory" (De la Piedra & Guerra, 2012, p. 629). For many heritage language learners, their communities and society at large have stigmatized the code they use (García & Kleyn, 2016). For example, saying in Spanish "pus no sé si haiga" may be considered "improper" or "uneducated" and index a rural area. Such forms typically originate in the country of origin and are perceived as deviations from a standardized form or a prestigious variety. As a result, many SHL students carry these feelings of stigmatization because they do not always understand the prevailing politics and ideologies that society has imposed on them and are often perpetuated in the classroom (Parra, 2016). This reality has propelled HL scholars and educators to develop knowledge and pedagogical tools to help maintain and revitalize heritage languages (Aparicio, 1997; Fairclough, 1992). Instead of perpetuating grammatical oriented and language-remedial models in the teaching of heritage languages, Spanish included, the field is advocating for a Critical Language Awareness focus where students examine and question the often-invisible ways in which linguistic inequality is reproduced and reinforced socially, politically, and educationally (Leeman & Serafini, 2016).

By the end of this activity, we began to see similarities between composition and SHL that led us to identify possible connectors for teaching.

IDENTIFY (POSSIBLE) CONNECTORS-FOR-TEACHING

Sharing translinguistic histories and adopting a translingual scholarly practice can help *transfronterizo* collaborators to identify what we call *connectors-for-teaching*, specific moments where collaborators are able to pinpoint possible areas where both disciplinary expertise can converge regarding language and writing issues.

In our case, one connector-for-teaching is the realization that our respective disciplines have historically imposed "prestige," "standard," or "academic" varieties in the teaching of heritage languages and writing alike (Horner, Lu, et al., 2011; Valdés, 1997, 2001). As a result, by centering on dominant monolingual ideologies, both the SHL and the composition classrooms have become sites where local varieties are directly or indirectly labeled as deficient (Aparicio, 1997; Hall, 2009). Another connector-for-teaching we identified is that both disciplines alike are challenging dominant conceptualization of language, language relations, and language use with "alternate pedagogical practices" (Hall, 2014b)—translingualism in composition studies and Critical Language Awareness (CLA) in SHL. Consequently, scholars in both fields have urged instructors to be careful not to mislead students by legitimizing one variety (i.e., the "standard") over another but to give all language varieties the same legitimization (Fairclough, 1992; Horner, Lu, et al., 2011).

We believe the preceding section exemplifies what connectors-for-teaching might look like in a transdisciplinary collaboration. For us, becoming aware of these connectors challenged us to think about the possible linguistic inclusive student activities we could design to raise our students' awareness of their linguistic agency, literacies, and cultural practices.

DEVELOP A STUDENT-CENTERED TRANSLINGUAL ACTIVITY

Identifying areas where disciplines intersect can assist *transfronterizo* collaborators in the design of more cultural and linguistic inclusive student activities and assessment. To do this, it is helpful to first read articles where the authors have implemented translingual pedagogies (Anderson & Lightfoot, 2018; Hartse et al., 2018; Kiernan et al., 2016; Lee & Jenks, 2016) and/or culturally sustaining pedagogies which center around linguistic-cultural issues (Paris & Alim, 2017). In "Sustained Communities for Sustained Learning: Connecting Culturally Sustaining Pedagogy to WAC Learning Outcomes" (this volume), Jamila Kareem provides an overview of culturally sustaining education and proposes learning outcomes for WAC educators intended to support curricula around cultural-historical realities of vulnerable and subjugated student populations. We believe her work supports the ideas proposed in our chapter.

The student-centered translingual activity we designed can be considered low-stakes for two reasons: we did not want students to stress over a grade and we are still considering how to best assess translingual writing in a way that is fair and promotes linguistic social justice (Lee, 2016). After aligning the activity to existing student learning outcomes, we devised the objective for the activity, which was twofold: that students saw their multiple languages as a resource, including the standardized academic forms (Ruecker, 2014), and that students gained an understanding that all linguistic, rhetorical, political, and institutional actions have impacts on others (Shapiro et al., 2016). To introduce students to these ideas, we chose a common reading titled "Challenging Our Labels: Rejecting the Language of Remediation," by Galindo et al., 2014. This article was written by five first-year composition students who were placed in a remedial writing course and labeled "not yet proficient" writers. Our goal using this reading was to direct our students' attention to the ways in which the different stakeholders (students, FYW professor, administrators, parents) negotiate, reflect, and recontextualize their identities through their linguistics practices.

The collaborative activity lasted seven weeks and moved rather slowly. It consisted of having both groups read, annotate, and discuss the common reading in their respective classes. After that, both groups of students had to respond to a prompt about the reading in a blog using their preferred language. To initiate the collaborative activity, Marcela compiled her students' blog responses in one Word document and shared the file with Yanina (students' full names were removed and replaced by initials). Yanina posted FYW students' responses on a Discussion Board in her online class and asked her students to choose and respond to one of the FYW students' posts. After that, Yanina gathered written responses, saved them in a Word document, and sent them back to Marcela. In class, FYW students received SHL students' responses to their blogs. Both instructors engaged their respective students in class discussion about what was interesting about their peers' responses and how they would continue the conversation if they could. To end the activity, students were asked to write a reflection about their experience participating in this activity and their perceptions on how language actions impact themselves and others (see Figure 14.2).

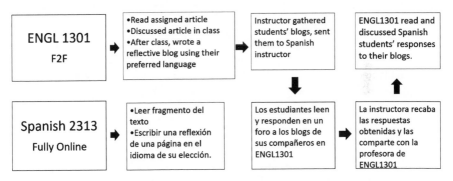

Figure 14.2. Translingual student activity descriptions for English 1301 and Spanish 2313.

After piloting the student activity, we analyzed students' final reflections. Notably, many SHL students wrote they identified with their FYW counterparts and the students/authors from the common reading in that they have been negatively labeled for speaking in Spanish, for being Hispanic, or for being undocumented. Even though a few SHL students questioned why they were given a reading in English in a Spanish language class, most noted it was a good experience reading FYW student reflections in English and responding to them in Spanish. While in need of revision, this cross-linguistic activity seemed to have heightened students' appreciation of the negotiation between two languages and raised their awareness of how linguistic actions impact others.

IMPLICATIONS AND CONCLUSION

Becoming *transfronterizo* collaborators can impact faculty in WAC/WID in at least three areas which include identity, teaching practices, and scholarship.

Regarding identity, engaging in transdisciplinary and translingual collaborations will assist WAC/WID practitioners to become more aware of the role language plays in shaping personal and professional identities (Dicker, 2003). For example, while exploring our translinguistic histories, we realize we are more relaxed in engaging in bilingual practices outside our work, but when it comes to our professions, we held what Rosina Lippi-Green (1997) called a "standard language ideology" (p. 64), a sustained commitment to native speaker idealization. Marcela tended to repress speaking Spanish at work because she believed that reflecting a proper identity as a teacher of first-year composition called for speaking and writing in English because traditionally the prefix used to designate these courses is ENGL 1301/1302: Rhetoric and Composition (Musanti & Cavazos, 2018), whereas Yanina felt that mixing her languages when communicating with her students portrayed her not as a good Spanish instructor. To foster a translingual ideology, monolingual faculty can reflect on their translinguistic histories and compare them to the linguistic experiences of their monolingual and multilingual students in their institution and local communities (Schwarzer & Fuchs, 2014). Doing this may lead monolingual faculty to shift from a deficit-based monoglossic ideology to a heteroglossic one where all students—including monolingual, are seen as full members of the classroom community (Blair et al., 2018).

Raising one's consciousness about language ideologies as a result of participating in translingual and transdisciplinary collaboration will impact and challenge our teaching practices. For example, while we introduce our students to language difference, we still cover and promote academic registers to help our students navigate the academic world (Ruecker, 2014). However, we also carve spaces where students can explore their linguistic repertoires without being penalized. Faculty in other disciplines interested in developing translingual student activities can also create spaces. For instance, WAC/WID practitioners collaborating with STEM faculty can engage their students in reviewing award winning articles written by non-native speakers in the field and have them pay attention to issues of structure, format, transitioning, content, and the use of world Englishes (Rozycki & Johnson, 2013). After the analysis, students may write a reflection on how learning about linguistic varieties challenges the dominant belief of using standard forms to write academically in college and/or for publishing in English-medium journals. Carving these spaces will encourage multilingual and monolingual students alike to see their linguistic repertoires as a resource. Another example may be a *transfronterizo* collaboration between sociology and Spanish as a heritage language faculty members where they design a translingual activity to have their students explore language discrimination in low-income housing.

Finally, becoming *transfronterizo* collaborators can expand and complicate participants' scholarship knowledge. For example, reading translinguality scholarship has helped us navigate and negotiate linguistic notions less familiar to us and has propelled our disciplinary discourses to come into contact with one another in a way that we have cultivated transborder thinking. As a result, we have submitted and presented transdisciplinary collaborative work in national conferences in each other's fields. While it has not been easy going out of our disciplinary comfort zone, by experiencing the "other" disciplinary environment at conferences, we have fostered elasticity——the capacity to move temporarily to the borderlands outside our disciplines to carry our project, as well as to have developed mutually respectful growth. Because we are preparing students for a world that is radically interdisciplinary and transdisciplinary (Rademaekers, 2015), WAC/WID practitioners collaborating with disciplinary faculty can develop scholarship exchanges that include scholarship about language and scholarship about writing. Doing this can complement/challenge one's views of writing and language by making "the language question" essentially unavoidable as well as help us explore and understand better our students' language use across disciplines and contexts (Donahue, 2018).

In conclusion, we believe that the linguistic and disciplinary borders in WAC/WID are ripe for translingual renegotiations because we know that solamente trabajando juntos haremos diferencia en la vida de nuestros estudiantes.

ACKNOWLEDGMENTS

The authors would like to thank Alyssa Cavazos for her support, comments and guidance with respect to this article.

REFERENCES

Anderson, J. & Lightfoot, A. (2018). Translingual practices in English classrooms in India: Current perceptions and future possibilities. *International Journal of Bilingual Education and Bilingualism.* https://doi.org/10.1080/13670050.2018.1548558.

Aparicio, F. (1997). La enseñanza del español para hispanohablantes y la pedagogía multicultural. In M. C. Colombi & E. X. Alarcón (Eds.), *La enseñanza del español a hispanohablantes: Praxis y teoría* (pp. 222–232). Houghton Mifflin.

Atkinson, D., Cursan, D., Matsuda, P. K., Ortmeier-Hooper, C., Ruecker, T., Simpson, S. & Tardy, C. (2015). Clarifying the relationship between L2 writing and translingual writing: An open letter to writing studies editors and organization leaders. *College English, 77,* 383–386.

Bakhtin, M. (1986). *Speech genres and other late essays.* University of Texas Press.

Bawarshi, A. (2016). Beyond the genre fixation: A translingual perspective on genre. *College English, 78*, 243–249. http://www.ncte.org/journals/ce/issues/v78-3.

Bazerman, C. (2012). From cultural criticism to disciplinary participation: Living with powerful words. In T. M. Zawacki & P. M. Rogers (Eds.), *Writing across the curriculum: A critical sourcebook* (pp. 239–245). Modern Language Association of America.

Blair, A., Haneda, M. & Bose, F. N. (2018). Reimagining English-Medium Instructional Settings as Sites of Multilingual and Multimodal Meaning Making. *TESOL Quarterly, 52*, (3), 516–539. https://doi.org/10.1002/tesq.449.

Block, D. (2003). *The social turn in second language acquisition.* Edinburgh University Press.

Canagarajah, S. A. (2011). Codemeshing in academic writing: Identifying teachable strategies of translanguaging. *Modern Language Journal, 91*, 401–417. https://doi.org/10.1111/j.1540-4781.2011.01207.x.

Canagarajah, S. (2016). Translingual writing and teacher development in composition. *College English, 78*(3), 265–273.

Cavazos, A. G., Hebbard, M., Hernández, J. E., Rodriguez, C. & Schwarz, G. (2018). Advancing a transnational, transdisciplinary, and translingual framework: A professional development series for teaching assistants in writing and Spanish programs. *Across the Disciplines, 15*(3), 11–27. https://wac.colostate.edu/docs/atd/trans/cavazosetal2018.pdf.

Ceballos, C. B. (2012). Literacies at the border: Transnationalism and the biliteracy practices of teachers across the US–Mexico border. *International Journal of Bilingual Education and Bilingualism, 15*(6), 687–703. https://doi.org/10.1080/13670050.2012.699948.

Cenoz, J. & Gorter, D. (Eds). (2015). *Multilingual education: Between language learning and translanguaging.* Cambridge University Press.

Cox, M. (2010). WAC-WID and second language writers: WPA-CompPile research bibliographies, no. 8. *WPA-CompPile Research Bibliographies.* https://wac.colostate.edu/docs/comppile/wpa/Cox.pdf.

Cox, M. (2011). WAC: Closing doors or opening doors for second language writers? *Across the Disciplines, 8*(4), 1–20. https://wac.colostate.edu/docs/atd/ell/cox.pdf.

Cox, M. & Zawacki, T. M. (Eds.). (2011). WAC and second language writing: Cross-field research, theory, and program development [Special issue]. *Across the Disciplines, 8*(4). https://wac.colostate.edu/atd/special/ell/.

De la Piedra, M. T. & Guerra, J. C. (2012). The literacy practices of *transfronterizos* in a multilingual world. *International Journal of Bilingual Education and Bilingualism, 15*(6), 627–634. https://doi.org/10.1080/13670050.2012.699944.

Dicker, S. J. (2003). *Languages in America: A pluralistic view* (2nd ed.). Multilingual Matter. https://doi.org/10.21832/9781853596537.

Donahue, C. (2018). We are the "other": The future of exchanges between writing and language studies. *Across the Disciplines, 15*(3), 130–143. https://wac.colostate.edu/docs/atd/trans/donahue2018.pdf.

Dryer, D. (2016). Appraising translingual. *College English, 78*(3), 274–283.

Ede, L. & Lunsford, A. (1990). *Singular texts/plural authors: Perspectives on collaborative writing.* Southern Illinois University Press.

Fairclough, N. (1992). The appropriacy of "appropriateness." In N. Fairclough (Ed.), *Critical language awareness* (pp. 33–56). Longman.

Ferris, D. & Thaiss, C. (2011). Writing at UC Davis: Addressing the needs of second language writers. *Across the Disciplines, 8*(4). https://wac.colostate.edu/docs/atd/ell/ferris-thaiss.pdf.

Fishman, S. M. & McCarthy, L. (2001). An ESL writer and her discipline-based professor: Making progress even when goals do not match. *Written Communication, 18,* 180–228. https://doi.org/10.1177/0741088301018002002.

Fránquiz, M. & Ortíz, A. (Eds.). (2017). Co-editors' introduction: Who are the *transfronterizos* and what can we learn from them? *Bilingual Research Journal, 40*(2), 111–115. https://doi.org/10.1080/15235882.2017.1329378.

Fredericksen, E. & Mangelsdorf, K. (2014). Graduate writing workshops: Crossing languages and disciplines. In T. M. Zawacki & M. Cox (Eds.), *WAC and second-language writers: Research towards linguistically and culturally inclusive programs and practices* (pp. 347–367). The WAC Clearinghouse; Parlor Press. https://wac.colostate.edu/books/perspectives/l2/.

Galindo, B., Castaneda, S., Gutierrez, E., Tejada, A. E., Jr. & Wallace, D. (2014). Challenging our labels: Rejecting the language of remediation. *Young Scholars in Writing, 11,* 5–16.

García O. (2009). *Bilingual education in the 21st century: A global perspective.* Blackwell/Wiley.

García, O. & Kleyn, T. (Eds.) (2016). *Translanguaging with multilingual students: Learning from classroom moments.* Routledge. https://doi.org/10.4324/9781315695242.

Geller, A. E. (2011). Teaching and learning with multilingual faculty. *Across the Disciplines, 8*(4). 1–19. https://wac.colostate.edu/docs/atd/ell/geller.pdf.

Gentil, G. (2018). Modern languages, bilingual education, and translation studies. *Across the Disciplines, 15*(3), 114–129. https://wac.colostate.edu/docs/atd/trans/gentil2018.pdf.

Gere, A. R., Knutson, A. V. & McCarthy, R. (2018). Rewriting disciplines: STEM students' longitudinal approaches to writing in (and across) the disciplines. *Across the Disciplines, 15*(3), 63–75. https://wac.colostate.edu/docs/atd/trans/gereetal2018.pdf.

Guerra, J. (2016). Cultivating a rhetorical sensibility in the translingual writing classroom. *College English, 78,* 228–233.

Hall, J. (2009). WAC/WID in the next America: Redefining professional identity in the age of the multilingual majority. *The WAC Journal, 20,* 33–49. https://wac.colostate.edu/docs/journal/vol20/hall.pdf.

Hall, J. (2014a). Language background and the college writing course. *Journal of Writing Assessment, 7*(1). http://journalofwritingassessment.org/article.php?article=77.

Hall, J. (2014b). Multilinguality across the curriculum. In T. M. Zawacki & M. Cox (Eds.), *WAC and second-language writers: Research towards linguistically and culturally inclusive programs and practices* (pp. 5–14). The WAC Clearinghouse; Parlor Press. https://wac.colostate.edu/books/perspectives/l2/.

Hall, J. (2018a). Rewriting disciplines, rewriting boundaries: Transdisciplinary and translingual challenges for WAC/WID. *Across the Disciplines, 15*(3), 1–10. https://wac.colostate.edu/docs/atd/trans/intro.pdf.

Hall, J. (2018b). The translingual challenge: Boundary work in rhetoric & composition, second language writing, and WAC/WID. *Across the Disciplines, 15*(3), 28–47. https://wac.colostate.edu/docs/atd/trans/hall2018.pdf.

Harklau, L. & Siegal, M. (2009). Immigrant youth and higher education. In M. Roberge, M. Siegal & L. Harklau (Ed.), *Generation 1.5 in college composition: Teaching academic writing to U.S.-educated learners of ESL* (pp. 25–34). Routledge.

Hartse, J. H., Lockett, M. & Ortabasi, M. (2018). Languaging about language in an interdisciplinary writing-intensive course. *Across the Disciplines, 15*(3), 89–102. https://wac.colostate.edu/docs/atd/trans/henghartseetal2018.pdf.

Hendricks, C. C. (2018). WAC/WID and transfer: Towards a transdisciplinary view of academic writing. *Across the Disciplines, 15*(3), 48–62. https://wac.colostate.edu/docs/atd/trans/hendricks2018.pdf.

Horner, B. (2018). Translinguality and disciplinary reinvention. *Across the Disciplines, 15*(3), 76–88. https://wac.colostate.edu/docs/atd/trans/horner2018.pdf.

Horner, B. & Hall, J. (Eds.). (2018). Rewriting disciplines, rewriting boundaries: Transdisciplinary and translingual challenges for WAC/WID [Special issue]. *Across the Disciplines, 15*(3). https://wac.colostate.edu/atd/special/trans/.

Horner, B., Lu, M.-Z., Royster, J. J. & Trimbur, J. (2011). Language difference in writing: Toward a translingual approach. *College English, 73*, 303–321.

Horner, B., NeCamp, S. & Donahue, C. (2011). Toward a multilingual composition scholarship: From English only to a translingual norm. *College Composition and Communication, 63*, 269–300.

Ives, L., Leahy, E., Leming, A., Pierce, T. & Schwartz, M. (2014). "I don't know if that was the right thing to do": Cross-disciplinary/cross-institutional faculty response to L2 writing. In T. M. Zawacki & M. Cox (Eds.), *WAC and second-language writers: Research towards linguistically and culturally inclusive programs and practices* (pp. 211–232). The WAC Clearinghouse; Parlor Press. https://wac.colostate.edu/books/perspectives/l2/ .

Jablonski, J. (2006). *Academic writing consulting and WAC: Method and models for guiding cross-curricular literacy work*. Hampton Press.

Johns, A. M. (2001). ESL students and WAC programs: Varied populations and diverse needs. In S. H. McLeod, E. Miraglia, M. Soven & C. Thaiss (Eds.), *WAC for the new millennium: Strategies for continuing writing-across-the-curriculum programs* (pp. 141–164). National Council of Teachers of English.

Jordan, J. & Kedrowicz, A. (2011). Attitudes about graduate L2 writing in engineering: Possibilities for more integrated instruction. *Across the Disciplines, 8*(4). https://wac.colostate.edu/docs/atd/ell/jordan-kedrowicz.pdf.

Kachru, Y. (1994). Multilingual bias in SLA research. *TESOL Quarterly, 28*(4), 795–800. https://doi.org/10.2307/3587564.

Kiernan, J., Meier, J. & Wang, X. (2016). Negotiating languages and cultures: Enacting translingualism through a translation assignment. *Composition Studies, 44*(1), 89–107.

Lacorte, M. (2016). Teacher development in heritage language education. In M. Fairclough & S. M. Beaudrie (Eds.), *Innovative strategies for heritage language teaching: A practical guide for the classroom* (pp. 99–119). Georgetown University Press.

Lee, J. W. (2016). Beyond translingual writing. *College English, 79,* 174–195.

Lee, J. W. & Jenks, C. (2016). Doing translingual disposition. *College Composition and Communication, 68,* 317–344.

Leeman, J. & Serafini, E. J. (2016). Sociolinguistics for heritage language educators and students: A model for critical translingual competence. In M. Fairclough & S. M. Beaudrie (Eds.), *Innovative strategies for heritage language teaching: A practical guide for the classroom* (pp. 56–79). Georgetown University Press.

Lippi-Green, R. (1997). *English with an accent: Language, ideology, and discrimination in the United States.* Routledge.

Lu, M. Z. & Horner, B. (2013). Translingual literacy and matters of agency. In A. S. Canagarajah (Ed.), *Literacy as translingual practice: Between communities and classrooms* (pp. 26–38). Routledge.

Makoni, S. & Pennycook, A. (2012). Disinventing multilingualism: From monological multilingualism to multilingual franca. In M. Martin-Jones, A. Blackledge & A. Creese (Eds.), *The Routledge handbook of multilingualism* (pp. 439–453). Routledge.

Matsuda, P. K. (1998). Situating ESL writing in cross-disciplinary context. *Written Communication, 15*(1), 99–121. https://doi.org/10.1177/0741088398015001004.

Matsuda, P. K. (2002). Alternative discourses: A synthesis. In C. Schroeder, H. Fox & P. Bizzell (Eds.), *ALTDis: Alternative discourses and the academy* (pp. 191–196). Boynton/Cook.

Matsuda, P. K. (2012). Teaching composition in the multilingual world: Second language writing in composition studies. In K. Ritter & P. K. Matsuda (Eds.), *Exploring composition sites, issues and perspectives* (pp. 36–51). Utah State University Press. https://doi.org/10.2307/j.ctt4cgjsj.6.

Matsuda, P. K. (2013). It's the wild west out there: A new linguistic frontier in U.S. college composition. In A. S. Canagarajah. *Literacy as translingual practice: Between communities and classrooms* (pp. 128–138). Routledge.

Matsuda, P. K. & Jablonski, J.. (2000). Beyond the L2 metaphor: Towards a mutually transformative model of ESL/WAC collaboration. *Academic writing: Interdisciplinary perspectives on communication across the curriculum.* https://wac.colostate.edu/aw/articles/matsuda_jablonski2000.pdf.

May, S. (Ed.). (2014). *The multilingual turn: Implications for SLA, TESOL, and bilingual education.* Routledge. https://doi.org/10.4324/9780203113493.

McCarthy, L. P. & Fishman, S. M. (1991). Boundary conversations: Conflicting ways of knowing in philosophy and interdisciplinary research. *Research in the Teaching of English, 25,* 419–468.

Mercier, L. (2015). Introduction to Serres on transdisciplinarity. *Theory, Culture & Society, 32*(5–6), 37–40. https://doi.org/10.1177/0263276415599118.

Mignolo, W. D. (2000). *Local histories/global designs: Coloniality, subaltern, knowledges, and border thinking.* Princeton University Press.

271

Motha, S., Jain, R. & Tecle, T. (2012). Translinguistic identity-as-pedagogy: Implications for language teacher education. *International Journal of Innovation in English Language Teaching, 1*(1), 13–28.

Musanti, S. I. & Cavazos, A. (2018). "Siento que siempre tengo que regresar al inglés": Embracing a translanguaging stance in a Hispanic-serving institution. *E-JournALL, EuroAmerican Journal of Applied Linguistics and Languages, 5*(2), 44–61. https://doi .org/10.21283/2376905X.9.147.

Osborne, P. (2015). Problematizing disciplinarity, transdisciplinarity problematics. *Theory, Culture & Society, 32*(5–6), 3–35. https://doi.org/10.1177/0263276415592245.

Paris, D. & Alim, H. S. (Eds.). (2017). *Culturally sustaining pedagogies: Teaching and learning for justice in a changing world.* Teachers College Press.

Parra, M. L. (2016). Critical approaches to heritage language instruction: How to foster students' critical consciousness. In M. Fairclough & S. M. Beaudrie (Eds.), *Innovative strategies for heritage language teaching: A practical guide for the classroom* (pp. 166–189). Georgetown University Press.

Pennycook, A. (2010). *Language as a local practice.* Routledge. https://doi.org/10.4324 /9780203846223.

Rademaekers, J. K. (2015). Is WAC/WID ready for the transdisciplinary research university? *Across the Disciplines, 12*(2). https://wac.colostate.edu/docs/atd/articles /rademaekers2015.pdf.

Rampton, B. (2011). From "multi-ethnic adolescent heteroglossia" to "contemporary urban vernaculars." *Language & Communication, 31*, 276–294. https://doi.org/10 .1016/j.langcom.2011.01.001.

Relaño Pastor, A. M. (2007). On border identities: "*Transfronterizo*" students in San Diego. *Diskurs Kindheits- und Jugendforschung, 2*(3), 263–277.

Rozycki, W. & Johnson, N. (2013). Non-canonical grammar in Best Paper award winners in engineering. *English for Specific Purposes 32*, 157–169. https://doi.org/10 .1016/j.esp.2013.04.002.

Ruecker, T. (2014). "Here they do this, there they do that": Latinas/Latinos writing across institutions. *College Composition and Communication, 66*(1), 91–119.

Russell, David. (2012). The writing-across-the-curriculum movement: 1970–1990. In T. M. Zawacki and P. M. Rogers (Eds.), *Writing across the curriculum: A critical sourcebook* (pp. 15–45). Bedford/St. Martin's.

Sandford, S. (2015). Contradiction of terms: Feminist theory, philosophy and transdisciplinarity. *Theory, Culture & Society, 32*(5–6), 159–182. https://doi.org/10.1177 /0263276415594238.

Schreiber, B. R. & Watson, M. (2018). Translingualism ≠ code-meshing: A response to Gevers' "Translingualism revisited." *Journal of Second Language Writing. 42*, 94–97. https://doi.org/10.1016/j.jslw.2018.10.007.

Schwarzer, D. & Fuchs, M. (2014). Monolingual teacher candidates promoting translingualism: A self-study of teacher education practices project. In Y. S. Freeman & D. Freeman (Eds.), *Research on preparing preservice teachers to work effectively with emergent bilinguals* (pp. 89–112). Emerald Group Publishing. https://doi.org/10 .1108/S1479-368720140000021003.

Shapiro, S., Cox, M., Shuck, G. & Simnitt, E. (2016). Teaching for agency: From appreciating linguistic diversity to empowering student writers. *Composition Studies, 44*(1), 31–52.

Shipka, J. (2016). Transmodality in/and processes of making: Changing disposition and practice. *College English, 78*(3), 250–257.

Siczek, M. & Shapiro, S. (2014). Developing writing-intensive courses for a globalized curriculum through WAC-TESOL collaborations. In T. M. Zawacki & M. Cox (Eds.), *WAC and second-language writers: Research towards linguistically and culturally inclusive programs and practices* (pp. 329–346). The WAC Clearinghouse; Parlor Press. https://wac.colostate.edu/books/perspectives/l2/.

Smith, H. P. & Murillo, A. L. (2012). Researching *transfronterizo* literacies in Texas border colonias. *International Journal of Bilingual Education and Bilingualism, 15*(6), 635–651. https://doi.org/10.1080/13670050.2012.699945.

Taczak, K. & Robertson, L. (2017). Metacognition and the reflective writing practitioner: An integrated knowledge approach. In P. Portanova, J. M. Rifenburg & D. Roen (Eds.), *Contemporary perspectives on cognition and writing* (pp. 211–229). The WAC Clearinghouse; University Press of Colorado. https://wac.colostate.edu/books/perspectives/cognition/.

Tarabochia, S. L. (2017). *Reframing the relational: A pedagogical ethic for cross-curricular literacy work*. National Council of Teachers of English.

Trimbur, J. (2016). Translingualism and close reading. *College English, 78*(3), 219–227.

Valdés. G. (1997). The teaching of Spanish to bilingual Spanish-speaking students: Outstanding issues and unanswered questions. In M. C. Colombi & E. X. Alarcón (Eds.), *La enseñanza del español a hispanohablantes: Praxis y teoría* (pp. 8–44). Houghton Mifflin.

Valdés, G. (2001). Heritage language students: Profiles and possibilities. In J. K. Peyton, D. Ranard & S. McGinnis (Eds.), *Heritage language in America: Preserving a national resource* (pp. 37–80). Routledge.

Worden, D. (2013). Afterword: Reflections from the ground floor. In A. S. Canagarajah (Ed.), *Literacy as translingual practice: Between communities and classrooms* (pp. 235–238). Routledge.

Zamel, V. & Spack, R. (Eds.). (2004). *Crossing the curriculum: Multilingual learners in college classrooms*. Lawrence Erlbaum. https://doi.org/10.4324/9781410609809.

Zawacki, T. M. & Cox, M. (Eds.). (2014). *WAC and second-language writers: research towards linguistically and culturally inclusive programs and practices*. The WAC Clearinghouse; Parlor Press. https://wac.colostate.edu/books/perspectives/l2/.

Zentella, A. C. (2009). *Speaker Series:* Transfronterizo *talk: Conflicting constructions of bilingualism among U.S.-Mexico border crossing college students* [Video file]. https://www.youtube.com/watch?v=VvrO1jHkcUg&t=1456s.

Zentella, A. C. (2016). "Socials," "Poch@s," "Normals" y *los demás:* School networks and linguistic capital of high school students on the Tijuana-San Diego border. In H. S. Alim, J. R. Rickford & A. F. Ball (Eds.), *Raciolinguistics: How language shapes our ideas about race* (pp. 327–343). Oxford University Press. https://doi.org/10.1093/acprof:oso/9780190625696.003.0019.

PART 4. ATTENDING TO THE HUMAN ELEMENT: ANTI-RACISM, EMOTIONAL LABOR, AND PERSONAL CONNECTION IN THE TEACHING OF WRITING

CHAPTER 15.

LETTERS ON MOVING FROM ALLY TO ACCOMPLICE: ANTI-RACISM AND THE TEACHING OF WRITING

Neisha-Anne S. Green
American University

Frankie Condon
University of Waterloo

In this epistolary chapter, based on our 2018 keynote address at the International Writing Across the Curriculum Conference, we name and challenge linguistic supremacy and its fundamental relationship to white supremacy and racism. We argue that teachers of writing across the disciplines should learn about code meshing: the practice of braiding or blending languages, discourses, and rhetorical traditions within a single text—particularly those historically marginalized or excluded languages, discourses, and rhetorical traditions such as African American and Chicanx Englishes. We argue that code meshing should not only be recognized as a legitimate writing practice, but also that it should be taught across the curriculum and in every discipline.

To begin, we would like to make the following territorial acknowledgment:[1] This address was first delivered at the International Writing Across the Curriculum conference, which convened in Auburn, Alabama on the traditional territory of the Chickasaw and Creek peoples, many of whom were forced from their lands

---

1   A territorial or land acknowledgment is an open recognition of the importance of the relationships between Indigenous peoples and their lands. Such an acknowledgment is aimed at foregrounding histories of these relationships that have long been denied or suppressed. A territorial acknowledgment recognizes the Indigenous peoples who continue to live in the spaces that non-Indigenous peoples have taken and now occupy and invites us to reflect carefully and critically on our own relationship to colonialism, imperialism, and their aftermaths. For more information about territorial acknowledgments, please see https://native-land.ca/territory-acknowledgement/ and https://www.teenvogue.com/story/indigenous-land-acknowledgement-explained?verso=true.

DOI: https://doi.org/10.37514/PER-B.2020.0360.2.15

in the 1830s during the Trail of Tears. Those who survived the journey were relocated in what is now Oklahoma. The traditional languages of the Indigenous peoples of Alabama were Muscogee, Mvskoke, and Hitchiti-Mikasuki.

Together we have worked hard to nurture a relationship built on respect, friendship, reciprocal mentoring, and a real desire to see each other be well and do better. We have tried, in other words, not merely to be allies to one another—providing safe(r) spaces for one another—but also to do the work associated with acting as what Neisha-Anne has termed, an accomplice (2018, p. 29). We have tried—are trying—to actively stand with and for one another, to name, interrogate, and intervene in racism as compatriots, co-conspirators, friends not merely in name but in what we be and do with and for one another. The essay which follows is a testament and living example of the ways in which we support and "take care" of each other, moving through the academy in our individual ways yet coming together with commitment and constancy, even and especially in the struggle to end racism, to promote acceptance, inclusivity and diversity especially in our practice of teaching writing.

Our essay is written in the form of an exchange of letters—a genre in which Dr. Vershawn Ashanti Young (Vay) and Frankie have been composing since they crafted an epistolary chapter for Frankie's book, *I Hope I Join the Band: Narrative, Affiliation, and Antiracist Rhetoric* (Condon, 2012). This genre enables us, we think, to both discuss and to model the honest, hard, and tender dialogue we believe is necessary to the work of anti-racism, whether that work is undertaken in our classrooms, our meeting rooms or offices, or beyond the confines of our campuses: in every community in and through which we move. We believe, further, that the epistolary genre enables us to engage anti-racism from our differing disciplinary positions—writing from where we stand as well as with an openness to change and be changed—even as we conjoin our voices in a single text. We hope you will take away from the letters that follow an understanding of the importance of storytelling as well as the necessity for deep listening that requires us to attend to one another's stories with humility even when we are uncomfortable. We hope you will take away a sense of curiosity about what it might mean in your work of teaching writing across the curriculum to value the many Englishes and rhetorical traditions in which our students speak and write. We hope you will begin to imagine what it might mean for you to teach rather than suppress the craft of mixing, blending, and braiding languages and rhetorical traditions well. We hope you will begin to recognize, as we do, that this work is, in all our fields, the work of anti-racism. We hope that, when asked by the naysayer in your department meeting, why the work of anti-racism is important to the teaching of writing across all disciplines that you will be able to say, without a doubt, that the current and future lives of all students of color (those who are holding onto their seat at the table for dear life and those who are waiting and hoping for some accomplice on the admissions committee to give them a shot at a seat at the table) matter—and that the work of anti-racism as it is enacted in those spaces where we teach writing is fundamental to making that mattering real. We hope that you will be able to say that anti-racism also matters to the lives of white students sitting beside students of color in our classrooms and writing centers, because if we are to ever rid ourselves of racism white folk must learn how and then do the work of dismantling the racism built by their ancestors and from which they continue to benefit.

THE LETTERS

Hey Frankie,

What it do? Sorry it took me so long to check-in, but as usual it's been crazy around here. The last couple of weeks go down in the history books as "them Manhattan days." You know what I mean? You know what I mean. I mean them days when you can't wait to go home and pour a strong one and just sit still!

The writing center is busy as usual and the tutors are keeping me on my toes. Yesterday in our practicum meeting we read one of Harris' classics and then drafted our first round of individual tutor philosophy statements. We worked backwards and looked carefully at some positive comments and feedback from students written specifically after they had met with a tutor. We really examined those comments and thought long and hard about the degree of kindness and the quality of feedback the tutors must have practiced to get that kind of feedback. There were even a few comments that got us thinking about how vulnerable some students can be in their sessions with us. It got deep for a min. I swear, Frankie, it's my time with the tutors that keep me doing this work! For real for real! And that's FACTS cause Lord knows I be needing all the encouragement I can get sometimes.

Remember I told you that Vay was doing a full day of workshops at a nearby campus and he invited me to come? Well I went and I'm glad I did. It was nice to talk through some of my ideas about this anti-racist work with other people who are also thinking about what to do and how to do it. I learned a lot from the tutors there too which was good cause their perspectives and questions helped me further understand my own tutors and their journey to awareness and then to practice. I think I realized that stepping away from my own campus can help me get a clearer view of home. I think I also learned something else. But I haven't quite figured out exactly what it is that I've learned; or maybe, I'm resisting it cause it hurt. Something else happened that I need to tell you about. It's been on my mind and it's bugging the piss outta me.

I thought everything was fine, Frankie. I was excited and happy to be on a campus that was new to me. The first event of the day was cool—I find it interesting and helpful to my own thinking and research to interact with folk as they unpack the phenomenon that is code-meshing. The second event was fun but challenging. Vay made it fun and he also made it challenging. Just like that. We walk into this auditorium and the room is packed with faculty and staff from all disciplines, writing center staff and tutors. They call Vay up on stage and give him a chair to sit in. Next thing I know Vay says "Can I get another chair? I want Neisha up here with me." Now you know me and my face. My face be telling on me. I was out there looking like Gary Coleman on some "whachu talmbout Vay?" LOL I'll forever be grateful for his active and purposeful demonstration of mentorship—of accompliceship—cause next thing I know there's an extra chair on stage and I can't say no cause everybody is watching. Vay indicated to all those folks that I have things to say that need to be heard and to me that this was the time to stand with him literally and figuratively. I got up and took the stage with Vay, and I'm glad I did. What I didn't realize though, was that he was taking a risk for me. Let me tell you how I figured it out.

So we get to the last event of the day, right. It's early in the evening, but late in the day. The event was intimate and at the house of one of the professors. Picture a fireside chat, but Vershawn Ashanti Young style. Anyway, Vay, the organizer of the entire day's events and myself walk into the spot. Real quick someone had organized a plate of snacks for me and had positioned a glass of wine in my hand. I'm grateful and walk over to the living room to find a place to sit. I can't stress just how intimate the last event was. Frankie, we were sitting in someone's living room! It was in this setting for all to hear, bare witness too, do nothing about but grimace and get red in the face that a much older woman who I hadn't met until that day, and who by academic standards is "respected" in the field looks up at me with disgust and says "Oh, so you're still here? Does your supervisor know that you're still out here?"

I instantly froze. I didn't know what to do or what to say in response. Eventually I mustered a "I was invited . . ."

Dazed and Confused,

Neisha

Dear Neisha-Anne,

I'm really glad you felt you could tell me this story and I'm so sorry that woman spoke to you that way. To tell the tale of having been treated so cannot be easy. I imagine this was one of those moments when—in the midst of your shock, embarrassment, and frustration at that attempted public humiliation—

you knew, just knew in your bones the way we do sometimes, that right there was racism. However unintentionally or dys-consciously wielded, that woman checked you. At the very least, her words were patronizing but there seems also an implied threat in them. You and I both know she wouldn't have spoken so had you been a white woman but this kind of "whiteliness"—the rhetorical practices that emerge from the conviction that one is best equipped to know, to speak, to judge, and to act—comes with the benefit of plausible deniability. "I didn't mean" "I didn't intend" "That's not who I am" (Condon, 2012, p. 34).

This morning, I read a terrific essay by James Sanchez (2018). He writes about what he calls "the versatility of white supremacy rhetoric." Sanchez theorizes the ways in which white supremacists in the age of Trump speak to two audiences at once. He says that rhetorical versatility is the vehicle that creates a white suprema-cist subtext for a message that otherwise might seem, in terms of white supremacy, ideologically inert. So, Sanchez says, a speaker or writer may address two audi-ences at once—affirming on the one hand a commitment to white supremacy and appealing on the other hand to that audience likely to be persuaded by what they perceive to be an ideal to which they ought to be committed (like patriotism, for example). Anyhow, your story makes me think that perhaps 'rhetorical versatility' is also the vehicle for the racist microaggression. Maybe your lady's utterance was a less than artful example. I mean I hope the folks in the room with you heard what she was doing right there and gave her some side-eye. But it seems to me that the racist microaggression works by appearing innocuous or even justified to whitely witnesses even as the speaker reasserts the Otherness and thus the unbelongingness of her target. The utterance affirms the superiority of the speaker, sliding in under-neath the assertion of the inferiority of that unbelonging Other.

I'm remembering a conversation you and I had not too long ago. We were talking about how that kindness that is so integral to the art of walking through the world as an anti-racist (the kindness that might be, in and of itself, insuf-ficient but is, in fact, so necessary) seems to us like common sense. Your story makes me think again about how common the everyday unkindness of racism is—not only in your life, but in the lives of our students of colour too. And I'm struck by how similar the apparent underlying assumptions of deficiency and profligacy are among the everyday microaggressions that compose the stories my students tell and the one you have told. Like that lady you told me about at CCCCs. Remember? What is that story again—the one about the woman with the imaginary pearl necklace?

Anyway, I'm thinking of you and always with you in spirit.

Love,

Shankie

Frankie,

Do I remember? I've got stories for days unwillingly stored up in my WTF memory bank. I swear I haven't been doing this long enough to have accumulated so many stories, but I have them.

No one ever said that any aspect of anti-racist work wouldn't be anything but hard. But it is as necessary as it is hard. Dr. King (1967) said that "in the end, we will remember not the words of our enemies, but the silence of our friends." That story that you're remembering became so very important to my readiness to speak up. That story broke my silence and gave rise to the public Neisha-Anne that folk have come to know. I hadn't really put these words to it before, but I see clear as day how that incident got me thinking and moving like a true accomplice and not an ally any more. Did I ever give you the full details on why things went down the way they did that day? The day before the lady clutched her nonexistent pearls Doug and I were in the audience of a panel about linguistic racism. We went because the title and aim seemed promising, but Lord did things go wrong. The presenter kept validating SRTOL while putting it in its place like an unruly child that only a mother could love. And then to make it worst, one of the most well known rhetoricians and compositionists walks into the room and folk instantly get to gawking and whispering. They do and do until he speaks, and then it happens. By the end of everything he has said, SRTOL, code-meshing, translingualism and the whole damn barnyard it seems was yet again reduced to being equal but separate. Doug and I were annoyed by this, but we were even more annoyed at ourselves for not being brave enough, or having our wits together enough to speak up in the moment. Right then there, we decided to let that be the last time we were caught off guard. We also decided that a pledge to act was not enough. We needed to act even if there was no offensive action. There is not safe(r) space; every space we live and move in is a space where racism may flourish. We right there, in the hot Houston sun, we started drafting the ideas that led to our panel the next year at Cs. That was the panel where you and I first worked together. We called that one Emotion and Anti-Racist Rhetorics in Writing Studies: Anger as Performance-Rhetoric (Green & Kern, 2015).

We were ready to act. Doug and I went about the remainder of the conference with this new mindset, not knowing that it would be tested the very next day in the Q&A of Doug's own presentation. As usual when folk get to talking about code-meshing and seeing value in others' Englishes and languages someone always gets upset because they see this validation as an invalidation of the ever fluid standard. They get mad or teary or both at once because they can't or won't see that teaching anti-racist moves such as code-meshing is important regardless of what discipline we're working from because many so many students of color are writing for our lives. They make their arguments against such moves personal in a way that they really don't have ownership of. They center themselves and what they see as their interests, needs, and "expertise" because their privilege allows it—demands it—instead of making it personal to those who of us whose lives are at stake. Let me explain what I mean. In the Q&A one person got up and started arguing not against the theory and practice of code-meshing, but against the man—Vershawn Young—and people like him, who believe in linguistic diversity and linguistic inclusion. Then Ms. Whiteliness herself got up and declared that while she sees the value in linguistic diversity that she can't fully endorse it. This is when she clutched her imaginary pearls, got all octaves of high pitched and started screaming that her students of color needed her permission to use their codes in her classroom.

Frankie, my heart started pumping and I swear to you if I could be red in the face I woulda been a red delicious apple shade of red. I knew I had to say something and even though I feared the outcome my hand shot up in the air and I anxiously waited my turn. I recalled my own experience of finally being aware that there was nothing wrong with my Englishes. I recalled the confusion I experienced negotiating this new truth with what I had been taught in school. I recalled the confusion I experienced as I started thinking and writing in a way that more resembled a linguistic celebration and not a linguistic incarceration. I professed that students needed to be made aware of the linguistic choices that they actually possess. In my own octaves of high pitched I begged for students to be made aware of their natural, mother-tongue, as well as learned-in-school linguistic abilities and given the chance to make what I call savvy rhetorical choices (to "funk up" their writing, as Dr. Young might say). I finally explained that in my writing center I teach the tutors to notice differences in choice of language, register, and rhetorical strategy rather than focusing on error narrowly (and erroneously) defined, because difference leaves room for conversation and understanding. We work hard at giving students the full picture. We say, "hey there is nothing wrong with this, but we can see why someone might want you to 'correct' it." We explain the potential consequences of being bold and embracing their difference as well as the rewards—and then we leave it up to the student, to the writer to choose the direction of their piece. Ownership of writing is in the hands of the writer at the end of the day. Permission can't be given where it was never required!

In full ownership of all that makes me ME,

Neisha

Neisha-Anne, you amazing woman!

Remember when you told us all back at the IWCA conference that if you said somethin it was okay to holler "Girl, you betta Preach"? Well, you just said somethin right there!

283

Under the heading of funny-not-funny, the similarity between the two whitely women you've been talking about is almost laughable. So, you need the permission of the first lady to attend an event to which you were invited? And the imaginary pearls lady says her students need her permission to speak and write their mother tongues! What the what!

I've been thinking of you as I read Austin Clarke's (2015) memoir, 'Membering. Clarke was a Caribbean Canadian novelist and poet. He died recently but his work has been famous here for some time and he is renowned as one of the great Canadian writers of all time. This passage in particular brings you to mind. Clarke writes about traveling to Canada for the first time from Barbados and the new kind of racism he encounters in the north. Clarke talks about writing his novel, The Polished Hoe, and the main character, Mary-Mathilde. In his book, Mary-Mathilde travels to the south from Buffalo with her white lover on a segregated train. Clarke writes of her experience, "To her, it was 'not normal.' She called this seating arrangement 'serrigated'" (2015, p. 19). And then he says this: "I chose the term 'serrigated' instead of the traditional spelling, because I wanted to invent a word that expressed the rawness of racism, like a wound made on the most delicate part of the body, a woman's belly, with a knife with a serrated blade" (2015, p. 20). Here, it seems to me, Clarke too is performing rhetorical versatility. But in this case his aim is to both represent in ways that affirm the visceral quality of the experience of racism for peoples of colour and make clear and plain to white readers the harm racism inflicts. Clarke was writing for his life, for sure!

Far too many of our colleagues seem to have no clue what code-meshing is. They haven't read a damn thing about it but they feel authorized somehow to be dismissive of what is now a rather large and compelling body of scholarship that explains and theorizes code-meshing both as a linguistic and a rhetorical practice and explores its pedagogical potential in the teaching of writing in every discipline.[2] So, they believe that code-meshing is really about ignoring "bad English" and letting "error" pass. They don't understand—or they refuse to understand—what you're saying about writing for your life, about rhetorical deliberation and the writerly practice of exercising choice. But we can see in Clarke's novel—as well as in Dr. Vay's writing and in yours—that code-meshing (the mixing, blending, braiding of multiple Englishes and rhetorical traditions) is careful, purposeful, and not in any sense a "mistake" on the part of the writer. If you're going to do it well, you have to understand so much more about both language and rhetoric than you do when you're all up in monolingual composing. Plus, if folks read a little bit they'd know cuz Young, and Young-Rivera, and Martinez,

---

2   We've included a reading list in the appendix that lists books and articles we think are important for folks to read.

and Villanueva, and Banks, and Kynard, and Richardson, and Smitherman, and Lunsford, and Horner and Lu and so many damn scholars I've lost count have told them that code-meshing is everywhere all the time. We all do it! In business and politics, in academic discourse across all the disciplines and in the public sphere, code-meshing is all around us and in us. The truth is—like Dr. Vay points out—that it's not code-meshed English that causes racism, it's racism that leads us to use the Englishes of racialized Others to justify discrimination.

Another famous Canadian writer, Tomson Highway, who is a Metis and Cree playwright and musician celebrates multilingualism and the ability to code-mesh among languages as "a suppleness of mind: a kind of intellectual and, notably, cultural dexterity" (Condon, 2018, p. 205). He says that "to learn another's language is to learn in a deep and sustained way who they are, how they have come to be, their history, their culture, their ways of seeing and of making meaning in and of the world. To speak (and we might add, to write) only one language, Highway writes, 'is like living in a house that has but one window . . . it is like sitting at a dinner table where you do all the talking and you talk about nothing but yourself. It means you're not listening to what the other person has to say. It means you are not interested.' And that, he notes, is 'not good for relationships'" (as cited in Condon, 2018, p. 205). Seriously, why wouldn't we want to encourage the suppleness of mind that comes with the ability to think and write within and across linguistic and rhetorical traditions: to code-mesh, and teach that to our students!

"Serrigated." Seems to me that whether the women in your stories knew they were wielding that knife or not, the wound remains and hurts! You and I both believe, I think, in our hearts that at some level they must have known or, at least, had available the means to know exactly what they're doing when they speak and act in such ways. In terms of impact, though, it little matters whether white supremacy so beclouds the vision of the whitely that they cannot discern the harm they do or whether they know exactly where and how to slice their words.

Love,

Frankie

Frankie,

I agree with Mary-Mathilde. There is nothing normal about racism. Her seating arrangement was not normal. Her seating arrangement was "serrigated." The academy was built on a "serrigated" mindset and not much has changed. MLK once said that "segregation is the adultery of an illicit intercourse between injustice and immorality." Just like Mary-Mathilde, stories like the ones we're talking about cut me like wounds made on my belly. Linguistic imperialism, rhetorical imperialism, epistemological imperialism ride our backs even when they aren't bent and as much as it is declared that diversity, inclusion, equality and equity are benchmarks that we now all, regardless of color, class and creed live by it really isn't so. There are still too many examples of folks who could otherwise make a positive difference acting like there's no language other than the imperial and ever fluid language that passes for a standard. There are still too many examples of discrediting and destroying the Englishes of communities of color. Still too many examples of ignoring and dismissing the rhetorical traditions of color. And Frankie, we haven't even really touched on the discrediting and destroying of the bodies of POC. We haven't talked about how I am judged by my hair, told how to dress, how to speak. We haven't talked about how I was denied the right to fully grieve my mother. How my timesheet is the only one that's scrutinized. Frankie, I am tired of working too many times as hard and getting a fraction of the recognition for my efforts. I am tired of being ignored or spoken at instead of to.

Frankie, these notions that people who look and talk like me need to be policed in every which way is real and actually being taught in schools. Just watch this instructional video from the Education Portal.[3]

> ▰Considering pronunciation, articulation, and dialect in public speaking (https://study.com/academy/lesson/pronunciation -articulation-and-dialect.html)

I believe James Baldwin (1961) was completely right when he said that "to be a Negro in this country and to be relatively conscious is to be in a constant stage of rage" (p. 205), but Baldwin didn't stop there as most people do. People like to forget that he then said that the next problem was controlling the rage so it doesn't destroy you. This control is one of the first lessons children of color get well before they've even entered pre-K! This video is a clear example of why this homeschooling is necessary. Children of color go to school and are taught that serious bodily harm could become them because of their accents, because of their dialects, because of their rhetorical traditions. White students are taught that it is okay to inflict that harm and hate.

Writing for my life,

Neisha

---

3   This video, produced by Study.com (Kadian-Baumeyer, n.d.), shows a series of cartoons. The first shows two students and discusses the difference between a teacher they admire who speaks with a British accent and another whom they dislike who "has an accent thicker than mud and a personality to match." The speaker in the video describes these differences between speakers as "vocal traits." The second cartoon shows a Black public speaker named Katie Bobbins who failed to "practice her pronunciation" and told her audience that if they "want to see the secrets of success they have to aks for it." Katie Bobbins is then struck in the head with an axe.

Dear Neisha,

That video is horrifying and maybe the most frightening aspect of its message is how widely and commonly its assumptions about linguistic and rhetorical diversity circulate. And there the threat against those who dare to speak and write their mother tongues is made explicit.

Neisha-Anne, you know I told you about the chapter I'm working on about Dr. Martin Luther King. Well, when I was in the King Archives in Atlanta a few years ago I found a little scrap of paper in one of the folders on the Birmingham struggle of notes Dr. King wrote while in jail there. And on this little scrap, Dr. King had written these lines: "Segregation is the invention of a God gone mad!" I read those words and I wept—not only because I imagined the moment of despair in which he must have penned them, but also because of Dr. King's courage in getting on up out of that despair to keep on keepin on.

Now, you and I know Dr. King wasn't thinking about linguistic and rhetorical segregation. But he was a master code mesher, moving fluidly and powerfully among and between Black English and the Englishes of his white audiences as well as between the Black evangelical rhetorical tradition and that of white protestantism, and of the liberatory and revolutionary rhetoric of the Black Power Movement. Dr. King understood, I believe, that in the face of united and unremitting resistance, in time the most entrenched ideas and practices must give way. Just as the course of rivers and the peaks of mountains yield to the forces of wind and water and time, so too must white supremacy in all its forms yield to our resistance if only there are sufficient numbers of us and we share a fierce determination to create racial justice.

When we talk about these matters in public, Neisha, I know the outrage, frustration, and hurt that many white listeners feel at the charges we lay against the predominantly white field of writing studies. If the lived experience of this pain is different than the pain you describe and that Dr. King expressed in the scrap of a note (and it is), the challenge to us is similar: to get on up out of that anger, hurt, and pain in order that we might yield on the one hand and join the struggle on the other. We, white folks, too need to learn to move and to keep on moving even in the face of our frustration and anger. We need to learn not to seek the amelioration of pain that can be achieved by the retreat to privilege; the real relief for the anguish of our implicatedness is to join the struggle. Dr. Vay says, "we gon win this battle fo sho!" I believe him, Neisha-Anne, but we all got some learning to do to figure out how!

Love,

Frankie

CONCLUSION

Dear Reader,

To define anti-racism you have to understand how racism operates. Racism is about power, it systematically disempowers people of color. It systematically privileges whites. It dehumanizes everyone. And racism accomplishes these things by utilizing systems and institutions to advance its purposes. Racism also accomplishes these things by disguising itself as abstraction (what Ian Haney Lopez, 2015, called "dog whistle" politics), as a very particular version of civility that excludes the rhetorical performances of racialized Others within and beyond the academy, or through a politics (and rhetoric) of respectability. In her chapter, "Sustained Communities for Sustained Learning: Connecting Culturally Sustaining Pedagogy to WAC Learning Outcomes" (this volume), Jamila M. Kareem calls this "an attitude of linguistic respectability."

Anti-racism, then, is active and determined resistance of structural and systemic racism in all its forms. We've just named linguistic racism and the policing of black bodies, whether those be the bodies of our colleagues or our students. So what do we do with all of this? How do we make a change?

Dr. Joni Jones (2010) gave us rules for being what she called an ally. If you've heard me talk before you know that my thinking has evolved and I now find the word ally problematic. In my experience in the academy, both as a student and now a scholar an ally is someone who is satisfied to QUIETLY PRETEND TO help and support someone else WHILE an accomplice, even if they aren't called that, is someone who helps and supports someone else through what they say/do. Accomplices actively demonstrate ally-ship. Accomplices take the necessary risks that really move towards inclusivity, diversity, equity, and equality.

And so, I hear Dr. Jones' rules and even though she uses the word ally I think her rules are spot on. Listen with me and tell me if you also hear what I hear. What I hear her really asking is for us to be accomplices, for us to take those necessary risks.

She says this:

> a. Allies know that it is not sufficient to be liberal, in fact the liberal position is actually a walk backwards. We must move towards a radical rather than a liberal approach. Allies must be willing to be warriors.

> b. Be loud and crazy so black folks don't have to be. Being loud doesn't mean be reckless, strategizing is important. Speaking up does mean being able to relinquish some privilege in order to create justice.

c. Do not tell anyone in any oppressed group to be patient—doing so is a sign of your privilege. Justice delayed is justice denied.

d. Recognize the new racism, the new sexism, the old homophobia. It is institutional and structural . . .

e. When called out about your racism, sexism, or homophobia don't cower in embarrassment, don't cry and don't silently think that "she" is crazy and vow never to interact with "her" again. Be grateful that someone called you out.

Tell me y'all ain't hear her say take risks in each one of those rules? I see risks as being important to actually getting this work done.

Minorities spend so much time checking ourselves to see if we're good enough to fit in and get in to do the work. I've long decided that I was giving you back this problem of racism cause it isn't of my invention, or that of my foreparents, so since I'm giving you your problem back to fix I've got a checklist for you—If you can't acknowledge the following then I got no time for you and you should keep out my way . . .

Cause I'll know you're an accomplice when

a. you can acknowledge your privilege—confession is good for the soul . . . and the movement.

b. you can take a back seat and let the voices of the marginalized be heard loud and clear

c. you have stopped expecting others to educate you on these issues—that's lazy and annoying

d. you don't have to give yourself a title. Titles are overrated

- —if you have to say that you're against oppression then chances are you're probably really not.

- —if you have to announce that you're an accomplice then I already don't trust you. All I really wanna see is that WERK!

Sincerely,

Neisha

ACKNOWLEDGMENT

We would like to thank Vershawn Ashanti Young for his tireless support, encouragement, and mentoring of us both as scholars, teachers, and activists. Thank you, Dr. Vay!

REFERENCES

Baldwin, J. (1961). The negro in American culture. *CrossCurrents, 11*, 205–224.

Clarke, A. (2015). *'Membering*. Tap Books.

Condon, F. (2012). *I hope I join the band: Narrative, affiliation, and antiracist rhetoric.* Utah State University Press.

Condon, F. (2018). The languages we may be: Affiliative relations and the work of the Canadian Writing Centre. *Canadian Journal for Studies in Discourse and Writing/ Redactologie, 28*, 196–211. http://journals.sfu.ca/cjsdw/index.php/cjsdw/article /view/627/672.

Green, N.-A. (2018). Moving beyond alright: And the emotional toll of this, my life matters too, in the writing center work. *The Writing Center Journal, 37*(1), 15–34.

Green, N.-A. & Kern, D. (2015, April 6–9). *Emotion and anti-racist rhetorics in writing studies: Anger as performance-rhetoric.* Paper presented at the Conference on College Composition and Communication, Houston, TX.

Jones, J. (2010). *Six rules for allies* [Video file]. https://www.youtube.com/watch?v= SZx6rgs21G0.

Kadian-Baumeyer, K. (Instructor) & Study.com (Producer). (n.d.) *Considering pronunciation, articulation, and dialect in public speaking* [Video-based online course]. https://study.com/academy/lesson/pronunciation-articulation-and-dialect.html.

King, M. L. (1967). *Conscience for change.* Massey Lectures [Radio series]. Canadian Broadcasting Corporation.

Lopez, I. H. (2015). *Dog whistle politics: How coded racial appeals have reinvented racism and wrecked the middle class.* Oxford University Press.

Sanchez, J. C. (2018). Trump, the KKK, and the versatility of white supremacy rhetoric. *Journal of Contemporary Rhetoric, 8*(1/2), 44–56.

APPENDIX: READINGS ON TRANSLINGUALISM AND CODE-MESHING, CRITICAL RACE THEORY, AND RHETORICS OF RACE

Canagarajah, S. (2006). The place of world Englishes in composition: Pluralization continued. *College Composition and Communication, 57*, 586–619. https://www .jstor.org/stable/20456910.

Canagarajah, S. (2007). Lingua franca English, multilingual communities, and language acquisition. *The Modern Language Journal, 91*, 923–939. http://www .personal.psu.edu/asc16/MLJ91.5LinguaFranca.pdf https://doi.org/10.1111 /j.1540-4781.2007.00678.x.

Canagarajah, S. (2009). Multilingual strategies of negotiating English: From conversation to writing. *Journal of Rhetoric, Culture and Politics, 29*(1/2), 17–48. https:// www.jstor.org/stable/20866885.

Canagarajah, S. (2011). Codemeshing in academic writing: Identifying teachable strategies of translanguaging. *The Modern Language Journal, 95*(3). https://onlinelibrary .wiley.com/doi/abs/10.1111/j.1540-4781.2011.01207.x.

Condon, F. & Young, V. A. (Eds.). (2017). *Performing antiracist pedagogy in rhetoric, writing, and communication.* The WAC Clearinghouse; University Press of Colorado. https://wac.colostate.edu/books/atd/antiracist/.

Essed, P. & Goldberg, D. T. (2001). *Race critical theories: Text and context.* Wiley-Blackwell.

Fields, B. J. & Fields, K. (2012). *Racecraft: The soul of inequality in American life.* Verso.

Green, N.-A. (2016). The re-education of Neisha-Anne S. Green: A close look at the damaging effects of "a standard approach," the benefits of code-meshing, and the role allies play in this work. *Praxis: A Writing Center Journal, 14*(1). http://www.praxisuwc.com/green-141.

Green, N.-A. (2018). Moving beyond alright: And the emotional toll of this, my life matters too, in the writing center work. *Writing Center Journal, 37*(1), 15–34.

Guerra, J. C. (2016). Cultivating a rhetorical sensibility in the translingual writing classroom. *College English, 78,* 228.

Horner, B. & Lu, M.-Z. (2013). Translingual literacy, language difference, and matters of agency. *College English, 75,* 586–611.

Horner, B., Lu, M.-Z., Royster, J. J. & Trimbur, J. (2011). Language difference in writing: Toward a translingual approach. *College English, 73,* 303–321.

King, L., Gubele R. & Anderson, J. R. (Eds.). (2015). *Survivance, sovereignty, and story: Teaching American Indian Rhetorics.* Utah State University Press. https://doi.org/10.7330/9780874219968.

LeCourt, D. (2004). *Identity matters: Schooling the student body in academic discourse.* State University of New York Press.

Lee, J. W. & Jenks, C. (2016). Doing translingual disposition. *College Composition and Communication, 68,* 317.

Leonard, R. L. & Nowacek, R. (2016). Transfer and translingualism. *College English, 78,* 258.

Marshall, S. (2013.) Thoughts on teaching as a practice of love. *Journal of the Assembly for Expanded Perspectives on Learning, 19,* 94–107. https://trace.tennessee.edu/jaepl/vol19/iss1/11/.

Matsuda, P. (2014). The lure of translingual writing. *PMLA, 129,* 478–483. https://doi.org/10.1632/pmla.2014.129.3.478.

Millward, J. (2010). Resistance to the "English Only" movement: Implications for two-year college composition. In B. Horner, M.-Z. Lu & P. K. Matsuda (Eds.), *Cross-language relations in composition* (pp. 221–229). Southern Illinois University Press.

Perryman-Clark, S., Kirkland, D. E. & Jackson, A. (2014). *Students' right to their own language: A critical sourcebook.* Bedford St. Martins.

Phillipson, R. (1992). *Linguistic imperialism.* Oxford University Press.

Smitherman, G. (2017) Raciolinguistics, "mis-education," and language arts teaching in the 21st century. *Language Arts Journal of Michigan, 32*(2). https://doi.org/10.9707/2168-149X.2164.

Wheeler, R. & Thomas, J. (2013). And "still" the children suffer: The dilemma of Standard English, social justice, and social access. *Journal of Advanced Composition, 33,* 363–396.

Young, V. A. (2007). *Your average Nigga: Performing race, literacy, and masculinity.* Wayne State University Press.

Young, V. A. (2009). "Nah, We Straight": An argument against code switching. *Journal of Advanced Composition, 29*(1/2), 49–76. https://www.jstor.org/stable/20866885.

Young, V. A. (2012). Should writers use they own English? In K. Rowan & L. Greenfield (Eds.), *Writing centers and the new racism* (pp. 61–74). Utah State University Press. https://doi.org/10.2307/j.ctt4cgk6s.7.

Young, V. A., Barrett, R. & Lovejoy, K. B. (2014). *Other people's English: Code-meshing, code-switching, and African American literacy.* Teachers College Press.

CHAPTER 16.

SUSTAINED COMMUNITIES FOR SUSTAINED LEARNING: CONNECTING CULTURALLY SUSTAINING PEDAGOGY TO WAC LEARNING OUTCOMES

Jamila M. Kareem

University of Central Florida

Central to WAC theory are the premises that writing is vital to the learning process across the curriculum and that learners bring diverse linguistic, literacy, and educational experiences to all courses. This chapter argues for applying culturally sustaining pedagogies to reinforce these premises as they relate to raciolinguistically marginalized communities, by applying a culturally pluralistic approach to teaching and learning writing in the disciplines. The chapter gives an overview of culturally sustaining education, discusses in what ways WAC theories have moved toward culturally sustaining practices, examines what major gaps exist between WAC and culturally sustaining practices, and describes how those gaps can be addressed through learning outcomes for WAC at the institutional or programmatic levels. The chapter concludes by examining possible culturally sustaining WAC outcomes and their advantages.

When I was a senior in college, I took a sociolinguistics course in the English department with a professor who studies pidgin and creole languages, and this was my first exposure to ideas about the social power and ideologies underscoring language practices. Throughout my childhood, I attended predominantly White public schools, with mostly White teachers or teachers who promoted Eurocentric epistemological perspectives, or views based in Eurocentric perceptions of the way things should and do work. Needless to say, I wasn't buying this professor's talk about linguistic cultural oppression. Standard English, or what Django Paris and H. Samy Alim (2017) called "Dominant American English" (p. 6), was the

DOI: https://doi.org/10.37514/PER-B.2020.0360.2.16

right English for me and my fellow Americans. According to Paris and Alim, Dominant American English is the normed language practice of the American White middle class. For me as a college senior, it was the English of intelligence, how we got jobs, how we were taken seriously. Two years after I took that sociolinguistics course, Black American Harvard professor and African American Studies scholar Henry Louis Gates, Jr. was accosted in his home by the police with the assumption that he must've been breaking into rather than living in such a beautiful home, despite how articulate he was in Dominant American English. But hindsight is 20/20. Yes, with my family and friends from the neighborhood, I code-meshed—or combined language practices in the same setting—with Black English Vernacular and Dominant American English, but those sites were hidden from the White-dominated world. In school and other dimensions of the public sphere, I needed to present a respectable portrayal of literacy.

This attitude of linguistic respectability is one of the major aspects of mainstream education that Paris and Alim (2017) aimed to challenge with the theory of culturally sustaining pedagogies (CSP) forwarded in the collection *Culturally Sustaining Pedagogy: Teaching and Learning for Justice in a Changing World*. The complication of linguistic respectability is an experience largely shared by students of color and other linguistically subordinated students at various intersectional identities. Culturally sustaining education works under the premise that if we want to vanquish social injustices in education, we must teach without relying on cultural hegemony of language, literacy, intelligence, and knowledge-making. This culturally pluralistic approach to teaching and learning affords teachers and administrators the opportunity to bring in ordinarily marginalized knowledge bases and ontologies. Doing so, educators can design curriculum around cultural-historical realities of our most vulnerable and subjugated student populations. Paris and Alim argued that it is essential for these student populations and the teachers who teach them to reimagine academic institutions as sites that engage with the many facets of students' cultures.

This chapter applies this basic premise of CSP to the knowledge and practices of WAC. I build on arguments about addressing the raciolinguistic illiteracy in WAC (Anson, 2012; Kells, 2007; Poe, 2013) to show that by understanding and articulating principles of culturally sustaining education practices, recognizing gaps in culturally sustaining education practices in current WAC outcomes at the institutional and programmatic level, and developing a critical dialogue about how to introduce culturally sustaining outcomes and curriculum in WAC, WAC administrators and teachers across the curriculum can produce practical tools and resources to apply culturally sustaining teaching and learning practices to WAC at their institutions. Critical to WAC right now is the globalization of higher education (see Frigo & Fulford, 2018; Horner & Hall, 2018) and transfer (see Baird &

Dilger, 2018; Driscoll & Daewoo, 2018). Therefore, CSP affords the capability to develop these tools such as culturally sustaining learning outcomes and assessment as well as resources such as culturally sustaining language support systems. In what follows, I provide an overview of culturally sustaining education, discuss in what ways WAC theories have moved towards culturally sustaining practices, examine what critical gaps exist between WAC and culturally sustaining practices, and describe how those gaps can be addressed through learning outcomes for WAC at the institutional or programmatic levels. I conclude by examining possible culturally sustaining WAC outcomes and their advantages.

WHAT ARE CULTURALLY SUSTAINING EDUCATION PRACTICES?

Culturally sustaining education enacts cultural pluralism in dynamic ways by sustaining communities of color "for positive social transformation" (Paris & Alim, 2017, p. 1) by perpetuating the customs of these communities. The goals of WAC are not "maintenance and social critique" (Paris & Alim, 2017, p. 5) of the curriculum but relevance for the purposes of assimilation. By remaining dedicated to assimilationist perspectives, WAC principles will continue to advocate the persistent exclusion of ever-expanding portions of the higher education population: multilingual, multidialectical, and international students. In "Letters on Moving from Ally to Accomplice: Anti-Racism and the Teaching of Writing" (this volume), Neisha-Anne S. Green and Frankie Condon argue against this culturally suppressive attitude toward marginalized rhetorical traditions, particularly those linked to raciolinguistic minority communities. Because CSP reveres the literate customs and traditions found in communities of color as important to the larger American culture, enacting CSP in WAC affords writing teachers across the curriculum the capability to understand and work with their students' cultural communities' discursive practices.

Within WAC, some scholars have argued for race- and linguistic-conscious approaches to programs (Anson, 2012; Kells, 2007; Poe, 2013). Such approaches to WAC programs resist practices that aim to assimilate the blackness and brownness out of students and instead see raciolinguistic diversity as a strength for students to draw on throughout their education experiences. Just as WAC pedagogy does, CSP has some basic principles that support writing learning outcomes. Drawing from Paris and Alim (2017), I see the central principles of culturally sustaining WAC pedagogy, or CSP-WAC, as those that

- decenter so-called "dominant gazes" in the curriculum (White, patriarchal, cisheteronormative, English monolingual, ableist, classist, xenophobic, Judeo-Christian) and challenge or critique Eurocentric dominance in the study and expression of disciplinary content

- investigate disciplinary language conventions in life, society, and community (Bucholtz et al., 2017)
- celebrate linguistic, literate, rhetorical and other discursive assets of marginalized communities
- resist systemic discrimination of communities of color and other marginalized communities through literate curriculum
- uphold students' ethnic and racial cultural identities through critical engagement and analysis (San Pedro, 2017) and recognize cultural fluidity of youth culture while also encouraging the critique of the culture

As indicated here, critical to CSP-WAC is the concept of moving beyond making writing curriculum relevant to making it include the discursive viewpoints of marginalized communities of color.

For example, looking at the contributions to the Cuban community by Cuban epidemiologist Dr. Carlos Juan Finlay (1937) provides a culturally sustaining approach to biology and can exemplify how Finlay used the genre of the scientific journal article to challenge dominant perspectives and to expose concerns from his community. Faculty in biology might incorporate this as part of their science literacy curriculum by having students reflect on the intersections between research, community culture, and writing. CSP expands on current linguistically inclusive WAC theories by emphasizing survival of cultures in all aspects of the writing curriculum rather than through final product alone.

CSP-WAC learning outcomes can offer teachers of writing ways to help students assess the rhetorical power of ethnic and racial cultures in the discipline, an element missing from the current WAC principles and WAC 2.0 approaches. As David G. Holmes (1999) suggested in "Fighting Back By Writing Black: Beyond a Racially Reductive Composition Theory," raciolinguistic inclusion in writing instruction should move beyond attributing language and dialect to specific racial groups but also examine the "rhetoricity of race [or ethnicity]" (p. 62) as it relates to writing. Holmes may contest the sociolinguistic approaches of CSP, because for Holmes, the link between racial-culture identity and dialect is greatly misconstrued in composition studies research (p. 63). However, his point that race and voice "can be used to map territory [and] community" (1999, p. 65) helps teachers of writing even in the disciplines develop practices that affirm students' racial communities in their curriculum and assignments, a key element of CSP-WAC.

CSP concerns exposing students to the importance of contributions by intellectuals of color in a variety of academic disciplines. Jason G. Irizzary (2017) demonstrated this aspect through a participatory action study with Latinx high school students. One student from Irizarry's study explains that in the traditional curriculum, he sees no evidence that Latinx people made any significant contributions to history (2017, p. 89). CSP focuses on communities of color because of their systematic erasure by mainstream education. CSP-WAC learning outcomes offer WAC a systemic route for cross-curricular community advocacy in order to combat commonplace assimilation through literacy and writing education, which is a defining feature of literacy practices in higher education.

NEARLY CULTURALLY SUSTAINING PEDAGOGIES IN WRITING ACROSS THE CURRICULUM

WAC scholarship advocates for cultural relevance and some inclusive pedagogy approaches through the strands of writing across communities (WAC 2.0) as well as anti-racist teaching practices and WAC assessment. Before delving into that, however, let's distinguish some terms and their relationships. Namely, I would like to look at the distinctions between culturally relevant pedagogy (CRP), WAC 2.0, and CSP. Figure 16.1 illustrates the overlaps and separations between these three critical approaches to writing pedagogy.

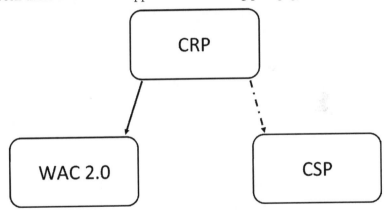

Figure 16.1.

Both WAC 2.0 and CSP have a foundation in CRP, but while WAC 2.0 is one example of CRP, CSP should be seen as a more evolved model of culturally sensitive teaching practices.

Readers may be familiar with the concept of CRP from education studies. Developed by Gloria Ladson-Billings (1995), this education theory asserts that cultural competence should not be at odds with academic achievement (p. 476). The goal of CRP is to "produce students who can achieve academically, produce students who demonstrate cultural competence, and develop students who can both understand and critique the existing social order" (Ladson-Billings, 1995, p. 474). While effective and a progressive move away from oppressive education practices, Paris and Alim (2017) argued that culturally relevant methods lack the community perpetuation goals of culturally sustaining practices. This missing element also contributes to the gap between WAC 2.0 and CSP.

Michelle Hall Kells (2007) advanced WAC 2.0 as a culturally conscious approach to WAC practices that perceives effective WAC programs as "organic (community-based), systemic (institutionally-distributed), and sustainable (flexible and responsive)" (p. 89). WAC 2.0 especially accounts for raciolinguistically varied student populations by recommending that WAC programs and practices help students learn to survive rhetorically in the many linguistic relationships they will participate in. Therefore, it links to culturally relevant practices that require what Ladson-Billings (2014) deemed "cultural competence" (p. 75). Cultural competence encompasses learning about the communities that a teacher or school serves and understanding their nuances (Ladson-Billings, 2017, pp. 143–144). In line with cultural competence, Kells (2007) proposed that "by promoting opportunities for context-based writing, WAC programs can facilitate students' civic, academic, and professional engagement with diverse discourse communities" (p. 88). Through advocating such opportunities, WAC programs might "foreground the values of community and sustainability [to] enhance students' initiation into a complex ecology of human relationships" (Kells, 2007, p. 89). Even as WAC 2.0 recognizes the need for cultural competence in teaching writing across the curriculum, its focus diverges from sustaining the communities of color.

According to Kells (2007), WAC 2.0 "emerges whenever we transgress the ethnocentric biases that permeate every field and discourse community" (p. 92), but such efforts toward ethnolinguistic cultural relevance and competence does not equate to the perpetuation of the traditions within communities of color. CSP involves more than enacting ethnolinguistically diverse discourses, as WAC 2.0 stresses; CSP also emphasizes managing the many avenues that our students of color have for representing and performing race through language. Although WAC 2.0 "foregrounds the dimensions of cultural and sociolinguistic diversity in university-wide writing instruction" (Kells, 2007, p. 90) and "attempt[s] to connect the college classroom to the students' other communities of belonging" (Guerra, 2016, p. xi), it does not "conten[d] in complex ways with the rich and innovative linguistic, literate, and cultural practices of . . . youth and communities of color" (Paris & Alim, 2017, p. 2). WAC 2.0 may be considered a culturally relevant approach to WAC and its outcomes, as its "cultural ecology approach seeks to cultivate critical awareness of the ways that literacy practices are shaped by ever-shifting sets of economic, political, social, cultural, and linguistic factors" (Kells, 2007, p. 93). Cultural ecology in WAC assists those teaching writing in any discipline understand the "dimensions of communicative competence" (Kells, 2007, p. 90), or the many factors involved successfully conveying information in different contexts. This concept is a culturally relevant rather than a culturally sustaining strategy for WAC, because it emphasizes competence with established ecosystems of written discourses not the social transformation of these ecosystems.

WAC 2.0 pedagogy could be sustaining, but that is not a requirement to learn to write "Appropriately (with an awareness of different conventions); Productively (to achieve their desired aims); Ethically (to remain attuned to the communities they serve); Critically (to learn to engage in inquiry and discovery), and Responsively (to negotiate the tensions caused by the exercise of authority in their spheres of belonging)" (Kells, 2007, p. 103) or to develop the necessary rhetorical resources for engaging with academic and their other communities of belonging (Guerra, 2016, p. xi). Kells' (2007) conception of WAC 2.0 does suggest that agents of WAC "should serve as advocates of literacy and language awareness for speakers of English as well as members of other ethnolinguistic communities present on and around campus" (p. 103), and advocacy is a key element of CSP. However, CSP also provides students, teachers, and program administrators with ways to remain productively critical of all their cultural community literacy and rhetorical practices.

WAC pedagogy that is culturally sustaining spotlights the experiential knowledge, linguistic preferences, and disciplinary social engagement of communities of color in the arts, humanities, sciences, and social sciences. Where WAC 2.0 provides a pedagogical basis to connect ethnolinguistically diverse students' many communities of belonging to academic discourse communities, CSP affords the means to study, understand, and learn to use writing in disciplines through the lens of complex discursive practices of communities of color, by decentering Eurocentrism in the curriculum. More than including the perspectives from these racial and ethnic cultures, CSP-WAC would ask: What if we begin the narrative of disciplinary knowledge from the position of a "[non-]White middle-class linguistic, literate, and cultural" (Paris & Alim, 2017, p. 6) community? Ladson-Billings (2014) suggested that culturally relevant pedagogy is "where the beat drops" for culturally sustaining pedagogy (p. 76), meaning that culturally sustaining education implements cultural relevance as its backing but departs from the goals of cultural relevance alone. For example, a culturally relevant pedagogy would consist of students reading about hip hop music and culture yet still expect students to compose analyses in the discursive practices of the academy. A CSP, on the other hand, would teach hip hop practices as forms of rhetorically effective means of communication. By emphasizing aspects such as writing as rhetorical and writing to learn, traditional WAC pedagogy and outcomes lean towards cultural relevance but not cultural sustainability.

With these distinctions now ascertained, the nearly-but-not-quite culturally sustaining strands of WAC are clearer. Besides WAC 2.0, Mya Poe (2013) and Chris Anson (2012) both argued that scholarship concerning racial identity is limited in WAC. Poe (2013) forwarded anti-racist teaching and curricular practices for WAC, suggesting that "if the goal is to help prepare students for real-world rhetorical situations, then teaching writing across the curriculum means preparing students for the multilingual spaces in which they will be writing and working" (p. 9). The idea here, to prepare students for multi-raciolinguistic rhetorical situations they will engage with in the real world, begins to flow into culturally sustaining approaches. In addition to urging administrators to prepare faculty and TAs for race and writing issues to intersect as they deliver and assess the curriculum, Poe recommended that WAC directors participate in consistent discussions about race with teachers and administrators across the curriculum (2013, pp. 2–3). Poe indicates that writing instruction across the curriculum must account for the intersections of racial histories and identities with written communication when instructors plan, deliver, and evaluate student writing. Such considerations can support CSP-WAC, as they lead to more robust understandings of what attitudes about students' racial, ethnic, and linguistic backgrounds we bring to writing instruction. Further, understanding our attitudes is the first step to recognizing that students from diverse backgrounds bring a multitude of socially constructed perspectives to traditional assessment practices such as rubrics and assignment prompts (Anson, 2012, p. 20).

Anson (2012) suggested that while assessment is not a place to start for WAC curricular intervention, it may be an ideal place to begin to examine the multiple literate experiences and resources students bring to the classroom (p. 20). The rhetorical act of writing is molded by our linguistic and sociocultural backgrounds, and as teachers in all disciplines, we must keep this in mind about our students. In line with CSP, Anson argued for teachers of writing to see students as individual learners (2012, p. 23) rather than possessing a homogeneous linguistic identity (Matsuda, 2006). As shown here, WAC programs have excellent foundation to foster culturally sustaining practices. Still, program outcomes center on writing practices guided by dominant gazes around the question "How can 'we' get 'these' working-class kids of color to speak/write/be more like middle-class White ones?" (Paris & Alim, 2017, p. 3). The next segment of the chapter details what I perceive as the critical gaps between current WAC theories and CSP to better understand how the field might begin to move towards CSP-WAC.

GAPS BETWEEN WAC AND CULTURALLY SUSTAINING PEDAGOGIES

For WAC to sustain communities of color, it should inspire all disciplines where writing is a part of the learning process to provide students of color with opportunities to recognize their ethnic, racial, and linguistic cultural histories and traditions. Even writing instruction in scientific, social science, and technical disciplines must create these opportunities. Anson (2012) put it this way:

> How students view their relationship to a discipline or major is a formulation of its institutional ideology, which includes its history of diversity or lack thereof, the presence or absence of role models, and how its various constituent communities look on the value of its work. (p. 23)

CSP-WAC can treat writing in most disciplines as a "generative spac[e] . . . to support the practices of youth and communities of color" (Paris & Alim, 2017, p. 10) through sustaining curriculum.

One way to enact this approach in scientific disciplines, for instance, is to implement the suggestion by Neisha-Anne Green and Frankie Condon (this volume) to amalgamate rhetorical traditions, such as the objectivity valued in scientific discourses and the community consciousness valued in Latinx discourses. Certainly, such an approach requires a shift in attitudes about the linguistic respectability of marginalized rhetorical practices, attitudes that comprise generations of sociocultural conditioning—that's not easy! WAC has traditionally "facilitate[d] students' civic, academic, and professional engagement with diverse discourse communities" (Kells, 2007, p. 88) and endeavored "to improve student learning and critical thinking through writing and to help students learn the writing conventions of their disciplines" (Thaiss & Porter as cited in Townsend, 2016, p. 118). A culturally sustaining approach to learning outcomes for writing across the curriculum examines and critiques disciplinary language and discourse as well as history of the discipline alongside students' literacies and language practices. Further, CSP-WAC transcends the learning and application of disciplinary writing conventions as the primary way to demonstrate intellectual prowess.

CSP-WAC treats the literate cultural perspectives from communities of color with the same respect, circulation, and criticism typically reserved for the mainstream Euro-Western cultural practices of the academy. Where WAC 2.0 offers "ways to connect students' home communities to college literacy education" (Kells, 2007, p. 90) and its auxiliary theory, writing across difference, pulls from the cache of discursive resources that students bring with them from each of their communities to connect to course writing content (Guerra, 2016; Hendrickson & Garcia de Mueller, 2016), CSP affords WAC the conceptual means to preserve cultural practices within disciplinary writing instruction. The current WAC principles and outcomes sustain disciplinary cultures but must do more work to show that WAC programs should value the literacy practices of sociopolitically oppressed communities.

Local college-level WAC outcomes and practices are often influenced by two sets of national guidelines: the *Statement of WAC Principles and Practices* (International Network of WAC Programs [INWAC], 2014) and the cross-curricular outcome recommendations found in the WPA Outcomes Statement for First-Year Composition (Council of Writing Program Administrators [CWPA], 2014). These guidelines support the central principles of WAC and should be localized to fit the context of each institution because in successful WAC programs, the director tends to have "an understanding of the local context, including: student educational, literacy, and language backgrounds; faculty values and goals; [and] institutional values and goals" (INWAC, 2014, p. 3). Both sets of outcomes act as guides as opposed to requirements. They were developed through "a distillation of fundamental principles and best practices based on some forty years of experience and research by professionals in the WAC field in the US" (INWAC, 2014, p. 1) and "what composition teachers nationwide have learned from practice, research, and theory" (Council of Writing Program Administrators, 2014, p. 1). While generalized to perhaps cater to no kind of student in particular, the outcomes actually sustain dominant cultural practices and disenfranchises the literacy and discursive practices of communities of color. For, the literate cultural practices of the academy, overall, are based in Eurocentric masculinist epistemological perspectives (Collins, 1991) and discourses of whiteness (Inoue, 2016), and these are perpetuated through the majority of curriculum. Eurocentric masculinist epistemological perspectives are ways of evaluating knowledge that proliferate White-centric ways of being (Collins, 1991, p. 271). For example, these epistemologies situate other knowledge bases, such as Afrocentric, women, or LGBTQ+ experiences, as specialized rather than normative. Discourses of whiteness have distinct features, including "hyperindividualism—self-determination and autonomy," an "individualized, [r]ational, [c]ontrolled [s]elf," "rule-governed, [c]ontractual [r]elationships," and "clarity, [o]rder, and [c]ontrol" (Inoue, 2016, p. 147). These features signify what Eurocentric ways of knowing privilege about discourse as well as what they hold in low esteem.

The prevalence of mainstream cultural values in learning outcomes illustrate what WAC directors and WAC theorists value about particular practices. Take, for example, the following remark from the *Statement of WAC Principles and Practices*:

> WAC refers to the notion that writing should be an integral
> part of the learning process throughout a student's education,
> not merely in required writing courses but across the entire
> curriculum . . . [and] is based on the premise that writing
> is highly situated and tied to a field's discourse and ways of
> knowing, and therefore writing in the disciplines (WID) is
> most effectively guided by those with expertise in that disci-
> pline. (INWAC, 2014, p. 1)

All of the above is certainly accurate and also demonstrates the importance of "those with expertise" in disciplines in fostering the rhetorical traditions and literate cultures of communities of color.

WAC program outcomes are complemented by the interdisciplinary outcomes on the WPA Outcomes Statement for First-Year Composition (CWPA, 2014; see Appendix). The important thing to note is that the WPA Outcome Statement reflects what the CWPA considers necessary for learning to write in any discipline. They too are devoid of raciolinguistic considerations that aim to sustain margin-alized cultures within higher education. In the next section, I suggest alterations to WAC program approaches that "sustain the cultural lifeways" (Paris & Alim, 2017, p. 1) of academically and socially marginalized communities.

ATTENDING TO THE CULTURALLY SUSTAINING GAPS IN WAC

WAC is rife with possibilities for sustaining the literacy practices of marginal-ized, oppressed, and underrepresented cultural communities. Consider the fol-lowing central principles of WAC:

- writing as rhetorical
- writing as a process
- writing as a mode of learning
- learning to write

Each student brings a set of personal and institutional vernacular histories that influences perceptions of disciplinary knowledge. Culturally sustaining learning outcomes for writing value those experiences while also encouraging students to use them as a way to understand new literacy experiences. CSP-WAC would expect students to understand and articulate how discourses are formed and practiced and how cultural experiences influence creation and reception of texts in any field. Table 16.1 shows the above principles alongside their CSP-WAC revisions.

Table 16.1

Current *Statement* Principles	CSP-WAC Principles
Writing as rhetorical	Writing conventions as rhetorical behaviors not classifications of correctness
Writing as a process	Writing practices as individual and communal
Writing as a mode of learning	Writing as a mode of learning cultural, political, and ethical implications
Learning to write	Writing as a cultural experience

I consider this comparison in Table 16.1 to be suggestive as opposed to prescriptive. These example outcomes exemplify how a change in our considerations about what WAC can do for sustaining raciolinguistic communities of students of color in college-wide writing curriculum. Rather than focusing on correcting the black, brown, indigeneity, and foreignness out of students' literacies, WAC programs have a responsibility to help students use these literacies as assets for writing across the curriculum. A focus on disciplinary conventions is critical to current WAC principles, yet without exploring or critiquing the cultural epistemologies embedded within the conventions, programs remain assimilationist (Kells, 2007, p. 92; Villanueva, 2001) and lack recognition "that students come to the classroom with a wide range of literacy, linguistic, technological, and educational experiences" (INWAC, 2014, p. 1).

As an example, the principle of "writing as rhetorical" (INWAC, 2014, p. 5) hints at cultural relevance, because it theorizes that "texts are dynamic and respond to the goals of the writer(s), goals of the reader(s), and the wider rhetorical context, which may include culture, language, genre conventions, and other texts" (p. 5). Yet educators in the disciplines habitually ignore the "wider rhetorical context" of written texts. Poe (2013) gave one example of such ignorance in the case of race and writing intersecting in a health policy and administration course:

> In professions such as Health Policy [sic] understanding linguistic diversity is enormously important. As John explained to me, hospital administrators as well as nurses, doctors, and other hospital workers interact with individuals from diverse backgrounds. Too commonly, misconceptions arise based on

patients' linguistic practices—misconceptions that are located at the intersection of a patient's linguistic and racial identities. Those misconceptions can lead to disastrous consequences, or at the very least, distrust of the healthcare system. (p. 8)

Poe illustrated that to sustain communities of color in disciplinary work, teaching the rhetoricity of writing needs to go a step further to examine the histories of race, ethnicity, and language that situate textual practices in the discipline. Race, ethnicity, gender, age and other defining aspects of an individual's culture weave their way into how researchers analyze, write up, and present data, even when those aspects are unapparent on the surface.

A culturally sustaining approach to the WAC principle "Writing as a mode of learning," for instance, moves beyond "mak[ing] thinking visible [and] allowing learners to reflect on their ideas" and the notion that "writing facilitates connections between new information and learned information, and among areas of knowledge across multiple domains" (INWAC, 2014, p. 5). It emphasizes these ideas while also revitalizing communities of color (Lee & McCarty, 2017; Paris & Alim, 2017) through the writing-to-learn process. This process could include prompts and assessments that use writing to apply concepts learned in a discipline (e.g., alternative therapies in counseling psychology) to their communities in specific ways to better understand the concepts.

To help students understand disciplinary rhetorical situations especially, "WAC recognizes that writing instruction is shaped to meet the needs of different contexts and disciplines" (INWAC, 2014, p. 5). The WAC Statement asserts that "WAC promotes engaged student learning, critical thinking, and greater facility with written communication across rhetorical situations" (INWAC, 2014, p. 1). Culturally sustaining learning outcomes give students the academic and sociocultural resources to bring their own discursive practices to many rhetorical situations. Being that WAC 2.0 seeks to use WAC to emphasize linguistic diversity related to racial, ethnic, and other cultural, social, and political ways of being and connect them to collective university writing instruction (Kells, 2007, p. 90), culturally sustaining practices transcend this objective by encouraging teachers and administrators to perpetuate students many discursive identities through all writing curriculum. I submit that this could begin with a shift in how we develop WAC program learning outcomes.

The implications of using WAC to sustain the "dynamic community practices" (Paris & Alim, 2017, p. 7) from communities of color in mainstream sites of higher education will not seem worthwhile to institutional representatives who see those practices as deficient. In the decade since I completed that undergraduate sociolinguistics course, I have replaced the goal of White-washing my writing to respectability with the goal of expressing ideas in the most appropriate manner possible for the content, genre, audience, and situation. I continually work towards doing so without sacrificing the rhetorically effective practices of my primary raciolinguistic community. It is a struggle. What helped me while I finished undergraduate work and graduate school was the encouragement and support of professors across disciplines to research and represent my own racial and language cultural histories within the context of the disciplinary content. For example, I worked with a professor in a classical archaeology course who helped me develop a project that looked at ancient African kingdom writing systems. Responsible faculty in graduate school courses humored my inquiries about the voices of color absent from readings in courses—yet not actually absent from the field—and then connected me with other scholars and resources who would have more knowledge about my inquiries. Through these situations, I was able to enact and contend with the complex linguistic cultural practices of the Black American language community and learn how to meaningfully respect and critique those practices. At this critical juncture in the higher education system, WAC practitioners need a theoretical basis for fostering the home and civic community raciolinguistic traditions of students like I was in college, in the way they foster and circulate the linguistic culture of White standard-English-speaking middle-class communities. CSP deserves further inquiry, critique, and empirical study from WAC to help the field continue to work ethically and responsibly with a student body that is steadily shifting racially and linguistically.

REFERENCES

Anson, C. (2012). Black holes: Writing across the curriculum, assessment, and the gravitational invisibility of race. In A. B. Inoue & M. Poe (Eds.), *Race and writing assessment*. Lang.

Baird, N. & Dilger, B. (2018). Dispositions in natural science laboratories: The roles of individuals and contexts in writing transfer. *Across the Disciplines, 15*(4), 21–40. https://wac.colostate.edu/docs/atd/articles/baird-dilger2018.pdf.

Bucholtz, M., Casillas, D. I. & Lee, J. S. (2017). Language and culture as sustenance. In D. Paris & H. S. Alim (Eds.), *Culturally sustaining pedagogies: Teaching and learning for justice in a changing world* (pp. 43–59). Teachers College Press.

Collins, P. H. (1991). *Black feminist thought: Knowledge, consciousness, and the politics of empowerment*. Routledge. https://doi.org/10.1086/229850.

Council of Writing Program Administrators. (2014). *WPA outcomes statement for first-year composition (3.0)*. http://wpacouncil.org/aws/CWPA/pt/sd/news_article/243 055/_PARENT/layout_details/false.

Driscoll, D. & Daewoo, J. (2018). The box under the bed: How learner epistemologies shape writing transfer. *Across the Disciplines, 15*(4), 1–20. https://wac.colostate.edu /docs/atd/articles/driscoll-jin2018.pdf.

Finlay, C. J. (1937). The mosquito hypothetically considered as an agent in the transmission of yellow fever poison. *Yale Journal of Biology and Medicine, 9*(6), 589–604.

Frigo, S. & Fulford, C. (Eds.). (2018). Internationalizing the WAC/WID curriculum [Special issue]. *Across the Disciplines, 15*(1). https://wac.colostate.edu/atd/special /internationalizing-wac/.

Guerra, J. (2016). *Language, culture, identity and citizenship in college classrooms and communities.* Routledge. https://doi.org/10.4324/9781315858081.

Hendrickson, B. & Garcia de Mueller, G. (2016). Inviting students to determine for themselves what it means to write across the disciplines. *The WAC Journal, 27,* 74–93. https://wac.colostate.edu/docs/journal/vol27/hendrickson.pdf.

Holmes, D. G. (1999). Fighting back by *writing* black: Beyond a racially reductive composition theory. In K. Gilyard (Ed.), *Race, rhetoric, and composition* (pp. 53–66). Boyton/Cook.

Horner, B. & Hall, J. (Eds.). (2018). Rewriting disciplines, rewriting boundaries: Transdisciplinary and translingual challenges for WAC/WID [Special issue]. *Across the Disciplines, 15*(3). https://wac.colostate.edu/atd/special/trans/.

Inoue, A. B. (2016). Whiteness as a discourse [Friday plenary address]. *WPA: Writing Program Administration, 40*(1), 134–154.

International Network of WAC Programs (INWAC). (2014). *Statement of WAC principles and practices.* https://wac.colostate.edu/principles/.

Irizzary, J. G. (2017). "For us, by us": A vision for culturally sustaining pedagogies forwarded by Latinx youth. In D. Paris & H. S. Alim (Eds.), *Culturally sustaining pedagogies: Teaching and learning for justice in a changing world* (pp. 83–98). Teachers College Press.

Kells, M. H. (2007). Writing across communities: Deliberation and the discursive possibilities of WAC. *Reflections: A Journal of Writing, Service-Learning, and Community Literacy, 6*(1), 87–108.

Ladson-Billings, G. (1995). Toward a theory of culturally relevant pedagogy. *American Educational Research Journal, 32,* 465–491. https://doi.org/10.3102/00028312032 003465.

Ladson-Billings, G. (2014). Culturally relevant pedagogy 2.0: The remix. *Harvard Educational Review, 84*(1), 74–84. https://doi.org/10.17763/haer.84.1.p2rj13148 5484751.

Ladson-Billings, G. (2017). The (r)evolution will not be standardized: Teacher education, hip hop pedagogy, and culturally relevant pedagogy 2.0. In D. Paris & H. S. Alim (Eds.), *Culturally sustaining pedagogies: Teaching and learning for justice in a changing world* (pp. 141–156). Teachers College Press.

Lee, T. S. & McCarty, T. L. (2017). Upholding indigenous education sovereignty through critical culturally sustaining/revitalizing pedagogy. In D. Paris & H. S. Alim (Eds.), *Culturally sustaining pedagogies: Teaching and learning for justice in a changing world* (pp. 61–82). Teachers College Press.

Matsuda, P. (2006). The myth of linguistic homogeneity in U.S. college composition. *College English, 68,* 637–651. https://doi.org/10.2307/25472180.

Paris, D. & Alim, H. S. (Eds.). (2017). *Culturally sustaining pedagogies: Teaching and learning for justice in a changing world.* Teachers College Press.

Poe, M. (2013). Re-framing race in teaching writing across the curriculum. *Across the Disciplines, 10*(3), 1–14. https://wac.colostate.edu/docs/atd/race/poe.pdf.

San Pedro, T. J. (2017). "This stuff interests me": Recentering indigenous paradigms in colonizing schooling spaces. In D. Paris & H. S. Alim (Eds.), *Culturally sustaining pedagogies: Teaching and learning for justice in a changing world* (pp. 99–116). Teachers College Press.

Townsend, M. A. (2016). What are writing across the curriculum and writing in the disciplines? In R. Malenczyk (Ed.), *A rhetoric for writing program administrators* (2nd ed., pp. 115–128). Parlor Press.

Villanueva, V. (2001). The politics of literacy across the curriculum. In S. McLeod, E. Miraglia, M. Soven & C. Thaiss (Eds.), *WAC for the new millennium: Strategies for continuing writing-across-the-curriculum programs* (pp. 165–178). National Council of Teachers of English.

APPENDIX: FROM THE WPA OUTCOMES STATEMENT FOR FIRST-YEAR COMPOSITION (CWPA, 2014)

Faculty in all programs and departments can build on this preparation by helping students to learn

- the expectations of readers in their fields
- the main features of genres in their fields
- the main purposes of composing in their fields
- the kinds of critical thinking important in their disciplines
- the kinds of questions, problems, and evidence that define their disciplines
- strategies for reading a range of texts in their fields
- ways to employ the methods and technologies commonly used for research and communication within their fields
- ways to develop projects using the characteristic processes of their fields
- ways to review work-in-progress for the purpose of developing ideas before surface-level editing
- ways to participate effectively in collaborative processes typical of their field
- the reasons behind conventions of usage, specialized vocabulary, format, and citation systems in their fields or disciplines
- strategies for controlling conventions in their fields or disciplines
- factors that influence the ways work is designed, documented, and disseminated in their fields
- ways to make informed decisions about intellectual property issues connected to common genres and modalities in their fields

CHAPTER 17.

EMOTIONAL LABOR, MENTORING, AND EQUITY FOR DOCTORAL STUDENT AND FACULTY WRITERS

Shannon Madden
North Carolina State University

Sandra L. Tarabochia
University of Oklahoma

Writing Across the Curriculum scholars are well positioned to improve educational access and maintain the free exchange of ideas by developing pedagogy, policy, and programming rooted in research on faculty and doctoral student writers' needs and experiences. This chapter uses results from a study of emerging scholars' writing development to examine the effects of emotional labor in mentorship experiences. Although emotion is a natural aspect of writing, learning, and development, our analysis reveals how institutional discourses impose normative expectations that create additional labor for writers in managing emotions; this labor impacts some groups of writers more significantly than others. The chapter concludes with recommendations and structural interventions for revising writing mentorship practices.

Historically, WAC researchers have not focused on graduate student and faculty writers. Two decades ago, *WAC for the New Millennium* (McLeod et al., 2001)—much like this volume—sought to document a moment in time. In that collection, "faculty writers" did not appear in the index at all. Faculty were treated as potential allies in cross-curricular writing instruction but not as writers in their own right. Graduate student writers garnered slightly more attention. Thankfully, interest in graduate student and faculty writers has expanded. The call for increased attention to graduate student mentorship, in particular, is represented in this collection; Rachael Cayley (this volume) describes a genre systems approach to mentoring publication-based thesis writers and Alisa Russell, Jake Chase, Justin Nicholes, and Allie Sockwell Johnston (this volume) highlight the need for mentorship as a factor leading to the founding of WAC's growing

DOI: https://doi.org/10.37514/PER-B.2020.0360.2.17

graduate student organization, WAC-GO. Acknowledging that many late-stage doctoral students and early-career faculty—a group we refer to collectively as "emerging scholars"—naturally struggle to navigate changes in their writerly habits and identities as they transition into high stakes writing situations, recent volumes offer programmatic strategies for supporting these writers (e.g., Baden-horst & Guerin, 2016; Geller & Eodice, 2013; Lawrence & Zawacki, 2019; Simpson, Caplan et al., 2016). Nevertheless, despite the established need and burgeoning scholarship, research findings do not inform writing support efforts as much as they should (Caplan & Cox, 2016; Simpson, 2016). Although researchers across disciplines provide struggling writers with strategies and hab-its to increase productivity (Silvia, 2007; Sword, 2017; Tulley, 2018), writers' needs are rarely addressed from a developmental perspective. As a result, WAC efforts focused on faculty and graduate students do not always support the holis-tic development of these writers. The effects are dire as the current climate of higher education marked by neoliberalism and austerity continues to intensify the stakes of the publication imperative. The consequences of failure impact not only individual careers but the advancement of knowledge; when scholars lack access to academic publishing, the free exchange of ideas suffers (Gray et al., 2018). Although WAC researchers and practitioners have historically paid little attention to graduate student and faculty writers, we are perfectly positioned to improve educational access and maintain the free exchange of ideas by support-ing these writers in meeting the demands of our historical moment. Empirical research is essential in this effort.

Toward that end, we present new findings from our ongoing study of gradu-ate student and faculty writers' development (Tarabochia & Madden, 2018). In this chapter, we explore one new insight: that writers perform significant emo-tional labor around mentoring. Drawing on Arlie Russell Hochschild (1983), we define emotional labor as the work writers do in handling emotions, others' and their own (p. 11). Emotional labor is not always negative but can be disruptive and have cumulative effects if not addressed from a structural perspective. Our study suggests that emotional labor in some cases hinders writers' development. Faculty and graduate student writers, their writing mentors, and WAC consul-tants who support these writers and their mentors know that writing involves emotion, but we are not always prepared to understand and engage with emotion in meaningful ways. Too often writing mentorship practices reinforce dominant discourses that treat emotions as barriers to writing success that individuals must overcome. Rather than framing emotion as a personal problem to be avoided or ignored, our analysis offers vantage points from which to rewrite this narrative of what writing-related emotions look like. It is essential for writing mentors across the disciplines, including WAC practitioners, faculty developers, administrators and dissertation advisors, to challenge problematic norms and engage in healthier ways with the range of emotions associated with high stakes writing demands. The time is right for this move as the WAC community attends more deliberately to the writing needs of emerging scholars and, we argue, empirical research focused on emotion and mentorship should drive the effort. Using data from our larger study of faculty and doctoral student writer development, we examine how emotional labor is legible in writers' mentoring experiences and offer strategies for revising mentoring structures to mitigate long term impacts of emotional labor. Before theorizing emotional labor and illustrating how it impacted writers from our study, we describe the methodology that led us to this insight.

STUDY DESIGN

To investigate emerging scholars' writer development, we cross-analyzed data from two separate studies, one on doctoral student writers (Madden) and one on faculty writers (Tarabochia).[1] Participants in the doctoral student study (N = 195) were writers from 19 different U.S. universities in the dissertation phase of their programs. Survey participants responded to several multiple choice (Likert scale) and open-ended questions. For the purposes of our cross-analysis, we focused on five of the seven open-ended questions. Of the respondents who self-identified, 68.9% (n = 93) identified as women, 29.6% (n = 40) identified as men, and 1.5% (n = 2) identified as trans or gender nonbinary; they were pursuing degrees in a range of fields such as geology, educational leadership, anthropology, and art history, among others. Respondents located their dissertation research in the social sciences (43.7%, n = 59), humanities (20.7%, n = 28), STEM (32.6%, n = 44), and design/creative disciplines (3%, n = 4). Study participants self-identified as white (80.3%, n = 94), Black/African American (2.6%, n = 3), Hispanic/Latinx (7.7%, n = 9), Indigenous/Native American (2.6%, n = 3), and Asian American/Pacific Islander (1.7%, n = 2). Several participants identified as multi- or biracial (4.4%, n = 5; [Black/white biracial 2.6%, n = 3; Asian/white 0.9%, n =1; Black/Indigenous/white 0.9%, n = 1]). Participants in the faculty study (N=9) were writers from a doctoral university with R1 Carnegie designation and represented the following disciplines: education (4), modern languages (2), architecture (1), social work (1), and geography (1).

---

1   The faculty study was approved by the University of Oklahoma IRB (#6811). The doctoral student study was approved by the University of Rhode Island IRB (#998118–4). Faculty consent forms allowed participants to specify whether to use their names or pseudonyms in published material. Their specifications have been honored here to respect participants' rights to claim authorship as well as their right to privacy.

Faculty participants identified as women (9), white (6), Black (1), Latina/Puerto Rican (1), and "no idea" (1); all but one were on the tenure track.[2] Faculty participated in one-hour qualitative interviews conducted using the Subject-Object Interview protocol (Lahey et al., 1988/2011), an approach based on Kegan's (1982, 1994) constructive-developmental theory, which centers on changes in what individuals treat as subject (part of self, unable to be seen or reflected on) vs. object (outside oneself, able to be critically considered). Faculty were given keywords (e.g., angry, torn, anxious/nervous, success) previously shown to elicit responses in which changes in subject/object orientation becomes visible, and asked to recall related memories from their writing lives. The interview was designed to shed light on faculty writers' developmental trajectories by identifying how they made sense of their writing-related experiences.

We combined these two data sets (doctoral students' survey responses and faculty interviews) and analyzed them by adapting Cheryl Geisler's (2004) method of verbal data analysis, Peter Smagorinsky's (2008) process of collaborative coding, and Johnny Saldaña's (2016) guide for magnitude and evaluation coding. As we explain elsewhere (Tarabochia & Madden, 2018), our methodology represents an innovative approach to studying writer development. Our goal was to learn about the developmental experiences of emerging scholars without relying on traditional longitudinal methods that demand time and resources not always feasible given career and institutional constraints. We argued that separate data collection protocols allowed us to respect the unique realities of each participant group while experimenting with the possibility of repurposing existing data to study development. Because both studies captured writer's lived experiences and both produced qualitative data, we saw an opportunity to combine the datasets in order to create a more texturized view of writers' experiences.

The overall data set included 721 segments of verbal data (350 segments from doctoral student surveys and 371 segments from faculty interviews). We segmented our data by topical chain, a unit of analysis bounded by the topic of discourse and typically identified by pronouns, demonstratives, and definite articles (Geisler, 2004, p. 35). Then, we used an iterative process of open and focused coding to identify the following writing-related concerns: mentoring, structure, social interaction, professional identity development, writing approaches/practices/routines, and life. A null category was used for segments that lacked sufficient detail to identify a dominant concern. "Concern," for our

---

2   We acknowledge that fewer faculty were included in the study than graduate students and do not claim that our findings are generalizable in a traditional sense. Instead, we suggest that our move to consider faculty and graduate student perspectives in relation to one another illuminates potential convergences and divergences in their experiences that deserve closer attention from researchers.

purposes, does not necessarily have a negative connotation. Therefore, we coded each segment a second time for positive, negative, or neutral magnitude in relation to the original concern (Saldaña, 2016).

We observed that emerging scholars' experiences with Mentoring and Structure were mostly negative, whereas all other concerns were mostly positive. We coded as Mentoring (M) any segments that were primarily concerned with writers' relationships with senior advisors, mentors, or their behavior, and we coded as Structure (S) segments concerned with institutional conditions that impact writing, including department culture or environment. We coded concerns as Negative (N) when participants described conditions of lack, problems, or struggle, or when they used negative terms (e.g., "burden," "anxiety"). Overall, 58% (52/89) of verbal data segments coded Mentoring were Negative (36/63 or 57% of doctoral student segments; and 16/26 or approximately 62% of faculty segments). The prevalence of negative experiences associated with mentoring concerns is significant given the important role that mentoring is known to play in supporting advanced writers' development and academic socialization (Casanave, 2016; Costello, 2015; Cox & Brunjes, 2013; Kim, 2016; Maher & Say, 2016; Morita, 2004; Simpson, 2016; Simpson, Ruecker et al., 2016; Stillman-Webb, 2016). At the same time, approximately 68% of segments coded Structure were Negative (135/200 total; 69/118 or approximately 58% of doctoral student Structure codes and 66/80 or approximately 83% of faculty Structure codes).

We used evaluation coding (Saldaña, 2016) to document the many different experiences reported in relation to Negative Mentoring and Negative Structure. Often used to assess programs or organizations, evaluation coding involves locating "patterned observations or participant responses of attributes and details that assess quality." Evaluation coding is not about identifying representative experiences; instead the goal is to use "attributes and details" in participants' responses to assess quality (of programs, policies, conditions; Saldaña, 2016, p. 141). We used evaluation coding to explicate the full range of negative experiences related to our codes of interest. When we considered evaluation codes related to Negative Mentoring and Negative Structure segments together, we discovered emotional labor as a recurring feature across these domains and realized that structure concerns shed light on the trends we noticed in writers' mentoring experiences. By interpreting writers' negative mentoring experiences through the lens of emotional labor, we highlight access and equity issues as well as structural factors that constrain writing and mentoring relationships. Our goal is not to generalize about the needs of all faculty and graduate students based on our findings; instead, we reveal several ways emotional labor can manifest in writing mentorship and call for WAC researchers and practitioners to attend more carefully to emotional labor in the context of writing and writer support.

THEORIZED FINDING: EMOTIONAL LABOR
AND WRITERS' DEVELOPMENT

To conceptualize emotional labor, we rely on cultural theorist Sara Ahmed (2004a, 2004b, 2010) and sociologist Hochschild (1983) who theorize emotion, as well as scholars in writing studies who study emotion in relation to teaching, learning, administration, and the job market (Micciche, 2002, 2007; Sano-Franchini, 2016; Stenberg, 2015; Worhsam, 1998). Emotional labor as it is explicated by these scholars is useful for our analysis because it treats emotion as socially constructed, rather than (only) located within the individual, and emphasizes the variable costs of emotions as they are performed and compelled within social interactions. Although emotions are commonly framed as psychological states individuals inhabit, the framework of emotional labor "challenges any assumption that emotions are a private matter, that they simply belong to individuals, or even that they come from within and *then* move outward toward others" (Ahmed, 2004a, p. 117). Emotions are produced through relationships among people and with objects (Micciche, 2016, par. 4); they are practices and interactions shaped by social and cultural systems that imbue meaning (Ahmed, 2004b; Micciche, 2002). In the context of our study, a view of emotion as socially constructed challenges the tendency to blame writers who express certain feelings (e.g., anxiety, anger, frustration, depression, self-doubt) and foregrounds the role of academic culture and institutional context in determining how writers should or shouldn't feel.

Although the social construction of emotion is not inherently value-laden, Hochschild (1983) pointed out that the work of "doing emotion" (Micciche, 2007, p. 2) always has a cost; the question becomes whether the cost is worthwhile. We perform emotions all the time and often find value in the relational effects of emotion management. For example, we see the personal and social "use value" in expressing sadness at a funeral or pretending to enjoy a boring party (Hochschild, 1983, pp. 7, 18). Rebecca Jackson, Jackie McKinney, and Nicole I. Caswell (2016) found that writing center administrators value many forms of emotional labor, including "mentoring, advising, making small talk, putting on a friendly face, resolving conflicts, making connections, delegating and following up on progress, working in teams, disciplining or redirecting employees, gaining trust, and creating a positive workplace" (par. 2). They discovered that emotional labor often "greases the wheel and makes other tasks easier, lighter, faster" (2016, par. 11). In these cases the cost of emotional labor seems necessary.

Problems arise, however, when an "instrumental stance" to our natural capacity for emotional labor is "engineered and administered by large organizations" (Hochschild, 1983, p. 20). In the context of our study, academic cultures implicitly communicate "latent feeling rules" (Hochschild, 1983, p. 18) through which writers are bound to experience and express only institutionally sanctioned emotions. Lynn Worsham (1998) called this "the schooling of emotion," a process that "inculcate[s] patterns of feeling that support the legitimacy of dominant interests" as emotions become "intertwined with issues of power and status" (p. 223; Micciche, 2002, p. 442). Popular self-help guides for dissertation writers and tenure-track faculty, for example, urge struggling writers to ignore or push through emotions that keep them from writing (Johnson, 2017). Such models favor productivity and publishing record—objectives that clearly serve universities' interests as they compete for funding and international recognition—but that may not cultivate healthy writing lives for emerging scholars.

The more institutions intervene in emotional management, the less individuals understand and trust their feelings. For example, a doctoral student who has internalized the norm that she should feel confident and able to write a dissertation independently, may distrust and redirect feelings of outrage she experiences when her advisor ignores her requests for support and assume she deserves her advisor's berating comments that take the place of meaningful feedback. Emotional estrangement is problematic because, according to Hochschild (1983) emotions serve an important "signal function" by providing clues to understanding who we are in relation to others (p. 30). When we are "schooled" to bury feelings or to pretend to feel a way we don't, we lose access to "reflection and spontaneous feeling" (Hochschild, 1983, p. 45). As a result, "we come to distrust our sense of what is true, as we know it through feeling" (Hochschild, 1983, p. 47). The graduate student who distrusts her legitimate feeling of outrage at her advisor's behavior may convince herself to feel unworthy of her advisor's attention and incapable of writing her dissertation. Thus, the cost of institutional emotion management "affects the degree to which we listen to feeling and sometimes our very capacity to feel" (Hochschild, 1983, p. 21). Moreover, restricting the signal function of emotions keeps people from recognizing the forces and circumstances that impact their ability to survive and thrive in their environments. Of course, power dynamics (related to age, race, gender, sexuality, ability, mental health, and institutional position, among others) affect the stakes of enduring emotion management. Emotions become "sites of social control" (Micciche, 2002, p. 440) as the culture of academia and institutional structures "nurture, stunt, and amplify certain emotional habits" (p. 453) and compel writers from marginalized groups to interpret feelings of anxiety or frustration as personal failures rather than indicative of a problematic reality.

By foregrounding the social construction and variable cost of emotion, emotional labor allows us to reconceptualize the relationship between the emotion work writers associate with mentoring experiences and larger institutional structures that can constrain mentorship and the work of writing. Highlighting the variable costs of emotional labor in mentoring interactions enables us to challenge dominant scripts of emotion in writer development and imagine mentoring structures that mitigate inhibitive emotional labor.

ANALYSIS: EMOTIONAL LABOR IN MENTORING EXPERIENCES

Analyzing comments from writers in our study through the lens of emotional labor suggests that mentoring experiences can trigger strong feelings and create additional work for writers. Writers frequently complained that not receiving timely feedback or not receiving feedback at all created affective complications for them. When asked to recount a memorable feedback experience, several doctoral students indicated they do not receive any feedback on their dissertation drafts. One participant stated, "My advisor asked me not to give him anything until I had a complete draft. I can understand his sentiment but it's also a little alarming to think that I'll have written three or four chapters without his having seen any of it until the end." Another doctoral student framed the lack of feedback in terms of their emotional wellness, saying, "My entire committee is very hands-off. I do not expect help or comments until my defense. This is not conducive to a healthy grad school experience." These responses index feelings of alarm and being unhealthy, showing how a negative "affective context circumscribes" the work of writing (Micciche, 2002, p. 443). In addition to struggling to write without guidance, these writers also must manage their feelings around doing so.

While lacking advisory feedback may understandably be difficult for dissertation writers, our study shows that the emotional labor caused by "hands off" mentoring can impact self-efficacy and confidence beyond graduate school. For example, Lorna, a faculty member, described feeling anguish when she mustered the courage to share a draft of an article with a mentor outside her department and did not hear back for months. She was convinced her writing was so bad that her mentor was embarrassed to discuss it, when in reality the mentor read the draft right away, made comments, and then was swallowed by the business of the semester and forgot to follow up with Lorna. The lens of emotional labor makes evident that mentoring relationships entail uneven power dynamics and that writers in transition are uniquely vulnerable. As institutional representatives, writing mentors "transmit meanings [they] may not intend or endorse" but nevertheless have significant costs when it comes to emotional labor (Micciche, 2002, p. 438). Lorna's mentor did not intend to generate self-doubt as a form of emotional labor in Lorna. Yet their actions exacerbated the cost of that labor, especially considering how Lorna had been historically "schooled" to feel about her writing ability.

Lorna's case demonstrates the cumulative effects of emotional labor as self-doubt and low confidence emerged in response to repeated lessons about herself as a writer. In her words, "I feel like I've been told that I'm not a good enough writer." As a writer for whom English is an additional language and who self-identifies as Latina/Puerto Rican, Lorna's experience aligns with scholarship that suggests that individuals from historically marginalized groups are more likely to feel like imposters in the academy (Burrows, 2016; Dancy & Brown, 2011; Dancy & Jean-Marie, 2014; Young, 2011). Identifying Lorna's comments as revealing emotional labor highlights the complex web of factors that shape how writers interpret their mentors' behaviors as well as the significant and lasting repercussions mentors' decisions have on individual writers' self-confidence.

As her comments show, Lorna's feelings of impostorship were exacerbated each time she received the message that she was a poor academic writer. In this light, it becomes evident that the particular feedback writers receive has the potential to incite emotional labor and have a lasting impact. For instance, Seema, a faculty writer in modern languages and linguistics, explained how negative interactions with her mentor in graduate school shattered her confidence: "[My dissertation advisor] would have one-on-one meetings with me and go page by page . . . [and] most of the time I went out of there crying. . . . She never had anything good to say." Seema emphasized the sustained impact of these meetings: "I don't think I had any confidence in my writing and the quality of my work." Similarly a doctoral student explained how their dissertation director's inconsistent advice inhibited their ability to develop a self-sustaining strategy for composing and revising their work:

> My committee Chair provides feedback, but then forgets
> what suggestions she gave. She then gives me counter advice
> in a few months [sic] time. This is very frustrating, and erodes
> confidence in the writing process. "Does my hair really know
> what she is doing when she gives counter advice" is the ques-
> tion I ask myself.

While writing feedback should evolve over the course of a long-term project such as a dissertation (Guerin, 2018), the writer in this case interpreted shifting feedback as contradictory and inconsistent as a result of the committee chair's forgetfulness. This suggests that writing mentors should be aware of—and communicate with their advisees about—writing and feedback as developmental processes so that writers and their supervisors can communicate openly about the kinds of feedback that are most useful at a particular moment in the process. These examples also reiterate that writing mentorship which is not rooted in a developmental perspective and responsive to writers' needs and perceptions of their experiences can have cumulative effects and set writers up to deal with the costs of emotional labor at various points throughout their developmental trajectories.

Because we gathered doctoral student and faculty writers' experiences of mentoring, we can see how emotional labor resulting from negative mentoring interactions in graduate school can follow writers into faculty positions. Significantly, most of faculty members' Negative Mentoring segments referred to graduate school (13 segments out of 16) rather than writing mentorship during their time as faculty. Faculty writer Julie traced her struggle to turn her dissertation into the book she needed for tenure to "a weird experience" with her committee. She described cryptic, demoralizing feedback; she believed several committee members went to the defense without having read her dissertation. One signed off on the project intimating that they would not have done so if they were chair, and another responded with vague, positive commentary that meant little to Julie. The reluctant approvals and lack of substantive feedback left Julie questioning the legitimacy of her project and wondering if she deserved to graduate. In her faculty position, those doubts made it difficult to write her book because she questioned the value of her research. At the time of her interview, Julie was immersed in the emotional labor of rewriting not only her book manuscript but the stories she told herself about her professional identity based on these troubling incidents. The fact that negative graduate school memories persist for faculty writers suggests that these experiences are prevalent and formative, which highlights an urgent need to address the costs of emotional labor in writing mentorship.

As we have shown, mentoring experiences can trigger powerful emotions that are not always conducive to healthy writer development. Participants in our study also revealed the cost of emotional labor when they were compelled to perform particular emotions in order to stay on good terms with advisors. According to Hochschild (1983), we all "act" sometimes when it comes to emotion. Through "surface acting," "we change how we outwardly appear" even if the appearance doesn't align with feelings we are experiencing; through "deep acting" we express "a real feeling that has been self-induced" (Hochschild, 1983, p. 35). In both cases, the feeling performed is separated from "the idea of the central self" (Hochschild, 1983, p. 36). Hochschild noted that estrangement becomes problematic when "the psychological costs of emotional labor are not acknowledged" (1983, p. 37). We discovered several such instances in writers' descriptions of performing emotion for mentors. Faculty writer Elizabeth described pandering to her dissertation advisor:

> So for an hour meeting I'll have 30 minutes of pandering and
> like self-flagellation you know like I'm worthless and then . . .
> the last 30 minutes would be nuggets of useful information

but it's just such an awful process. [. . .] I mean I'm just eating
poo until (laughing) making to the end of this process and
then that's it. I'm just like wash my hands and just walk away.

Doctoral students similarly described emotional labor in power imbalances with mentors. In answering the question, "What can be done to improve support for doctoral student writers at your institution?" one student recommended, "cut down on extra service that one feels indebted to participate in in fear that professors will pull away if the grad student doesn't agree to help with service." These responses highlight how uneven power dynamics generate emotional labor. Study participants illustrate how individuals lose agency over their feelings when "the locus of acting, of emotion management, moves up to the level of the institution" (Hochschild, 1983, p. 49). The loss of agency is particularly troubling given that emotions are an important way we perceive reality and constitute identity. Academic institutions, and mentors as institutional agents, control how writers perceive development and success—the possible ways of doing and being available to writers—and shape not only feelings but experiences to align with institutional objectives.

Of course, the work of sustaining relationships has a natural affective dimension; performing emotion can be a useful tool for relational work. However, writers in our study often described emotional labor that was not mutually productive. Instead, it was leveraged to meet the demands of inequitable conditions or to alleviate disenfranchising relationships. In such cases emotional labor was not undertaken as an investment in relationships but because writers were compelled toward institutionally sanctioned performances. Thus, writers in our study reveal the exchange value of emotional labor (Hochschild, 1983); they show how emotions are not merely internal, personal problems but "circulate and are distributed across a social as well as a psychic field" (Ahmed, 2004a, p. 120; Ahmed, 2004b, p. 10). Moreover, because emotions "are intertwined with issues of power and status in the work world" (Micciche, 2002, p. 442), the value and effects of circulation are not neutral or evenly distributed.

Faculty writer Seema illustrates how emotional labor can become a form of social control. As mentioned above, Seema felt degraded by interactions with her dissertation advisor. Additionally, Seema explained how her advisor deliberately put up obstacles to thwart her progress in the program, even refusing to sign Seema's immigration papers. Although the relationship was abusive, Seema rationalized her advisor's behavior and performed the dutiful student. In her interview, Seema cited cultural differences between them as one explanation for their fraught relationship and convinced herself it was up to her to find a way to learn from the situation. It was not until another faculty member named her experience as abusive that Seema recognized that the relationship was dysfunctional. Seema's experience exemplifies how emotional labor can become habituated over time; because she had low confidence as a result of repeated negative mentoring encounters, she was predisposed to read the situation from that perspective and assumed it was her responsibility to sustain the mentoring relationship despite its impact on her well-being. Acknowledging emotional labor in mentoring experiences reveals the vicious cycle of disempowerment perpetuated by problematic mentoring relationships.

So far, the lens of emotional labor has highlighted how mentoring moments can provoke costly affective work and compel writers to perform emotions to the point where estrangement limits their ability to trust feelings as clues for interpreting reality. Emotional labor also reveals how institutional discourses demand particular kinds of emotional performances. In *The Promise of Happiness,* Ahmed (2010) described the "sociality" of emotion, in her case happiness, as a phenomenon in which social bonds determine the objects of our emotions and emotions become objects shared among others (p. 56). She identified the happy housewife and the feminist killjoy as figures that orient women to definitions of happiness and shape their perceptions of themselves and others based on whether or not they fit those definitions. Similarly, writers in our study described emotional work around assumptions about others' perceptions of their work habits and writerly identities in relation to tacit institutional ideals. The need to appear busy in front of others is one example of this type of emotional labor. For instance, Julie indicated a need to hide her struggles with writing and procrastination: "I really feel the hierarchy of [people in my department who] are going to be voting on my tenure case, and I don't know how much weakness I can show as far as I don't know where my writing is going, or I am having trouble writing." Later, Julie mentioned the need for appearing productive to faculty colleagues: "I sometimes feel like oh I should just only be writing and advancing, and I feel like I have to put up a very good front and be really positive about how I am advancing." Responses like Julie's reveal institutional discourses that compel academics to appear busy, competent, and confident as writers. The discourse has material effects as writers like Julie expend emotional labor hiding natural feelings of uncertainty and the often slow evolution of writing projects. We see this as distinct from emotional performances compelled directly by mentors because whereas the latter is rooted in interpersonal relational work, this type of emotional labor is compelled implicitly by academic culture.

Relatedly, several doctoral students shared a perception that faculty were too busy to give them feedback. One student wrote, "My professors are often too busy with their own research to offer quality feedback." Given the pressures on faculty writers to publish and produce, these perceptions are likely correct. Additionally, the institutional discourses that compel faculty to appear busy likely exacerbate emotional labor for their doctoral student mentees. One doctoral student expressed this advice for faculty mentors: "Don't cause students to feel as if they are a burden for the work that their dissertation is causing for the members of the department." The perception that mentors are too busy may lead writers to feel guilt over asking for help or prevent them from asking for help at all. At the same time, it reinforces the "latent rul[e]" (Hoschild, 1983, p. 18) that successful academics are busy, as writers are "schooled" to perform similarly as graduate students and faculty, perpetuating a problematic "pedagog[y] of emotion" (Worsham, 1998, p. 216). Foregrounding how institutional discourses regulate writers' feelings in the context of mentoring reveals how "academic institutions function at the affective level to generate loyalty, create perceptions of good workers, and suggest what workers should be willing to contribute to the professional community" (Micciche, 2002, p. 442). Just as Betty Friedan's happy housewife "is a fantasy figure that erases the signs of labor under the sign of happiness" (Ahmed, 2010, p. 50), the figure of the perpetually busy, competent, productive academic writer becomes a way to hide and justify emotional labor. Productive mentorship is difficult to achieve when professional discourses make writers' and mentors' natural feelings seem inappropriate.

Moreover, the emotional labor incited by institutionally sanctioned success narratives and evaluative structures places undue strain on writers from marginalized groups whose identities and perspectives challenge the status quo. Sadie described feeling like her work, which used Black feminized frameworks to study Black women faculty, was dismissed by colleagues in her department and by one department leader in particular. As a Black woman whose research is tied to her embodied identity, Sadie described experiencing these circumstances as "a general lack of support—and almost resistance to support, even beyond a lack of support." Sadie reported that the pattern of undervaluing her research impacted her self-worth and sense of capability. In her words, these "constant onslaughts . . . create[d] a space where I get very anxious about my writing; I get very fearful about whether or not I will make it." Sadie explained that this lack of support also materialized in the formal annual review process:

> On paper if you look at my annual evaluations I always get
> very satisfactory progress but the qualitative feedback in those
> conversations . . . I always have to fight when the annual
> evaluations come; I always have to fight with my [tenure
> committee]. I always feel like I have to gear myself up and . . .
> I have to really argue for myself and for some people that is—
> you know I have colleagues, particularly male colleagues, who
> enjoy the banter, they gear up—

Perhaps Sadie's male colleagues could revel in the challenge of defending their work during annual review because a positive outcome was likely. However, because Sadie's work was constantly discredited, she experienced emotional labor disproportionately as she worried that she did not belong in the academy. Sadie was not supposed to feel the emotions she did (self-doubt) and was compelled to engage in self-advocacy that she believed her white male colleagues likely experienced as playful banter. Sadie's situation demonstrates how the costs of emotional labor can be disproportionate for writers from minoritized groups.

As these examples show, writers are compelled to perform emotions on multiple levels within their mentoring relationships. Sometimes writers value emotional work; at other times, emotional labor can be disempowering and dehumanizing. Our study suggests that regardless of the cost, emotional labor is rarely acknowledged, appreciated, or supported. By analyzing doctoral student and faculty writers' mentoring experiences in relation to one another, we challenge the assumption that negative mentoring experiences are the result of poor individual mentors alone, surfacing broader structural issues that limit access to mentoring and that compel particular emotional performances as the cost of participation in institutional discourses.

RECOMMENDATIONS: REVISING WRITING MENTORSHIP

Based on our analysis of emotional labor in graduate student and faculty writers' mentoring experiences, we offer the following practical recommendations for writing mentors, including dissertation advisors, writing center directors and consultants, faculty developers, journal editors, and WAC leaders working with writers and their mentors.

First, writing mentors should acknowledge emotional labor and be mindful of how mentoring behaviors may cause unintended emotions. Respecting writers' emotional labor might take the form of small changes in practice, such as clear expectations about turnaround time and open communication about developmental support needs. Mentors who recognize the emotional impact of giving or withholding feedback can alleviate the additional work writers do in establishing self-confidence. Further, because emotional labor reported by emerging scholars too often stems from experiences of systemic disempowerment and because U.S. writing policies and pedagogies reflect Western, "whitely" values (Inoue, 2016), we call for mentoring structures that center the needs of writers from historically marginalized groups. In other words, we must acknowledge that writing "mentorship is about equity" (Costello, 2015, p. 3) and do more to create mentoring relationships that reflect the experiences of marginalized writers.

Second, emotion should be intentionally and explicitly addressed in professional development and mentoring contexts. For example, Lisa Russell-Pinson and M. Lynne Harris (2019) described "psychoeducational" dissertation support groups "founded on the strengths-based goal of building resilience" (p. 64). These groups help graduate students address the sources and repercussions of anxiety related to dissertation writing. Although they focus in their article on multilingual writers, Russell-Pinson and Harris asserted—and our study confirms—that all writers experience writing-related emotional stressors and must learn how to navigate complicated emotional situations in their academic relationships and writing lives.

Although these changes in practice are essential, our study suggests that acknowledging emotion in one-with-one and professional development mentoring situations will only be partial solutions unless we challenge the broader structural forces that compel emotional performances and create emotional labor (see also Tang & Andriamanalina, 2020). For example, as Jill Belli (2016) suggested, the popular movement toward "well-being," seems to respect emotional needs but actually stands to reinscribe a neoliberal agenda that encourages individuals to achieve happiness so they can be incorporated into dehumanizing structures. Likewise, Lesley Erin Bartlett and Brandon L. Sams (2017) asserted that practices such as mindfulness that are becoming more popular in the context of self-care "can become oppressive in their emphasis on individual action (or lack thereof), leading people to understand their circumstances strictly as a personal failing and to ignore the influence of institutions and culture" (pp. 6–7). Our analysis draws attention to how emotional labor in the context of mentoring always operates within problematic structures that constrain relationships and limit access. Thus, we advocate redressing the problems of the broader system rather than merely encouraging individuals to adapt to bad situations.

One way to address emotional labor from a structural perspective is to revise traditional approaches that too often associate emotions with individual behavioral causes and solutions (Johnson, 2017). We advocate for support that goes beyond strategies for dealing with anxiety or other negative emotions around writing to include explicit discussion of how writers internalize the need to hide or overcome their emotions, perpetuating a "survival of the fittest" mentality that characterizes higher education (Boice, 1990; Geller, 2013). Talking in support groups about emotion as constructed can transform individual experiences of emotional labor into what Mara Holt, Leon Anderson, and Albert Rouzie (2003) called "emotional work," which involves "building emotional solidarity in groups, and using one's own or others' outlaw emotions to interrogate structures" (cited in Jackson et al., 2016, para. 3). In this way, writing groups might do more than provide emotional support and become sites of collective and individual empowerment.

Another way to address systemic issues impacting writer support is to revise traditional mentoring structures toward collectivist approaches. According to Beth Godbee (2018), "Multiple mentoring relationships can disperse the concentrated power associated with a single supervisor [and] can help [writers] with reclaiming personal power and becoming empowered to stand tall in one's research and professional identity" (para. 8). Dispersed mentoring models might include co-mentoring communities and peer-to-peer support initiatives. Jeannette D. Alarcón and Silvia Bettez (2017) called for inclusive mentoring efforts such as nonhierarchical mentoring, the development of partnerships and coalitions, and valuing "community cultural wealth." Michelle Maher and Brett H. Say (2016) promoted more collaborative authorship among faculty and students and co-chaired committees. The MiSciWriters group at the University of Michigan (see https://misciwriters.com/) and the North Carolina State University Catalyst group (see https://transforming-science.com/catalyst) provide good models of student-led co-mentoring structures that are created for and by graduate students. In addition to alleviating the labor burden of individualized mentoring, co-mentoring also mitigates the danger that one-with-one mentoring relationships may become abusive or toxic, as was reflected in responses to our study.

As we suggested, revised writing mentorship models will have limited impact unless we challenge the climate in which mentoring relationships are constituted. Indeed, the value of mentoring is embedded in institutional practices such as professionalization, tenure, and promotion. For that reason, we agree with Lisa A. Costello (2015) that campus actors must work to change how "chairs, deans, and provosts . . . formally recognize this mentoring as crucial to the hiring, retention, and promotion of strong faculty members" (p. 22). Without more global structures in place, the recommendations we make will never be fully realized.

CONCLUSION

By focusing on emerging scholars, an understudied population of writers, we were able to consider how high-stakes mentoring situations create emotional labor that can interfere with development and productivity. Our project reveals how writers' emotional labor is inseparable "from social contexts and power relations" (Stenberg, 2015, p. 46) and makes evident problematic assumptions about what writing a dissertation or publishing for tenure should *feel* like. The lens of emotional labor uncovers "naturalized conceptions of emotion as individualized, internally located, and privately experienced" (Stenberg, 2015, p. 48), which in our neoliberal educational climate can result in blaming writers for negative emotions and requiring them to overcome those feelings in order to succeed. We argue that interrogating emotional labor is necessary because "it shows that an affective context circumscribes how we work—how we function on a daily basis, how we envision the possibility of creating changes, and how we develop a sense of efficacy and purpose in our [writing] work lives" (Micciche, 2002, p. 443). Acknowledging "the reality of negative experiences that frequently structure our [writing] work lives" is vital if WAC's mission is to promote strong cultures of writing. Our research findings should urge WAC leaders as well as writing mentors and writers across disciplines to repurpose the inevitable emotion involved with writing and cultivate responsive and empowering mentorship experiences.

ACKNOWLEDGMENTS

The authors would like to thank the research participants for sharing their stories and experiences with us. We appreciate very much the helpful feedback provided by Jacob Babb, Lesley Bartlett, Andrea Olinger, and one anonymous reviewer in several rounds which helped us develop the ideas presented here. Thanks always to Michele Eodice for her mentoring and support of these projects. This research was funded by the National Council of Teachers of English.

REFERENCES

Ahmed, S. (2004a). Affective economies. *Social Text, 79, 22*(2), 117–139. https://doi .org/10.1215/01642472-22-2_79-117.

Ahmed, S. (2004b). *The cultural politics of emotion* (2nd ed.). Routledge.

Ahmed, S. (2010). *The promise of happiness*. Duke University Press. https://doi.org /10.1215/9780822392781.

Alarcón, J. D. & Bettez, S. (2017). Feeling brown in the academy: Decolonizing mentoring through a disidentification "Muxerista" approach. *Equity and Excellence in Education, 50*(1), 25–40. https://doi.org/10.1080/10665684.2016.1250234.

Badenhorst, C. & Guerin, C. (2016). Post/graduate research literacies and writing pedagogies. In C. Badenhorst & C. Guerin (Eds.), *Research literacies and writing pedagogies for masters and doctoral writers* (pp. 3–28). Brill. https://doi.org/10.1163 /9789004304338_002.

Bartlett, L. E. & Sams, B. L. (2017). Telling time: Practicing clock wisdom in audit culture. *English Leadership Quarterly, 40*(2), 6–8.

Belli, J. (2016). Why well-being, why now?: Tracing an alternate genealogy of emotion in composition. *Composition Forum, 34.* http://compositionforum.com/issue/34 /why-well-being.php.

Boice, R. (1990). *Professors as writers: A self-help guide to productive writing.* New Forums Press.

Burrows, C. D. (2016). Writing while Black: The Black tax on African American graduate student writers. *Praxis: A Writing Center Journal, 14*(1), 15–20.

Caplan, N. A. & Cox, M. (2016). The state of graduate communication support: Results of an international survey. In S. Simpson, N. A. Caplan, M. Cox & T. Phillips (Eds.). *Supporting graduate student writers: Research, curriculum, and program design* (pp. 22–51). University of Michigan Press.

Casanave, C. P. (2016). What advisors need to know about the invisible "real life" struggles of doctoral dissertation writers. In S. Simpson, N. A. Caplan, M. Cox & T. Phillips (Eds.), *Supporting graduate student writers: Research, curriculum, and program design* (pp. 97–116). University of Michigan Press.

Costello, L. A. (2015). Standing up and standing together: Feminist teaching and collaborative mentoring. *Feminist Teacher, 26*(1), 1–28. https://doi.org/10.5406/femteacher.26.1.0001.

Cox, M. & Brunjes, A. (2013). Guiding principles for supporting faculty as writers at a teaching-mission institution. In A. E. Geller & M. Eodice (Eds.), *Working with faculty writers* (pp. 191–209). Utah State University Press. https://doi.org/10.2307/j.ctt4cgs6g.16.

Dancy, T. E. & Brown, M. C. (2011). The mentoring and induction of educators of color: Addressing the impostor syndrome in academe. *Journal of School Leadership, 21*(4), 607–634. https://doi.org/10.1177/105268461102100405.

Dancy, T. E. & Jean-Marie, G. (2014). Faculty of color in higher education: Exploring the intersections of identity, impostorship, and internalized racism. *Mentoring and Tutoring: Partnership in Learning, 22*(4), 354–372. https://doi.org/10.1080/136112 67.2014.945736.

Geisler, C. (2004). *Analyzing streams of language: Twelve steps to the systematic coding of text, talk, and other verbal data.* Pearson/Longman.

Geller, A. E. (2013). Introduction. In A. E. Geller & M. Eodice (Eds.), *Working with faculty writers* (pp. 1–18). Utah State University Press. https://doi.org/10.2307/j.ctt4cgs6g.5.

Geller, A. E. & Eodice, M. (Eds.) (2013). *Working with faculty writers.* Utah State University Press. https://doi.org/10.2307/j.ctt4cgs6g.

Godbee, B. (2018). The trauma of graduate education. *Inside Higher Ed.* https://www.insidehighered.com/advice/2018/07/09/how-trauma-affects-grad-students-their-career-search-opinion.

Gray, T., Madson, L. & Jackson, M. (2018). Publish and flourish: Helping scholars become better, more prolific writers. *To Improve the Academy: A Journal of Educational Development, 37*(2), 243–256. https://doi.org/10.1002/tia2.20081.

Guerin, C. (2018). Why do supervisors contradict themselves? Development of feedback. *Doctoral Writing SIG.* https://doctoralwriting.wordpress.com/2018/09/11/why-do-supervisors-contradict-themselves-development-of-feedback/.

Hochschild, A. R. (1983). *The managed heart: Commercialization of human feeling.* University of California Press.

Holt, M., Anderson, L. & Rouzie, A. (2003). Making emotion work visible in writing program administration. In D. Jacobs & L. Micciche (Eds.), *A way to move: Rhetorics of emotion and composition studies* (pp. 147–160). Boynton/Cook.

Inoue, A. (2016). Afterword: Narratives that determine writers and social justice writing center work. *Praxis: A Writing Center Journal, 14*(1). http://www.praxisuwc.com/inoue-141.

Jackson, R., McKinney, J. G. & Caswell, N. I. (2016). Writing center administration and/as emotional labor. *Composition Forum, 34*. http://compositionforum.com/issue/34/writing-center.php.

Johnson, K. (2017). Writing by the book, writing beyond the book. *Composition Studies, 45*(2), 55–72.

Kegan, R. (1982). *The evolving self: Problem and process in human development.* Harvard University Press.

Kegan, R. (1994). *In over our heads: The mental demands of modern life.* Harvard University Press.

Kim, K. M. (2016). Post/graduate feedback in second language writing: The feedback network on the dissertation proposal. In S. Simpson, N. A. Caplan, M. Cox & T. Phillips (Eds.), *Supporting graduate student writers: Research, curriculum, and program design* (pp. 238–256). University of Michigan Press.

Lahey, L., Souvaine, E., Kegan, R., Goodman, R. & Felix, S. (1988/2011). *A guide to the subject-object interview: Its administration and interpretation.* Minds at Work.

Lawrence, S. & Zawacki, T. M. (2019). *Re/writing the center: Approaches to supporting graduate students in the writing center.* Utah State University Press. https://doi.org/10.7330/9781607327516.

Maher, M. A. & Say, B. H. (2016). Doctoral supervisors as learners and teachers of disciplinary writing. In C. Badenhorst & C. Guerin (Eds.), *Research literacies and writing pedagogies for masters and doctoral writers* (pp. 277–294). Brill. https://doi.org/10.1163/9789004304338_016.

McLeod, S. H., Miraglia, E., Soven, M. & Thaiss, C. (Eds.). (2001). *WAC for the new millennium: Strategies for continuing writing across the curriculum programs.* National Council of Teachers of English.

Micciche, L. (2002). More than a feeling: Disappointment and WPA work. *College English, 64*, 432–458. https://doi.org/10.2307/3250746.

Micciche, L. (2007). *Doing emotion: Rhetoric, writing, teaching.* Boynton/Cook.

Micciche, L. (2016). Staying with emotion. *Composition Forum, 34*. https://compositionforum.com/issue/34/micciche-retrospective.php.

Morita, N. (2004). Negotiating participation and identity in second language academic communities. *TESOL Quarterly, 38*(4), 573–603. https://doi.org/10.2307/3588281.

Russell-Pinson, L. & Harris, M. L. (2019). Anguish and anxiety, stress and strain: Attending to writers' stress in the dissertation process. *Journal of Second Language Writing, 43*, 63–71. https://doi.org/10.1016/j.jslw.2017.11.005.

Saldaña, J. (2016). *The coding manual for qualitative researchers* (3rd ed.). Sage.

Sano-Franchini, J. (2016). "It's like writing yourself into a codependent relationship with someone who doesn't even want you!": Emotional labor, intimacy, and the academic job market in rhetoric and composition. *College Composition and Communication, 68*(1), 98–124.

Silvia, P. J. (2007). *How to write a lot: A practical guide to productive academic writing.* American Psychological Association.

Simpson, S. (2016). Introduction: New frontiers in graduate writing support and program design. In S. Simpson, N. A. Caplan, M. Cox & T. Phillips (Eds.), *Supporting graduate student writers: Research, curriculum, and program design* (pp. 1–20). University of Michigan Press. https://doi.org/10.3998/mpub.8772400.

Simpson, S., Caplan, N. A., Cox, M. & Phillips, T. (Eds.). (2016). *Supporting graduate student writers: Research, curriculum, and program design.* University of Michigan Press. https://doi.org/10.3998/mpub.8772400.

Simpson, S., Ruecker, T., Carrejo, D., Flores, B. C. & Gonzalez, H. C. (2016). Leveraging development grants to create graduate writing support at three Hispanic-serving institutions. In S. Simpson, N. A. Caplan, M. Cox & T. Phillips (Eds.), *Supporting graduate student writers: Research, curriculum, and program design* (pp. 171–191). University of Michigan Press. https://doi.org/10.3998/mpub.8772400.

Smagorinsky, P. (2008). The method section as conceptual epicenter in constructing social science research reports. *Written Communication, 25*(3), 389–411. https://doi.org/10.1177/0741088308317815.

Stenberg, S. J. (2015). *Repurposing composition: Feminist interventions for a neoliberal age.* Utah State University Press. https://doi.org/10.7330/9781607323884.

Stillman-Webb, N. (2016). Writing beliefs and mentoring practices: Advisor perspectives on post/graduate writing instruction in the sciences. In C. Badenhorst & C. Guerin (Eds.), *Research literacies and writing pedagogies for masters and doctoral writers* (pp. 257–276). Brill. https://doi.org/10.1163/9789004304338_015.

Sword, H. (2017). *Air and light and time and space: How successful academics write.* Harvard University Press. https://doi.org/10.4159/9780674977617.

Tang, J. K. & Andriamanalina, N. (2020). "I cut my hand off and gave it to you, and you gave it back to me with three fingers": The disembodiment of doctoral student writers of color in the US nation state. In S. Madden, M. Eodice, K. T. Edwards Williams & A. Lockett (Eds.), *Learning from the Lived Experiences of Graduate Student Writers.* Utah State University Press.

Tarabochia, S. L. & Madden, S. (2018). Writing in transition: Researching the development of graduate student and faculty writers [Special issue: Writing Development Across the Lifespan, Charles Bazerman, Ed.] *Writing & Pedagogy, 10*(3), 423–452. https://doi.org/10.1558/wap.34576.

Tulley, C. (2018). *How writing faculty write: Strategies for process, product, and productivity.* Utah State University Press. https://doi.org/10.7330/9781607326625.

Worsham, L. (1998). Going postal: Pedagogic violence and the schooling of emotion. *JAC: Journal of Advanced Composition, 18*(2), 213–245.

Young, V. (2011). *The secret thoughts of successful women: Why capable people suffer from the impostor syndrome and how to thrive in spite of it.* Crown.

CHAPTER 18.

MEANINGFUL WRITING AND PERSONAL CONNECTION: EXPLORING STUDENT AND FACULTY PERSPECTIVES

Michele Eodice
University of Oklahoma

Anne Ellen Geller
St. John's University

Neal Lerner
Northeastern University

Even with a focus on acquiring academic discourses, WAC efforts can lead to meaningful writing experiences for students if students' personal connections are valued. Writing in any discipline can include opportunities for personal connections to self, others in community, and to subjects of study. Implications for WAC include understanding both faculty and student perceptions of what is meaningful for them as writers.

Teaching writing in higher education occurs through a range of pedagogies and with varied motivations.[1] Most pervasive are those that emphasize mastery of academic discourse and disciplinary conventions (Melzer, 2014) or what Thaiss and Zawacki (2006) characterized as writing marked by "the dominance of reason over emotion or sensual perception" (p. 16). When describing their goals for writing across the curriculum initiatives, institutions routinely invoke a set of outcomes, including learning disciplinary conventions, transferring writing knowledge, and developing critical thinking skills. Writing across the curriculum often focuses on the learning of these academic discourses and reduces the

---

1   This chapter is based on a keynote for IWCA 2019 and draws on research findings specifically developed for an article in *Research in the Teaching of English*, "The Power of Personal Connection for Undergraduate Student Writers" (Eodice et al., 2019).

scope of attention to students' needs and desires as language users. This focus on acquiring academic discourse is potentially at odds with attending to pedagogies inclusive of students' identities and experiences—recognizing what students bring with them and where they are in their own development of academic literacies (Guerra, 2015; Ivanic, 1998; Kareem, this volume; Kells, 2018; Lea & Street, 2006; Lillis & Scott, 2007). As Kells (2007) argued, "Traditional models of WAC too narrowly privilege academic discourse over other discourses and communities shaping the worlds in which our students live and work" (p. 93). While we understand the risk of positioning "academic discourse" versus "student agency"—after all, many students might be motivated to become expert in particular academic discourses—in this chapter, we focus on a particular kind of agency, one we label "personal connection," as a means for students to make meaning from their writing, drawing on personal resources and connecting to academic writing tasks that are "framed expansively" (Engle et al., 2012). Our intent is to offer faculty from any disciplinary context the means to create writing tasks that students will find meaningful.

We also see this chapter speaking to the present moment when much of the focus in WAC and WID research and practice has been on student mastery of knowledge, whether it is the "threshold concepts" (Adler-Kassner & Wardle, 2015) that define disciplinary discourses or particular vocabulary that might lead to "teaching for transfer" (Yancey et al., 2014). Our concern in these dominant approaches is that students are positioned as mere consumers of curriculum and pedagogy, rather than active agents in their own learning. The goal of ensuring that the writing students do will be meaningful—and that all of our assigned tasks will lead to meaningful writing—might be too optimistic, but fully understanding the elements students and faculty bring to those tasks is a first key step, one built on students as knowledge makers rather than merely knowledge consumers.

In what follows, we explore the role of personal connection through the data we collected for *The Meaningful Writing Project* (Eodice et al., 2016), a multi-institutional research initiative drawing on data from 707 student surveys, 27 one-to-one interviews with those students, 160 surveys of faculty named as having taught the class in which the meaningful writing project took place, and 60 follow-up interviews with those faculty (with all interviews conducted by undergraduate researchers trained with a common interview protocol). Our motivation for research was rooted in understanding how students describe writing projects of their undergraduate years they name as meaningful and how faculty who assigned those projects describe the learning and teaching of those writing tasks. When it comes to the writing that students and faculty identify as most meaningful, looking closely at how students and faculty describe their experiences sheds light on the features of meaningful writing, revealing how these features were activated by the writer, the instructor, the assignment, the context, or relationships, and thus provide implications for future teaching and research.

Personal connection to the writing, through individual interest, social relations, or subject matter, emerged as a primary element in both students' meaningful writing projects and the ways faculty designed those writing tasks (see Eodice et al., 2019). It was the power of these personal connections that led us to dig deeper into its significance across disciplines—learning from a range of faculty and students. The questions we address in this chapter are as follows: (a) How do students and faculty describe the role of personal connection in the making of meaningful writing? (b) What are the significant similarities and differences between student and faculty experiences of meaningful writing? (c) What are the implications of these findings for learning and teaching writing across the curriculum?

BACKGROUND OF THE MEANINGFUL WRITING PROJECT

The Meaningful Writing Project traces its start to conversations circulating within and beyond writing studies about student writing and the ways student work is so often framed in a deficit model. In addition, and perhaps even more importantly, we too often fail to hear from students themselves about the experiences they have with writing while in higher education. After receiving a Conference on College Composition and Communication Research Initiative grant, we offered a survey to all seniors at our three institutions in Spring 2012, and, as we noted above, we received 707 responses. At the center of our survey was the following prompt and related questions:

> Think of a writing project from your undergraduate career
> up to this point that was meaningful for you and answer the
> following questions:
> - Describe the writing project you found meaningful.
> - What made that project meaningful for you?

Our initial focus of analysis was on the latter question—the reasons students offered for what made their writing projects meaningful. Our grounded theory, qualitative analysis (Glaser & Strauss, 1967; Saldaña, 2012) of these responses yielded 22 codes (see Appendix) or descriptors of reasons students found their writing meaningful. We discovered that while students write projects that they describe as meaningful in diverse contexts, genres, and majors, that meaningfulness is focused within a set of conditions that most frequently included opportunities to make a personal connection, see the potential for current or future relevance, engage in research, and learn new content.

These most frequently occurring factors reach across writing projects written from first-year to senior year, representing almost 100 different majors writing in disciplines from archeology to zoology. More specifically, while 52% of the seniors in our study reported that they wrote their meaningful writing project in their major, 52% also said they wrote it within a required course. Only 17% said their meaningful writing project had been written in an elective course, and 29% of the seniors said their meaningful writing project developed in a general education course. In other words, the possibilities for meaningful writing to happen are broad though the reasons for that meaningfulness coalesce around the four most frequently occurring factors that we name above.

THE POWER OF PERSONAL CONNECTION

One key factor—personal connection—was the most frequently occurring code across the 707 student survey responses, appearing in 36% of all responses. To triangulate student and faculty perspectives, we administered a two-question survey to instructors whom students named as having assigned the meaningful writing projects. For the first question, we were able to pull information that the student supplied describing the meaningful writing project and asked faculty the following:

> We're sending you this survey because a student named a writing project written for your course as the most meaningful of their undergraduate career. Why do think that was so?

To analyze these responses, we collaboratively applied the 22 codes that we derived from our analysis of students' descriptions of what made their writing projects meaningful. In other words, we wanted to analyze faculty responses through the lens of students' own perceptions of meaningful writing. As was true for the student survey, for faculty describing their assignments, personal connection was the most frequently occurring code (41% of all responses). This meant faculty may have been intentional enough in their assignment design to allow student personal connection.

Given this frequency and our curiosity about the kinds of personal connections students and faculty described, we decided to explore these data more fully. For the student data, we collaboratively recoded the personal connection set of responses, asking ourselves, "personal connection to what?" Our analysis revealed three primary kinds of personal connections:

- Individual, including the ways students connect to their development as writers, their sense of authorship, their vision of future writing or identities, their need for self-expression, and their individual experiences;

- Social, including family, community, and peers;
- Subject-matter, namely students' interests in and passion for their writing topics, and their sense of the importance of those topics.

For the purposes of this chapter, we applied the same subcodes of personal connection to faculty responses, acknowledging any points of similarity and difference between the kinds of personal connections students make to their meaningful writing projects and the kinds of personal connections that faculty ascribe to those same projects. Tables 18.1 and 18.2 offer the results of this analysis from the student and faculty data sets, including examples of each subcode. It is important to note that these examples do not come from the pairing of students and faculty (i.e., a student telling us about a meaningful writing project and the faculty member who taught that class telling us why they believed the student chose that project). We offer them to give some sense of how these representative samples compared.

Table 18.1. Personal connection subcode frequencies and examples of student survey responses

Code	Response %	Example
Individual connections		
development	16%	In order to accomplish this paper, I really needed to dig deep and decide where I stand as a person. There are many approaches that could be taken on this project, I had to decide which one I agreed with morally.
authorship	12%	I got to choose what topics I was interested in, and incorporate real research with real thought and creativity.
future	8%	It directed me to a field I was very interested in and eventually to the field that I will be studying in my masters.
self-expression	7%	It was a relevant topic to our society and government today and I was able to express my personal opinion.
experience	3%	This project was meaningful because I could relate to the subject being relevant to my area of interest (marketing and supply chain management) and also my years of experience working within the retail industry as a whole.

Code	Response %	Example
Social connections		
family/ community/ others	16%	The project was meaningful to me because it was touched home for me being from the area where the wind farm was proposed to be built. I found it very interesting that a project like this had the ability to do so much good for the environment as well as the economy. This particular project could help create cleaner air quality as well as help the area save on electricity costs. At the same time it was interesting to see how the people against the project were directly affiliated with the oil and gas industries.
Subject-matter connections		
interest/ passion	18%	We were allowed to choose a topic that was interesting to us, and then motivated to elaborate on it much deeper.
topic importance	8%	[I] could pick a topic that was important to me.

Table 18.2. Personal connection subcode frequencies and examples of faculty survey responses

Code	Response %	Example
Individual connections		
develop- ment	8%	The use of writing in my curriculum has always been important to me, from the standpoint of craftsmanship as well as a tool for reflection. In my capstone course this takes on special signifi- cance as the students transition from undergraduate work to graduate education. I myself am a professional writer and author in addition to my research writing. The students gain apprecia- tion of themselves and others as they grow through writing.
authorship	12%	The project was based on a short experiment that students designed and conducted in the laboratory portion of a cell biology class. I think they found it meaningful because: a) it was based on their own independent work (intellectual ownership); b) was in the style of a scientific manuscript (i.e., relevant to their professional goals), c) was manageable in length (5–10 pages); and d) required revision and re-submission following review by peers and by their TA (opportunity to improve).
future	0%	N/A

Code	Response %	Example
self-expression	9%	I believe the assignment the student referred to asked them to begin to define those values that are most important to them as designers. My sense is this assignment was one of the few opportunities they have to attempt to stake out their own position in contemporary architectural practice and discourse.
experience	3%	In assigning this particular project—which I have used successfully for MANY years—I attempt to personalize the experience to the student's individual perspective. It is a somewhat subjective assignment, albeit with an established, applied behavioral science foundation. Also important, it absolutely requires individual thought, so cannot be downloaded or culled from outside sources. Students learn the cumulative meaning of consumer behavior through this one assignment.
Social connections		
family/ com- munity/ others	6%	The assignment asked students to make connections between their family stories and their personal identities. I think students may find value in this assignment because they are invited to define themselves against the tapestry of family background in unique ways—race, gender & class. Students interview their family members as part of their work and engage in important conversations that they otherwise might miss.
Subject-matter connections		
interest/ passion	44%	Well, I'm certainly glad to hear that the student got something out of the assignment. Perhaps the appeal lay in the fact that I worked with each student to explore individual interests and develop unique research topics. I suggested two or three sources to each student, but after that essentially got out of the way and let them work. Each student presented his or her study to the class.
topic importance	15%	This course, "Capstone in Anthropology," is a class in which the students choose a research topic that relates to their interests in the discipline and spend the semester preparing a final research paper. I think it is meaningful in that students see this as a culmination of the education within their major subject, the topic is completely of their choosing, and the paper is an integral, major part of the course (not just a small part that is peripheral to the rest of the class).

One purpose of this analysis was to compare the frequency of personal connection subcodes in faculty survey responses with the frequency of those subcodes in student survey responses, essentially exploring if faculty and students might value different kinds of personal connections and believe different kinds of personal connections lead to meaningful writing. Figure 18.1 describes this comparison. For students, "individual connections" constitute 46% of all responses; for faculty, these connections add up to 32% of all responses. "Social connections" also revealed differences: we coded 16% of student responses as social in nature while only 6% of faculty responses reflected this connection. Finally, a significant difference is in the connections to subject matter or topics for writing: While 26% of student responses reflected this connection, 59% of faculty responses did; this is not surprising given that faculty prioritize their subjects as integral to their work.

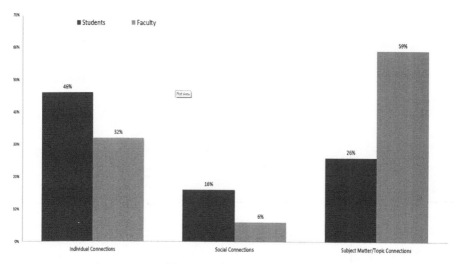

Figure 18.1. Comparison of frequency of types of personal connections by student and faculty.

We dig more deeply into these differences in Figure 18.2, which compares the frequency of specific faculty subcodes to the frequency of subcodes of personal connection in student surveys. A key difference is that faculty believe that students found their writing projects meaningful because of personal connections to subject matter interests and passions. We were not too surprised by this finding. As writing teachers ourselves and having worked with faculty across the disciplines on teaching with writing for many years, we have seen how faculty are focused on their subject matters and the ways they might invite students to write about those subjects.

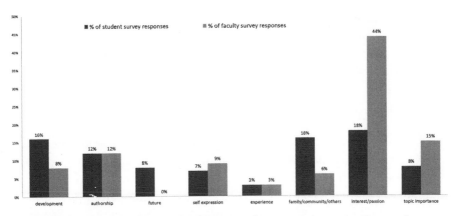

Figure 18.2. Faculty subcodes of personal connection compared to student subcodes: IC = individual connections, SC = social connections, SMC = subject matter connections.

What stands out here for us is that faculty were describing the personal connection they wanted students to make to disciplinary or course subjects. In other words, it wasn't simply what Dan Melzer (2014) described as "the purpose of more than 8 in 10 assignments," the "transactional" assignments that are "informative" rather than "persuasive"—with a teacher-examiner as the primary intended reader (pp. 21–23). Transactional assignments often sound like: "Use three examples from the course reading to explain x," or "Compare two theories we've studied this month." Instead, as one faculty member said: "I worked with each student to explore individual interests and develop unique research topics," or as another faculty said: "The second paper is solution-oriented of the student's own choosing, and again requires a theoretical explanation of why they think the solution proposed in the paper is necessary. So, the paper assignments offer students the flexibility to explore their own interests but still draw upon the material presented in class." We believe that these deliberately designed personal connections to students' interests and passions for the subject matter represent a form of "expansive framing" in the term that educational psychologist Randi Engle and colleagues (2012) used to describe learning tasks in which the following occurs:

> In an expansive framing of roles, learners are positioned as active participants in a learning context where they serve as authors of their own ideas and respondents to the ideas of others. Within this sort of learning environment, students' authored ideas are recognized and integrated into class discussions and other activities. (p. 218)

Further, Engle et al. have found that expansively framed learning tasks lead students to more successful transfer of their learning to new contexts, representing "an initial discussion of an issue that students will be actively engaging with throughout their lives" (2012, p. 217).

CHOICE/ALLOW AND REQUIRE

In addition to the 22 codes we applied to students' explanations for what made a writing project meaningful, one element we saw repeatedly in student survey responses was whether the instructor, or the assignment itself, offered opportunities for exploration (choice) or allowed for some degree of freedom in undertaking the assignment (allow), another manifestation of "expansive framing" (Engle et al., 2012). This choice/allow component was often balanced by a corresponding description of required elements. Faculty, similarly, included in their descriptions of assignments notions of choice/allow and require.

As we show in Table 18.3, for the student survey responses that we coded specifically for personal connection, elements of choice/allow and particular requirements played a greater role as compared to all other survey responses, differences that are statistically significant. Perhaps this finding is driven by students' choice of topics or subject matter for writing, but we also believe that for some students, the "expansive framing" of personal connection represents the agency to make a variety of choices in writing projects students name as meaningful.

In faculty survey responses that we coded personal connection, choice/ allow and require were also common features. However, the frequency of those elements differed between student and faculty responses, as shown in Table 18.4. More specifically, faculty were much more likely than students to name an assignment as giving students choice or that it allowed students room to maneuver, as well as to describe required elements.

Table 18.3. Frequency of choice/allow and require in student survey responses coded personal connection as compared to all other responses

	Choice/Allow	Require	Both
Personal Connection responses	45%	38%	18%
All other responses	22%	33%	7%

Note: All differences statistically significant at p < .05.

Table 18.4. Comparison of frequency of choice/allow and require in student and faculty survey data coded personal connection

	Students	Faculty
% of responses with choice/allow	45%	70%
% of responses with require	38%	44%
% of responses with both	18%	32%

Note: All differences are statistically significant at p < .05.

In several survey responses, faculty attempted to describe what it means to give students freedom to explore yet offer some useful structure for students in order to help them succeed:

> I try to come up with writing assignments that are open-ended enough to allow students to explore things that interest them yet are guided enough that the students don't get lost in choice.

> I believe the project was meaningful to the student because it honestly attempted to allow for as much freedom and self-direction as possible while still providing parameters necessary for focus and communication.

> While it is very structured, [the assignment] allows the student to tap into their altruistic passions to change their world.

> I don't assign topics to the students but look to support topics they are passionate about. This freedom can be a huge burden to some students, but it also provides an opportunity for students to consider a topic that really interests them—one that they want to explore/know more about/question.

> I believe the students chose this assignment because it is for many of them the first time they become active and critical researchers in their field, the first time they are allowed to follow their own curiosity, and it allows them to genuinely begin to participate in the conversation they hope to join professionally.

That so many faculty who completed our survey understand student opportunities to choose as essential to why projects were meaningful tells us that they recognize the power and potential of student agency. Perhaps the more frequent presence of this element in the faculty responses as compared to students' responses is indicative of our need to be transparent about our goals for writing projects and the ways we might connect the open-ended nature of the task to students' interests, passions, and experiences, or what Behizadeh (2014) described as "authentic" writing tasks. Still, these projects occurred in contexts in which requirements were also present, and those requirements were not necessarily onerous burdens to students but instead may have offered a type of scaffolding to support student learning.

FACULTY STORIES OF MEANINGFUL WRITING PROJECTS

In their interviews with faculty, our research team of undergraduates asked faculty members about the most meaningful writing project they produced when they were undergraduates. Our curiosity, in part, was driven by the possibility of a relationship between a faculty member's meaningful writing experience and the assignments students named in our survey. In teaching with writing, a powerful influence—often one we do not realize—is our own experience as writers (Thaiss & Zawacki, 2006) and the "folk theories" (Windschitl, 2004) we come to tell ourselves about writing. While in this chapter we do not trace the possible through line between students' meaningful writing projects, the tasks that led to those projects, and faculty's undergraduate meaningful writing experiences, in this section we explore how faculty members' experiences with meaningful writing as undergraduates might be similar or different than what their students told us. In a sense we're asking, "How similar and different are faculty and students when it comes to their experiences with meaningful writing?" One particular finding that follows is how far less important personal connection was to faculty's stories of their meaningful writing than in their students' accounts.

In some instances, faculty members claimed that memories of meaningful writing as an undergraduate were not so easily conjured as we heard from the St. John's professor who told his interviewer, "When I was an undergraduate, the dinosaurs walked the Earth, and we used the hammer and chisel on the cave walls. What do you mean by my writing assignment? Ha ha." In most cases, however, faculty easily related stories from their undergraduate years. To analyze these stories, we collaboratively coded faculty members' responses using the codes we developed from students' descriptions of their meaningful writing projects, once again using student perspective to make sense of this data set.

As shown in Table 18.5, the factors most frequently cited by faculty for what made their undergraduate writing projects meaningful were quite different than the factors students offered. For undergraduates the two most frequently occurring codes were *personal connection* and *app+* (application, relevancy, future, pragmatic, authentic, professional), but for faculty the two most frequently occurring codes were *accomplishment* (milestone, gaining confidence) and *engagement* (with instructor/with peers) and, proportionally, more faculty than seniors reported having no meaningful writing projects while undergraduates.

Table 18.5. Most frequent codes for faculty members' meaningful writing projects

Code	Occurrence %
accomplishment	41%
engagement	33%
content learning	26%
researching to learn	24%
new	17%
personal connection	17%
app+	15%
length	15%
process	15%

When faculty described their meaningful writing projects to their interviewers, their experiences involved noteworthy accomplishments, and those accomplishments were often connected to engagement with their own faculty mentors, as the following examples describe:

> She read my final paper in the class as an example of one that she thought was good.

> When I wrote a paper for that class, . . . I was very pleased at the reception that I was in there with the big boys writing this paper, and understanding more of this author that I found very difficult.

> [The instructor] was like, "This is wonderful. You should be writing like this. You're a good writer. You should submit this." That was the first time that anybody had said something like that.

> That was satisfying, to get that written down, and be a part of that, and do some of the research for that, and then writing up those results.

As we speculate about the reasons for these differences between the most frequently cited factors for students and faculty, we do wonder if they say something about a particular subgroup of professionals—teachers in higher education—and the motivations that propel someone to that destination. Perhaps those who seek academic work are more likely to have been set on that course because of mentors who shepherded their academic pursuits and because of academic accomplishment expressed in writing. Perhaps the importance of "applicability" is more urgent for seniors—immersed as they are in thinking about who they are, what they need to do and know, and how to reach those goals. Certainly, there were students in our study who saw themselves as future researchers and academics and who describe the connections between their meaningful writing projects and those goals. Many other seniors described the relationship between future goals and careers that were not connected to higher education or research. What faculty named are in fact the very *app+* factors that make up their academic careers. Whatever the speculation, putting faculty members' and students' meaningful writing projects alongside each other reminds us of the uniqueness of these experiences, as well as their shared traits. After all, less than 2% of the U.S. population currently holds a doctoral degree (Wilson, 2017).

RECOMMENDATIONS FOR TEACHING MEANINGFUL WRITING

We hope this chapter offers an opportunity to reflect on how our students might both meet our course goals and have experiences with meaningful writing. For some readers, that might mean the need to re-orient assignment design toward the student writer and their potential personal connections and an emphasis on expansive framing. This approach is an inclusive one, inviting and valuing the "learning incomes, i.e.,—what students bring with them when they come to school" (Guerra, 2008, p. 296) and acknowledging students as "writers who need and want to participate as active and engaged citizens in a multiplicity of intersecting communities of belonging" (Guerra, 2015, p. 150).

We also believe that writing across the curriculum leaders and researchers can begin to move WAC models away from what Lillis & Scott (2007) describe as "deficit discourses . . . in order to consider the impact of power relations on student writing; the contested nature of academic writing conventions; the centrality of identity and identification in academic writing, [and] academic writing as ideologically inscribed knowledge construction" (p. 12). Looking at teaching practices from the perspective of student writers, as we have, can inform future work in WAC and WID for students and faculty. We should ask: how are "identity and identification bound up with rhetorical and communicative practices in the academy?; to what extent and in which specific ways do prevailing conventions and practices enable and constrain meaning making?" (Lillis & Scott,

2007, p. 9). For example, in "Listening to Stories: Practicing Cultural Rhetorics Pedagogy: A Virtual Roundtable," Cedillo et al. (2018) advocate for a cultural rhetorics pedagogy that centers what both students and faculty bring to learning and writing contexts across disciplines. Learner-centric and writer-centric approaches could inform our understanding of both what it means for students to learn to communicate in (and critique) disciplinary discourses and for faculty to design learning contexts in ways that meet course goals and provide experiences students name as meaningful.

Informed by what we learned from faculty and students in our research, we offer the following recommendations to enhance the prospect of a meaningful writing project.

Explicitly offer options and choices for students in terms of content or other potential connections. Over 50% of faculty who assigned meaningful writing projects believed they offered choices and allowed options in the writing assignment. Yet only 31% of students named choice as a factor influencing their meaningful writing project. Perceptions differ for several possible reasons. It may be that faculty offered more options around topic and content, while students let the invitation for options open a channel for connections beyond content, to the realm of the personal (family, community, etc.) and their future selves. For example, in an assignment about climate change, offer options for students to imagine direct impacts on their own communities.

Create more varied ways for students to connect with content. Faculty most often named subject-area connections as factors they believed made the writing project meaningful. Students, however, named personal and social connections most often. As we design for meaningful writing, offering options in content exploration is one way to engage students, but surely, we can imagine prompts that also open the way for individual and social connections. With some fresh intentionality, we might design so students can and do make more personal and social connections with the content. This can simply take the form of letting students choose among an array of book chapters or topics, so they can explore more deeply what resonates with them.

Consider what learners might want to do—not just what you want them to do. When mentoring student writers, keep in mind your own formative writing experiences while understanding that a small percentage of our students will take that same path to the professoriate. Knowing the features of meaningful writing for faculty and students, across time and space, can inform what makes an assignment appealing, motivating, meaningful for yet unknown futures and allow faculty to mentor student writers for more futures than they had imagined for themselves. Overall, our research taught us that students have a great deal to tell us about the writing we assign; we urge faculty to ask for feedback on an assignment—ask students to describe both the barriers and opportunities they experienced while completing a project. To offer students opportunities for agency and find the writing they do meaningful, we can be more intentional and inclusive in our assignment design.

Writing Across the Curriculum efforts are often programmatic and structured to fit institutional initiatives. Models are borrowed or born; but whatever shape the WAC effort takes it will necessarily involve faculty development because no matter how higher education contexts understand and enact WAC, and no matter how well or poorly the curriculum itself supports WAC, the individual instructor holds a key to the student experience with writing in the discipline. Any faculty development designed to strengthen the teaching of disciplinary writing can capitalize on this entry point and help faculty consider how students learn and experience more meaningful writing for themselves and their futures.

ACKNOWLEDGMENTS

This chapter is based on a keynote address for the 2019 IWAC conference. We thank the conference planning committee for inviting the Meaningful Writing Project to take part in this way.

REFERENCES

Adler-Kassner, L. & Wardle, E. A. (Eds.). (2015). *Naming what we know: Threshold concepts of writing studies.* Utah State University Press. https://doi.org/10.7330/9780874219906.

Behizadeh, N. (2014). Adolescent perspectives on authentic writing instruction. *Journal of Language and Literacy Education, 10*(1), 27–44.

Cedillo, C. V., Del Hierro, V., Epps-Robertson, C., King, L. M., Male, J., Perryman-Clark, S., Riley-Mukavetz, A. & Vidali, A. (2018, May). Listening to stories: practicing cultural rhetorics pedagogy. *Constellations: A Cultural Rhetorics Publishing Space.* http://constell8cr.com/issue-1/listening-to-stories-practicing-cultural-rhetorics-pedagogy/.

Engle, R. A., Lam, D. P., Meyer, X. S. & Nix, S. E. (2012). How does expansive framing promote transfer? Several proposed explanations and a research agenda for investigating them. *Educational Psychologist, 47*, 215–231. https://doi.org/10.1080/00461520.2012.695678.

Eodice, M., Geller, A. E. & Lerner, N. (2016). *The meaningful writing project: Learning, teaching, and writing in higher education.* Utah State University Press. https://doi.org/10.7330/9781607325802.

Eodice, M., Geller, A. E. & Lerner, N. (2019). The power of personal connection for undergraduate student writers. *Research in the Teaching of English, 53*, 320–339.

Glaser, B. G. & Strauss, A. L. (1967). *The discovery of grounded theory: Strategies for qualitative research.* Aldine. https://doi.org/10.1097/00006199-196807000-00014.

Guerra, J. C. (2008). Cultivating transcultural citizenship: A writing across communities model. *Language Arts, 85,* 296–304.

Guerra, J. C. (2015). *Language, culture, identity and citizenship in college classrooms and communities.* Routledge. https://doi.org/10.4324/9781315858081.

Ivanič, R. (1998). *Writing and identity: The discoursal construction of identity in academic writing.* John Benjamins. https://doi.org/10.1075/swll.5.

Kells, M. H. (2007). Writing across communities: Deliberation and the discursive possibilities of WAC. *Reflections, 6,* 87–108.

Kells, M. H. (2018). Writing across communities. In J. I. Liontas & M. DelliCarpini (Eds.), *The TESOL Encyclopedia of English Language Teaching.* Wiley. https://doi.org/10.1002/9781118784235.eelt0152.

Lea, M. R. & Street, B. V. (2006). The "Academic Literacies" Model: Theory and Applications. *Theory Into Practice, 45,* 368–377. https://doi.org/10.1207/s15430421tip4504_11.

Lillis, T. & Scott, M. (2007). Defining academic literacies research: issues of epistemology, ideology and strategy. *Journal of Applied Linguistics, 4*(1), 5–32. https://doi.org/10.1558/japl.v4i1.5.

Melzer, D. (2014). *Assignments across the curriculum: A national study of college writing.* Utah State University Press. https://doi.org/10.7330/9780874219401.

Saldaña, J. (2012). *The coding manual for qualitative researchers* (2nd ed.). Sage.

Thaiss, C. & Zawacki, T. (2006). *Engaged writers and dynamic disciplines: Research on the academic writing life.* Boynton/Cook.

Wilson, R. (2017, April 3). Census: More Americans have college degrees than ever before. *The Hill.* https://thehill.com/homenews/state-watch/326995-census-more-americans-have-college-degrees-than-ever-before.

Windschitl, M. (2004). Folk theories of "inquiry": How preservice teachers reproduce the discourse and practices of an atheoretical scientific method. *Journal of Research in Science Teaching, 41,* 481–512. https://doi.org/10.1002/tea.20010.

Yancey, K. B., Robertson, L. & Taczak, K. (2014). *Writing across contexts: Transfer, composition, and sites of writing.* Utah State University Press. https://doi.org/10.2307/j.ctt6wrr95.

APPENDIX: CODES USED TO DESCRIBE WHY STUDENTS CHOSE A PROJECT AS MEANINGFUL

- accomplishment (milestone, gaining confidence)
- affect (enjoyment, excitement, pleasant, pain, safe)
- app+ (application/relevancy/future/pragmatic/authentic/professionalization)
- audience (awareness of rhetorical situation)
- citation/documentation

- collaboration
- content learning
- creative
- deepen/fragmentary
- engagement (of professor/of students)
- failure/limitations
- length
- metacognition (thinking about writing process)
- new/new appreciation/new attitude
- personal connection (incomes & prior knowledge)
- process (describes writing or research process/sequence as meaningful)
- re-see with academic or analytical lens (from outside-of-school to in-school)
- reflection/recognition (of turning point experience)
- researching to learn (use of sources)
- time/timing/timeliness
- transfer (strategies, skills, knowledge transferred to meaningful writing project)
- writing to learn (knowledge, skills, and process)/writing to think
- writing to realize (something about oneself)/identity

CONTRIBUTORS

Jaena Alabi is the English and psychology librarian at Auburn University. Her research interests include information literacy and peer review of teaching, as well as diversity in academic libraries.

Lesley Erin Bartlett is Assistant Professor of English at Iowa State University, where her scholarship and teaching focus on composition theories and pedagogies. Her work has appeared in *English Leadership Quarterly, Feminist Teacher, International Journal of ePortfolio, Journal of the Assembly for Expanded Perspectives on Learning, Journal of Interactive Technology and Pedagogy*, and *Teaching/ Writing: The Journal of Writing Teacher Education*.

Christopher Basgier is Acting Director of University Writing at Auburn University, where he helps faculty integrate writing and high impact practices into courses and curricula and leads professional development experiences for writing center consultants. His scholarship focuses on WAC, writing program administration, threshold concepts, and rhetorical genre theory. In addition to faculty academies, he teaches courses in research writing and writing center theory and practice.

Catherine G. P. Berdanier is Assistant Professor of Mechanical Engineering at The Pennsylvania State University. As an NSF CAREER recipient, her research expertise is in engineering education, focusing on engineering writing and communication, particularly for academic genres, and doctoral engineering student attrition and persistence.

Rachael Cayley is Associate Professor, Teaching Stream at the Graduate Centre for Academic Communication at the University of Toronto, where she teaches academic communication to graduate students. She blogs about academic writing for graduate students at *Explorations of Style*.

Jake Chase is an English and creative writing teacher at AIM Academy in Conshohocken, PA. His teaching focuses on making literary texts accessible to students with language-based learning disabilities.

Frankie Condon is Associate Professor in the Department of English Language and Literature at the University of Waterloo. Frankie's recent books include *Performing Anti-Racist Pedagogy in Rhetoric, Writing and Communication* (co-edited with Vershawn Ashanti Young), and *I Hope I Join the Band: Narrative, Affiliation and Antiracist Rhetoric*. She is currently completing a monograph on the history of the metaphor of colorblindness for racial justice as well as an edited collection on intersectionality in writing center studies (co-edited with Wonderful Faison).

Phyllis Conn is Associate Professor in the Institute for Core Studies in the College of Liberal Arts and Sciences at St. John's University. She teaches and writes about New York City history and undergraduate history education.

Michelle Cox is the inaugural director of the English Language Support Office in the Knight Institute for Writing in the Disciplines at Cornell University, where she develops programming and pedagogy that support international multilingual graduate and professional students as writers, speakers, and language users. Her scholarship focuses on WAC, graduate writing, and multilingual writing.

James Croft is Assistant Professor in the Division of Criminal Justice, Legal Studies and Homeland Security in the College of Professional Studies at St. John's University. He frequently speaks and writes on topics including U.S. bankruptcy law and undergraduate legal education.

Malcah Effron is in the Writing, Rhetoric, and Professional Communication Program (WRAP) in the Comparative Media Studies/Writing Department at MIT. Her articles appear in journals such as *Narrative* and *Women & Language*, and she has edited *The Millennial Detective* (McFarland & Co, 2010) and co-edited *The Function of Evil across Disciplinary Contexts* (Lexington Books, 2017).

Michele Eodice is Senior Writing Fellow in the Center for Faculty Excellence at the University of Oklahoma.

Heather M. Falconer is Assistant Professor of Writing at Curry College. Her teaching and research focus on the intersections of culture, discipline, and pedagogy, with a special emphasis on discursive identity development.

Bridget Farrell is Assistant Professor at the University of Denver, where she serves as the Coordinator of Library Instruction and Reference Services. She has written articles in *portal: Libraries and the Academy, Reference Services Review,* and the *Journal of Library Administration.*

Gracemarie Mike Fillenwarth is Assistant Professor of Writing Arts at Rowan University. Her research focuses on writing pedagogy across a range of contexts, including second language writing and writing in the disciplines.

Jeffrey Galin is the founding director of the University Center for Excellence in Writing, Writing Across the Curriculum Program, and Community Center of Excellence in Writing at Florida Atlantic University. His scholarship and teaching focus on WAC, writing program administration, FYC, copyright in higher education, and multimodal teaching and learning.

Anne Ellen Geller is Professor of English and Director of Writing Across Communities at St. John's University.

Angela Glotfelter is a Ph.D. student in Composition and Rhetoric at Miami University of Ohio, where she serves as a graduate assistant director in the Howe Center for Writing Excellence and teaches classes in Professional Writing. Her research focuses on the intersection of emerging technologies with writing and communication.

Christy Goldsmith is Assistant Director of the Campus Writing Program—the Writing Across the Curriculum initiative at the University of Missouri—where she also teaches education methods and disciplinary literacy courses in the College of Education. Through her research into teachers' identities as writers *and* as teachers of writing, she explores the tensions inherent in teaching writing in secondary schools. Extending her work beyond the university campus, Christy is the Missouri Writing Project Summer Institute Director and the President-Elect of the Missouri Council of Teachers of English.

Neisha-Anne S. Green is a multidialectal orator and author proud of her roots in Barbados and Yonkers, NY. Director of the Writing Center and Academic Student Services in the Office of Undergraduate Education at American University, Neisha-Anne is also a Faculty Fellow in the Frederick Douglass Distinguished Scholars program. Her articles include "The Re-education of Neisha-Anne S. Green: A Close Look at the Damaging Effects of 'A Standard Approach,' the Benefits of Code-Meshing, and the Role Allies Play in this Work" and "Moving beyond Alright: And the Emotional Toll of This, My Life Matters Too, in the Writing Center Work." She is currently collaborating on book chapters focused on anti-racism and anti-racist pedagogy.

Al Harahap is Visiting Lecturer in Critical Theory and Cultural Studies at the University of Oklahoma. His scholarship focuses on institutional critique, political economy, and writing ecologies. He nuances the "C" in WAC with "Cultures" and "Communities."

Marcela Hebbard is Lecturer at the University of Texas Rio Grande Valley where she teaches first-year composition, linguistics, and teacher preparedness courses. Her research interests include online writing pedagogy, language and identity, first-year writing, translingual and transnational writing, writing across the curriculum, and second language writing. She has published articles in several academic journals.

Brian Hendrickson is Assistant Professor of Writing Studies, Rhetoric, and Composition at Roger Williams University, where his work explores equitable and culturally responsive approaches to teaching and assessing writing, cultivating community-based writing partnerships, and integrating high-impact, writing-intensive educational practices across and beyond the curriculum.

Yanina Hernández is Lecturer at the University of Texas Rio Grande Valley, where she teaches beginning-level Spanish courses for second language learners and for heritage language learners. Currently, she is co-coordinator of the User-Generated Material for Heritage Spanish in the Center for Open Educational Resources and Language Learning of the University of Texas at Austin.

Allie Sockwell Johnston is a doctoral student in Rhetoric, Writing, and Linguistics at the University of Tennessee, Knoxville. Her research focuses on writing center studies, specifically on student dispositions towards campus support services. She currently serves as Chair for the Writing Across the Curriculum Graduate Organization.

Jamila M. Kareem is Assistant Professor of Writing and Rhetoric at the University of Central Florida, where she serves as the Assistant Director of Composition and teaches first-year writing and upper-division courses in writing and rhetoric. Her essays have appeared in the *Journal of College Literacy and Learning, JAC: A Journal of Rhetoric, Culture, and Politics, Teaching English in the Two-Year College,* and the collection *The Good Life and the Greater Good in a Global Context.*

Jose Lai is Director of the English Language Teaching Unit at The Chinese University of Hong Kong. She is also the Principal Investigator of the English Across the Curriculum (EAC) project funded by the Teaching Development and Language Enhancement Grant (TDLEG). Her professional interests include EAC, learner autonomy, service-learning, program development, evaluation, and validation.

Neal Lerner is Professor and Chair of English at Northeastern University. He has published on the history, theory, administration, and practice of teaching writing in classrooms, laboratories, and writing centers, and is a five-time recipient of the IWCA Outstanding Scholarship Award. His book *The Idea of a Writing Laboratory* won the 2011 NCTE David H. Russell Award for Distinguished Research in the Teaching of English. He is also the co-author with Mya Poe and Jennifer Craig of *Learning to Communicate as a Scientist and Engineer: Case Studies from MIT,* winner of the 2012 CCCC Advancement of Knowledge Award, and co-author with Paula Gillespie of *The Longman Guide to Peer Tutoring,* 2nd ed. With Beth Boquet, he was co-editor of *Writing Center Journal from 2002–2008.*

Shannon Madden is Director of Graduate Writing at North Carolina State University, where she facilitates workshops, retreats, non-credit courses, and faculty development efforts geared toward supporting graduate students and postdoctoral scholars across the disciplines as writers. Her research on inclusive pedagogies for writers from historically oppressed groups has been presented in invited keynotes at the Consortium on Graduate Communication, funded by the National Council of Teachers of English, and awarded by Computers and Composition Digital Press.

Jennifer Price Mahoney is Senior Lecturer in English at Indiana University-Purdue University Indianapolis, where she teaches composition with a focus on professional writing and new media. She also serves as Associate Director of the Writing Program.

Laura Man is Lecturer in the English Language Teaching Unit at The Chinese University of Hong Kong, where she teaches undergraduate foundation courses, English for Academic Purpose (EAP) courses, and English for Specific

Purpose (ESP) courses. Her article, titled "From Second Language to Third Language Learning: Exploring a Dual-motivation System among Multilinguals," has appeared in *Australian Review of Applied Linguistics*.

Margaret J. Marshall began her teaching career as a Peace Corps volunteer in Kenya and migrated to college-level teaching of reading and writing as an adjunct at West Texas State, now a part of the Texas A&M system. After earning her Ph.D. from the University of Michigan's English and Education program, she has taught and held a variety of writing administration positions at the University of Pittsburgh, the University of Miami, and Auburn University where she served as the Director of University Writing from 2010–2019. She describes hosting the 2018 IWAC conference as both exhausting and exhilarating and loves the rich conversations that happen when scholars of writing interact with faculty and students from other disciplines.

Mary McCall is Assistant Professor of English at North Dakota State University. Her research focuses on professional and technical writing, writing across the curriculum, and women's, gender, and sexuality studies.

Dan Melzer is Director of First-Year Composition at the University of California, Davis. He teaches first-year composition, advanced composition, and graduate courses in composition theory and practice. His scholarship focuses on WAC and writing program administration.

Elaine Ng is Lecturer of the English Language Teaching Unit at The Chinese University of Hong Kong. She began pursuing an area of specialty in research and education for ESL, bilingual and biliterate students in 2007. Her publications as the sole author include "Bilingualism, Biliteracy and Cognitive Effects: A Review Paper" in *University of Sydney Papers in TESOL* and a manuscript in preparation on formulation processes of bilingual, biliterate, and monolingual writers.

Justin Nicholes is Assistant Professor of English at the University of Wisconsin-Stout. His teaching and research center on writing's role in constructing disciplinary identities, enhancing disciplinary learning, and supporting retention efforts.

Andrea R. Olinger is Assistant Professor of English and Director of Composition at the University of Louisville, where she studies disciplinary writers' representations and practices of style. Her articles have appeared in publications such as *Research in the Teaching of English*, *Rhetoric Review*, and *Linguistics and Education*.

Mike Palmquist is Associate Provost for Instructional Innovation, Professor of English, and University Distinguished Teaching Scholar at Colorado State University. His scholarly interests include writing across the curriculum, the effects of computer and network technologies on writing instruction, and new approaches to scholarly publishing.

Mya Poe is Associate Professor of English and Director of the Writing Program at Northeastern University. Her books include *Learning to Communicate in Science and Engineering* (CCCC Advancement of Knowledge Award, 2012), *Race and Writing Assessment* (CCCC Outstanding Book of the Year, 2014), and *Writing, Assessment, Social Justice, and the Advancement of Opportunity*. She is series co-editor of the Oxford Brief Guides to Writing in the Disciplines.

Chris Rozendaal is Lecturer of the English Language Teaching Unit at The Chinese University of Hong Kong, where he teaches foundation English, EAP for Science and Engineering students, and EPP courses. In addition to several academic presentations on English Across the Curriculum, he has conducted a number of workshops, usually in technology and language learning.

Alisa Russell is a doctoral candidate in rhetoric and composition at the University of Kansas, and she has also served as founder, Chair, and Past Chair for the Writing Across the Curriculum Graduate Organization. Her work has appeared in *Composition Forum*, *The WAC Journal*, and *The Clearing House*.

Joseph Serafin is Associate Professor in the Department of Chemistry in the College of Liberal Arts and Sciences at St. John's University. He teaches, writes about, and engages in research in the area of physical chemistry and has been involved in university efforts to incorporate high-impact practices into the STEM curriculum.

Stacey Sheriff is Director of the Writing Program at Colby College and Assistant Professor of Writing. She primarily teaches first-year writing and rhetorical theory. Her scholarship focuses on writing program administration, WAC, and rhetorical theory and historiography.

Sandra L. Tarabochia is Associate Professor of English at the University of Oklahoma, where she regularly participates in and facilitates faculty writing groups. Her book *Reframing the Relational: A Pedagogical Ethic for Cross-Curricular Literacy Work* is part of the National Council of Teachers of English series Studies in Writing and Rhetoric. Her scholarship has appeared in *WPA: Writing Program Administration*, *Across the Disciplines*, *WAC Journal*, *Writing & Pedagogy*, and *Composition Forum*.

James C. W. Truman was Assistant Director of University Writing responsible for the Miller Writing Center at Auburn University. As part of a university-wide initiative, he worked with students and faculty to enhance the culture of writing and writing instruction across campus. He is currently a Visiting Assistant Professor at Trinity College in Hartford, CT.

Ann Updike is Associate Director of the Howe Center for Writing Excellence at Miami University, where she assists faculty who use writing in their classrooms to help students learn course content and disciplinary ways of knowing. She has taught courses in composition and rhetoric, professional writing, and writing center theory and methods. Her research investigates non-textual literacy practices that speak to and across cultural literacy boundaries.

Elizabeth Wardle is the Roger and Joyce Howe Distinguished Professor of Written Communication and Director of the Howe Center for Writing Excellence at Miami University. She is the co-author or editor of *Writing About Writing* (4th edition, 2019), *Naming What We Know* (2015), *Composition, Rhetoric, and Disciplinarity* (2018), and *(re)Considering What We Know: Learning Thresholds in Writing, Composition, Rhetoric, and Literacy* (forthcoming 2019). She has directed writing programs since she was a graduate student. Her interests include transfer of writing-related knowledge, genre theory, writing program design, and threshold concepts of writing.

Misty Anne Winzenried is Associate Dean of Teaching and Learning at The Seattle School of Theology & Psychology in Seattle, Washington. She has taught a wide range of writing, education, and research methods courses, often with an interdisciplinary approach. Her current work involves faculty development, curricular alignment, and Writing in the Disciplines at the graduate level. Her scholarship has appeared in *Across the Disciplines* and *Composition Forum*.

Rebecca Wiseheart is Associate Professor of Communication Sciences and Disorders at St. John's University, where she currently serves as "Faculty-in-Residence" in the Writing Across Communities program. Her disciplinary research and teaching focuses on language, literacy, and dyslexia.